STUDIES IN MEANING 2

STUDIES IN MEANING 2: BRIDGING THE PERSONAL AND SOCIAL IN CONSTRUCTIVIST PSYCHOLOGY

Edited by
Jonathan D. Raskin
State University of New York at New Paltz

and

Sara K. Bridges
The University of Memphis

Pace University Press
2004

Table of Contents

PART III
THE PERSONAL AND SOCIAL IN RESEARCH

PART IV
DIALOGUE, REFLECTION, AND ANTICIPATION: FUTURE DIRECTIONS

Contributors

Contributors

Lynne Angus, Department of Psychology, York University, Toronto, Ontario, Canada

Marla Arvay, Department of Educational and Counselling, Psychology and Special Education, University of British Columbia, Vancouver, Canada

Beverley Bouffard, Department of Psychology, York University, Toronto, Ontario, Canada

Sara K. Bridges, Department of Counseling, Educational Psychology and Research, The University of Memphis, Tennessee, USA

William E. Cabanillas, Comisión Nacional para el Desarrollo y Vida Sin Drogas-DEVIDA, Lima, Peru

Gabriele Chiari, Centro Studi in Psicoterapia, Florence, Italy

Jay S. Efran, Department of Psychology, Temple University, Philadelphia, Pennsylvania, USA

Franz R. Epting, Department of Psychology, University of Florida, Gainesville, Florida, USA

Louis A. Gamino, Scott & White Clinic and Memorial Hospital, Texas A&M Health Science Center College of Medicine, Temple, Texas, USA

Matthew Graham, Graduate Program in Counselling Psychology, Trinity Western University, Langley, British Columbia, Canada

Stephanie Lewis Harter, Department of Psychology, Texas Tech University, Lubbock, Texas, USA

Lara Honos-Webb, Department of Counseling Psychology, Santa Clara University, Santa Clara, California, USA

Patrice Keats, Department of Educational and Counselling Psychology, and Special Education, University of British Columbia, Vancouver, Canada

Derrick Klaassen, Graduate Program in Counselling Psychology, Trinity Western University, Langley, British Columbia, Canada

Marvin McDonald, Graduate Program in Counselling Psychology, Trinity Western University, Langley, British Columbia, Canada

Sheila McNamee, Department of Communication, University of New Hampshire, Durham, USA

Spencer A. McWilliams, College of Arts and Sciences, California State University, San Marcos, California, USA

Sanjay R. Nath, Department of Psychology, Temple University, Philadelphia, Pennsylvania, USA

Robert A. Neimeyer, Department of Psychology, The University of Memphis, Tennessee, USA

Maria Laura Nuzzo, Centro di Psicologia e Psicoterapia Construttivista, Rome, Italy

Mark Eliot Paris, Department of Counselor Education, University of Florida, Gainesville, Florida, USA

Kati A. Phillips, Department of Educational Psychology, Baylor University, Waco, Texas, USA

Jonathan D. Raskin, Department of Psychology, State University of New York at New Paltz, New York, USA

Kenneth W. Sewell, Department of Psychology, University of North Texas, Denton, Texas, USA

Jerrold Lee Shapiro, Department of Counseling Psychology, Santa Clara University, Santa Clara, California, USA

Sunwolf, Department of Counseling Psychology, Santa Clara University, Santa Clara, California, USA

Richard E. Watts, Department of Educational Psychology, Baylor University, Waco, Texas, USA

Preface

Issues surrounding the personal and social have garnered a great deal of attention from constructivist psychologists over the last few years. In keeping with the title of a 2002 symposium at the 110th Annual Convention of the American Psychological Association (APA), this volume marks an attempt to "bridge the gap" between personal and social perspectives within constructivism. Several of the chapters within this book were originally presented as part of that symposium (Paris & Epting, McNamee, Harter). Others still originated at the Tenth Biennial Conference of the North American Personal Construct Network (NAPCN), which was held on the campus of the University of British Columbia in Vancouver from July 10-14, 2002 (Honos-Webb et al., Angus & Bouffard, Keats & Arvay, Efran & Nath, Sewell & Gamino, Klaassen et al., Watts & Phillips, McWilliams). Like the works originally presented at APA, the chapters whose origins began at the 2002 NAPCN Conference also stress the emerging integration of personal and social aspects of constructivist theories as they apply to therapy, research, and theory development. Two of the chapters were not presented at conferences, but rather written specifically for this volume (Neimeyer & Cabanillas, Bridges). Finally, two more recently presented papers at the 15th International Congress on Personal Construct Psychology (Chiari & Nuzzo, Raskin) round out the volume. Because NAPCN has historically stressed personal construct psychology, many (but not all!) of the chapters focus specifically on issues facing personal construct psychologists as they come face to face with the personal/social dynamic within the broader arena of constructivist psychology. While the chapters span a wide swath of psychological terrain, they also are thematically related in that all of them have an integrative kind of emphasis, wherein a variety of constructivist theories are incorporated and special attention is paid to addressing the personal/social dimension in new and less dichotomous ways.

On a more personal note, we are thankful to a variety of people who helped us tremendously as we developed this second volume in the Studies in Meaning series. We thank Mark Hussey of Pace University Press, whose patience and encouragement have once again helped us immensely. We also thank our respective spouses (Shay and Eric) and children (Ari, Noa, and Jacob) for their enduring support—especially the kids, who every once in a while even went to bed early enough for us to call each other on the phone as we coordinated our editing of this collection (and exchanged parenting tips!).

We expect this volume to continue an already vibrant scholarly dialogue about personal and social aspects of constructivist psychology. As psychotherapists, researchers, and psychologists, it is our belief that the chapters in this book stand on their own as unique contributions, while also expounding on important personal/social themes. We proudly share these contributions with you.

Jonathan D. Raskin   Sara K. Bridges
New Paltz, New York   Memphis, Tennessee

October, 2003

Note: There are two version of Kelly's seminal two volumes, The Psychology of Personal Constructs. There is the original 1955 Norton edition and the 1991 Routledge reprint. The page numbers are different in each version. Thus, in this book, when citing from The Psychology of Personal Constructs, both editions' page numbers are provided—1955 page numbers first, 1991 page numbers second. Also, volume 1 is distinguished from volume 2, with Kelly (1955/1991a) referring to volume 1, and Kelly (1955/1991b) referring to volume 2.

PART I

THE PERSONAL MEETS
THE SOCIAL

CHAPTER 1

Social and Personal Construction: Two Sides of the Same Coin[1]

Mark Eliot Paris and Franz R. Epting

Because we both believe in the importance of context, we want to begin by putting into context this effort to synthesize what have often been considered two very different, if not opposed ways of thinking. Our notion that social constructionism and personal construct psychology represent "two sides of the same coin" comes out of much more than a professional collaboration. It is an outgrowth of our relationship as life partners, of the many conversations about these subjects that have taken place between us at home, in the car, at restaurants. In a sense, this project arose out of our efforts to understand (and convince) each other, and our realization that, more often than not, we were in agreement. The more we talked, the more we came to feel that each of us was saying something that was very important, and that the different theoretical frameworks we were using to describe how "realities" are constructed (rather than found) were not only not opposed, but were complementary. While each of us continues to have a particular locus of interest, our position now is that social constructionism and personal construct psychology are interdependent frameworks that are both useful and necessary, especially when applied in the context of the practice of psychotherapy.

Mark is the social constructionist in the family. He believes that we are always participating in larger contexts of meaning-making, contexts that are interpersonal, social, institutional, cultural and political, and that it is our participation in these contexts that makes

[1] A version of this chapter was originally presented as part of a symposium entitled *Constructivism versus Constructionism-Bridging the Gap*, which was conducted at the 110th American Psychological Association Convention, Chicago IL, August 2002.

3

meaning itself possible. That is, meaning-making does not begin with isolated, atomized individuals encountering a world "out there" about which they, then, try to make sense. Rather, the sense we make of ourselves (and the world) depends on our participation in ongoing conversations that are taking place in this particular culture at this particular point in time about what it means to be a person and about what counts as knowledge of the world. Mark's passion for social constructionism is a result of a long-standing interest in the philosophy of Michel Foucault and the ways in which Foucault's particular kind of social constructionist thinking has informed, and in many ways made possible, contemporary queer theory and gender theory. Mark's perspective also owes a lot to the way narrative therapy theorists such as Michael White and David Epston have integrated social constructionist thinking into a therapeutic practice that works towards helping people liberate themselves from oppressive or constraining stories about themselves and others. The idea is that the stories that problematize clients' realities are interpersonal or social constructions and that therapy is about "co-constructing" new stories that help enact "preferred realities" (White & Epston, 1990; Freedman & Combs, 1996).

Franz, on the other hand, has devoted his professional life to the dissemination and elaboration of George Kelly's personal construct psychology. His fascination has been with the exquisitely personal and intimate meanings that people live their lives by and upon which their very existence depends. Constructs may take shape in the space between people, but according to Franz, they also come to have a peculiarly and intensely personal meaning for the individual. They represent a uniquely personal set of commitments without which it would be impossible for any of us to negotiate our way through the otherwise impenetrable mysteries of our own being in the world. Personal constructs represent the person's road map to reality, making that reality negotiable and, ultimately, sane. To come unmoored from our own constructions of reality invites an extreme sense of personal dis-ease, a feeling that the integrity and coherence of our relation to self and others has disintegrated. At the same time, personal constructions represent what is most especially important and meaningful to the person; that is, they are the basis of and means for a unique and genuine commitment to a particular set of life choices. During the course of our frequently lively conversations about these seemingly contrasting sets of ideas, we have each learned a great deal from the other and have together come to a place where

4

we feel like we're talking about two complementary aspects of the same process: the construction of meaning.

However, we recognize that both sides of this social/personal divide have regarded the other as being antithetical to their own point of view. Social constructionism, in particular, has often struck non-initiates as being alien, elusive, painfully abstract, and contrary to their most basic assumptions. In our earlier conversations, Franz himself expressed deep reservations about social constructionism, seeing it as robbing the personal and reducing it to a simple intercept of the social, which made such constructionism appear to him like a sociological determinism similar to other kinds of external determinism. Viewed in this light, social constructionism has seemed to some distasteful, if not impossible to swallow.

In addition to these concerns, arguments about social constructionism have tended to get hung up on questions about the nature of reality, including whether or not there is a human nature that is real apart from our efforts to construe it. It is our position that debate about these impossibly large and mysterious questions, while perhaps interesting and entertaining in its own right, serves ultimately to obscure the value and utility of constructionist (and constructivist) approaches behind a smokescreen of metaphysics and ontological point-making. English philosopher Ian Hacking (1999) calls differences around these sorts of questions "sticking points," because they represent incommensurate metaphysical assumptions. The question of the realness of reality is the perfect example of a sticking point. Any answer to such a question hinges on a person's deepest personal convictions about the nature of existence and on the range of ambiguities and uncertainties he or she is willing to tolerate. A contest around the validity of such feelings cannot be resolved because *all* answers depend on some kind of leap of faith, even the most emphatically empirical or doggedly logical ones. However, this contest does not need to be resolved in order for legitimate arguments in favor of constructionism to be put forward and evaluated. A constructionist perspective does not depend on a specific ontology, but rather on how we come to understand our own processes of meaning-making and the role of meaning-making in the formation of life-worlds, or specifically *human* realities. While we do maintain, following Stojnov and Butt (2002), that anti-essentialistism is a key feature of both social constructionism and personal construct psychology, our hope is that we are able to bracket any

5

other sticking points without compromising our argument for the usefulness of social constructionism.

We do want to attend carefully, however, to those obstacles we perceive as being most in the way of readers accommodating a social constructionist perspective, seeing its enormous value for attending to concerns that are otherwise marginalized, and appreciating our own contention, that a greater awareness of the social actually deepens understanding of the personal. Our purpose in this chapter is threefold: (1) to make a case for social constructionism as a powerful and indispensable analytical framework for talking about the construction of meaning and for making sense of the experience of persons, particularly as these concerns relate to the practice of psychotherapy; (2) to open space for those committed to a social constructionist perspective to integrate into their own framework a more whole-hearted interest in and concern for the personal; (3) to begin to show how well social constructionism and personal construct psychology work together.

We believe that George Kelly anticipated social constructionism in his own writings about personal construct theory but that he was also able to develop a *psychology* of the person around specifically personal processes of meaning-making. In doing so, he neither excluded the social nor minimized its primacy and power in the meaning-worlds of persons. At the same time, he provided a way of talking about meaning-making at the level of the person that may help those of us who are social constructionists develop a more nuanced and multi-layered understanding of how "realities" are constructed. Our hope is to utilize insights gained from both a social constructionist and personal construct perspective in order to facilitate the elaboration of a theoretical framework that takes in the full scope of the social without denying or devaluing the passionate idiosyncrasies and existential vicissitudes of the personal.

WHAT IS AT STAKE WHEN WE SPEAK OF THE "INDIVIDUAL"

In speaking of the complementarity of the social and personal in the construction of meaning, it is important to first disentangle our notion of the personal from the kind of individualistic conceptions of the self that social constructionism clearly argues against. When we speak of individualism, we are referring to a set of bedrock assumptions that are often unacknowledged and unrecognized, assumptions that ground what might be called the traditional Western worldview. For instance, Gergen (1994) speaks of the way that traditional models of explanation tend to bypass cultural and/or relational modes of understanding human phenomena in favor of an exclusive focus on

> the nature of individual minds–their states of well-being, their tendencies, their capacities, and their shortcomings. Individual minds have served as the critical locus of explanation, not only in psychology, but in many sectors of philosophy, economics, sociology, anthropology, history, literary study, and communication. (p. 3)

Social constructionism (Gergen, 1994; Gergen, 2001; McNamee, 2002; Raskin, 2002) sets itself up against the assumptions of individualism by replacing an individual level of analysis with a mode of inquiry that highlights processes that occur *between* people, in relationships and in society. Those committed to an individualistic, even person-centered, perspective often do not see the enormity of the social or recognize the extent to which the relational is constitutive of our very sense of ourselves as *individuals*. Individualism, as a worldview, leads to a decontextualized understanding of the person, to a belief in individual selves with self-contained "cognitions," self-contained emotional worlds, and self-contained problems. This represents a distortion of the fundamental relatedness of human beings and the inescapably social nature of meaning-making, a distortion to which social constructionism can serve as a powerful corrective.

At the same time, social constructionism, as a mode of analysis, sometimes has the effect of concealing what we think are the very legitimate claims of the personal. In talking of the personal, as opposed to the individual, we are thinking very much in terms of the Heideggerean notion of being-in-the-world (Frede, 1993), wherein person and world are so inextricably bound together that they constitute a gestalt. At the same time, we mean to invoke by the personal that sense in which our lives are necessarily grounded in our own feelings, desires, hopes, dreams, and existential commitments, which, no matter where they come from, we experience as deeply intimate, as exquisitely or excruciatingly necessary to our own person. The personal is, in a sense, a space within the social, a space that is not *separate* from the social but one that is constituted within relationships between people. The personal is not bounded, a unit unto itself, but it names that which feels like the stuff of our own lives.

However, as Kath Weston, author of *Families We Choose: Lesbians, Gays, Kinship* (1991) says, "In the United States people often tend to image social organization as the additive end-product of a series of voluntary choices: individuals create groups (like families) which in turn create society" (p. 200). That is, "the individual" is a monad-like unit, self-contained but, in aggregate, foundational of and responsible for the social order of the things. If individuals *are* both the builders of and building blocks for all other social units, from the family to society itself, then it only makes sense to examine the nature of this individual, what makes him or her tick, so to speak, be it bio-genetic make-up, the dynamics of the individual's unique intra-psychic processes or even his or her personal construct system, when this is conceived of as analogous to a set of "cognitive structures" (Stojinov & Butt, 2002, p. 99). If we then examine the "social surround," it is only to surmise what impact the environment has had in shaping or directing these individual processes. While explanations for the individual's thoughts, feelings, and behaviors may vary, the notion of the individual itself appears to be self-evident, transparent—it is what we *are* after all—*individuals*. Yet, as Weston implies, this conception of "the individual" is a culturally and historically specific way of creating a version of "self" that is individualistic, self-contained, free and, therefore, responsible for its own choices, a self that precedes and grounds the social, rather than the other way around.

One consequence of this way of thinking about people is that if an individual is unable to live successfully within the bounds of what is presumably a free, rational and responsible self, then it can only be surmised that her or his particular self is, in some way, disordered. That is, the person is thought to be suffering from a problem that is psychological in origin, that has as its root cause some maladaptation or dysfunction on the part of the individual. Since dysfunctions and maladaptations originate within the individual, feelings of distress or problems in living are not understood to be indicative primarily of problems occurring *between* persons or between persons and larger social systems.

This view of the self as a kind of "concrete 'thing,' a recognizable entity...with specific psychological boundaries" (Cushman, 1995, p. 259) leads to the provision of mental health services aimed primarily at the remediation or correction of individual processes. It leads to a cataloguing of the various symptoms of distress and problems in living as discrete pathologies of the individual that fall into naturally occurring, internally consistent categories of disorder. An individualistic conception of distress precludes consideration of what possible stories "disorders" might be telling about relations between people. In this view, there is simply no need to refer to an individual's relationships or social context in order for her or his disorder to be understood accurately and subjected to the appropriate technological (psychotherapeutic or biological) intervention. Furthermore, there is no reason to reflect on the ways in which both clients and clinicians are necessarily situated in larger social, cultural, institutional, and political domains of meaning-making. However, if we were to step back from our focus on the individual, we might see how these larger domains of meaning-making serve to organize (make visible and coherent) those meanings that *construct* both clients' presenting problems and clinician's own practices and ways of understanding those problems (Early, Nazario & Steier, 1994). From our own perspective, individuals are like the trees that prevent us from seeing the forest.

We believe that meaning-making is, fundamentally, a process that occurs between people. There is no way to pull the person apart from his or her meaning-filled relationships without hypothesizing a kind of "empty self" (Cushman, 1995), a self that can be described in terms of structure, needs, function or dysfunction, but is otherwise devoid of any relational context in which "self" is actually a meaningful construction. (After all, I can only be recognizably *me* in relation to some others who are most decidedly not me—it is the relationship that makes the recognition possible.) Taken out of context, human distress and problems in living are reduced to a set of individual symptoms that are, in themselves, identifiable but meaningless. That is, they are not fundamentally *about* anything but themselves. Distress is stripped of its relationship to the world, including the world of other people. At best, distress is conceived of as an effect caused by factors in a world that is "external" to the individual. Distress is not understood to be, itself, a meaning-full kind of *relationship* with other people, with the larger social order (and even with existence itself), in which there are always multiple partners interacting with and impinging upon one another. Recognizing distress and other problems in living as kinds of relationships, rather than as the disorders, dysfunctions, and maladaptations of a monadic self, makes it possible to see those persons and *larger systems* who are partners in the construction of distress. It makes it possible to investigate how interpersonal and systemic processes of meaning-making serve to constitute distress as a meaning-full relationship. We can begin to inquire into how we might be able to *deconstruct* those meanings (i.e., narratives and discourses) that sustain relationships of distress so that we can open space for alternative meanings that help us construct more preferred relations with others and the world (Freedman & Combs, 1996). All of which is to say that there is actually a great deal at stake socially, politically and personally in what we agree to mean by terms such as "self" and "the individual" (terms that are not, by the way, a part of George Kelly's formulation of personal construct psychology.)

THE POWER OF SOCIAL CONSTRUCTIONS

The power of a social constructionist framework is that it allows us to see meaning-making as a collaborative process that is necessarily situated in and informed by larger cultural, socio-political, and historical contexts. As Raskin (2002) points out, not only are there many varieties of constructivism in general, but also social constructionism itself is an umbrella term covering a number of different approaches. In fact, we are offering our own version of social constructionism, a version we hope highlights what is most valuable and useful in this approach while making room for people to adopt a "both/and" rather than an "either/or" position.

Social constructionism is most often portrayed as being, first and foremost, an anti-realist, anti-essentialist epistemological position. It seems specially designed to say "no!" to the treasured verities of the traditional Western worldview. There is no "reality"–"realities" are merely socially constructed. There is no essential human nature–"personhood" is merely "a matter of how people are talked about, the social practices they engage in, and the particular relationships they find themselves in" (Raskin, 2002, p. 18). In a sense, this is a matter of social constructionists parrying the epistemological thrusts of an entrenched positivism that has dominated the social sciences since their inception. The point is that the search for essences and the cold, hard, facts of an independent "reality" blinds us to the ways in which we are only able to see ourselves, other people, and the world through those meanings and ways of making sense that are salient for us. The world of perception is not simply "given" to us. It becomes visible, so to speak, through some framework of meaning that allows us to find order in what we perceive, a paradigm that makes the world make sense to us.

These frameworks or paradigms are forms of *intelligibility* that, according to social constructionists, arise from and depend on already existing communities of meaning. As McNamee (2002) says, "One cannot constitute meaning alone, nor engage in a rational choice among competing goods, without having absorbed the intelligibilities of a community" (p.147). To say that reality is socially constructed means that our own sense of "reality" depends on the intelligibilities available in those communities of meaning in which we participate. Different frameworks of meaning, different forms of intelligibility inevitably provoke, incite, and *construct* different "realities," different versions of what it means to be human. As George Kelly (1955/1991a, 1955/1991b) pointed out almost fifty years ago, however we describe "reality" or "human nature," alternative constructions are always possible. A social constructionist position underlines the ways in which processes of construing are necessarily interactive and participatory. Even alternative constructions arise out of, if only as a response to, those frameworks of meaning that are already available to us. Different frameworks of meaning lead to the possibility of different constructive alternatives and each alternative opens space for meanings that may not have been previously accessible. The point is that the "realities" we are able to see depend on the range of meanings that are available to us, which are, in turn, dependent on "the intelligibilities of a community."

Furthermore, as McNamee (2002) says, "meaning emerges as communities of people coordinate their activities with one another. The continual coordination required in any relationship or community eventually generates a sense of common practices, a vocabulary if you will" (p.156). We can only name, describe, and, ultimately, perceive what we call reality using the "vocabulary" generated by the "common practices" of the communities in which we participate. This is the pragmatist face of social constructionism—knowledge is comprised of those understandings that are useful to us within the context of our social practices.

SOCIAL CONSTRUCTIONSIM AS A MODE OF INQUIRY

The anti-realist, anti-essentialist epistemology associated with social constructionism most aptly characterizes its stance in relation to those questions that have dominated positivist scientific investigations. What is the nature of reality? What are the laws of human nature? What is important here is not that the answers to these questions are "there is no reality" or "there is no human nature" but that it is time to focus on different questions. However, it is tempting to interpret social constructionism in terms derived from more traditional approaches and to see it as giving answers to questions that are not appropriately within its purview as a mode of inquiry. For instance, Raskin (2002) argues, "social constructionism

is relativistic in emphasizing how contextual, linguistic, and relational factors combine to determine the kinds of human beings that
people will become and how their views of the world will develop"
(p. 17). This statement is indicative of a fairly common understanding of social constructionism (Burr, 1995) as positing a kind of environmental determinism in which individual psychology is a by-
product of exposure to a particular set of "contextual, linguistic, and
relational factors." However, it is pertinent to ask whether social constructionism is really concerned with the question of what factors
determine "the kinds of human beings that people will become and
how their views of the world will develop."

As social constructionists, we would be more interested in
asking how people together *decide* what kinds of human beings there
are, in what kinds of ongoing conversations are such decisions negotiated, who gets heard in these conversations and who never gets a
chance to speak, what stories and discourses convey the most powerful and resonant meanings about different kinds of people, what
kind of life possibilities do dominant narratives open space for, what
alternatives are available within these narratives, and what life possibilities are precluded or left "unstoried?" Our assumption is that the
meanings we ascribe are the meanings we live by, but that meaning
is constantly being negotiated within an ongoing relational process
in which meanings are never, in themselves, *determinate*. The process
of negotiation may be prematurely terminated so that positions
become reified, or one's entry into these conversations may be
blocked, or one's role may be highly constrained. Nevertheless,
meaning-making is an open-ended process in which realities are not
determined but are always *under construction*, so to speak. What comes
next is always related to but not necessarily determined by our previously or currently held constructions of reality. There are always
constructive alternatives and every change in meaning makes it possible to conceive of new alternatives that were previously unthinkable.

While social constructionism cannot be equated with a
determinist perspective, neither does it subscribe to the kinds of
notions about human agency and free will typically associated with
humanistic psychology, notions which embody the biases of individualism (Gergen, 1994). Instead, social constructionism adopts a
constitutionalist perspective that highlights and investigates the ways
in which persons are constituted as *subjects*, as beings having particular kinds of *identities* within a given set of discourses or socially con-

structed narratives. A constitutionalist perspective such as social constructionism can look sometimes a lot like the old environmental
determinism wrapped inside a package of fancy, new, intimidating
abstractions.

For instance, Foucault (1980), in his analysis of the operations of power, warns us against trying to answer "why certain people want to dominate, what they seek, what is their overall strategy"
(p. 97). This would be an inquiry guided by the biases of individualism, one that seeks to answer questions about power in terms of
individual purposes and motivations. Instead, Foucault instructs us
to ask

> how things work at the level of ongoing subjugation, at the level
> of those continuous and uninterrupted processes which subject
> our bodies, govern our gestures, dictate our behaviors, etc. In
> other words...we should try to grasp subjection in its material
> instance as a constitution of subjects. (Foucault, 1980, p. 97)

One way to interpret this statement is to see it as saying that our very
nature as "subjects," as individual subjectivities, is *determined* by the
operations of power, by "uninterrupted processes" of "ongoing subjugation." However, to say that we are *constituted* as subjects through
our ongoing "subjugation" does *not* mean that "subjection" *determines*
who we are (although subjection, in this sense, certainly obstructs
some possible pathways for the elaboration of self while, in effect,
producing others.) Instead, a constitutionalist perspective is concerned with how various kinds of subject *positions* (Burr, 1995) are
produced (or constituted) through the use of language and the generation of *meaning* within relational and/or cultural contexts. The idea
of subject positions refers to how kinds of persons or identities are
constituted within discourse (Burr, 1995), or put more simply, how
they are construed within those social arenas in which people find
themselves. Because we invariably participate in the systems of
meaning that are available to us, we are, in a sense, intelligible to
ourselves and others only in terms of those subject positions that can
identify us as having a place in the known universe of kinds of people. This is a long way from individualistic notions of agency (where
meaning itself seems to arise, ex nihilo, from within the interior of
the individual), but it is also a long way from determinism. The
problem here is that a constitutionalist perspective rests on an entirely different conceptual foundation than do cause and effect explanations.

According to The Oxford Dictionary of Philosophy (Blackburn, 1994), determinism is "the doctrine that every event has a cause. The usual explanation of this is that for every event, there is some antecedent state, related in such a way that it would break a law of nature for this antecedent state to exist yet the event not to happen" (p.102). This same volume also has a section discussing what it calls "regulative" and "constitutive" principles: "The distinction was taken over [from Kant] by the 20th century American philosopher J.R. Searle, to describe the way rules (such as those of chess) may not only regulate the activity but actually constitute it" (Blackburn, 1994, p. 78). Following Searle, we can say that the activity of chess and the role of chess player, are constituted by the rules that make up the game of chess, and without which it would not be chess. We can only think and do chess by first knowing the rules. However, the way we play the game, the particular moves that we, as well as our opponents, decide to make, the very outcome of the game, are not determined in the sense that the rules of chess cannot be said to cause any particular move, strategy, or outcome of any particular game. There is never some "antecedent state" within the game of chess "related in such a way that it would break a law of nature for this antecedent state to exist yet the event [move, strategy, or outcome] not to happen" (Blackburn, 1994, p. 102). At the same time, all moves, strategies, and outcomes, as such, are constituted by and through the rules of the game; i.e., that which makes them chess moves, strategies, and outcomes.

To elaborate this notion further, this is what the Oxford Dictionary of Philosophy (Blackburn, 1994) has to say about the concept of the "language game:"

> The pattern of activities and practices associated with some particular family of linguistic expressions. The notion is associated with the later philosophy of Wittgenstein, encouraging us to think of the use of language in terms of a rule-governed, self-contained practice. (p. 211)

It should be noted that Wittgenstein is here rejecting the idea that language corresponds to an external reality which it endeavors to faithfully represent and is, instead, proposing that language is like a tool (Wittgenstein, 2001) in that meaning is synonymous with use, and the use of language is governed by the rules that structure a community's social practices (i.e., conventions for using the tool of language.) Following Wittgenstein, we can say that we are constituted as players (so to speak) within any language game through our participation in it and we can only participate by knowing and following the rules that govern the game. Wittgenstein (2001) goes on to say that language games taken together within a particular social context make up what he calls "forms of life" (p. 192).

If we then say that we find ourselves as "selves" through our participation in the meanings that are available to us, this means that we can come to some kind of understanding of ourselves only by following those social practices that govern the construction of meaning within our community. We are "constituted" as subjects through our participation in those rule-governed language games (i.e., constructions, narratives, discourses) and those forms of life, in which we find ourselves. The rules do not determine who we are, any more than the rules of chess determine how one decides to play any particular game, but they do make it possible to have some kind of identity or meaningful sense of self in the first place. It is very important to see how inextricably bound the ascription and experience of identity is to those rule-bound language games (or social constructions) that make it possible for identities to have meaning. At the same time, the rules that govern and thereby constitute language games are simply socially agreed-upon practices that represent human interventions, not laws of nature. As George Kelly (1955/1991a, 1955/1991b) says, it is always possible to enter into alternative constructions, although alternatives are, likewise, necessarily situated within the context of social practices.

The purpose of social constructionism as a form of inquiry is to interrogate the rules of the game so to speak, to show what the rules do as something distinct from the intentions and actions of individuals, and to unpack and make visible those rules (i.e., social practices) that enable certain kinds of identities while rendering others impossible or unlivable (at least without violating the rules and thereby making one unfit to play the game.) A social constructionist framework allows us to talk about whose interests are served by which rules, to explore how we came to agree (or disagree) on certain ways of understanding the world and to situate what we call knowledge within the specific cultural, institutional, political, and historical practices that enable the asking of certain kinds of questions while simultaneously suppressing other possible questions. It allows us to bring to the surface practices of inclusion and exclusion that inform those narratives and discourses we certify as true, to examine the social and personal consequences of dominant constructions of reality and to investigate what alternatives have been hidden or suppressed

15

by the truths we take for granted. Social constructionism is, itself, a kind of language game that takes the form of a critical inquiry (Scheman, 1996) into rule-governed meanings that both enable and disable persons who are bound together in shared forms of life.

WHAT'S REAL: DOES IT MATTER?

It can be difficult sometimes for people to appreciate the critical thrust of this inquiry because the debate around social constructionism (and constructivism in general) so often founders on the question of whether reality is really real or whether we have, more or less, made it all up. If we say that reality is constructed, this is only to point out that in order for us to be able to *name* something as "reality," we must already be seeing that something from within a system of meaning-making that is a human artifact. We are only able to have a "reality" *because* we are able to construct one. As Stojnov and Butt (2002) put it, "we have to watch the universe through the transparent patterns we produce, because otherwise it would not make any sense to us" (p. 106). We are not forced to conclude, on this basis, that there is not a reality "out there" that is really real, only that our perceptions of an "out there" are necessarily encapsulated within our own constructions. This means that, at best, we can only know our constructions of reality, whether there is a really real reality on the other side of them or not. However, we would like to argue that what may or may not be on the other side of our constructions is not, ultimately, as important a question as it may appear to some. What matters is that we attend to our own constructions, to where they come from and what they do (for us and to us.)

There are a couple of other arguments that we can make that may help us find our way around (and beyond) this debate about the realness of reality. The first is to be mindful of the original protest of the pragmatists (such as William James and John Dewey) to the effect that questions about the existence of an "external" reality inevitably land us in a epistemological quagmire, that these are questions that can never be answered satisfactorily and ought to be set aside. What we call knowledge are those understandings that are useful to us, so that usefulness becomes our epistemological standard. This is very much the tradition that George Kelly aligned himself with and one that contemporary social constructionists such as Kenneth Gergen (1994, 2001) and Sheila McNamee (2002) draw on as well. The second comes from Ian Hacking (1999), who points out that different applications of social constructionist arguments involve making dif-

16

ferent sorts of claims about the nature of reality, so that it matters what it is we are saying is socially constructed. It makes a difference whether we are maintaining that the rocks and the stars are socially constructed or insisting that the categories of disorder listed in the *DSM-IV* are socially constructed. The former entails a different set of epistemological claims than the latter. We do not necessarily have to accept the idea that rocks and stars are socially constructed in order to agree that Attention-Deficit/Hyperactivity Disorder or Borderline Personality Disorder might well be social constructions. (There are arguments to be made for the social constructedness of rocks and stars; however, it is not inappropriate to bracket this question and move on.)

Hacking (1999) makes a distinction between what he calls "natural kinds" and "interactive kinds." Put simply, natural kinds do not change as a result of the terms we use to label or describe them. A rose by any other name would smell as sweet (and a rock would be just as hard). However,

> Terms for interactive kinds apply to human beings and their behavior. They interact with the people classified by them. They are kind-terms that exhibit a looping effect, that is, that have to be revised because the people classified in a certain way change in response to being classified. (p. 123)

Hacking's notion that terms that "apply to human beings and their behavior" interact with the people who use them (which includes both those who classify and those who are classified by these terms) is as relevant to the social construction of everyday life as it is to elite discourses such as the social sciences. This is the crux of the matter. How we experience what we call reality is isomorphic with how we go about making sense of our lives and ourselves and with what sense we make of the world. The terms we use to describe ourselves and others (and that others use to describe us) come loaded with definitions, implications, and connotations, around which we spin the stories that we live by. In this way, these descriptive terms are standing invitations to construe others and ourselves in ways that are consistent with them. This is true for those terms that are authorized for usage by the social sciences and for those vernacular terms we use in everyday life.

At the same time, our experience of self, others, and the world has a way of interacting with the terms we have settled on as providing accurate descriptions of what is real and true. As we wind our way along the chain of implications and connotations derived

17

from our original definitions of reality, we sometimes discover our-selves moving toward unexpected changes, and suddenly we are for-aging around for new terms on which to live (so to speak). Or some-times we are confronted by powerful new terms that seem to nail us to the spot where we are told we belong. These are terms authorized for use by established institutions (medicine, psychiatry, the church, etc.) that designate the proper category in which we are to find our place (e.g., the DSM-IV). We are given and adopt as our own official-ly sanctioned identities that interact with our constructions of who we thought we were, who we think we can be now, and with oth-ers' constructions of who they see when they are looking at us. Sometimes our terms fail us—they simply do not work within the context of our relationships and life struggles. We are faced with a crisis that seems to force us to alter the terms we live by or find new ones altogether. Whatever the case, when we change terms we alter the existential terrain on which we go about fashioning our day-to-day lives, which then changes who we are (how we construe our sense of identity) and what we do. Therefore, the terms we use to describe "human beings and their behavior" interact with the lives being lived on those terms. As lives shift and change due to interac-tion with these defining terms, the terms used to define those lives change as well. Looked at this way, at least in relation to "interactive kinds," we are only being realistic when we say that reality is con-structed.

GOING ON TOGETHER

The social constructionist move allows us to address ethical as well as epistemological concerns that may otherwise be outside the range of our consideration. For instance, writers such as Sheila McNamee and Kenneth Gergen are very concerned with the social and ethical consequences of the assumptions of individualism that have been implicit (and often explicit) in Western thought at least since the time of Descartes. McNamee (2002) argues that

> individualist discourse is our dominating tradition (conven-tion). It affects cultural life by valorizing the self as the origin of action. The result is that the self is prioritized. We value our own goals, needs, wants, and rights...We only examine other's actions as they affect our own...In this realm, individual gain is impoverishment for the community...On both local and global levels, individualism promotes interminable conflict among incommensurate moral or ideological commitments. *Is this a use-ful path for the future?* (pp. 147-148)

For Gergen (2001), social constructionism, as a framework for viewing the world through the prism of relationships rather than from within the enclosure of monadic individual selves, "lends itself to a re/visioned political agenda" (p. 174). That is, it lends itself to what he calls a "*relational politics*" (p. 175). This means

> a politics in which the self/other, we/them binaries are replaced by a realization and appreciation of the significance of the relational process. It is in those practices that break free from the parochial coagulation of meaning, and set disparate discourse into common orbit that we shall locate the source of viable social change. (pp. 174-175)

Whether in the domains of politics, the social sciences, or everyday life, the bottom line for these writers is that, as McNamee (2002) puts it, "Social construction, by placing our attention on what people do together, allows us to ask different questions" (p. 158). For McNamee (2004 [this volume]), the most pressing question is one asked by the philosopher Ludwig Wittgenstein: *How do we go on together?*

We are very much in agreement with the idea that meaning is always relational, that meaning is only possible as something that occurs between people, as something that people do together, and not as some mystical emanation from within the confines of an isolated Cartesian *cogito* (this is a point with which George Kelly would also agree.) We also believe that this focus on how we make meaning together, and on how people necessarily participate in the meanings circulating between them, has profound implications for what kinds of questions we decide to ask and for how we understand the political dynamics inherent in the practice of the social sciences as well as in the communal realities of everyday life.

However, as therapists, we are also concerned with the experience of individual persons, for how the relational (or the social) resonates within the personal. We are inclined to see the social and the personal as a gestalt so that when we are talking about the personal, we are also, in one way or another, talking about the social and when we speak of the social, we are also referring to aspects of experience that might be thought of as personal. There is no definitive way to tease apart the social and the personal so that they can be set into ontologically distinct categories, but at the same time, it is convenient to be able to talk about one or the other as a way of prioritizing a particular set of immediate concerns. Ultimately, however, these concerns fit together. We cannot talk about our personal experience without simultaneously talking (implicitly or explicitly) about our relations with other people and with the social order, so that the social and the interpersonal are always implicated in those pressing concerns that feel most deeply and intimately personal to us. Conversely, it is pointless to valorize the relational if we dispense with consideration of the impact of various kinds of relationships on the experiences and meaning-making processes of individual people. This is why we advocate using, and in some way integrating, both social constructionist and personal construct frameworks. Social constructions are ultimately experienced in a personal way and personal constructions are always formed through and informed by relational processes of meaning-making.

Another way of talking about this is to say that we reject a decontextualized reading of personal constructs. The social construction of meaning is the context for (and part and parcel of) the personal construction of meaning. By emphasizing the importance of reading context into meaning, we are underscoring the usefulness of social constructionism as a form of critical theory, particularly for those classes of persons who have traditionally been culturally disenfranchised. In moving from an individualistic to a relational perspective, we believe that it is important not to read "relationship" as indicating only the interpersonal or a simple notion of community. Relationships are embedded in a whole social, cultural, institutional, political, and historical *apparatus* of relationships that we think of as being *systemic*; that is, those relations that have evolved over time into complex social systems that form large, powerful, overarching contexts to the relationships of everyday life. Systemic relationships are structured around often-powerful discourses or culturally sanctioned narratives that become the larger contexts of meaning in which we all participate.

THE CONTEXTUAL NATURE OF DAY-TO-DAY LIFE

To a large extent, we discover our "selves" and each other through our participation in these larger systemic contexts in which we find dominant constructions of reality already in circulation. In a sense, we find ourselves already invented within these contexts, with an identity affixed that positions us within various hierarchies of cultural value organized around a whole host of socially constructed distinctions, from class to race to gender, ethnicity, culture, sexual orientation, gender expression, ability, educational status, occupation, age, size, health, temperament, and many others (Early, Nazario

& Steier, 1994; Nazario, 1998). The discourses that construct these hierarchies of value have tremendous cultural resonance and weight. They tend to saturate more "local" interpersonal and personal meaning-making processes with their own residue, to make their own implications and connotations organizing principles around which we form the meanings by which we live our daily lives.

This is not to say that dominant discourses and cultural hierarchies of value *determine* who we are, but that they set up certain parameters for the construction of meaning within which more "local" practices of meaning-making operate. This does not preclude constructive alternatives; in fact, alternatives are always present in whatever constructions prevail at any particular time, even if only through a process of negation. However, it is not a simple or easy thing to embrace alternative constructions or to believe in their viability within the network of relationships that sustain us, or even, sometimes, to locate them within the range of what is thinkable to us. This is because what is at stake is our very sense of belonging to a community that includes us, the risk being exile, psychological homelessness, an insurmountable feeling of disconnection from others. We are often more inclined to collude with a prevailing meaning (narrative, discourse) that assaults our very sense of worth as human beings rather than accept an alternative that may be far more validating but seems to threaten us with expulsion or estrangement from those communities that matter to us most. Here we are talking about processes of meaning-making that are profoundly personal and yet, profoundly social as well.

Alternative constructions that challenge or attempt to subvert the power of dominant social constructions become viable only when we encounter other persons who can join with us in substantiating a different way of construing reality or who can act as witnesses to our testimony about that which was previously unspeakable. (These encounters do not necessarily have to be face-to-face. For instance, both of us used reading books by and about other gay people as a way of substantiating the reality and validity of our own feelings.) Constructive alternatives that can live and breath in the world require alternative communities which can sustain the viability of stories that have no place in the dominant constructions of reality. In fact, this is a good description of what post-modern therapies such as narrative therapy (White & Epston, 1990; Freedman & Combs, 1996) try to accomplish–the co-construction of preferred stories that are to be circulated amongst those who figure most

21

importantly in the client's life. It is the circulation of preferred mean-ings (constructions) within the context of the client's significant relationships that helps to turn these "stories" into realities. We might add that we see narrative therapy as being consistent with and an elaboration of a way of thinking that begins with George Kelly's per-sonal construct psychology. Both see shifts in meaning, be it alterna-tive constructions or new stories, as central to any process of change.

One of the things we mean when we talk about discourses and other culturally sanctioned narratives having tremendous reso-nance and weight is that it often appears to us that everyone who knows or matters has agreed that the construction of reality repre-sented in a particular discourse is, in fact, the way things really are. Depending on where we are situated in the larger culture, our per-ception of who knows and/or who matters will vary, as will our sense of the authority and social import of different discourses. In time, we may move between competing discourses so that a way of making sense that we used to take for granted loses its authority while a previously rejected or unnoticed alternative becomes the basis for us to authorize significant and meaningful change in our lives.

To reiterate, discourses, as dominant versions of reality, tend to position people in hierarchies of value (e.g., upper-middle class people are more valued than poor people, thin people are more val-ued than fat ones, masculine men are more valued than effeminate ones, etc.). As a result, some of us experience positions of privilege and inclusion in the activities and conversations of our communities while others of us are marginalized and excluded, and experience invalidation as a sort of organizing principle in our relations with our social world. We occupy positions in many different cultural hier-archies of value so that our experience of these socially constructed realities may be very complex, ambiguous, and conflicted. Nevertheless, certain hierarchies tend to be particularly salient because they occur in relation to identity distinctions that are espe-cially loaded with cultural meaning, for instance, race, gender, class, religion, culture, ethnicity, and sexual orientation. Those of us whose cultural location, as defined by these identity distinctions, is privi-leged may not perceive our privilege as obvious or even noticeable. Privilege is the ground against which the unique particulars of our individual attributes and personal relationships emerge as figure. However, for those of us on the other side of the cultural equation, our race, class, gender, or sexual orientation may appear as a sort of omnipresent figure, a problematic and inescapable focal point in the relational calculus of our social world.

THE APPARATUS OF DESCRIPTION

Without a social constructionist framework, it is very difficult to talk about the ways in which cultural discourses insinuate themselves into our everyday processes of meaning-making and become an integral part of our interpersonal and *psychological* realities. Social constructionism is also an invaluable tool for *deconstructing* previously taken-for-granted cultural truths that have served to marginalize or cover up the interests, experiences and points of view of various subaltern peoples (i.e., non-whites, low-income people, women, non-heterosexuals, transgender people, etc.). In particular, social constructionism provides an analytical framework for identifying otherwise unseen relationships between regimes of knowledge, such as the social sciences, and the interests, values and worldview of those who hold positions of power and/or privilege in the larger society (Dreyfus & Rabinow, 1982).

This framework (which represents one kind of social constructionism) derives from the work of the French philosopher Michel Foucault. Foucault brings to the surface those historically and culturally specific relations of power actualized in the production of knowledge. As Foucault (1980) says,

> Truth is of this world; it is the product of multiple constraints...Each society has its own regime of truth, its general politics of the truth...There is a combat for the truth, or at least around the truth, as long as we understand by the truth not those true things which are waiting to be discovered but rather the ensemble of rules according to which we distinguish the true from the false, and attach special effects of power to "the truth." (p. 131)

It is precisely in the formulation of that "ensemble of rules according to which we distinguish the true from the false" that those empowered to decide what the rules are become empowered to decide what counts as the truth. For instance, those who have the power to determine the form and function of the DSM-IV also have the power to determine (1) what is and is not to count as being *mentally disordered*, and (2) that distress and problems in living are, *in fact*, symptomatic of some actuality that we can call a "mental disorder." To put it very simply, many people might wish to construe their problems in living differently, but lack access to any sort of larger cultural apparatus that could give their own descriptions the power of truth. Once they find themselves absorbed into the mental health discourse, they are faced with little choice about the construction of their "disorder" (Gergen, 1994; McNamee, 2002; Raskin & Lewandowski, 2000; Szasz, 1974).

The project of deconstructing the epistemological assumptions that prop up the ordered universe of the DSM-IV (and other claims to objective, systematic knowledge about human beings and their behavior) has had a special relevance for those classes of persons who suffer from what David Halperin (1995) calls "social liabilities." Social liabilities are characteristics or aspects of persons that are outside of or contrary to what a culture designates as normal or acceptable and that feature centrally in the social construction of *identities*. Such attributes are *liabilities* because they are either not privileged in the social order and/or serve to fundamentally discredit the individual in the context of dominant culture. These attributes can include, among other possibilities, being poor, black, non-Christian, elderly, gay, transgendered, physically disfigured, or even simply being female. Social liabilities have a way of becoming irrevocably attached to the identities of individuals, so that the identity of the person cannot be thought of apart from the existence of the liability (either by others or by the person themselves). Liabilities always take the form of obstacles blocking access to an otherwise seemingly taken-for-granted individuality and/or normalcy (which is not to say that such liabilities cannot sometimes be *transformed* into sources of resistance, resilience, creativity, or wisdom).

Traditionally, many social liabilities have been interpreted as symptoms or sources of pathology within the supposedly objective descriptions of human nature generated by the social sciences. Halperin speaks passionately of the "peculiar terror" experienced by individuals who, by virtue of their social liabilities, are subject to what he calls

> the apparatus of unchallengeable description. To be, and to find oneself being, known and described—rationally (or so it can be made to seem) and therefore definitively, more objectively (or so one is told) than one is capable of describing oneself...with an instantaneous finality that...defeats any attempt on one's own part to intervene in the process by which one becomes an object of knowledge, and that renders one helpless to stave off the effects of a knowledge one has had no share in creating—that is an experience whose peculiar terror is hard to convey to those who have never suffered from the social liabilities that cause the

rest of us to be continually and endlessly prey to it. (Halperin, 1995, p. 176)

The "apparatus of unchallengeable description" works by preserving the interests, experiences and worldview of the privileged at the center of purportedly accurate descriptions of those with "social liabilities," whose own interests, experiences, and points of view are thereby pushed to the margins or completely outside of these constructions of their own reality. This "centering" operation may be invisible to both the propagators and objects of these descriptions precisely because the point of view of the former is privileged, and therefore *assumed* to be consistent with a principled and objective search for the truth. To put it another way, a privileged point of view is the ground against which social liabilities figure as forms of "deviant behavior." In this context, the power and utility of a social constructionist approach is that it provides an analytical framework which, by revealing the dependence of knowledge claims on the contingencies of specific historical, cultural, and political practices, serves to deconstruct the unchallengeable (i.e., universally true) nature of such descriptions.

Having no say in the supposedly "true" description of who we are, or having our say have no weight in that description, or believing that description because we have lost the capacity to believe in ourselves, is, as Halperin says, a strangely terrifying experience. Being gay men of a certain age, we have both experienced how what were once widely circulated and seemingly unchallengeable descriptions of homosexuality (as something that was *obviously* unacceptable, unnatural, and pathological) insinuated themselves into our most intimate processes. Social constructions became personal constructions. Seemingly objective descriptions became incarnated as subjective experiences of panic, of feeling psychologically "sick" or as a desperate determination not to let socially and *personally* unacceptable feelings be acted upon or known by anyone.

For anyone who has ever had her or his viability as a person thoroughly subjugated to the dominant culture's prescriptive definitions for healthy and appropriate personhood, and who has, furthermore, found these prescriptions backed by the authority of scientific truth, survival can sometimes be measured in terms of an ability to successfully challenge this authority and unravel the threads that hold this "truth" together. By doing so, we forge a clearing (personal, interpersonal, social, cultural, and/or political) in which to tell new stories that position at the center of our constructions of "reality" precisely those interests, experiences, and points of view (our own or those of people like us) that had been pushed to or beyond the margins of the dominant account. In this clearing we may see the personal strengths, resiliency and resistance to oppression that went unnoticed and untold in what were previously unchallengeable descriptions of our "true" nature. All of which is to say that there is a great deal at stake, particularly for those of us with "social liabilities," in who gets to speak what truth.

THE FINDING AND MAKING OF A "SELF"

As social constructionists, we believe that we all, quite literally, find our selves through our entry into and participation in the ongoing conversations of our communities and culture (which is to say we always arrive in the middle of the conversation and find our place or role in it.) However, these are frequently not free and open conversations among equal participants. Rather, these are conversations in which certain points of view have already gained ascendancy, in which some classes of persons hold positions of privilege, while others are marginalized or silenced. Those who are privileged get to decide, in a sense, what the rest of us are talking about (or hearing), what terms are used, how they are defined and, therefore, what things mean within the context of the conversation. They generally determine who gets to speak, whose voices are heard and, consequently, whose interests are most clearly and forcibly represented in the conversation. Of course, this is particularly true of cultural conversations (or discourses) that are organized around dominant views of reality.

For instance, as a young gay man, I (Mark) found my "self" within the context of my participation in larger cultural conversations in which the dominant group, heterosexuals, most often depicted homosexuals, i.e., folks like me, as sick, pathetic and despised. Therefore, I could not help but find a "self" that was stigmatized, pathologized and defined as irrevocably "other" to the community of meaning in which I participated. Heterosexuality was obviously natural, normal, and healthy, while homosexuality was equally obviously a deformity of psyche, soul and sex. There were other voices saying something different, but they seemed to me to be whispering inaudibly to each other in some secret conversation amongst dubious people that was taking place well outside the bounds of the conversation I found my "self" in. I therefore participated in a socially constructed "reality," which also became, sadly, a "therapeutically" constructed reality, in which I was a developmentally impaired, emotionally deformed person, even to myself. In narrative terms, this was the story I told myself, the story that constrained me to live by its terms, although it was certainly not a story that I simply invented nor one I chose. Rather, it was a story that organized the meanings that were then available to me into a coherent sense of reality, a story that sustained my sense of continuing connection to other people, even as it, ironically, profoundly constrained my actual relationships with them. In terms of my homosexuality, the only possible narrative that could connect me to others was the dominant homophobic discourse circulating between us, so that connection seemed possible only if I understood myself in similarly homophobic terms. This was my socially constructed reality.

As long as I continued to find my "self" in relation to this particular, yet seemingly omnipresent community of meaning, there seemed to be only two positions that I could occupy that would allow me to participate in their conversation. One was to take a position of open opposition and defiance, in which case my role in the conversation would have been that of the rebel who was also a pariah and an outcast. I could try to reject the terms of the conversation but then I was faced with either wandering alone in the wilderness or trying to find connection with the only people who would still be available to me (I thought), those other pariahs who had been cast out from their communities because of their freakishness, because they had been found so thoroughly and completely unacceptable. Both of these prospects terrified me. The other position was to collude with the meanings generated in this conversation about people like me, to take them as my own, to belong to this community of meaning by hiding, disavowing or disowning that aspect of my being-in-the-world, my attraction to other men, that had been marked as unacceptable. Or perhaps I might somehow try to occupy both positions, scuttling back and forth on a high wire strung between self-repudiation and exile from my community, a truly vertiginous balancing act. These were unhappy positions to occupy.

Impelled by the emotional pain of feeling trapped in these utterly hopeless positions, I began eventually to listen more closely to the whisperings of that other conversation where people were saying radical things like "gay is okay" and "we are being oppressed." For awhile I moved back and forth between these two different conversations until I seemed to find my "self" within the context of this new community of meaning, the one that resided at an alternative

27

location. It is not so much that the self I found was more real or true (i.e., my essential nature) as that I was able, for the first time, to join unrestrainedly in the mutual construction of meaning around my "self," instead of feeling intimidated or silenced while others went about constructing the terms I was to live by. This was a different kind of conversation in which the possibilities of "gay" and "me" could be brought forth and elaborated, instead of stifled and crushed. But "gay" was not something I could just decide to be on my own, a natural substance to be thrust into the world from out of the dark cave of my bounded individual self. Rather, I needed to join with others to open space in the world for something called "gay," to construct together a new story that carried with it the weight of a genuinely possible and livable "reality." My decision to "come out of the closet" was simultaneously a decision to join a community of others for whom "gay" was at the center of their relational and meaning worlds instead of at the margins. Since then, being gay has often meant unpacking the many possible meanings contained (or created) by the term "gay" so that the meaning of "gay," for me, has been continually elaborated, redrawn, and reconnected to my relational world. As I have elaborated the meaning of the word "gay," I have also elaborated myself (and vice versa) so that being gay and being me means something quite different (and, I think, better) now than it did when I first "came out."

Because the meaning of homosexuality has been (and still is) so contested, because the negotiation of its meaning is so visible and so visibly subject to political vicissitudes, we can easily see how definitions of homosexuality are inevitably products of social processes. Our contention is that homosexuality is not a special case but rather a case whose controversial character makes visible general and ubiquitous processes of social construction that in less controversial cases are less easily seen. Privileged identities (such as heterosexuality) that are taken-for-granted and deemed normal and natural are no less socially constructed—it is just that they are socially constructed as taken-for-granted identities that are normal and natural. Of course, most of us participate in multiple conversations taking place within our communities and cultures, conversations that often seem to place us in varying positions and degrees of privilege and/or marginalization, which weave different, sometimes contradictory meanings around our relationships and our sense of self, meanings that come together in complex storylines that are often fragmented, that don't quite add up.

As a result, it ultimately falls upon the person to fashion a coherent (if not necessarily consistent) sense of her or his own being-in-the-world, to construe self and world in a way that manages to be both intelligible and viable for the project of living. As an individual, I (Franz) certainly don't invent the meanings I live by, ex nihilo, from within the interiority of my own being. Rather, the systems of meanings in which I participate each day sift down and "sediment" in my body, my thoughts, my feelings, my desires, where they become transformed into meanings that are not so much "individual" as meanings that feel exquisitely and sometimes excruciatingly personal. It is my desire, my suffering, my joy, my relationships, my viability, my life that are at stake in my personal constructions of reality. Our personal constructions are the form of our own existential commitment to a particular way of living and being-in-the world. They are the form of our engagement with the conversations at hand, and as engaged participants we may well make our own distinct, even original, contribution to the conversations in which we participate. In fact, we mark ourselves as us by the particular and sometimes, peculiar, contributions we make. So we need to have some way to talk about this aspect of the construction of meaning as well.

PERSONAL CONSTRUCTIONS AND SOCIAL MEANING

George Kelly's personal construct psychology speaks to this personal level of meaning-making and to the existential project of fashioning a viable self in the world that all of us must undertake. By our very participation in relational contexts, we are able to clear a space wherein we lay claim to meanings that we call and make our own. In this space we can make choices between the various constructive alternatives that are available to us—certainly "coming out of the closet" is an example of this. Personal constructions are both idiosyncratically personal and arise through social interchange. We see PCP as a bringing together of the personal, the existential and the pragmatic within a framework that in no way precludes or contradicts insights generated by social constructionism into the larger collaborative, systemic, and cultural nature of meaning-making. At the same time, Kelly's (1969) theory allows us to talk about personal processes without resorting to conventional ideas about entities such as traits, motivations, and various other purely internal states or dynamics that tend to be posited within the context of cause and effect explanations of individual behavior. According to Kelly, we are fundamentally construing beings whose processes of construction are always, and necessarily, in motion. We cannot not construe events in some fashion or another. For Kelly then, there is no need to posit internal structures or dynamics existing prior to and as causal agents of personal constructions. Rather, the only meaningful question is–in what direction do our constructions take us? Whatever direction we happen to be going in, it will necessarily be a direction co-constituted within the space between ourselves and other people.

Core constructions, the very heart of Kelly's theory, are defined in such a way that formally includes the social—in fact, he calls these role-governing core constructs (Epting, 1984); that is, the most salient and emotionally compelling ways in which we construe our relationships with others. In this way, Kelly speaks to how our most personal constructions are necessarily infused with social meaning and intimately bound up with our relationships, to how that which is most fundamentally personal is also that which most clearly connects us to other people.

This fundamental connection between the social and personal can be very aptly illustrated by focusing on the way Kelly portrays the experience of guilt. Let us start this exploration by examining what Kelly means by core constructions. For Kelly, core constructs are the most precious meanings we hold about who we are and what our world is like. In Kelly's words, "Core constructs are those which govern a person's maintenance processes—that is, those by which he [sic] maintains his identity and existence" (Kelly, 1955/1991a, p. 482/356, italics in original). These are the notions that are the most personal and, at the same time, the ones that most closely tie us to our social world. This unavoidable and necessary fusion of the social and the person is illustrated by Kelly's conception of guilt, which he defines as the "Perception of one's apparent dislodgment from one's core role structure" (Kelly, 1955/1991a, p. 502/370).

For Kelly, "role" is understood as a relationship we set up with others based on our best understanding of them as people who are different from ourselves, yet somehow still comprehensible. We are said to be in a role relationship with another person when we interact with that person on the basis of our best attempt to understand what the world is like for her or him. A role therefore involves our treating the other person as someone who has a whole life perhaps not totally dissimilar from our own. We interact with this other person on the basis of his or her being a whole human being rather than an object for us to manipulate, fix, dispense with, or ignore. Being dislodged from a core role structure, or more simply put, being dislodged from an important *core role*, means that we have somehow slipped away (or been driven away by powerful forces) from important social/personal moorings and have started literally to lose a crucial part of what we have always taken ourselves to be. Kelly goes on to elaborate his concept of guilt in the following way:

> We are dependent for life itself upon an understanding of the thoughts of certain other people. The psychology of personal constructs emphasizes the essential importance of *social construc-tions*. It emphasizes the fact that a role is not always a superficial thing, a simple mask to be taken off; rather, that there is a core role, a part one plays as if one's life depended on it. Indeed, one's life actually does depend on it. Finally it is the loss of sta-tus within the core role constructions which is experienced as guilt. (Kelly, 1955/1991a, pp. 503/370-371; emphasis added)

He later asserts:

> If the whole truth were known, it is likely that we would learn that the sustenance of life in the face of extreme guilt is difficult in any cultural group, including our own. It is difficult, not only because it interferes with the adequate distribution of our dependencies, but also because it interferes with the sponta-neous elaboration of all our psychological processes, including the so-called "bodily" processes. (Kelly, 1955/1991b, p. 909/246)

Here Kelly is referring to the kind of profound guilt that might be experienced by a young person, in his early teens, grow-ing up in a fundamentalist Christian home, who becomes increas-ingly aware of the fact that he is sexually attracted to some of the other boys in his school. The dislodgment from his core role as a good Christian would be profound and the resulting guilt feelings massive, and might extend not only to personal distress but also to a gut-wrenching pain, as if the body itself was enacting the agonies of his expulsion from that crucial role which had previously defined him. In fact, it is not uncommon to learn that a young man, so estranged from his primary community, cannot find a way to go on living. As Kelly says:

> There are records of outcasts who soon die, apparently as a result of the loss of their core role...Our constructions of our relationships to the thinking and expectancies of certain other people reach down deeply into our vital processes. Through our constructions of our roles we sustain even the most autonomic life functions. These are indeed *core role structures*. (Kelly, 1955/1991b, p. 909/246, italics in original)

31

By taking such a position in order to account for the feeling of guilt, Kelly is tying together not only the psychological identity but also the bodily existence of the person with social meaning. He is saying that there are, in fact, unbreakable bonds among what is in the realm of personal meanings, what is in the realm of the social meaning of events, and what is in the body. Kelly is further asserting that the social is primary in terms of giving a context for the person to be in a body. We are using the experience of guilt to illustrate Kelly's way of fusing the social with the personal, but the same case could be made for his portrayal of anxiety, hostility, fear, and threat, to mention only a few of the concerns we might have in looking more carefully at the young man in our example. In undertaking this illustration based on Kelly's work, we are very much in accord with Stojnov and Butt (2002) who assert "it is our deep belief that personal construct systems are not situated 'in the head' but between people. It seems that Kelly made the person a 'crossroads' of interacting human individuals" (p. 88). We would go even further to make the case that Kelly extended this "crossroads" to include the body and the literal existence of people. It is not too uncommon to find that people, on the basis of their constructions of life, have despaired to the point of a sickness unto death. To say that realities are socially (and interpersonally) constructed does not mean that our constructions of reality are not frequently a matter of life and death for us.

IN CONCLUSION

Playwright Tony Kushner (2002), author of *Angels in America*, speaks eloquently of the intimate and powerful connection between the personal and the social:

> For the truly imaginative mind, for the truly adventuresome spirit, for the truly living heart, introspection, memory, interiority do not lead one into isolation and implosion. Self-exploration is revealed to be only another path, perhaps the highest, truest path, to the world at large, to other people, to the communal, the social, the political. (pp. x-xi)

What Kushner is saying is that the more we search for those truths lodged within the innermost recesses of our being, the more we will find ourselves discovering our essential and unbreakable connectedness to other people, to our social world, to the stories that define the particular time and place in which we live.

Kushner's statement serves to underscore the central argument of this chapter, that what is most deeply personal is, at the same

time, profoundly social. Once we let go of the individual as somehow being the foundation of all we know and do, once we recognize
that an individual self can have no understanding of either self or
world without first belonging to the world, without already participating in a web of social connections that bring definition to both
self and world, then we can embrace the personal without denying
the primacy and power of the social. As we said earlier, we see the
personal, the relational, and the social as forming a gestalt. Social
constructs and personal constructs are two sides of the same coin:
the construction of meaning. Furthermore, we see social constructionism and personal construct psychology as offering two different
levels of analysis of human meaning-making, both of which are necessary for generating a comprehensive framework that genuinely
engages with the complexity and significance of persons, relationships and social context. In addition, we see engaging with the person in context as essential for fashioning a meaningful and a most
especially helpful therapeutic encounter.

REFERENCES

Blackburn, S. (1994). *The Oxford dictionary of philosophy*. Oxford: Oxford University Press.

Burr, V. (1995). *An introduction to social constructionism*. London: Routledge.

Cushman, P. (1995). *Constructing the self, constructing America: A cultural history of psychotherapy*. Reading, MA: Addison-Wesley.

Dreyfus, H. L. & Rabinow, P. (1982). *Michel Foucault: Beyond structuralism and hermeneutics*. Chicago: University of Chicago Press.

Early, G., Nazario, A. & Steier, H. (1994, April). *Oppression-sensitive family therapy: A health-affirming model*. Paper presented at the meeting of the American Orthopsychiatric Association, Washington, DC.

Epting, F. R. (1984). *Personal construct counseling and psychotherapy*. Chichester: John Wiley.

Foucault, M. (1980). *Power/Knowledge: Selected interviews and other writings of Michel Foucault, 1972-1977*. New York: Pantheon Books.

Frede, D. (1993). The question of being: Heidegger's project. In C. Guignon (Ed.), *The Cambridge companion to Heidegger* (pp. 42-69). Cambridge, UK: Cambridge University Press.

Freedman, J. & Combs, G. (1996). *Narrative therapy: The social construction of preferred realities*. New York: Norton.

Gergen, K. J. (1994). *Realities and relationships: Soundings in social construction*. Cambridge, MA: Harvard University Press.

Gergen, K. J. (2001). *Social construction in context*. London: Sage.

Hacking, I. (1999). *The social construction of what?* Cambridge, MA: Harvard University Press.

Halperin, D. M. (1995). *Saint Foucault: Towards a gay hagiography*. New York: Oxford University Press.

Kelly, G. A. (1969). The autobiography of a theory. In B. Maher (Ed.). *Clinical psychology and personality: The selected papers of George Kelly* (pp. 46-65). New York: John Wiley.

Kelly, G. A. (1991a). *The psychology of personal constructs: Vol. 1. A theory of personality*. London: Routledge. (Original work published 1955)

Kelly, G. A. (1991b). *The psychology of personal constructs: Vol. 2. Clinical diagnosis and psychotherapy*. London: Routledge. (Original work published 1955)

Kushner, T. (2002). Foreword. In T. Miller, *Body blows: Six performances* (pp. ix-xii). Madison, WI: University of Wisconsin Press.

McNamee, S. (2002). The social construction of disorder: From pathology to potential. In J. D. Raskin & S. K. Bridges (Eds.), *Studies in meaning: Exploring constructivist psychology* (pp. 143-168). New York: Pace University Press.

McNamee, S. (2004 [this volume]). Relational bridges between constructionism and constructivism. *Studies in meaning 2: Bridging the personal and social in constructivist psychology* (pp. 37-50). New York: Pace University Press.

Nazario, A. (1998). Counseling Latina/o families. In W. M. Parker (Ed.), Consciousness-raising: A primer for mulicultural counseling (2nd ed., pp. 205-222). Springfield, IL: Charles C. Thomas.

Raskin, J. D. (2002). Constructivism in psychology: Personal construct psychology, radical constructivism, and social constructionism. In J. D. Raskin & S. K. Bridges (Eds.), *Studies in meaning: Exploring constructivist psychology* (pp. 1-25). New York: Pace University Press.

Raskin, J. D. & Lewandowski, A. M. (2000). The construction of dis order as human enterprise. In R. A. Neimeyer & J. D. Raskin (Eds.), *Constructions of disorder: Meaning-making frameworks for psychotherapy* (pp. 15-40). Washington, DC: American Psychological Association.

Scheman, N. (1996). Forms of life: Mapping the rough ground. In H. Sluga & D. G. Stern (Eds.). *The Cambridge companion to Wittgenstein* (pp. 383-410). Cambridge, UK: Cambridge University Press.

Stojnov, D. & Butt, T. (2002). The relational basis of personal construct psychology. In R. A. Neimeyer and G. J. Neimeyer (Eds.), *Advances in personal construct psychology: New directions and perspectives* (pp. 81-110). Westport, CT: Praeger.

Szasz, T. (1974). *The myth of mental illness: Foundations of a theory of personal conduct* (rev. ed.). New York: Harper & Row.

Weston, K. (1991). *Families we choose: Lesbians, gays, kinship.* New York: Columbia University Press.

White, M. & Epston, D. (1990). *Narrative means to therapeutic ends.* New York: Norton

Wittgenstein, L. (2001). *Philosophical investigations: The German text, with a revised English translation.* Oxford, UK: Blackwell Publishers.

CHAPTER 2

Relational Bridges Between Constructionism and Constructivism[1]

Sheila McNamee

A good deal has been written about the distinction between constructivist and constructionist versions of psychology. At worst, the two are viewed as competing orientations; one—constructivism—whose focus is on internal, cognitive processes of individuals, the other—social constructionism—whose focus is on discourse or the joint (social) activities that transpire between people. At best, the two are viewed as similar because of their focus on meaning-making processes. George Kelly (1955/1991a, 1955/1991b), a central name in constructivism, can be described as focusing a good deal of attention on the internal processes by which individuals construe their worlds. He was interested in how a person makes *personal meaning*. Yet, as Kelly developed his corollaries (moving from the fundamental postulate to the sociality corollary) he arrived firmly located within the social, performative world of the relational (the focus of social construction). Viewed in historical context, we could easily see that Kelly, influenced by the dominance of the period's individualist discourse of social science and psychology, used this discourse as his *starting* place. He was attempting to understand how it is that people make meaning, how meaning changes and evolves, how it becomes sedimented, and so forth. His central metaphor, *person as scientist*, clearly is in keeping with the trends in psychology at the time.

It is interesting to me that much of the work that has emerged since Kelly (1955/1991a, 1955/1991b) published The *Psychology of Personal Constructs* has placed central attention on *personal* (read: individual) meaning making processes. I wonder if this focus

[1] A version of this chapter was originally presented as part of a symposium entitled *Constructivism versus Constructionism-Bridging the Gap*, which was conducted at the 110th American Psychological Association Convention, Chicago IL, August 2002.

is in some way predetermined by the power of Kelly's metaphor of person as scientist. Yet, probably the most interesting aspect of Kelly's work, to me, is how he eventually pulled himself from inside the head of the person into the social arena. As a constructionist, I would critique any approach that builds from the internal, individual to the social. Yet, one could also recognize the bold moves Kelly was suggesting at the time of his writing by moving into a relational realm to explore the human activity of meaning making.

Beyond this historical reading of Kelly's work, we must recognize that other noted constructivists, such as Mair (1988; 1989) and Neimeyer (2000) have also amplified and extended the relational aspects of Kelly's constructivism and more and more so let the residual individualism recede quietly into the background. One can question whether such attempts might simply be renamed as constructionism—we are most happy to welcome you into the club—but since there appears to be some commitment to constructivism, let us put issues of naming aside and explore in more depth the relational as the most significant bridge between constructivism and constructionism.

If we only focus on a person's construct system (as many constructivists do—particularly in the work of psychotherapy where the temptation is strong to focus on the individual), we are left with a view that, "Each individual's construct system is...private, ideographic, and personal in the way it makes meaning out of the world and the individual's experience in it" (Rosen, 1996, p. 12). In addition to placing all attention on an ideographic, individualist, private view of meaning, we can see in Rosen's words (above) an objectification of the personal construct system through his reference to it—as if a personal construct system were a separate entity from the person and his or her experience. This echoes a common constructivist theme that locates meaning within a foundational structure of the person (see McLeod, 1997 for an excellent discussion of this) and ultimately proposes that a construct system is an entity and thus can be objectively examined.

Again, if we shift our focus to the social—recognizing that it is easier for us to do so at this point in history than at the time of Kelly's writing when the idea of psychology as a science dominated—we begin to find a way for two previously incommensurate ways of approaching an understanding of meaning making to, in Wittgenstein's (1953) words, go on together. For me, an important point of connection between constructivism and constructionism is the shared desire to engage in transformative dialogue. In other words, whether in psychotherapy or in our academic conversations, I believe that both constructivism and constructionism are most concerned with how social and personal change can emerge such that we are able to co-exist and thus continue to co-create a world and a life together.

What social construction adds to this conversation, I think, is of great significance. Rather than focus attention on mental processes (construct systems, cognition), constructionism urges us to explore the ways in which people engage *together* in their activities. To the constructionist, meaning making is a relational activity (McNamee, 2002, in press-a, in press-b; McNamee & Gergen, 1999). Knowledge and understanding are not in the person but in the *performance*. Thus, interest in constructs—a hypothetical, abstract notion—is replaced with an interest in communication, discourse, and dialogue. It is not what is *in the head* but what people are *doing together* that concerns us. With this as our focus, we enter the domain of the relational. I suspect that this is what Kelly was pointing our attention towards in his sociality corollary. If we focus on what people do together, we are taking as our starting point the *relational* as opposed to the individual. Rather than explore an individual in his or her context, we are exploring relational configurations (contexts of many kinds with historical, cultural, and situational traditions and implications) *that give rise to (i.e., construct) any sense of individuality or privateness that we have*. So, as constructionists say over and over again, rather than *start* by examining individuals in order to understand the relational, we propose that meaning-making is a relational process through which we *accomplish* the creation of a sense of individuality.

From this perspective then, our "private thoughts," the deep-rooted images and beliefs we hold, can be described as internalized *conversations* (relations) with others. Again, we place the meaning making process in the relational, conversational domain. The distinction I see between constructivism (in all its colors and shapes) and constructionism (in the color and shape that I describe it) is rooted in liberating oneself from the modernist discourse where isolated individuals become the unquestioned focus of attention. As I have noted elsewhere (McNamee, 2002), it makes perfect sense to focus on self-possessed individuals because we have definable, distinguishable, non-contiguous bodies. When I look at you, I see your body and your gestures; I hear your words. Yet, if we could see the transfer of heat molecules, we would see that our bodies actually co-mingle. It is hard, a scientist friend of mine tells me, to determine where one "entity" ends and another begins. So, we might now understand the unquestioned belief that we are self-contained individuals as an illusion fed by our limited visual abilities. How might our understandings, our theories of human, social life be different if we could see the ways in which our bodies, our entities blur into one another? Would we then be inclined to fully embrace the relational as our starting point and begin to see individuality as a constructed accomplishment?

One of the primary premises of social constructionism is that, within any community, values and forms of practice will vary from other communities' constructions depending upon the ways in which participants coordinate their activities. Very much in keeping with this premise then, I would like to embrace the "difference" of constructivism, appreciate that difference, and begin to build the means for "going on together" (i.e., for making meaning about the social world in general and psychology in particular). A relational focus provides a way to go on together. The specific relational focus I am suggesting, however, is not a simple attention to relationships as entities. Rather, I am arguing for a more subtle form of relational engagement—the sort identified with dialogic process.

THE CENTRALITY OF DIALOGUE

> Sampson (1993) distinguishes between dialogue and monologue. When I construct a you designed to meet my needs and desires, a you that is serviceable for me, I am clearly engaging in a monologue as distinct from a dialogue. Although you and I may converse and interact together, in most respects the you with whom I am interacting has been constructed with me in mind. Your sole function has been to serve and service me. (p. 4)

Bakhtin (1981) describes this self-contained individual of monoligism as "a hermetic and self-sufficient whole, one whose elements constitute a closed system presuming nothing beyond themselves, no other utterances" (p. 273). Dialogue, on the other hand, "requires that there be two separable presences, each coming from its own standpoint, expressing and enacting its own particular specificity" (Sampson, 1993, p. 15). Yet, the "expressing and enacting" that can be distinguished as dialogue is a *coordinated* expressing and enacting. Perhaps Sampson's description of dialogue does not sufficiently underscore this central aspect. It is the coordination of "two separable presences" that characterize the relational engagement that is necessary for dialogue (as opposed to monologue) to transpire.

My attention here to dialogue and the ways in which participants coordinate their activities together in order to create a context where they are relationally engaged is purposeful on two fronts. First, I believe that both constructivism and constructionism might initiate generative conversation within the common discourse of dialogue. Second, I believe that an invitation to engage in dialogue, as opposed to traditional academic debate, might provide constructionists and constructivists with interesting points of connection while it simultaneously putting the focus of personal and social transformation (that both orientations champion) into practice. As Sampson argues,

> To celebrate the other is not merely to find a place for her or him within a theoretical model. Nor is it simply to analyze the role that conversations and talk play in all aspects of human endeavor. Rather, celebrating the other is also to recognize the degree to which the dialogic turn is a genuinely revolutionary transformation . . . (P. 15)

Taking Sampson's words seriously then, I would like to not only "find a place" for constructivism within my attempt to bridge the gap between constructivists and constructionists. I would like to utilize the centrality of dialogue—of what people do together—in the meaning making process for both constructionists and constructivists. Dialogue requires coordination. Narrative is one useful way to talk about the coordination necessary for transforming our academic debates into generative dialogue.

NARRATIVE AS RELATIONAL MEANING

Both constructionists and constructivists have embraced the notion of narrative (Neimeyer, 2000; Gergen and Kaye, 1992). Narrative requires relationships. No story is told in a vacuum. No story is devoid of intermingling beliefs, images, and meanings. Stories might be seen as *offerings* into a way of living a life. I say this because it differs so radically from the scientific tradition we inherent from modernism. In science, we *tell it like it is*. Objectivity and reason reign. With narrative, we populate our rationalities—our ways of making sense out of the world—with people, events, context, history, culture, family, and all the quirky things that go along with that. Science depends on rational individuals. Stories, on the other hand, depend on characters, storytellers, audiences. They shift and vary as these elements shift and vary.

I think that the use of narrative points to the relational commonalities between constructionism and constructivism. Rather than argue about the individualist hangover inherent in constructivism or critique social construction for the relinquishing of individual responsibility (as many critics do), attention to the relational aspects of meaning making *can* give us a common focus. A focus on the relational aspects of both allows us to bridge what could be seen as incommensurate differences. We can make a choice: to focus on differences and maintain the discourse of debate (who has the truth and who doesn't) or to focus on threads of similarity thereby creating the possibility to engage in dialogue (relational coordination). While some constructionists and some constructivists disagree about whether meaning making resides in the social domain (performance) or in the private recesses of individual minds, both agree that *what people do together* is central to the meaning making process. Dialogue, then, plays a central role for both. Mair (1988) suggests, in fact, that if Kelly's metaphor of "person as scientist" was transformed into "person as storyteller," we might capture what Kelly was most interested in capturing: the complexity of personal and social meaning. If we use recent constructivists' attempts (Neimeyer, 2000; Drewery, Winslade, & Monk, 2000) to focus on narrative, not as a structure, but as a process of meaning making, then we find the gap between constructivism and constructionism recede.

Yet, as rich as the metaphor of narrative may appear, it raises problems that could potentially prolong the chasm between constructivism and constructionism. Gergen and Kaye (1992) point to the common understandings of narrative as either a lens that determines how we see the world or as an internal model of the world that guides our behavior. Since constructivists come from a tradition of privileging the private, cognitive description of meaning-making, there are ample cases where narrative is used also in this private, individualist manner (see Goncalves, 1995; Goncalves, 2002).

The constructionist understanding of narrative is ultimately relational. Here, we shift from a focus on cognitive features of the person to the ways in which people engage with each other. Such a focus directs our attention to language practices as opposed to private thoughts. Neimeyer (2000) identifies the constructivist narrative as intrapersonally focused while constructionist narrative is interpersonally focused. Constructionists describe narratives as forms of action, as social performances. They are not, as more cognitively oriented constructivists would claim, causal schemas explaining our actions. By offering the intra-interpersonal distinction, Neimeyer attempts, as I am here, to bridge constructionist and constructivist positions. His attempt to do so, in my view, underscores the relational focus that might bridge these seemingly incommensurate discourses in two ways. First, it clarifies the *different* senses of narrative as they are used by constructivists (cognitive, intrapersonal scheme) and constructionists (dialogic performances with others). Second, in clarifying the distinctions (rather than arguing for one over the other) Neimeyer, himself, *performs* just the sort of transformation that I am interested in and, in doing so, offers a connection between the two approaches. For me, a nice way to expand this common link in the relational is to go back to the words of Kelly (a forefather of constructivism, but not the only one) and Wittgenstein (a forefather of constructionism). Kelly, as mentioned above, uses the metaphor of "person as scientist." He describes a scientist's "ultimate aim is to predict and control" (1955, p. 5). Whether or not we can predict and control the social world, isn't it possible for us to see a link between Kelly's image of the person—a person wishing to make his or her way through life in a way that is coherent (by some relational standards)—and Wittgenstein's (1953) orienting question, "How do we go on?" Both were concerned with the future. And, perhaps it is in this future (not the past) that the relational commonalities between constructivism and constructionism might flourish. Their shared narrative focus provides a common means for moving away from pathology toward potential, for expanding our resources for action as psychologists and psychotherapists, and for attending to processes of relating as opposed to forestructures of the mind. Our interest is not in *why* a narrative is told but *how* it is told and who populates that narrative.

Narrative can be described as a common means for expanding our resources for action. Much of the debate between constructionists and constructivists centers on the personal/social (or otherwise stated, the cognitive/performative) distinctions. But, as I mentioned earlier, we can easily describe our private, inner construct systems as a myriad of relations that we carry with us (see McNamee and Gergen, 1999, p. 11-13). Of course, this way of putting things is consistent with the historical and cultural focus of meaning in which constructionists are interested. What we take to be private thoughts now become the confluence of conversations—real, imagined, virtual—with which we have in some way engaged over time.

Having deconstructed the private/social split that has divided constructionism and constructivism, we must turn our attention to how such a deconstruction—how such a focus on the relational—expands our resources for action. In the remainder of this chapter I would like to address the common focus on narrative that has emerged in both constructivist and constructionist work. Yet, it is important to clarify that narrative, as I use the term, refers to embodied, coordinated activities among people. This view of narrative differs from discussions of narrative as a cognitive structure through which we view and make sense of the world.

FROM NARRATIVES AS STRUCTURE TO NARRATIVES AS PERFORMANCE

Specifically, and practically, I would like to propose that the common issue is how the relational aspect of narrative underscores coordination and in so doing provides us with generative ways of focusing on the future and thereby constructing alternative paths for "going on together."[2] To do so, we must move from a view of narrative as structure to a view of narrative as performance. As a performance, narrative requires coordination with others, and is, therefore, relational. However, I would like to propose that this view of narrative does not require an abandonment of what Neimeyer refers to as the constructivist attention to the intrapersonal coherence.

Earlier I suggested that what we have come to describe as private, inner thoughts can be refigured as *internal conversations* (McNamee and Gergen, 1999) that we carry with us. Whether the conversations we carry are actual, imagined, or virtual, they are relational. They require the voices of others. It might be helpful to grasp the relational nature of our private narratives by thinking of the ways in which we rehearse our anticipated performance in a setting. As I try out *my lines*, my moves, my stance, I hear the voices of other relevant players. Some of those players might be my actual partners in conversation. Others might well be voices of significant people in my life. When we talk about our beliefs, our thoughts, our private mean-

---

[2] For philosophical reasons, I am choosing Wittgenstein's focus on *how we go on together* rather than Kelly's focus on *person as scientist predicting and controlling* because it allows us to operate outside of the discourse of science.

ings, we are really giving voice to our inner dialogue. And dialogue, we know, is populated with others—it is, ultimately, relational.

This description simultaneously allows us to hold on to the focus on narrative coherence that constructivists privilege while envisioning the *private, inner narrative* as a form of relational coordination. Psychological processes are social actions as are all the interpersonal constructions of meaning. One is not more or less relational. One is not more or less performative. And we can use this formulation to fashion therapeutic questions. We can ask, "How many voices/conversations/relationships do I carry?" and "How would these other voices tell this story?" In doing so, what we have been characterizing as a form of cognitive coherence can be described as inherently relational. In this way, the static image of narrative structure takes on a performative, active quality. It is, in addition, a quality that engenders coordination with others (again, either actual, imagined, or virtual) and by so doing, remains within a deeply relational frame. Coordination, as an important aspect of narrative, highlights our interdependencies on others. Additionally, when cast as a network of internal others who we carry in conversation with us, the personal is re-situated as social. Our private inner reaches are fashioned as polyphonic. And, once again, the emphasis on coordination with others—an inherently relational activity—is required in order to *construct a narrative* that plays with the multiplicity of voices.

How might we actually put these ideas into practice and in so doing create a bridge between constructionism and constructivism? Are there any resources upon which we can draw to facilitate such a bridging? Let me suggest three as only an opening to further conversation among constructionists and constructivists interested in dialogues of transformation.

There are, I believe, a variety of ways we can make the intrapersonal, the private, the individual and cognitive structures into more dynamic, relational dialogues that require social coordination. The forms of discourse identified below are not meant as an exhaustive list but rather as a means of generative possibility. My hope is that the following discursive options open us to a view of narrative that collapses the personal/social dichotomy and offers the relational bridge between constructivism and constructionism.

Narratives of Legitimation

What are the stories that lend coherence to a situation or a relationship? In the face of conflicting views or sedimented narratives we can note a tendency for abstraction in our stories. Phrases

45

such as "That's just the way I am," or "This is the way it should be done" seem to flourish. Doesn't it seem likely that we speak from these abstract positions because they appear to carry more rhetorical force? After all, the idea of *a way things should be done* or *a way I can't help but be* seem powerful features of social life—too powerful to overcome. It would be interesting to explore in a focused and detailed manner the relationship between sedimented narratives and narratives of abstraction. But for the moment, let us note that the connection between the two is common (if not properly documented).

It is in precisely these instances that an invitation to a narration of legitimacy could open the door to more fruitful coordinations. Can we engage clients in therapy in detailing a story about how they see their relationship to their present circumstances? I draw here from the work of the Public Conversations Project (Roth, Chasin, Chasin, Becker, and Herzig, 1992). In their attempt to move groups and individuals locked in heated debate on important, "hot" issues, they suggest that opening with a question about each person's *personal* relationships to the issue invites a move toward dialogue (coordination among disparate views). Couldn't this same discourse—what I propose here as *the discourse of legitimation*—be generative in psychotherapy? Wouldn't such a question invite a story, populated by significant others, and illustrative of sincere coordination among participants? And wouldn't such a question and the story it invites move everyone beyond the notion that people have their private belief systems and instead toward a recognition of our beliefs and meanings as conversations that require relational coordination?

Narratives of Difference

Another range of relational coordination can be energized by inviting clients to coordinate their own narrative of legitimacy with the stories of legitimacy they have either heard others offer or imagine they might offer. This could be others who are in some way related to the difficulty being discussed. They could also usefully be others who the client might not typically connect with the current situation/issue. Imagining how these "unrelated others" might legitimate a particular scenario, situation, or relationship can facilitate an appreciation for the variation in perspectives on a given issue. Such appreciation resonates with the complexity of social life and avoids the simplistic parsing of life events into dualities such as "right or wrong" or "good or bad." Once confronted with such a broad range of legitimacy narratives, participants might engage in attempts to coordinate the multiplicity rather than distill the complex into the simple. This form of coordination ensures that multiple voices and relationships in some way (perhaps imaginatively or virtually) participate in personal and social transformation.

Narratives of Uncertainty

Once we open dialogue on how others might offer stories that legitimate a particular belief, activity, or situation, we are poised to reflect on our own narrative with a healthy sense of uncertainty. In other words, once we move into dialogue (i.e., coordination) with diverse stories, our own story becomes less sedimented. In the process of transformation, I find that entertaining doubt about one's own narrative is useful. Here I am not suggesting doubt or uncertainty that is self-critical or likely to create yet another dichotomy (I'm good/I'm not good). Rather, I am referring to the ways in which we might invite our clients in therapy into constructing complex narratives that by definition require relational coordination. For example, we could say that sexual abuse can be narrated in many different ways. To the perpetrator, there is one story (the story of legitimation). To the victim there is a very different story (the story of right and wrong). If we employ this idea of uncertainty, might we be encouraged to start our conversations differently. Rather than invite the narrative of legitimation or the narrative of justice, might it be useful to engage in a dialogue about the multitude of possible stories and the local coherence of each? Might we construct transformation in questioning the dominance of any one story and instead exploring what story helps us coordinate all the narratives of legitimation with each other. Narratives of uncertainty encourage us to ask (ourselves and our clients), How else might we describe this? This sort of self reflexive inquiry also underscores the relational nature of our own dialogues with ourselves. It illustrates the generative ways in which we can draw upon our own multiple voices in the construction of change.

Narratives of Possibility

Finally, we might consider how dialogue about the future, about possibilities rather than pathologies (McNamee, 2002) might underscore meaning making as relational. Here we might consider if there are any narrative possibilities for a different future. In some instances, these stories might be stories of ideal scenarios. In other cases, they might be more "pragmatic" but yield a narrative of possibility simply in shifting the conversation from the past to the future. It is important to note here that dialogue about the future does not ignore or replace narratives of the past. Rather, stories about the past are integrated into the imagined future. Here, it is worth noting that there is a significant difference between positions that disregard the past (a common and misplaced critique of some versions of social construction) and the position I offer here. As a constructionist, I am *very* concerned with the past. However, I am not interested in how or why the past causes the present. Rather, I am interested in the conversational traditions and conventions that are woven into the fabric of the interactive moment by virtue of our emersion in relational networks. And, more directly to the present point concerning possibility and future potential, I am interested in how our conversational traditions, conventions, and narrations of our past are *imagined* into our futures. In other words, how do we invite others into coordination of potential? It should be clear that narratives of possibility are not simply "pollyanna-ish" fantasies. They are, instead, emblematic of action that is relational in nature. They are emblematic of the interconnectedness of all our narratives as well as emblematic of the diversity of voice we all carry.

Relational Coordination

The narrative genres suggested here stand only as invitations to the many ways we can engage in dialogue—and thus, relational coordination—among constructivists and constructionists. Narrative is a social performance and as such, narrative can be seen as the coordination among relationships. The narrative genres identified above are not new. They simply stand as potential openings to dialogue. I have tried to sketch here the common bond between constructionism and constructivism by carefully selecting the ways in which both theories can optimize a dialogic focus. Our common interest as constructionists and constructivists is on meaning-making. In particular, we concern ourselves with generative and transformative processes of meaning-making that allow people to "predict and control" their lives in ways that facilitate "going on" with others. It is in these areas that I find constructionists and constructivists can embellish each other's conversations. Surely there are many topics each group can discuss that create and continue incommensurate and divisive debate. My attempt here is not to say such debate is wrong, nor to suggest it is damaging. I wish only to propose some common threads that might help us join in dialogue and thus in the communal construction of meaning about personal and social life.

REFERENCES

Bakhtin, M. M. (1981). The dialogic imagination. Austin: University of Texas Press.

Drewery, W., Winslade, J., & Monk, G. (2000). Resisting the dominating story: Toward a deeper understanding of narrative therapy. In R. A. Neimeyer & J. D. Raskin (Eds.), Constructions of disorder: Meaning-making frameworks for psychotherapy (pp. 243-264). Washington, DC: American Psychological Association.

Gergen, K. J., & Kaye, J. (1992). Beyond narrative in the negotiation of therapeutic meaning. In S. McNamee & K. J. Gergen (Eds.), Therapy as social construction (pp. 166-185). London: Sage Publications.

Goncalves, O. F., Korman, Y., & Angus, L. (2000). Constructing psychopathology from a cognitive narrative perspective. In R. A. Neimeyer & J. D. Raskin (Eds.), Constructions of disorder: Meaning-making frameworks for psychotherapy (pp. 265-284). Washington, DC: American Psychological Association.

Goncalves, O. F. (1995). Cognitive narrative psychotherapy. In M. J. Mahoney (Ed.), Cognitive and constructive psychotherapies (pp. 139-162). Elmsford, NY: Pergamon Press.

Kelly, G. A. (1991a). The psychology of personal constructs: Vol. 1. A theory of personality. London: Routledge. (Original work published 1955)

Kelly, G. A. (1991b). The psychology of personal constructs: Vol. 2 . Clinical diagnosis and psychotherapy. London: Routledge. (Original work published 1955)

Mair, M. (1988). Psychology as storytelling. International Journal of Personal Construct Psychology, 1, 125-137.

Mair, M. (1989). Kelly, Bannister, and a story-telling psychology. International Journal of Personal Construct Psychology, 2, 1-14.

McLeod, J. (1997). Narrative and psychotherapy. London: Sage Publications.

McNamee, S. (2002). The social construction of disorders: From pathology to potential. In J. D. Raskin & S. K. Bridges (Eds.), Studies in meaning: Exploring constructivist psychology (pp. 143-168). New York: Pace University Press.

McNamee, S. (in press-a). Therapy as social construction: Back to basics and forward toward challenging issues. In D. Pare and T. Strong (Eds.), Furthering talk: Advances in the discursive therapies. New York: Kluwer Academic/Plenum Press.

McNamee, S. (in press-b). Social construction as practical theory: Lessons for practice and reflection in psychotherapy. In D. Pare & G. Larner, Critical knowledge and practice in psychology and therapy. New York: Haworth Press.

McNamee, S., & Gergen, K. J. (1999). Relational responsibility: Resources for sustainable dialogue. Thousand Oaks, CA: Sage.

Neimeyer, R. A. (2000). Narrative disruptions in the construction of the self. In R. A. Neimeyer & J. D. Raskin (Eds.), Constructions of disorder: Meaning-making frameworks for psychotherapy (pp. 207-242). Washington, DC: American Psychological Association.

Rosen, H. (1996). Meaning-making narratives: Foundations for constructivist and social constructionist psychotherapies. In H. Rosen & K. T. Kuehlwein (Eds.), Constructing realities: Meaning-making perspectives for psychotherapists (pp. 3-51). San Francisco: Jossey-Bass.

Roth, S., Chasin, L., Chasin, R., Becker, C., and Herzig, M., (1992). From debate to dialogue: A facilitating role for family therapists in the public forum. Dulwich Centre Newsletter, 2, 41-48.

Sampson, E. E. (1993). Celebrating the other. Boulder, CO: Westview Press.

Terrell, C. J., & Lyddon, W. J. (1995). [Narrative and psychotherapy.] Journal of Constructivist Psychology, 9, 27-44.

Wittgenstein, L. (1953). Philosophical investigations. New York: Macmillan.

CHAPTER 3

Steering Personal Construct Theory Toward Hermeneutic Constructivism[1]

Gabriele Chiari and Maria Laura Nuzzo

Previously we contrasted epistemological constructivism with hermeneutic constructivism (Chiari & Nuzzo, 1996a, 1996b). Both constructivist metatheoretical assumptions share the view that what we believe to know about reality is a personal construction. This common aspect differentiates them from the perspective we called *limited realism*, implied by all the traditional cognitive perspectives and centered on the notion of a (better or worse) representation of one reality rather than of personal constructions of realities.

According to *epistemological constructivism*, a person is supposed to look at an independently existing world, but personal (as well as scientific) knowledge does not (can not) reflect an "objective" ontological reality: it reflects none other than a viable ordering of a world constituted by our experience within the constraints of the "real" world. In other words, epistemological constructivism holds a subjective view of experience, and therefore presupposes a separation between subject and object—a subject-object duality. The radical constructivist epistemology that von Glasersfeld (1974, 1982) recognizes in Piaget's genetic epistemology embodies what we mean by epistemological constructivism.

On the other hand, *hermeneutic constructivism* rejects both a subjectivist and an objectivist view in favor of an interdependence of a mutual specification between subject and object—a subject/object complementarity. This kind of relation is similar to the relationship between a text and its reader envisioned by contemporary hermeneutic phenomenology (Gadamer, 1960). The text has no intrinsic meaning, independent of an interpretation. Interpretation

[1] A version of this chapter was originally presented at the 15th International Congress on Personal Construct Psychology, Huddersfield, England, UK, July 2003.

arises from the interaction between the "horizon" supplied by the text and the "horizon" given to the text by the interpreter. In the same way each person—in understanding the world, him or herself, and other people—is continuously involved in a process of interpretation. Many representatives of social constructionism (Gergen, 1985), as well as Maturana and Varela's (1980, 1987) theory of autopoiesis, appear to fit this latter metatheory. Here, knowledge is not knowledge of something, but a proper bringing forth of things as the result of the making of distinctions by an observer within a linguistic domain generated from and in the reciprocal interaction among self-organizing systems during their ontogenesis.

Kelly's (1955/1991a, 1955/1991b) personal construct theory (PCT) has been recognized as a forerunner of contemporary psychological constructivism (Chiari, 2000). Notwithstanding this, if we pay attention to the above distinctions we observe that prominent scholars and researchers in the field of PCT (quoted in Raskin, 2002, pp. 9-10) interpret it in terms of a limited realism rather than according to an epistemological, not to mention a hermeneutic, constructivism. That is, they argue that some personal constructions are better than others if they conform more adequately to a supposedly external reality independent from the observer. On the other hand, we have already pointed out (Chiari & Nuzzo, 1996a, 1996b) that PCT can be easily regarded as embracing an epistemological constructivist metatheory. The very philosophical assumption of constructive alternativism fulfills the fundamental requirement of epistemological constructivism to the extent that it suggests the possibility of construing the world in many equally legitimate ways (Chiari & Nuzzo, 2003).

Moreover, Kelly pointed out that a feature of any good scientific theorizing is its modifiability "which is not so much a property of theories themselves as it is of those who use them" (1955/1991a, p. 30/22). The sentence can be rephrased in a hermeneutic way, recognizing a relation of complementarity between the theory and its users: *the modifiability of a theory arises from the encounter between the theory and those who use it*. In other words, PCT is open to further elaborations (that is, it is permeable) to the extent that one can read it in a propositional way. We are trying to elaborate PCT as a hermeneutic constructivist theory, in the direction already shown by Butt (1998a, 1998b) and ourselves (Chiari & Nuzzo, 2000).

We aim to offer some hints in this direction, stressing what we regard as three of the most important, distinctive features of hermeneutic constructivism. We can find them extensively treated in hermeneutic phenomenology under the headings of historicity, embodied subjectivity, and language—dimensions dealt with in particular by Gadamer, Merleau-Ponty and Heidegger, respectively. We shall illustrate them by resorting to somewhat similar notions pertaining to the disciplinary domains of cognitive science and psychology. This will make easier to show their role in our tentative interpretation of PCT as a hermeneutic constructivist theory.

HISTORICITY , RECURSIVENESS , AND RECURSIVE CONTRUING

According to Gadamer's (1960, 1986) philosophical hermeneutics, any interpretation is bound and embedded in history because understanding deploys the knower's effective-history (that is, his or her personal experience and cultural traditions) to assimilate new experiences. In other words, the initial structure of an effective-history constrains the range of possible interpretations, excluding some possibilities and calling forth others. Effective-history constitutes the prejudices brought to bear in understanding, and implies the historicity of any interpretation.

Gadamer's notion of effective-history reminds us of Pepper's (1942/1970) world hypothesis of contextualism whose root metaphor is the historical event. History is here an attempt to re-present events, in that "the very integration of the conditions of an event will alter the context of a future event which appears to have a similarity to a preceding event" (Sarbin, 1977, p. 6). Even von Foerster's (1982) distinction between trivial and non-trivial machines, characterized by their independency/dependency from history, addresses a similar notion in the highly abstract language of cybernetics. The input to a non-trivial machine determines the output and, at the same time, modifies the machine's internal state, thus modifying the output at a subsequent occurrence of the same input.

Generally speaking, when the operations of a process are based on the results of its preceding operations, as in the cases reported above, the process itself can be regarded as recursive. Maturana (1995) offers a more strict definition of recursion: "there is a recursion whenever the observer can claim that the reapplication of an operation occurs as a consequence of its previous application" (p. 153). Recursion can be contrasted with repetition or iteration:

> There is a repetition whenever an observer can claim that a given operation is realized again independent of the consequences of its previous realization...Whenever the observer sees

53

a repetition he or she sees that everything remains otherwise the
same, and...whenever the observer sees a recursion he or she
sees the appearance of a new phenomenal domain. (Maturana,
1995, p. 153)

In everyday life we can find many examples of recursive
processes and contrast them with iterative processes. For instance, we
perform an iterative process if we make several photocopies of the
same original, whereas we use a recursive process if we make a photocopy of a photocopy of a photocopy (and so on) of an original.

It is easy to show examples of recursive processes in mathe-
matics and geometry. Factorial numbers represent a simple example,
where the recursion relationship is $n! = n\ (n-1)!$ More suggestive
examples are Fibonacci numbers (0, 1, 1, 2, 3, 5, 8, 13...), where
each number is the sum of the preceding two numbers, and the
Mandelbrot set, that is, the set of all the points that remain tied for
each iteration of $z = z*z+c$, where the initial point of z is 0 and c is a
constant. Both Fibonacci numbers and the Mandelbrot set (at the
basis of the geometry of fractals) are used in the natural sciences as
a general basis from which models can be produced to represent
such things as plant growth, the structures of various organs in the
body, the structure of molecules or the fractal nature of coastlines.
Graphically, the repetitive/recursive distinction can be represented
by contrasting a circle with a spiral—and this suggests to us
Waddington's (1977) distinction between homeostasis and its
dynamic extension, homeorhesis, consisting of the maintenance of
stability through change.

Given that historicity refers to the unavoidability to found
any new interpretation on the constrained possibilities offered by the
current structure of the knower, historicity can be viewed in terms
of recursiveness. The plausibility of such a translation is illustrated in
the best possible way in psychology by Piaget's theory of cognitive
development in terms of adaptation. In fact, according to Piaget, any
form of knowledge always includes a process of assimilation to previous structures. It is founded on an individual's prior knowledge,
consistently with a recursive process of development from sensori-
motor schemes (coordination of actions) to formal operations
(coordination of internalized actions). Piaget understands knowledge in terms of historicity, and Sarbin (1977), coherently, considers his theories of psychological functioning illustrative of the use of
a contextualist paradigm. Interestingly, Sarbin sees in Kelly a similar
use of the contextualist worldview, even though "Kelly's contextual-

ism did not go far enough…Kelly did not follow the implications of his apparent departure from prevailing mechanistically oriented theories" (Sarbin, 1977, p. 12).

Actually, we see in Kelly's work an abundant recourse to the notion of recursiveness. The recursive nature of the evolution of a person's construction system appears clear to us in the Modulation Corollary, where it is specified that "the progressive variation must… take place within a system" (Kelly, 1955/1991a, p. 77/54). As a result, "even the changes which a person attempts within himself must be construed by him" (p. 78/55). It is worthwhile reporting the following quotation:

> The new outlook which a person gains from experience is itself an event; and, being an event in his life, it needs to be construed by him if he is to make any sense out of it. Indeed, he cannot even attain the new outlook in the first place unless there is some comprehensive overview within which it can be construed. Another way of expressing the same thing is to say that one does not learn certain things merely from the nature of the stimuli which play upon him; *he learns only what his framework is designed to permit him to see in the stimuli*. (Kelly, 1955/1991a, p. 79/55, italics added)

Recursiveness is connected to an understanding of living systems in terms of their autonomy. In fact, rephrasing the above notion in more modern terms, we can easily say that Kelly considers a person's construction system as an autonomous system and, as such, as organizationally closed: that is, a system whose processes are related as a network so that they recursively depend on each other in the generation of the processes themselves. These same processes constitute the system as a unity recognizable in the domain in which the processes exist.

Such self-referentiality of processes implies in its turn a consideration of a person's construction system as determined by its structure instead of by its environment. We refer to a previous paper of ours to provide documentation of a feature of structural determinism in Kelly's work (Chiari & Nuzzo, 1996a). What we wish to emphasize is that the choice to stress Kelly's resort to recursiveness in his understanding of personal knowledge affords us a first strong cue for locating PCT within a hermeneutic constructivist framework.

EMBODIMENT AND EMBODIED PERSONAL CONSTRUCTIONS

By *embodiment*, a second important feature of hermeneutic constructivism, we refer to an understanding of the mind as inherently embodied: that is, as arising from the structure of our brains, bodies, and bodily experience, in their turn molded by our history of interactions with the world, on the basis of a relation of complementarity between organism and environment (see also Chiari & Nuzzo, 2001).

This approach, seen in Merleau-Ponty's (1945) analysis of perception, is one of the most important phenomenological elaborations. In the field of cognitive science, outside the dominant representationalist paradigm, the notion of embodiment has been particularly developed in Maturana's understanding of knowledge as a biological phenomenon; in Varela's (Varela, Thompson & Rosch, 1991) *enactive approach* and his notion of knowledge as *embodied action* (with explicit reference to Merleau-Ponty); and in the re-opening of central Western philosophical questions in terms of *embodied mind* by Lakoff and Johnson (1998).

The last two authors suggest that even the process of categorization is a consequence of how we are embodied (Lakoff & Johnson, 1998). We have evolved to categorize; if we had not, we would not have survived. Categorization is, for the most part, not a product of conscious reasoning: we categorize as we do because we have the brains and bodies we have and because we interact in and with the world the way we do. The categories we form are part of our experience. They are the structures that differentiate aspects of our experience into discernible parts. Categorization is thus not a purely intellectual matter, occurring after the fact of experience. Rather, the formation and use of categories is the stuff of experience: it is part of that in which our bodies and brains are constantly engaged.

Embodiment can be regarded as an implication of the recursive development of cognitive systems. It corresponds to the stronger or weaker rootedness in the body of the structures arising from the continuous elaboration of the system, up to the emergence of language (more on this to follow). However, if recursiveness appears to us at the surface of Kelly's theoretical position, we had to unearth the presence of embodiment from the "inner body" of PCT. Can personal constructions be regarded as embodied? A first affirmative answer can arise from the very nature of "personal construct" as specified by Kelly: "Human discrimination may take place also at levels which have been called 'physiological' or 'emotional'. Nor is discrimination necessarily a verbalized process. Man discriminates even at a very primitive and behavioral level" (Kelly, 1969a, p. 219).

Here, Kelly seems to assert that some personal constructs are closer to "bodily" processes than others; these are less abstract than the *verbal* constructs. In the language of PCT, in a person's construction system there are also *pre-verbal* and *non-verbal* constructs. At the same time, his reference to different "levels of discrimination" can be meant as a loose sign of recursiveness.

A second, stronger suggestion comes from his account of the disorders involving guilt:

> The sustenance of life in the face of extreme guilt is difficult...not only because it interferes with the adequate distribution of our dependencies, but also because it interferes with the spontaneous elaboration of all our psychological processes, including the so-called "bodily" processes. Our constructions of our roles are not altogether superficial affairs—masks to be put on and taken off for the sake of social appearances only. Our constructions of our relationships to the thinking and expectancies of certain other people reach down deeply into our vital processes. Through our constructions of our roles we sustain even the most autonomic life functions. There are indeed *core role structures*. (Kelly, 1955/1991b, p. 909/246)

Here, the vital connotation of core role structures derives not so much from their particular nature, as from their "historical" (recursive) derivation from more primitive structures. Our understanding in terms of recursive processes of Kelly's progressive evolution of the person, as well as the presence in Kelly's theory of a dimension of embodiment, are validated by his inclusion in a person's construction system of what he termed "core constructs," "*those which govern a person's maintenance processes*—that is, *those by which he maintains his identity and existence*" (Kelly, 1955/1991a, p. 482/356; italics in original). Even though outside the range of convenience of a psychological theory, the maintenance processes are supposed to be affected by the interaction of the person in a social domain. In this very sense, some personal constructs—core and core role constructs, whether or not they are put into words—are embodied.

LANGUAGE, OBJECTS, AND SELVES

The crucial importance of language in the construction of realities and selves is a third mark of hermeneutic phenomenological perspectives. Kelly does not appear to have adequately dealt with the topic of language. The above-mentioned distinction between *non-verbal*, *pre-verbal* and *verbal constructs*, combined with the warning not to confuse a personal construct with its verbal label, appear to be almost the only references to language in PCT. This notwithstanding, we think it worthwhile to draw attention to some passages of Kelly's work in order to compare them with more recent constructivist accounts, and to stress at least their coherence with the elaboration we are presenting here.

The emergence and the role of language have been described in some constructivist explanations—In particular in Maturana (1978, 1995)—in terms of the outcome of progressive recursions following recurrent interactions in a particular class of living systems (human beings) endowed with a sufficient structural plasticity. In other words, language—as well as the subsequent distinction of objects and the emergence of self-consciousness—can be regarded as the possible results of the system's conservation of an adaptation with the environment in a social domain.

According to Maturana, the whole process starts from the consensual coordination of behavior between two living systems as a result of their living together (see Figure 1). One instance of this *linguistic behavior* is the consensual coordination of a cat scratching a door to be let out of the house by its owner.

Following a first recursion in the coordination of consensual behavior (that is, in presence of consensual behavior about consensual behavior), a new phenomenon emerges: *languaging*. Only with language, objects and self can emerge: they do not preexist language. In fact, *observing* arises as an operation in a second recursion that distinguishes a distinction, thus allowing the specification of objects. In a third order recursion, that is, in the distinction of observing, the *observer* appears. *Self-consciousness* arises in a fourth order recursion in which observing the observer takes place. In general terms, "since at any level of recursion the consensual behaviors coordinated become objects, and thus a fundament for further recursive distinctions, any level of recursion may recursively become a domain of objects that operates as a ground level for further recursions" (Maturana, 1995, p. 155).

The style of Maturana can appear obscure, and his arguments far from those of PCT. But consider how Kelly described how we can "talk" to one another with our behavior:

> Two people, say a mother and a newborn child, may not have a full intellectual meeting of minds the first time they try to enter into a discourse with each other in the maternity ward. But by sharing their encounter with events—including their own behavior—some mothers and daughters do develop a fair

understanding, each of what the other is talking about. (Kelly, 1969b, p. 28)

We recognize in the above sketch an instance of linguistic behavior (see Figure 1). And here is how Kelly describes the psychologically crucial event of the emergence of self in a section on the personal construction of one's role:

> [T]he *self* is...a proper concept or construct. It refers to a group of events which are alike in a certain way and, in that same way, necessarily different from other events. The way in which the events are alike is the self...The self, having been thus conceptualized, can now be used as a thing, a datum, or an item in the context of a superordinate construct...When the person begins to use himself as a datum in forming constructs, exciting things begin to happen. (Kelly, 1955/1991a, p. 131/91, italics in original)

In the process described above it is possible to recognize three distinct orders of recursion. Like in Maturana's account, the order of recursion constituted by "a group of events" (distinctions in observing, according to Maturana) operates as a ground level for a further recursion leading to the construct "self" (the observer in the terminology of Maturana), in its turn liable to be used as an element, a datum, a ground level for another recursion: the "personal construction of one's role" (that is, self-consciousness). Hereafter, "much of his social life," Kelly (1955/1991a, p. 131/91) writes, "is controlled by the comparisons he has come to see between himself and others." This last sentence can be used as a starting point for outlining the clinical and psychotherapeutic implications of the choice to bring to the front of PCT the three topics of recursiveness, embodiment and language that we indicated at the beginning as characteristic of a hermeneutic constructivist metatheory.

RECURSIVENESS, ADAPTATION, AND DISORDERS

As soon as language emerges as a recursion in consensual coordination of behaviors, the domain of discourses that we generate becomes part of our domain of existence and constitutes part of the environment in which we conserve identity and adaptation. In other words, the person's relationships with other people—to the extent that they are connected to core aspects of him/herself—become tied to his or her identity and, eventually, to his or her existence. From the emergence of self-consciousness on (that is, in Kellyian terms, from the personal construction of one's role on), the conservation of an adaptation within the social domain depends on the conservation of his or her identity (core role). This is why "the sense of having lost one's core role structure" (a transition of guilt) leaves the person without "guide-lines for staying alive" and makes him/her suffer "the inner torment most of us know so well" (Kelly, 1970, p. 27).

How can we explain the relation between the conservation of identity and the perturbations to the maintenance ("bodily") processes that can jeopardize the conservation of existence? Consider the aforementioned, effective expression of Kelly: "Through our constructions of our roles we sustain even the most autonomic life functions" (Kelly, 1955/1991b, p. 909/246). We can resort to the understanding that objects pertaining to a given domain can be elements of a higher domain (that is, can be used as grounds for further recursions). In Maturana's language, there can be a structural intersection between different phenomenal domains. In Kellyian language, superordinate role constructs can also be core constructs.

This is why some words are like a caress and other words are like hammerings in the head: quoting again Maturana, "we kill or elate with words because, as co-ordinations of actions, they take place through body interactions that trigger in us body changes in the domain of physiology" (Maturana, 1988, p. 48). This is why some conversations are indeed healing conversations and there are people trained to have these kinds of conversations. This opens the way to an analysis of the implications of the above said for psychotherapy.

The psychotherapist operates in the linguistic domain of conversations. He or she has relationships with persons who experience distress both in the linguistic domain and in the domains of their bodyhood. The first task of the psychotherapist should be to help the client by interacting with him or her in the domain of conversations. Therefore, the psychotherapist will look for a relation (a structural intersection) between the client's superordinate role constructs and core constructs. The psychotherapist has some useful guides starting from the above understanding.

The client has difficulty in conserving a role in relationships with other people. In other words, there is a loss of social adaptation, or the anticipation of a loss of social adaptation in the client. In our opinion, the psychotherapist's understanding of the client's complaint is likely to be inadequate as long as he or she is not able to trace back the client's complaint to a difficulty in maintaining a social adaptation: in other words, any personal problem is a problem in the social domain.

If the conservation of an adaptation requires the possibility of undergoing structural recursive changes, it becomes clear why Kelly defines a disorder as a *"personal construction which is used repeatedly in spite of consistent invalidation"* (Kelly, 1955/1991b, p. 831/193; italics in original). Note Kelly's use of the word "repeatedly." The person is no longer able to conserve an adaptation through *recursive* changes. His or her processes become *repetitive*, iterative—as if the person tried to maintain the old kind of adaptation.

If it is the client's core role that is threatened—that is, the embodied construction of his or her role (as is usually the case)—then his or her maintenance processes will be affected. And, if it is a loss, or a possible loss that the client experiences, what the psychotherapist has to understand to help the client is "what can follow from that." It is here that the anticipatory nature of personal constructs, as well as transitions (one of Kelly's most revolutionary inventions) enter the scene in the attempt to open alternative ways of relating with other people—that is, to explore alternative ways of being.

REFERENCES

Butt, T. W. (1998a). Sociality, role and embodiment. *Journal of Constructivist Psychology*, 11, 105-116.

Butt, T. W. (1998b). Sedimentation and elaborative choice. *Journal of Constructivist Psychology*, 11, 265-281.

Chiari, G. (2000). Personal construct theory and the constructivist family: A friendship to cultivate, a marriage not to celebrate. In J. W. Scheer (Ed.), *The person in society: Challenges to a constructivist theory* (pp. 66-78). Gießen: Psychosozial Verlag.

Chiari, G., & Nuzzo, M. L. (1988). Embodied minds over interacting bodies: A constructivist perspective on the mind-body problem. *The Irish Journal of Psychology*, 9, 91-100.

Chiari G., & Nuzzo M. L. (1996a). Personal construct theory within psychological constructivism: Precursor or avant-garde? In B. M. Walker, J. Costigan, L. L. Viney, & B. Warren (Eds), *Personal construct theory: A psychology for the future* (pp. 25-54). Melbourne: Australian Psychological Society Imprint Series.

Chiari G., & Nuzzo, M. L. (1996b). Psychological constructivisms: A metatheoretical differentiation. *Journal of Constructivist Psychology*, 9, 163-184.

Chiari G., & Nuzzo M. L. (2000). Hermeneutics and constructivist psychotherapy: The psychotherapeutic process in a hermeneutic constructivist framework. In J. W. Scheer (Ed.), *The person in society: Challenges to a constructivist theory* (pp. 90-99). Gießen, Germany: Psychosozial-Verlag.

Chiari, G., & Nuzzo, M. L. (2001). Penetrating the sphere of between: The adoption of a framework of complementarity and its implications for a constructivist psychotherapy. *The British Psychological Society, Psychotherapy Section Newsletter*, No. 30, 30-51.

Chiari, G., & Nuzzo, M. L. (2003). Kelly's philosophy of constructive alternativism. In F. Fransella (Ed.), *International handbook of personal construct psychology* (pp. 41-49). Chichester, UK: John Wiley.

Gadamer, H. G. (1960). *Wahrheit und Methode*. Tübingen: J.C.B. Mohr (Paul Siebeck).

Gadamer, H. G. (1986). *Wahrheit und Methode II*. Tübingen: J.C.B. Mohr (Paul Siebeck).

Gergen, K. J. (1985). The social constructionist movement in modern psychology. *American Psychologist*, 40, 266-275.

Kelly, G. A. (1969a). The psychotherapeutic relationship. In B. Maher (Ed.), *Clinical psychology and personality: The selected papers of George Kelly* (pp. 216-223). New York: John Wiley.

Kelly, G. A. (1969b). Ontological acceleration. In B. Maher (Ed.), *Clinical psychology and personality: The selected papers of George Kelly* (pp. 7-45). New York: John Wiley.

Kelly, G. A. (1970). A brief introduction to personal construct theory. In D. Bannister (Ed.), *Perspectives in personal construct theory* (pp. 1-30). London: Academic Press.

Kelly, G. A. (1991a). *The psychology of personal constructs: Vol. 1. A theory of personality.* London: Routledge. (Original work published 1955)

Kelly, G. A. (1991b). *The psychology of personal constructs: Vol. 2. Clinical diagnosis and psychotherapy.* London: Routledge. (Original work published 1955)

Lakoff, G., & Johnson, M. (1998), *Philosophy in the flesh: The embodied mind and its challenge to western thought.* New York: Basic Books.

Maturana, H. R. (1978). Biology of language: The epistemology of reality. In G. A. Miller & E. Lenneberg (Eds), *Psychology and biology of language and thought: Essays in honor of Eric Lenneberg* (pp. 27-63). New York: Academic Press.

Maturana H. R. (1988). Reality: The search for objectivity or the quest for a compelling argument. *Irish Journal of Psychology, 9,* 25-82.

Maturana, H. R. (1995). Biology of self-consciousness. In G. Trautteur (Ed.), *Consciousness: Distinction and reflection* (pp. 145-175). Napoli, Italy: Bibliopolis.

Maturana, H. R., & Varela, F. J. (1980). *Autopoiesis and cognition: The realization of the living.* Boston: Reidel. (Original work published 1970-1973)

Maturana, H. R., & Varela, F. J. (1987). *The tree of knowledge: The biological roots of human understanding.* Boston: New Science Library. (Original work published 1984)

Merleau-Ponty, M. (1945), *Phenomenologie de la perception.* Paris: Gallimard.

Pepper, S. C. (1970). *World hypotheses: A study in evidence.* Berkeley: University of California Press. (Original work published 1942)

Raskin, J. D. (2002). Constructivism in psychology: Personal construct psychology, radical constructivism, and social constructionism. In J. D. Raskin & S. K. Bridges (Eds), *Studies in meaning: Exploring constructivist psychology* (pp. 1-25). New York: Pace University Press.

Sarbin, T. R. (1977): Contextualism: A world view for a modern psychology. In A. W. Landfield (Ed.), *Nebraska symposium on motivation 1976* (pp. 1-41). Lincoln: University of Nebraska Press.

Varela, F. J. (1979). *Principles of biological autonomy.* New York: Elsevier North Holland.

Varela, F. J., Thompson, E., & Rosch, E. (1991), *The embodied mind: Cognitive science and human experience.* Cambridge, MA: MIT Press.

von Foerster, H. (1982). *Observing systems.* Seaside: Intersystems.

von Glasersfeld, E. (1974). Piaget and the radical constructivist epistemology. In C. D. Smock & E. von Glasersfeld (Eds), *Epistemology and education* (pp. 1-24). Athens, GA: Follow Through Publications.

von Glasersfeld, E. (1982). An interpretation of Piaget's constructivism. *Revue Internationale de Philosophie, 36,* 612-635.

Waddington, C. H. (1977). *Tools for thought: How to understand and apply the latest scientific techniques of problem solving.* New York: Basic Books.

FIGURE 1. LEVELS OF RECURSION IN
MATURANA (BOLD) AND KELLY (ITALIC)

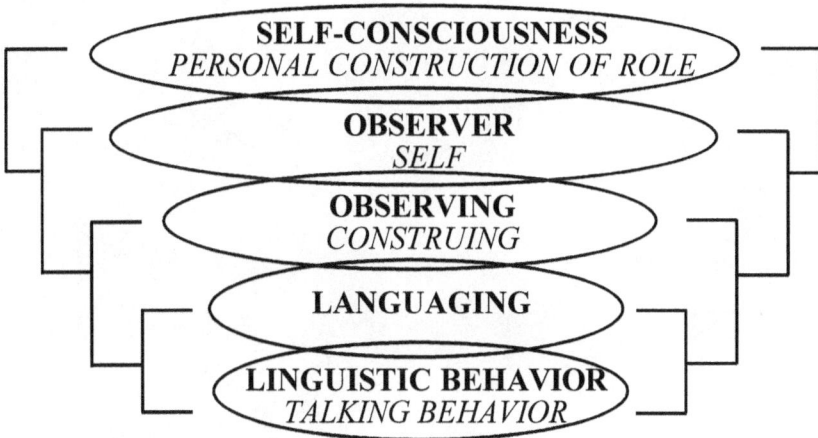

SELF-CONSCIOUSNESS
PERSONAL CONSTRUCTION OF ROLE

OBSERVER
SELF

OBSERVING
CONSTRUING

LANGUAGING

LINGUISTIC BEHAVIOR
TALKING BEHAVIOR

PART II

THE PERSONAL AND SOCIAL IN PSYCHOTHERAPY

CHAPTER 4

Epistemology and Psychotherapy: A Constructivist Conversation

Robert A. Neimeyer and William E. Cabanillas

Perhaps one of the most pervasive metaphors for meaning making in constructivist circles is that of "conversation." The idea that meaning emerges between people, rather than within them, resonates with constructivists who emphasize the intersubjective origins of self-knowledge as well as social constructionists who view efforts after meaning as inevitably drawing upon a fund of culturally available symbols and discourses into which any given individual is born. Recent advances in "dialogic" conceptions of the self even suggest that meaning, at its most personal levels, arises from conversations (whether cooperative or conflictual) between or among different "I-positions" within us, which in their give-and-take constitute a dialectically developing sense of identity across time.

This chapter therefore adopts a conversational structure, not merely as a metaphor, but as a method for exploring the inter-braiding of epistemology (the study of knowledge) and psychotherapy that is distinctive to constructivist practice. It arose from an actual conversation—albeit an electronically mediated one—initiated by a Peruvian psychologist interested in the growing influence of constructivism in his part of the world, and an American psychologist with a long-term commitment to fostering and disseminating constructivist concepts and methods. This paper preserves the format of their planned correspondence, carried out through a series of occasional probing questions and earnest answers, over a period of nearly two years. To maintain the conversational, interview-based flavor of the exchange, the authors mutually decided to suspend the usual trappings of academic discourse (including extensive citation of literature) and instead speak spontaneously, but not casually, about the significance of constructivism's unique epistemological commitments, and their implications for psychotherapy theory, practice, and

research. Seven such questions and answers follow, culminating in a
joint closing reflection on the conversational exchange as a whole.[1]

> 1. Constructivism is widely understood as an epistemological posi-
> tion that emphasizes an image of human beings constructing the
> meaning of their experience, without the necessity of validating it
> against the external criterion of "objective reality." What implica-
> tions does this epistemological vision carry for psychotherapy?

In adopting an image of persons as actively engaging life
experiences in a way that renders them meaningful in human terms,
constructivism postulates both an (implicit) ontology and an
(explicit) epistemology that carry profound implications for psychotherapy. In the first instance, constructivism rejects the "ontology
of the observer" that pervades many traditional perspectives, which
views human beings as passively mirroring and reacting to the fac-
tual contingencies of an external world. Instead, constructivism
embraces an "ontology of the actor," which construes people as
punctuating, organizing, differentiating, and symbolizing the
unending flow of experience in order to anticipate events and pursue important goals in the social world. In this view, the fundamental form of human "being-in-the-world" is one of *situated interpretive
activity*, positioning ourselves within schemes of meaning and action
that we construct individually, negotiate interpersonally, or appropriate from the cultural and linguistic network of signs and symbols
that surrounds us like an atmosphere. This ontological position car-
ries with it a corollary epistemology, which acknowledges that
human constructions need only be pragmatically *viable*, not transcendentally *valid*, in order to function as proactive frameworks for
attributing meaning to our past, positioning ourselves in the present,
and orienting us toward the future in useful ways.

What implications does this philosophical stance carry for
psychotherapy? At a heuristic level, it suggests that the basic goal of
therapy—and life—is to "transcend the obvious," to liberate ourselves from a single hegemonic view of the way things are or should
be, and instead to cultivate the flexibility to envision alternative
"possible worlds" and "possible selves" that could permit us to live

---

[1] All questions were framed by WC, and answered by RAN; RAN was also responsible for translating each of the questions from the original Spanish.

in more satisfying ways, individually and collectively. At a strategic level, it implies that psychotherapy is more a *creative* than a *corrective* enterprise, insofar as it prompts clients toward new meaning symbolization, behavioral experimentation, and social negotiation rather than critiquing their cognitive errors, neurotic tendencies, or lack of social skills. In keeping with a constructivist epistemology, psychotherapy would be more concerned with the *emotional truth* of clients' deeply held convictions about self and world, rather than the *literal truth* of their core beliefs. Stated differently, constructivism allows us to ask the question, "What might psychotherapy look like if freed from the quest to improve the client's degree of 'reality contact'?"

> 2. Suppose we can distinguish two types of reality, a "perceived reality" (based principally on sensory perception of the physical world) and an "interpreted reality" (whose referent is unclear, and is characterized by judgments and interpretations of a personal character). On which of these two types of reality does constructivist psychotherapy concentrate?

In some respects this is a difficult question to answer as it is written, in so far as it constructs a distinction between physical and interpretive realities that constructivists edge away from, or in some cases, reject outright! Indeed, this distinction is at the core of many objectivist epistemologies, which acknowledge the "psychological reality" of human judgments, but also presume a pristine "real world" that can be accessed relatively unproblematically by the senses, and which provides the ultimate warrant for our knowledge claims. From such a position, it is only a short step to construe psychotherapy as a procedure that promotes better "adjustment" through improving a client's degree of contact with this objective reality.

Not only does this ontological distinction support more authoritative (and even authoritarian) forms of psychotherapy, but it also creates a mischievous fragmentation at the level of epistemology, which requires completely different theories of knowledge to account for our negotiation of the physical and social worlds. On the one hand, this view requires a "doctrine of immaculate perception," according to which we have immediate knowledge of a world of objects through our senses. On the other hand, it presumes that human interpretations, opinions, values, and the like represent

71

mediated forms of knowing, which introduce error and distortion into our perception of patterns in the environment that surrounds us. Yet a moment's serious reflection calls these propositions into question. At what point in the hierarchy of abstraction, from the most elementary nerve impulse to the formulation of visionary cosmologies, does human mentation lose its presumed grounding in a secure sensory world? Likewise, at what point of concreteness does there exist the consensus among observers required to establish a reality as objectively physical, given, uninterpreted? Constructivists would deconstruct such questions by challenging the binary distinction that sustains them, arguing instead that the boundary between "perception" and "interpretation" can be usefully blurred.

In the place of this binary contrast between sensation and judgment, constructivists would erect a continuum of meaning making, ranging from the concrete to abstract. For example, I may be impressed by the apparent collegiality, friendliness, and common purpose displayed by a group of South American colleagues, in contrast to the competitiveness and individualism I perceive in similar work groups in the U.S. On close inspection, this construction represents a complex composite of schemes for organizing social experience, including abstract anticipations concerning expected differences between North and South American cultures, my own sometimes awkward and provisional attempts to extract meaning from interactions with new colleagues, our mutual efforts to infer one another's views and negotiate a shared social setting, my sense of the rhythm and emotional resonance of Latin American Spanish and the way it modulates relationships, etc. This everyday example suggests that even such common "acts of knowing" represent sophisticated perceptual/cognitive/affective schemes for engaging the world that do not reduce easily to a binary distinction between the sensory and interpretive domains. Instead, human sense making, from its most concrete to its most abstract expressions, represents *a means of configuring an experiential world in which we can find both meaning and direction.*

This epistemology leads me, in my role as a psychotherapist, to attend to the often subtle ways in which people struggle for, find, impose, and become constrained by the meanings they (co)construct as they engage the world. Consider the quite different accounts of their interaction given by two spouses referred for therapy because of domestic violence. To the extent that each feels free to formulate his or her own version of events (a consideration that itself emphasizes the social and interpersonal dimensions of reality construction), each partner is likely to draw on different "facts"[2] to sub-stantiate his or her narrative of their discord, embedding these in different cultural discourses about the appropriate roles of husbands and wives, the nature of anger and self-control, etc. While neither partner may have access to a transcendentally valid conception of gender roles or an indisputable set of facts that proves one person right and the other wrong in some conclusive sense, this does not mean it is a matter of indifference whose version of the relationship wins out. The role of the constructivist psychotherapist confronting these contested reality claims is to grasp, articulate, and deconstruct the hidden assumptions that sustain such social constructions, help each person experience these constraints and contradictions in a compelling way, and reach toward more hopeful accounts of self and relationships that do not reinforce and replicate this dominant narrative.

> 3. There is no single "cognitive therapy," but rather a great range of "cognitive psychotherapies," so that we encounter a huge variety of theoretical positions and practical procedures, all of which bear the label "cognitive." Within this broad spectrum, we find constructivist therapies, which are themselves diverse in principles and procedures. Taking into account their significant differences with "rationalistic" therapies, is it appropriate to place constructivist approaches within the "cognitive" spectrum?

Yes, and no. On the one hand, a (substantial) subset of cognitive therapies have strong constructivist leanings, insofar as they (a) emphasize phenomenological, rather than "objective" criteria for the validity of an individual's constructions, (b) promote the exploration and extension of the client's meaning system rather than its correction and conformity to presumed principles of rationality, and (c) view any given construction as part of a (largely tacit or non-conscious) network of associated meanings, rather than as simply an isolated and easily verbalized "thought unit" subject to modification. For example, approaches that respectfully attend to "core ordering processes" in clients' worlds of meaning, that promote the coherence

---

[2] It is interesting in this connection to note that the term "fact" derives from the Latin root meaning "to do or make." This active interpretation of fact as something constructed is preserved in Spanish, for example, where it is translated as "el hecho," literally, something done or made.

of a client's self-knowledge at the level of both experience and explanation, and that support clients in articulating and expanding their personal construct systems might all be considered "cognitive" in these terms, while also being clearly constructivist.

On the other hand, many therapies with unmistakable constructivist commitments do not easily fit within the compass of cognitive therapy, even in a broad definition. This is because constructivism does not represent an identifiable "camp" or "school" of therapy, so much as a general postmodern trend that is revolutionizing many traditions of therapy from within. For example, strong constructivist trends can be discerned in the psychodynamic tradition, especially in those approaches that emphasize intersubjective and adaptive features of psychic life, and that dethrone the analyst from a privileged position of authority over the "narrative truth" of a patient's experience. Likewise, constructivism has proven a comfortable "fit" for many experiential/humanistic therapies, which find the more holistic orientation toward "personal knowing" espoused by constructivists more congenial than the "tighter" definitions and procedures preferred by cognitive therapists. Finally, and perhaps most radically, several forms of family therapy draw inspiration from a social constructionist perspective on meaning as residing principally *between*, rather than *within*, individuals. Proponents of this latter, more relational perspective would be especially resistant to being described as "cognitive," instead identifying themselves as narrative, solution-oriented, or structure-determined therapists. Perhaps the clearest image of the relationship between constructivist and cognitive therapists would be in terms of a Venn diagram, in which two overlapping circles of similar size represented the two positions, and the area of their intersection symbolized those therapists who have strong constructivist, as well as cognitive leanings. The "constructivist" circle would simultaneously intersect with other traditions (such as the psychodynamic, humanistic, and systemic, as discussed above), all of which would also show only partial overlap with a constructivist orientation. This poses interesting implications for the integration of psychotherapies, but perhaps this is another question!

> 4. With the great number of psychotherapeutic approaches available, it has become difficult for therapists to adhere strictly to the procedures of a particular school, prompting a necessary eclecticism. On one hand, this liberates the therapist from the theoretical and applied limitations of a single orientation, to the ultimate benefit of the

> client. On the other hand, however, this situation can lead to an
> arbitrary and unsystematic aggregation of techniques and para-
> digms. What contributions does constructivism make to a more
> coherent form of integration in psychotherapy?

The question of integration can be posed at least two levels:
the abstract level of psychotherapeutic theory, and the concrete (and
in some respects more urgent) level of psychotherapeutic practice.
From a constructivist standpoint, each poses unique problems and
possibilities for a more eclectic approach to psychotherapy.

At the level of theory, constructivism would draw attention to
the limitations of many of the most popular paths to integration. For
example, a *common factors* approach, which emphasizes the extent to
which all therapies make use of shared principles in facilitating
change (e.g., fostering client trust in the therapist's rationale, providing a credible therapeutic ritual) would be seen as deficient both
because it fails to attend to how each therapy achieves these general
aims, and because it ignores unique features of specific approaches
that are not represented in others. Thus, the ironic outcome of a
common factors model is that it might actually reduce the flexibility of therapeutic practice by focusing only on their "shared variance." *Common language* models, which argue that integration of
diverse schools can be accomplished by ignoring the technical "jar-
gon" associated with each, and instead communicating in a single
vocabulary (such as "plain English" or the terminology of cognitive
psychology) encounter similar problems. Not only do such
approaches risk the reduction of theoretically rich discourse to the
"lowest common denominator," but they also privilege the "common language" over others. Such apparently straightforward
approaches neglect the subtle entailments of natural language (e.g.,
how might psychological distress be understood differently if the
common language selected were Spanish—or Chinese—rather than
English?), as well as the way in which different technical languages
(e.g., cognitive psychology vs. systems theory) suggest very different
approaches to human problems an their treatment.

Constructivism is likewise cautious about the prospects of
theoretical integration, defined as the combining of features of one psychotherapy tradition with those of another, without regard to their
compatibility (e.g., incorporating psychodynamic concepts into a
family systems model). On close inspection, this kind of eclecticism
seems to be based on an objectivist epistemology, which presumes

that each theory reveals one aspect of the underlying reality of human existence, much as the blind men in the traditional parable are all considered to be contacting different parts of the same elephant. But in a constructivist view, the "realities" constructed by different therapeutic paradigms might well be incommensurable, resisting simple synthesis into a larger whole. For example, there is no "in principle" reason to believe that adding features of an object relations approach to a conditioning model, and augmenting both with a consideration of family coalitions, would produce a therapeutic model that would be viewed as more adequate, either from the perspective of psychotherapy theory, or that of the bewildered client subjected to a barrage of incoherent interventions!

A more *theoretically progressive* approach to integration would consider the compatibility of the two (or more) candidates for integration, defined in terms of their convergence at the levels of metatheory (e.g., their explicit or implicit epistemology, ontology, ethics, etc.) and formal theory (e.g., their perspective on human behavior and the meaning of disorder). Using this criterion, some theories would offer the prospect of a coherent, progressive integration, as when the cross-fertilization of narrative therapy concepts with personal construct therapy produces a hybrid model that better accounts for the interplay of personal and cultural constraints on self-change than either approach taken alone. On the other hand, the marriage of some theories might produce offspring whose viability could be threatened by the incompatibility of their inheritance from both parents. For example, wedding a rationalist cognitive therapy to a narrative model could be regressive in this sense, perhaps encouraging the therapist to invite the client to express an intimate story of painful personal experiences at one moment, only to critique the "cognitive distortions" in this account a moment later. Instead, an ideal integration would bring together models with compatible metatheories, but rather different strategies of change at a more technical level, so that the practicing therapist would be able to coordinate his or her use of a wide range of tools and methods within a coherent case conceptualization.

Viewed in this way, a theoretically progressive integration of approaches can assist the practicing therapist in reaching toward a more flexible, but nonetheless coherent therapy. But ultimately, an eclectic form of practice must be integrated concretely in the *style of the therapist*, rather than only at the abstract level of principles. In other words, it makes little difference whether a post-rationalist model of therapy can be integrated with a structure-determined model, unless a specific therapist knows how to do it! In this sense, psychotherapy integration is a challenge to any therapist who wants to augment the scope and flexibility of his or her practice, rather than simply being the concern of theorists and academicians. Moreover, it extends beyond the concerns of mental health professionals, per se, insofar as successful psychotherapy requires coherence between the therapist's constructions and those of the client. In the final analysis, it is the client's ability to integrate particular conceptualizations of the problem with his or her pre-existing meanings that determines which approaches to change will be welcomed or resisted, which leads logically to a consideration of therapeutic strategy and technique.

> 5. It is quite clear that there are multiple theoretical and practical differences among different schools of psychotherapy, which suggests the importance of three closely related questions. First, from a constructivist standpoint, who is the client who seeks consultation? Second, what is psychotherapy? And third, what is the ultimate objective of treatment?

At a literal level, the client in constructivist therapy is any person or group that seeks consultation from a constructivist therapist. Although this might seem obvious, it is important to acknowledge, because such consultation might be sought not merely by individual adults, but also by couples, families, businesses or other organizations, and even entire communities, such as socially marginalized youth seeking to foster their personal and collective development. Accordingly, constructivist counselors have worked with all of these groups, and more, to help them identify the web of meanings and practices that both constrains and supports them in important activities, and to assist them with developing a broader, deeper, and richer way of engaging the social world.

Accordingly, at a more philosophical level, the client in constructivist therapy is viewed as an agent or group of agents, whose distinctive means of organizing life embody unique resources as well as constraints that need to be understood as a precondition to psychotherapeutic change. For example, the client who constructs a life that centers on compulsive self reliance in the face of life challenges can be viewed as having developed a distinctive, and largely adaptive style for managing adversity, but one that simultaneously limits his

77

or her degree of intimate trust in relationships with important others. Respectfully grasping the unique meanings of this core construction requires an appreciation of the developmental utility of this way of patterning relationships, as well as a subtle recognition of its positive and negative implications for the client's current life with others. Furthermore, exploring these often tacit meanings and implications with the client typically moves beyond intellectual contemplation on unsatisfying outcomes, to the experiential "encounter" with such tacit meanings through visualization, enactment, and other methods. For instance, the client described above might be asked to close his eyes and envision a recent, vivid occasion when he felt threatened or challenged by a major life problem or crisis, but to refrain for a moment from responding in a self-reliant way. Holding this image might well trigger an emotional recognition of the deep purpose served by his "symptomatic" self-possession, such as avoiding the prospect of abandonment or vulnerability to loss to which it represents a preferred alternative. This then sets the stage for a consideration of whether the predominant pattern is still crucial for survival in the client's current life.

Thus, the question of who each specific client is importantly shapes what therapy must be. In general terms, therapy represents an attempt to "structurally couple" with the meaning system of the client in such a way that the therapist can graft his or her interventions onto these very meanings, fostering the client's receptivity, rather than resistance. This implies a delicate attunement to not only the relevant content of the client's concerns, but also to the client's preferred style of working in therapy. For example, some clients might require an initial focus on the concrete particulars of their life narratives, while others might invite an immediate focus on their attendant emotions or reflective attempts to make sense of these same events. Therapy typically proceeds best by first matching, and then systematically mismatching the client's preferred processing styles, so as to prompt early connection followed by eventual growth in the client's ability to engage old problems and patterns in new ways.

In a real sense, there is no "ultimate objective" of constructivist psychotherapy. As essentially a form of "accelerated living," the process of therapy is one that invites the exploration of emotionally significant material in one's life story, in a way that fosters greater reflexive self-awareness and experimentation with new solutions or practices. All of these represent valuable proximal outcomes, whose goal is not to bring about some hypothetical state of "adequate adjustment" or "self-actualization," but an ongoing process of self-exploration, reflexivity, sociality, and development. Fostering these shifts constitutes the art of psychotherapy.

> 6. In standard psychotherapeutic practice, each "patient" is assessed and diagnosed. This process typically involves fitting the person into categories based on objective (and sometimes quantitative) criteria. Given that much of this process seems alien to a constructivist vision of persons, how does constructivist psychotherapy understand "assessment" and "diagnosis?"

As a metatheory, constructivism does not preclude the application of other professional constructs to a given clinical case; indeed, the "constructive alternativism" that informs personal construct theory and many other constructivist approaches explicitly encourages this. Thus, it would not be inappropriate for a constructivist clinician to ask, "How might this patient's sense of resignation, hopelessness, and self-criticism be understood as a response to a constricted form of meaning-making? A disrupted attachment relationship? A breakdown in problem-solving? A clinical depression? An abusive marriage? Racial or gender oppression?" In other words, many different "diagnostic" frameworks might be useful at different points in treatment, including the quasi-medical diagnostic system that forms the framework of the ICD or DSM.

What constructivism contends against is the hegemony of any one system to the marginalization of all others, particularly when that system wraps itself in the mantle of "science" in a rhetorical move to silence its critics. Constructivists view all diagnostic systems as potentially useful and potentially constraining fictions, simplifications of a vastly complex set of relationships within and among the various systems that jointly constitute human functioning. As such, the ontological "reality" of human life owes no special allegiance to any of them, and can often be helpfully assessed in more than a single framework. Thus, although psychosis might be seen as—among other things—an attempt to loosen one's meaning system to ward off further invalidation of one's hypotheses about the world, this does not also mean that a more medical diagnosis that leads to the administration of antipsychotic medication might not also be useful. Conversely, just because some of the diffuse anxiety of someone struggling with a panic disorder can be ameliorated by

anxiolytics does not mean that a psychotherapeutic attempt to evaluate the meaning of these symptoms is not also a clinical priority.

This being said, constructivist psychotherapists are particularly drawn to forms of assessment that are coherent with their own
constructions of disorder. For example, those working from a personal construct standpoint might use laddering or repertory grid
techniques to identify important hierarchies of linked meanings that
point to core identity commitments, commitments that might seem
threatened by the prospect of significant impending life changes.
Construct theorists of a more experiential persuasion might instead
attend to the subtle nonverbal ways in which a patient protectively
withdraws from intimate "role relationships," in which he or she
might be known, and potentially invalidated in profound ways by
another. Depth-oriented brief therapists might empathically affirm
the pain of clients' conscious presenting problem, but then engage
in a form of "radical inquiry" in session, using visualization methods, incomplete sentences, and imaginary symptom removal, to help
the clients experientially encounter powerful non-conscious positions they hold that make these same distressing symptoms compelling to maintain. Developmentally oriented constructivists might
attempt to reconstruct significant scenes from a client's biography
that are linked to critical, "under-referenced" emotions, moving the
client through a "slow motion replay" of these significant events to
make their tacit meaning explicit. Narrative therapists might engage
in "curious questioning" to reveal the adverse effects of problem stories on the lives of persons, as well as their relationships to others.
Social constructionist therapists might work directly with whole
families or communities of concern to promote "open dialogue"
about quite serious presenting problems such as psychosis in a family member, bringing to light the resources in the community that
can support them through the crisis. And radical critical theorists
might "diagnose" even the pathologizing tendencies in our own
profession, and promote forms of social action with disadvantaged
groups that permit them to foster their own development. Although
I weave most of these evaluation and intervention strategies into my
own practice, my central tendency is to attend carefully to the
nuances of a client's language and self-narrative to guide my attention to important metaphors that invite elaboration, and the themes
that require experiential attention to reveal their sustaining and constraining role in the client's social world. Thus, a central concern of
constructivist diagnosis and evaluation—however it is expressed in

various approaches—is a focus on vividly articulating (inter)personal meanings and the openings they suggest for a revised or expanded relational self.

> 7. To the extent that traditional psychotherapy research is rooted in objectivism and experimental control, it is questionable whether it can assimilate the insights generated by constructivists. In view of this tension, do you think that constructivism can make a significant contribution to the otherwise encouraging development of research in psychotherapy?

Constructivist scholars already have contributed to the field of psychotherapy research in both a positive sense—by adding directly to what is "known" about psychotherapeutic process and outcome—and in a negative sense—by critically calling into question the very conceptual and methodological paradigms by which most psychotherapy research is pursued. The result has been an ambivalent, but energetic engagement with the empirical study of psychotherapy, which both augments and questions the "body of knowledge" resulting from the field.

On the one hand, constructivists have mounted ambitious research programs concerned with therapeutic process and outcome. For example, personal construct investigators have delineated conceptual changes experienced by clients in psychotherapy using repertory grid technique, documented the salutary effects of matching clients and therapeutic approaches based upon clients' conceptualization of their presenting problems, traced the relationship of identification with group therapists and members to symptomatic improvement in group therapy, and adduced evidence for the efficacy of specific procedures, such as fixed role therapy. Narrative researchers have developed detailed and reliable taxonomies for coding transcripts of therapy sessions, determining shifts in external/objective, internal/emotional, and reflexive/meaning-oriented narrative styles associated with therapeutic progress or impasse. And process-experiential investigators have identified "markers" of critical client tasks in therapy, mapping the specific change processes that facilitate their resolution. Unlike most psychotherapy research, which seeks to demonstrate the superiority of the investigators' preferred approach, studies by constructivists tend to examine basic change processes in a great variety of therapeutic traditions, from psychodynamic to behavioral, and from process experiential to cognitive. In this sense, the direct contributions of constructivism to contemporary psychotherapy research are varied, shedding light particularly on the elusive linkage between therapy process and outcome.

Complementing constructivist contributions to traditional psychotherapy studies are those that call into question the very methodology by which such research is conducted, and propose alternatives. Like others in the "human science" arena, constructivists have played a role in the diversification of methodology, helping develop qualitative, hermeneutic, and narrative procedures for investigating the meaning of silence in psychotherapy, the generation of insights, the cultivation of reflexivity, and the revision of self-theories in the crucible of therapeutic conversation. The result has been an expanded repertory of concepts and methods for understanding the construction and consolidation of therapeutic change.

These positive contributions notwithstanding, constructivist and social constructionist therapists have been among the most vocal opponents of traditional psychotherapy research, especially that which tends to privilege dominant schools of "scientific" therapy while marginalizing others. Thus, constructivists have joined humanists in their skeptical reception of the "empirically supported treatment" movement, in view of overwhelming evidence that, although psychotherapy is demonstrably effective, few if any differences in efficacy exist between treatments once investigator allegiance is controlled. In light of these findings, repeatedly replicated in meta-analytic studies, the accrual of evidence for disorder-specific efficacy for a given approach says more about the political clout of dominant perspectives that adopt a medicalized view of both diagnosis and treatment than it does about the relative effectiveness of different therapies.

Still more trenchantly, the most radical of critical, narrative, and social constructionist theorists indict the very frameworks that sustain the "psy-complex," that intricate network of discourses and social structures that localizes disorders within people, and that grants a privileged status to culturally appointed "healers" who have the power to diagnose and "cure" mental illness. Such a position is naïve at best, and pernicious at worst, insofar as it distracts attention from the institutional and cultural processes by which disorders are socially constructed, as well as from the necessity of taking action against the economic, discursive and political forces that create and sustain such oppression. In this sense, the postmodern cultural critique to which constructivism contributes militates against the presumed authority of psychotherapy research, narrowly conceived, keeping open spaces for alternative understandings of human distress and development in the margins of our profession.

Coda

In recent years the constructivist "conversation" has spread beyond the field of psychotherapy, per se, to stimulate fresh and fertile exchanges in other domains of psychology, as well as other areas of the human sciences. Simultaneously, the distinctive epistemology associated with constructivism has proven attractive to scholars and practitioners across national as well as disciplinary boundaries, with theorists of many countries participating in the energetic exchange and elaboration of ideas and practices. This paper stems from one such exchange, whose goal was to explore the implications of the unique philosophical commitments of a constructivist perspective for psychotherapy.

In the course of our conversation, we found ourselves transitioning naturally from one topic to another as we traversed a broad field of interconnected issues, including a constructivist approach to clinical diagnosis, the helping relationship, the establishment of therapeutic goals, psychotherapy integration and research. Our questions took as their point of origin the core vision of constructivism regarding human beings, a concern that transcends the traditional (and occasionally superficial) frameworks propounded by academic theorists and researchers. We have to acknowledge the temptation to continue formulating further questions and venturing further answers, a temptation that in itself suggests something of the spirit of inquiry inherent in constructivist psychology. We hope that the attempt to articulate and address this series of open questions provides a point of orientation for those therapists new to the field, and helps shed light on the sometimes daunting terrain of constructivist epistemology, and its implications for the theory and practice of psychotherapy.

CHAPTER 5

The Healing Power of Telling Stories in Psychotherapy[1]

Lara Honos-Webb, Sunwolf, and Jerrold Lee Shapiro

Telling stories is one therapeutic intervention that is consonant with constructivist approaches to psychotherapy. According to
constructivist approaches, clients come to therapy with a set of personal constructs imposed on the world that have failed to serve them.
The process of therapy thus entails a therapist-facilitated healing
based on the clients' re-construction of life events and self-defini-
tions. Although personal construct psychotherapy is its own brand-
name approach (Kelly, 1955/1991a, 1955/1991b), the broader
philosophical constructivist approach to psychotherapy has incorporated elements from a wide sampling of approaches, such as cognitive, behavioral and psychodynamic.

Here we delineate a theory for explaining the healing power
of storytelling in psychotherapy by the therapist. The right story may
help clients to tolerate tragic life events and the attendant emotional
fall-out. Suggestions are provided for integrating storytelling into
constructivist, emotion-focused, feminist, cognitive, behavioral,
existential, psychodynamic and family systems approaches to treatment. It is argued that stories serve to synthesize the dialectical tension between validating the client and using persuasive or enticing
interventions to effect change. Stories may facilitate clients' transitions from searching for immediate pain relief and problem solutions toward an openness and willingness to examine and change
their characteristic ways of attributing meaning to the world that
may have contributed to creating problems. By offering the client a
story, which is open to a myriad of interpretations by the client—
rather than an interpretation—the therapist honors the constructivist

[1] A version of this chapter was originally presented at the Tenth Biennial
Conference of the North American Personal Construct Network, Vancouver, British
Columbia, July 2002.

value of opening up a plurality of meanings (G. J. Neimeyer & Rood, 1997) to the client based on his or her constructions of the story. As an example, the therapist can recount a story that contains many characters and it may be left ambiguous which character in the story the client is intended to learn from. Like fixed-role therapy, wherein a therapist offers a client an alternative course of behavior to experiment with, stories offer character sketches that model different ways of acting in the world. However, the telling of a story with multiple characters allows the client to draw from many different possibilities.

While storytelling takes its place in constructivist theory next to narrative reconstruction approaches, it is emphatically distinct from narrative therapies, such as those as traditionally constructed by Freedman and Combs (1996) or Gardner (1993). Both storytelling and narrative approaches rely on the use of alternative stories as a method for shifting personal constructs. In the seminal narrative approach developed by White and Epston (1990), a paradigmatic shift from "clients with problems" to "problems with clients" is facilitated through narrative tools that allow clients to get in touch with their lived-stories. The storytelling approach suggested in this chapter is different. In narrative approaches, the therapist facilitates clients' re-telling their own stories (Eron & Lund, 1996). By contrast, in the storytelling intervention we are elaborating in this chapter, the therapist initially generates the therapeutic story. Whereas narrative approaches emphasize clients constructing alternative emplotments of their own life stories, the therapist's use of storytelling allows a more tentative approach, which permits the client to play with reconstruing life events that are held at a safe distance. Thus, storytelling by the therapist allows the client to approach initially the material for reconstruction, in a somewhat displaced manner. Told stories often happen "once upon a time" or, in "a place far, far away," thus evoking fictional characters in fictional settings. Such an approach may be particularly useful when life events are traumatic and direct exposure to personal material may become aversive or threatening to the client. We will elaborate a specific model that articulates how storylistening can be healing for the client. We will also explore the importability of this one technique across an array of mainstream therapeutic approaches. Finally, we will briefly describe the reasons for therapists' resistance to the use of therapist storytelling in psychotherapy.

A friend and colleague, Dr. Roger Karlsson, a Swedish psychoanalyst who is particularly interested in the treatment of psychosis through psychotherapy, gave us an excellent example of the healing power of stories in psychotherapy. Dr. Karlsson was struggling with a severely disturbed client who threatened suicide in one of the very first meetings. The therapist had just begun treating this client, so the therapeutic alliance was insufficiently strong. He feared hospitalizing the man might result in rupturing beyond repair the tentative alliance that did exist. Hospitalization was also an undesirable choice because of the valuable progress that had already been made by this patient (just showing up for the sessions!). This patient had never before accepted any offers of psychotherapeutic treatment, and had been difficult to handle in psychiatric care. Yet he was now reporting hearing voices with dangerous messages. During his reverie, the therapist began to reflect upon why such a man would want to kill himself. He remembered this distressed man had once been the president of a corporation; he had been powerful, wealthy, and happily married. Now the man had lost his power, wealth, and family as a result of his mental disorder. The therapist speculated that the client had lost hope because he had lost everything that had seemed meaningful to him.

Although the therapist had used folktales in therapy previously, he did not consider himself to be a storyteller. He was surprised to find the old tale of the Bremen Town Musicians coming to mind. He hesitated to tell the story, fearing the client might find a child's folktale patronizing, but he took the risk, sharing the story in great detail. This tale, an ancient oral tale collected by the Brothers Grimm in the 1800s, was a model for the plot of the "Wizard of Oz," as characters in distress travel together in search of something that can make them complete. In "The Bremen Town Musicians," each character feels cast off, hopeless, unappreciated, facing death, as they join forces in search of hope. The last to be invited to join the motley traveling group is the rooster, who was given the same invitation as the others: "You had much better go with us, Chanticleer. We are going to Bremen to become musicians. At any rate, that will be better than dying. You have a powerful voice and when we perform together, it will have a good effect."

Upon hearing these words, the client's eyes closed. He seemed to be sleeping during the telling of the story and when the therapist finished the client did not say much except, "That was an interesting story." However, the next week the client returned and reported that he no longer feared he would kill himself. When he heard a voice telling him to kill himself he responded to the voice with a refrain from the story that "anything is better than dying." This client stayed in treatment for many years and over the course of therapy made frequent references to the importance of this refrain in holding at bay the destructive voices he heard.

THE CONTAINER MODEL

According to the container model of storylistening (Honos-Webb, Sunwolf, & Shapiro, 2001), stories heal clients by serving as a container for both intolerable affect and multiple conflicting voices or impulses. We use the term *containers* in a way that parallels the object relations use of the term, in the sense that introjected objects can serve to contain affect and internal experience (Klein, 1948). Klein also introduced the notion of projective identification, whereby clients project unwanted experiences onto others as if the other identified with the projection would thereby contain the unwanted experiences. So it is for stories, as clients can project unwanted or desirable experiences and characteristics onto fictional others. In this way, therapist storytelling is an important therapeutic intervention that has the potential for expanding the client's capacity to assimilate and integrate otherwise painful or intolerable experiences.

Storylistening as Expanding Tolerance of Painful Experiences

Stories may also expand the client's capacity to tolerate painful experiences by increasing the flexibility of the self to contain contradictory and/or overwhelming internal and external experiences. A story may thus offer an internal mechanism by which a tragic event can be more successfully re-experienced. Unlike a filter that blocks out or allows certain components of a trauma to enter, this mechanism expands the self. Such a technique addresses a glaring omission in the common psychotherapeutic repertoire: how to increase the capacity of the self to bear unwanted traumatic experiences. The provision of stories by the therapist offers the possibility of changing the self so that tragic events are borne, thereby mitigating their shattering impact.

We offer a story to illustrate the container model of storylistening:

> A story was told of an aging Hindu master who asked his student to pour a handful of salt into a glass and taste it. After the student spit out the bitter water, the master asked him to pour the salty water into the lake. After confirming the freshness of the lake water, the master said "The pain of life is pure salt; no more, no less. However, the amount of bitterness we taste

depends on the container we put the pain in. So when you are
in pain, the only thing you can do is to enlarge your sense of
things. Don't be a glass. Become a lake."

We assume that increasing clients' capacity to bear painful
experiences is a legitimate goal of psychotherapy, though this
appears antithetical to much of current thinking about the goals of
therapy: to eliminate, reframe, suppress, or avoid pain. The Container
Model of storying suggests that therapeutic success is represented by
the client's increased capacity to endure their burdens, struggles and
human frailties.

On the Importance of Being StoryStoned

Another therapeutic characteristic of storytelling as psychotherapeutic treatment is that it can provoke an altered state of
consciousness. When a story is told artfully, the audience is trans-
ported into a story-listening trance. Storied trance, in fact, may be a
form of light hypnosis. Much of conventional trauma work entails
exposure, which can be re-traumatizing or lead to therapy high drop
out rates because of the anxiety associated with such interventions.
The "storystoned" state that results frequently from listening to stories is, by contrast, anxiety reducing. This also increases receptivity
and an enhanced therapeutic bond, making therapeutic progress
more likely. An altered state of consciousness may facilitate a loosening of constructions, which may be a necessary precursor to the
reconstruction of one's life thereby allowing for therapeutic change.

While the specific pleasurable, soothing altered state of an
adult's storylistening mind, "storystoned," has only recently been
applied to psychotherapy (Honos-Webb, Sunwolf, & Shapiro, 2001),
the "storylistening trance" was first identified by Stallings (1988),
who was interested in the biophysiology of adults listening to told
tales. It was later investigated by Sturm (2000). Adult listeners to
folktales were found to be aware of their own profound altered states
of consciousness, including a sense of experiencing the fictional
story as real, identifying with story characters, plots, or roles ("I'm
no longer sitting in a tent listening to someone tell a story, I was in
those woods, I saw those animals." Sturm, 2000, p.290). More
recently, storylistening was found to reduce clinically significant
anxiety in college students, immediately following the September 11
terrorist attacks (Honos-Webb, Sunwolf, Hart, & Scalise, 2002).

ASIMILATIVE INTEGRATION

Why does therapist storytelling in psychotherapy offer a compelling solution for the therapist's and the client's heroic journey? Stories move clients into reconstruing their plight in one fundamental way: Healing occurs as clients change their personal perspectives from that of "victims" to one of "seekers." The perceived "dead-ends" become transformed into a call for personal transformation. There are many pathways for effecting this reconstruction and we will review the use of storytelling interventions along these different "pathways"—also considered as distinct theoretical interventions.

Assimilative integration (Lazarus & Messer, 1991) suggests that when an intervention is imported into a "brand-name" theoretical orientation, its incorporation must be consonant with the dominant orientation. The use of storytelling in psychotherapy is, therefore, current with recent developments in the field toward integrative and multicultural approaches to psychotherapy. Below, storylistening is discussed in terms of its assimilative integration into a variety of constructivist and related therapeutic approaches.

Personal Construct Therapies

According to George Kelly, the most important therapeutic change involves the development of new constructs to be applied to life circumstances (Kelly, 1955/1991a, 1955/1991b). Storytelling by the therapist is one intervention the therapist can use for offering new possible constructs. Stories told by the therapist not only provide content for informing new constructs, but the process of telling stories and inducing a storystoned state may allow for a loosening of former constructs. According to Epting (1984), loosening of constructs effects change by permitting movement in the personal construct system, broadening the client's ability to consider previously unnoticed aspects of the world and increasing the client's openness to new experiences. Storytelling by the therapist has an additional benefit over other techniques for loosening (i.e., relaxation, recounting dreams) in that a story well told induces a loosening of constructs in the therapist, as well as the client. As noted by Epting (1984), "It is sometimes necessary for the counselor to purposefully loosen his or her own construct system in order to understand the loosened construction of the client" (p. 121).

Storytelling in therapy also is consonant with the goals of constructivist approaches to balance interventions that honor the client's current system of constructs while opening up possibilities for alternative methods of construing life. As Mahoney (2000) writes,

> The perspective of constructivism questions the wisdom of interventions that seek to quickly dampen or eliminate expressions of systemic disorganization...the living logic of the person is honored, and his or her personal realities are fundamentally affirmed as creative solutions to a complex history of life challenges. Such life logic may need to be explored and expanded to accommodate new possibilities of experiencing, but it is still the hand—and foothold from which such explorations and expansions must be based...This is a balancing act." (p. 45).

It may be difficult for a therapist to determine if the client at a particular moment is more in need of validation or more in need of interventions that offer alternative constructions. Because of the complexity of a story, the client can often choose whether to attend to and identify with plot lines or characters that either validate current constructions or open up different possibilities. In short, clients can either identify with story characters that reflect the client's current predicament or be inspired by characters who have overcome the client's existential tangles. The ambiguousness of a story told not only permits responsiveness to the client's needs at any given moment; it allows the therapist to assess the client's needs, which may change from moment to moment. Thus, if a client responds to a tale of unrequited love with comments suggesting identification with the pain of the hero, the therapist is alerted to the fact that the client is demonstrating a need for interventions that honor and contain emotional pain and predicament. However, if a client responds to the same tale by noting the elements of transformation that were effected in the hero by an experience of unrequited love, the therapist may infer that the client is indicating a willingness to explore alternative modes of construing current life predicaments.

Personal construct therapies seek to find alternatives to systems of diagnosis such as the *Diagnostic and Statistical Manual of Mental Disorders* (American Psychiatric Association [APA], 2000) for construing disorders. A recent compilation (R. A. Neimeyer & Raskin, 2000) offers a wide array of constructivist alternatives to diagnosis for understanding the meaningfulness of clients' presenting predicaments. The use of storytelling in psychotherapy is consonant with the bias against diagnosis. Characters in stories are cast as being caught in complex circumstances and as having the power to make meaning of or work themselves out of such predicaments. Whereas diagnoses convey to clients that their problems are static unchanging entities (Honos-Webb & Leitner, 2001), stories present problems as having an interesting developmental history and as having a resolution in the next act or scene. In story, struggles are cast in epic proportions and may be understood as eternal conflicts between an individual and him or herself, or a conflict among humans, or a conflict between humans and nature. In stories, these archetypal conflicts are not problems to be eliminated as soon as possible, but the very essence of life itself. Character is built through these confrontations, not through the elimination of the pain and symptoms aroused in the confrontation with these existentially unavoidable conflicts.

In terms of meeting the need for assessment of the client's current level of functioning, rather than global diagnostic labels that are, more often than not, insults as well as diagnoses, the therapist can use the client's response to a told story to judge the client's most pressing needs at any moment in therapy. Just as the Rorschach provides a method of assessment by judging the construction of an ambiguous stimuli, so too does the ambiguous nature of stories allow for the therapist to assess clients by their responses to, elaboration of, or lack of elaboration of stories.

The capacity of storytelling to evoke and contain intense emotion might be particularly relevant to experiential personal construct psychotherapy (EPCP), an elaboration of personal construct psychotherapy, developed by Larry Leitner (cf. Leitner, 1988; Leitner & Dill-Standiford, 1993). EPCP has as its foundation the understanding of therapy as an intimate relationship between the therapist and client that directly engages existential struggles, including the conflict between the terror and richness involved in true intimacy. Leitner advocates for understanding disorders that often get DSM diagnoses as existential struggles that evoke intense feelings of fear, anxiety, hostility, guilt, and despair. By Leitner's account, these intense experiential states are meaningful reactions to invalidation in intimate relationships.

The central theory behind EPCP maps well onto the use of storytelling as an intervention in psychotherapy. Stories may allow for clients to process the horrors of their invalidations in a displaced manner by identifying with story characters. This displaced processing may allow for clients to re-organize their constructions to such an extent that they progress to being capable of directly processing their own relational traumas.

The use of telling a story may be particularly helpful in the treatment of severely disturbed clients who are most threatened by intimacy and potentially disorganized by therapist empathy. The use of a story to reflect and amplify a client's experience of loss or threat may allow a therapist to provide validation to a disturbed client without presuming to enter into the client's mind which may be felt as invasive to an individual with a long history of exposure to abuse in intimate relationships. In this way, the use of storytelling by the therapist can be used in the service of one of the core tenets of EPCP—the therapist's achievement of optimal therapeutic distance in relation to the client.

Feminist Psychotherapeutic Approach

Feminist therapists have advocated a collaborative style of therapy that focuses on meaning-making, rejection of absolute neutrality, and an insistence that all realities are not created equal (Hare-Mustin & Marecek, 1978; Nichols & Schwartz, 2001). Looking through a lens of gendered-socialization, feminists contend that psychopathology (i.e., insecure, controlling, emotional, ineffective female clients) may be understood by examining the historical, political, and economic positions women have traditionally occupied (Goldner, 1985). Hence, feminist therapy examines the sociological influences that create problems for individuals, in particular social and occupational role-strain (i.e., gender schema theory, Bem, 1987, 1993), moral decision-making styles (Gilligan, 1977, 1982; Walker, 1984), and issues of abuse and violence (Avis, 1992; Rinfret-Raynor & Cantin, 1997). At the same time, however, feminist therapy is usually coordinated with other theories of psychotherapy, including psychoanalytic, behavioral, cognitive, Gestalt, and brief therapies (cf. for example, Sharf, 2000).

Assessment issues in feminist therapy include attention to and rejection of negative labeling potential and artificial pathologies of the major diagnostic system (DSM-IV) (Brown, 1994). For example, Worall and Remer (1992) promote obtaining information about a client's social power, making a gender-role analysis, and using interventions that reframe and relabel, accordingly. The role of the therapist is one of listener, collaborator, and cheerleader, who strives to validate the individual, encourage drawing needed boundaries, and coach healthy assertiveness. Storytelling is an unusually consonant intervention with those values, techniques, and roles. Storytelling offers important opportunities, including selection by the therapist of particular stories, parables, or folktales that will validate a client's experiences by providing parallel fictional models; a tool for gender-role analysis, as a client's shared reactions to a story provide diagnostic and history-taking functions; a basis for collaborative intervention, as clients are encouraged to critique the character behaviors and choices, reframe outcomes, and change points-of-view from tales told in sessions, as clients go beyond analysis of a tale towards recreation of new possibilities; and a vicarious learning by identifying with heroines who overcome dilemmas.

One psychotherapist successfully imported interpretive folktales into her work with women facing gendered issues of mid-life and aging (an issue that holds important challenges for feminist psychotherapists) (Thomas, 1997). Of particular note was that Thomas found the wisdom of folktales seemed to touch her female clients emotionally long after the tales were first told, as clients called or wrote to say, "Such and such was happening to me, and I remembered that story you told me about..." (p. viii). Other therapists report powerful personal connections female clients draw from multicultural tales (e.g., Peseschkian, 2000). One woman gained new self-understanding after listening to one version of an ancient Persian tale about a man's intolerable burdens (Sunwolf, 2003):

> Once there was a traveler who was loaded with many burdens. Around his neck an old millstone dangled; a heavy sack of sand hung on his back; a water hose was draped around his body. In his hands he carried a boulder. Chains dragged heavy weights around his ankles. On his head, the man balanced a rotten pumpkin. Moaning and groaning, he moved forward but complained of the weariness that tormented him. A farmer met this traveler and asked, "Why do you load yourself down with this boulder?" The wanderer was surprised, "Awfully dumb, but I hadn't noticed it before." He threw the rock away and felt much lighter. Then he met a merchant who asked, "Tell me, why do you trouble yourself with the rotten pumpkin on your head and those heavy weights you drag behind you?" The wanderer was surprised again, "Awfully dumb, I'm glad you pointed it out." He took off the chains and smashed the pumpkin. Again, he felt lighter. Yet he continued to suffer. A housewife from a field watched him in amazement and said, "Tired wanderer, you are carrying sand in that sack, but what you see in the distance is more sand than you could ever want. Your big water hose is not needed, when there's a clear stream flowing alongside you." The wanderer dropped the hose and the heavy sand. Then he stood there and glanced down, seeing for himself the heavy millstone around his neck that caused him to walk bent over. He threw it into the river. Freed from his unnecessary burdens, the traveler wan-

dered on, now delighting in the cool of the evening—and soon found both comfort and lodging.

A 42-year old mother of three had presented with severe depression. She listened to this story, then brought notes to her next session of her reactions to it, which demonstrated her connections with specific events and symbols, not just the "moral" of the tale (Peseschkian, 2000):

> The wanderer walking down the seemingly endless road was myself, loaded down with all sorts of burdens: in a heavy sand-bag on my back hung my false egotism, my low self-esteem, and my mostly feigned coldness. Full of unsatisfied sexual expecta-tions and other unrealizable needs...a thick water hose was wrapped tightly around my body. In my right hand I carried the oddly shaped stone of dishonesty and in my left hand the boul-der of discourtesy...Truly moaning and groaning I moved for-ward (or backward), step by step, pleasantly wrapped up in the wadding of my morbid self-pity, and beautifully lulled by my well-nourished neuroses, complaining of my fate and my weari-ness. (p. 187)

This client was not only collaborating in her own diagnosis through storylistening, but providing a powerful assessment tool for her therapist—grounded in her new perceptions about powerless-ness and gender role strain.

Behavior Therapy

Stories may shift perspectives by containing implicit pre-scriptions for alternative courses of action. Comparable to a behav-ioral approach, stories may spur clients to try new behaviors that will improve the likelihood of solving problems. Additionally, the indirect approach of giving a fictional story to the client may provide oppor-tunities for vicarious learning.

The goals of behavior therapy are client and situation specif-ic, depending upon the desired behavior change. A distinguishing characteristic of behavior therapy is its emphasis on the specificity of goals and a focus on changing target behaviors (Sharf, 2000). The basic principles relied upon in modern behavioral therapies include reinforcement (positive or negative), extinction, generalization, dis-crimination, shaping, and observational learning (Spiegler & Guevremont, 1998). Three traditional approaches (operant condi-tioning, classical conditioning, and social learning theory) provide the foundation for assessment and intervention. Behavior therapies focus primarily on increasing the frequency of behavior (positive or negative reinforcement) or reducing it (punishment or non-rein-forcement). The therapist and client collaborate together for improvement in psychological functioning, with the therapist also serving in roles as informational teacher or coach.

Behavioral therapists have developed a wide variety of treat-ment methods, generally focusing on reducing fear and anxiety in order to change unwanted behaviors. A prime example is Wolpe's (1990) desensitization method, making use of progressive relaxation and gradual imaginal strategies. Contrary to the gradual process of desensitization, imaginal flooding therapies introduce continual, immediate images that frighten or induce anxiety (e.g., Stampfl's implosive therapy, 1970, where scenes are exaggerated rather than realistic). Symbolic modeling techniques, based on social learning theory, recognize the inconvenience of providing live modeling, and rely upon films, photographs, books, and plays to allow the client to usefully observe someone else's behaviors (e.g., Bandura, 1977), as well as covert modeling, when a client visualizes a model's behavior (e.g., Krop & Burgess, 1993, using covert modeling on a 7-year old deaf girl who imagined another little girl who felt good about mak-ing decisions).

As Sunwolf and Frey (2001) note, storytelling and storylis-tening are interventions that can be imported into behavioral thera-py to provide relaxation, desensitization, imaginal strategies and flooding, and symbolic modeling (such stories function as recipes for behaving, creating attitudes, beliefs, values, and actions). Storytelling offers specific opportunities for behaviorists to provide an engaging method of relaxation to that of physical progressive relaxation (e.g., the Jacobson procedure, which progressively addresses different parts of the body). Sturm (2000), for example, has shown that storytelling provides a calming trance for listeners (Sturm, 2000). Further, storytelling allows the therapist to choose and frame specific tales to provide novel images and scenes in the context of story for client desensitization or inoculation (in which a client prepares for an anticipated similar real life experience), as well as offering new tools for imaginal flooding, where a story's plot gives mental images of a frightening object or event and maintains that sequence until the client is better able to tolerate it. In addition, stories provide indirect symbolic modeling that may be more less burdensome than reading, less time-consuming than watching films, and more mentally-engaging than passively receiving images (videos, photographs), while at the same time providing a convenient and vivid method of fictional role playing and rehearsal, as therapists invite clients to switch roles with various characters in the tale in order to gain different perspectives, obtain insights, or safely experience the effects of new choices.

Cognitive Therapy

Stories may also offer alternative constructions on life events and current struggles. Consistent with a cognitive model of psychotherapy, the storyteller can offer stories that provide a concrete intervention for reframing thought processes that are prone to cognitive distortions. Many stories offer tales of heroes escaping from impossible predicaments or overcoming overwhelming odds to succeed in improbable feats. These tales can point clients to the possibility that their sense of hopelessness is a distortion, or at least does not serve them in overcoming current problems. Stories may offer a way of visioning a future that before was not available to the client.

Cognitive therapy as promoted by Beck (1976, 1991) is based on the view that behavior is impacted by automatic thoughts, cognitive schemas, and cognitive distortions that contribute to psychological distress. Key constructs for the cognitive approach include automatic thoughts (which are inaccurate, exaggerated, or distorted and occur spontaneously, without effort or choice), and cognitive schemas (adaptive or maladaptive beliefs and assumptions about people, events, and social worlds), many of which render clients vulnerable to repeated distress. Both of these constructs affect information processing and render it inaccurate or ineffective (Freeman, 1987). The basic goal of cognitive therapy is to remove distortions in thinking to help individuals live more effectively, with less distress, so attention is paid to challenging the ways clients process information. Therapists typically take a collaborative approach towards goal setting, but are willing to be more authoritarian in confronting the false or ineffective beliefs.

Cognitive therapists favor guided discovery, and shared storytelling as a less-threatening tool to help clients discover new ways of thinking or behaving and challenge belief systems, as clients analyze the behavior of characters in the tale. Stories have been found to teach new attitudes and belief systems in cognitive therapy (Dwivedi, 1997; Dwivedi & Gardner, 1997). When imported into cognitive therapeutic approaches, stories, parables, and multicultural wisdom tales can provide unique tools to help change dichotomous thinking, inaccurate inferences, tendencies to catastrophize events, overgeneralizations, mislabeling, magnification or minimiza-

97

tion of their own qualities, and personalization of unrelated events. Told stories facilitate the imagining of future possibilities as well as the contemplation of hypotheticals (Sunwolf & Frey, 2001). Storytelling offers opportunities for cognitive therapists to assess client thoughts, through sampling during or directly after story listening. This occurs as therapists dialogue with clients regarding client beliefs and assumptions about events in the tale. Further, storytelling provides models for more positive imagining of anticipated events, when clients are given access to outcomes beyond their own experiences. Additional benefits for this therapeutic perspective include offering a vehicle for less-threatening confrontation of a client's distorted thinking, as therapist and client collaboratively explore the possibilities presented in stories that parallel issues in a client's life; creating opportunities to choose and share tales that exaggerate or magnify qualities or events that are significant for individual clients; and offering a useful way to guide clients towards decatastrophizing, by sharing stories that expand a client's dysfunctional "what if" and obsessive thinking about possible outcomes. Finally, therapeutic storytelling creates fictionalized opportunities for clients to cognitively rehearse behavioral choices and anticipated emotions, as more successful outcomes and alternative choices are offered in stories, while providing a new method for self-monitoring through homework assignments, by which a client can keep a record of feelings and thoughts about stories shared in therapy sessions.

Emotion-Focused Treatments

Emotion-focused therapy (Greenberg, 2002) implicates emotional processing styles in the cause and cure of psychopathology. Over-controlled emotional processing styles can lead to depression and anxiety disorders whereas under-controlled emotional processing can lead to personality and/or conduct disorders. Traditional interventions in emotion-focused treatments include Gestalt-inspired empty chair work for unfinished business and focusing exercises in which clients are encouraged to attend carefully to emerging here-and-now experience. Modern EFT therapists have added interventions to facilitate leaving emotions and soothing existing disturbed emotional states.

Therapist storytelling can be used in the service of many of these aims. Stories may serve to intensify emotional reactions of clients by offering dramatic portrayals of situations parallel to client life events. Additionally, stories may serve as a container for apparently intolerable affect resulting from traumatic life events. Finally,

98

the trance-like state induced by storytelling may also be soothing, allowing clients to overcome internal agitation and progress in emotional expression work.

Stories could be used to amplify emotional themes uncovered in focusing work. Often during a client's increasing awareness to emerging experience, vivid images arise which provide "handles" for the unclear feeling. Elaboration of these images often yields themes that evoke mythical and cultural stories. In one instance, a woman who was focusing on an experience of being trapped shared an image of being locked away in a tower. She perceived that her husband had complete control over her and that she was powerless to free herself. It was clear to the therapist that she was dependent on the husband in many inescapable ways. The client was perpetually feeling hopeless. In discussing this case in consultation, it came up that an appropriate story might be that of Rapunzel, a woman in distress who escaped from an evil witch who locked her away in a tower. Depending on the version of this story which is selected, such a story can be used to amplify and validate the client's current emotional experiencing through the use of archetypal images of folklore and an experience of universality. Alternatively, a story with a happy ending can be used to inspire hope to encourage a client in the leaving phase of emotional expression, where the task is to move beyond being overcome by an emotional state that has adequately been expressed and processed.

In processing emotions of grief and shock after tragic loss, stories of others who have gone through similar situations may be helpful in enabling clients to endure barely tolerable emotional states that are not ready to be soothed or fully processed. The story of another's loss may allow the client to approach in a displaced manner, current emotion themes without becoming overwhelmed. In this way, a story may serve a function similar to social support in group therapy. Simply knowing that others have endured similar situations can ameliorate secondary negative emotions of alienation and inspire hope that life can go on in the face of loss or trauma.

Existential Psychotherapy

Existential psychotherapy, with roots in European philosophy, Jewish mysticism, and American notions of freedom, is predicated on the construction and attribution of meaning and the salience of personal choice. From an existential perspective, psychotherapy is focused on the meaning individuals give to their experience. The content of actual life events is considered less important than the reaction clients have or the meaning they give to events. In existential therapy, the focal point is the moment-by-moment, here and now reactions of clients. Therapeutic movement is fueled by continually working on the tension between the choice of living with the stagnation of the status quo and facing the fear of the unknown. From this orientation, health is more associated with clients' choosing to face the fear of change. Of course, embedded in this choice is the ultimate fear of the unknown: death.

In order to do this, therapists must help the client distinguish between healthy and neurotic anxiety about coming face-to-face with the unknown. The latter may be understood as a paralyzing anxiety that represents a fear of the fear of the unknown. A client's symptoms are often representative of this neurotic anxiety. For example, a phobia may well represent a client's defense against facing a greater unknown. Thus, agoraphobia may protect a patient from facing intimacy or unknown challenges in a new setting. After all, if one cannot leave the house, there is a severe reduction in possible new encounters. Existential therapy is successful to the extent that the client may face the true fear and make a choice.

It is precisely here that a well-placed therapeutic story may underscore the importance of facing the actual fear (albeit, in a once-removed manner). It is most important to note that from the existential framework, the facing of the fear and understanding, changing or creating meaning is the goal. Counter-phobic behavior may not be considered successful.

The following example of an existential story may underscore this point. After months of working with a client who was procrastinating endlessly about necessary career and relationship decisions, the therapist told the following story.

> I used to live on the island of Oahu in Hawaii. On the North Shore of the island is a beach with a huge rock jutting out into the ocean. It is a place where teenagers often climbed to the top of this very high rock and dove into the ocean. The top of the rock was higher than a high diving board and the ocean was often churning beneath. I knew two people who decided independently that they had to take the challenge of the big rock. One was a woman. She was about 40 when she climbed up to the top of the rock and without much delay, took a running start and "cannonballed" off the rock and into the ocean. She emerged from the water with a delighted smile on her face and much new found confidence. Later the same month, a man in his mid thirties also made the trip to the rock. He slowly climbed to the top, spent some time looking at the rock, the

ocean below and indeed, himself. After much consideration, he
climbed down, never jumping off the rock. What was most
interesting was that he was as delighted with himself as she was.

The client initially scoffed at the man's reaction and saw him
as a failure, but then asked why would he feel good. The therapist
replied, "because he looked into the eye of one of his personal
demons and made a choice that was right for him. He could overcome some fears and needed to respect others." The client kept trying to reconsider the personal belief that any non-overcoming of fear
was a failure. He subsequently spontaneously reported that to him all
failures were the same and any failure meant that he was a total failure. That was his neurotic anxiety. Then he said that if this guy did-
n't jump off the rock and wasn't a failure then maybe he needed to
reassess some of his own decisions.

The therapist inquired about what fears he was experiencing
at the moment. The client replied, "I wonder about if I marry the
woman I'm seeing, maybe it won't turn out well and we'll get
divorced." The therapist pondered, "so better to have avoided altogether than to have loved and lost." When the client chuckled and
asked, "Did you just come up with that, or is it a standard line?" The
therapist replied, "So you are also concerned about being close
enough to me to be influenced." This led to a rich exploration of the
intimacy concerns in the here-and-now, and ultimately to a decision
about relating in newer, more anxiety provoking ways with the
woman friend and perhaps facing the question of marriage.

Psychodynamic Approaches

Storytelling by a therapist will likely promote a regressive
transference as many storylisteners report evocation of childhood
memories of being told stories. This experience of the transference
may transport the client into another time and place, shifting perspective away from the here-and-now. Not only the process of storytelling, but also the story itself frequently evokes a time and place
"long ago and far, far away." This offers the client a historical perspective, allowing for a shift in perspective, such that the presenting
problem becomes seen as a moment in time, one of a series of seemingly unsolvable problems. This pathway to a changed perspective is
consonant with psychodynamic approaches to psychotherapy.

Psychodynamic theories emanate from the late nineteenth
and early twentieth century work of Breuer, Freud, and a host of oth-

ers. There are many varieties of psychodynamic therapy, including classic psychoanalysis, neo-analytic approaches, ego psychology, and object relations theories. The psychodynamic approaches have produced the most clinical writing and reported case studies of any of the major psychological approaches. Until the ascendancy of behavioral approaches to clinical work in the mid-twentieth century, psychodynamic approaches held sway over the entire mental health field.

Psychodynamic theories are predicated on a few crucial constructs. One is that behavioral and emotional problems are caused by unconscious factors. These factors frequently represent early childhood experiences that could not be understood, absorbed, or handled by the child. Thus the child represses (keeps from conscious awareness) these painful experiences. In the process they become influential as unconscious drives and defenses in later life. It is believed that making these factors conscious and "working them through" in a therapeutic environment is healing.

Psychodynamic therapy focuses on uncovering the unconscious causes of current discomfort through a very unique relationship in which the therapist is experienced by the client as significant others in his/her past and the issues that were defended against previously may be handled directly in this healing relationship. This process is called transference. The therapist becomes the object of repressed and fantasized feelings, attitudes and desires.

Therapeutic stories may play a powerful role in uncovering the unconscious material and in enhancing the potency of the transference relationship. Thus, stories about children in acts of discovery, conflict and adventures may well activate long unconscious memories that may be discussed in the therapy sessions. Many fables, fairy tales and epics are particularly prone to generating a regressed state and produce memories.

One client was a self-described "workaholic," who claimed in therapy to have succeeded at making money as CEO of two companies, but failed at relationships. During the first session, he related that his third wife was about to leave him because he never had time for "fun." "For me," he confided, "my work is fun. When I go to Hawaii, I sit on the beach and scheme business plans." He was alienated from his family and children and described himself as just like his dad.

After several sessions, the patient told of a takeover of another company "against all odds. I just knew I could do it if I kept at it and I did." The therapist opined that the patient's "favorite childhood story must have been, 'The Little Engine That Could.'" Almost instantly the client teared-up and together they began reciting portions of that book. As he talked about it, he remembered that it was the only story his father would read to him. He was most touched that the therapist would share it with him. Of course, this increased the positive "father" transference with the therapist.

Later, the therapist, using the extra weight occasioned by this enhanced transference, began to suggest another train story he thought the client would appreciate. The next session, he told the client the story of "Tootle," a train that went off the track to play. The client was obviously troubled by this story. In the next three sessions he railed against the ethic of play over hard work and accomplishment. He wondered if the therapist was himself, serious enough about working to be able to actually help him. During the third session he began to weep and said, "I am way too afraid to play. That's when people leave you." This allowed for the movement into the exploration of abandonment and loss, the next phase of the therapy.

Systems Approaches: Structural Family Therapy

According to Minuchin (1974), Kantor and Lehr (1975), and others, every family operates within a structure; an invisible set of functional demands by which family relationships are governed. Within such a structure there are sub-units between family members. These consist of boundaries, hierarchies and sub-systems that govern the patterns of interactions within which adaptations are made. The family structure is pushed to limits with developmental or situational crises.

For structural family therapists, symptoms are best understood within the framework of the family structure and corrections are best made at the structural-system level. To do this, therapists must first join and understand the system, then create disequilibrium in the system to unbalance the problematic methods of dealing with stress. Next, the therapist helps the family restructure the boundaries and patterns of interaction. Finally, the therapist helps the family develop an understanding, necessary communication skills and reassurance that they can replicate the changed interactions in the future.

In Minuchin and Fishman's (1981) terms, some of the most common and difficult boundary violations are those that involve emotional coalitions by members of two different generations against a third family member. Thus, when there is a greater alle-

103

giance between a parent and a child than between the two parents, it is the job of the therapist to help the family establish appropriate boundaries and allegiances and to minimize the cross-boundary allegiances.

A therapeutic story may be employed at any phase of structural family therapy. It may be used to join the family in a collaboration. It may provide the unconscious means to dis-calibrate the current family boundaries and structure or it may provide guidance for restructured boundaries.

One example of the use of story in this form of therapy occurred in a marital therapy case. In this family, the husband came into the therapy after a job-related injury that had him home in bed for almost a month. He complained that since the birth of their two children, his wife wanted "nothing to do" with him and instead placed all of her energy and time with the children. He claimed that she was a great mother, but had ceased being a wife. She complained that he was "selfish, was only interested in sex, and wasn't child oriented." Because one of the children had asthma, she had taken to sleeping in the bed with the two youngsters (aged 4 and 6) and he ended up sleeping alone. She claimed to be "completely worn out, with nothing to give." The therapist was able to join the current boundary situation by telling a story about a shortage of wheat to feed a village and the reaction of the villagers to exile those members who were seen as able to survive on their own without further depleting the village stores for the winter.

Later in the process of unbalancing and focusing on the unconscious meaning of the asthma, the therapist commented to the mother that he had just taken a trip and while on the trip he had thought about her. He said, in a slow and intricate manner, "it was when the flight attendant began to talk about any potential problems in cabin pressure. She said, if you are traveling with small children, put your oxygen mask on first before helping your child put the mask on."

As the therapist finished, the husband of the couple automatically and gently took his wife's hand in his and looked at her in a most supportive manner. The therapist seized on the moment to reinforce the couple's togetherness and the importance of the parental sub-system.

In summary, the potential impact of therapist storytelling that is highlighted by each distinct theoretical orientation provides a review of the important healing potential of stories in a more general sense. For example, that story listening promotes a "regressive transference" or a "relaxed receptive state" will be true regardless of the therapeutic approach. Awareness of each of these potential therapeutic impacts could benefit therapists from every orientation.

THE CLIENT'S HEROIC JOURNEY

While some current trends in the field (managed care, empirically supported therapies) underscore the crisis intervention mode of symptom reduction as the primary aim of psychotherapy, constructivist approaches might well re-plot this storyline of successful treatment and suggest that, when a specific solution to the presenting problem has been achieved, another more salient journey begins. The problems that bring clients into therapy are often the culmination of longstanding patterns of behavior across many domains. Getting fired from a job may bring an individual with narcissistic traits into therapy. The client's history may be littered with failed relationships and chronic underemployment due to the typical environmental response incurred by a person who exudes a sense of entitlement.

The first layer of therapy can be viewed as clients gaining understanding of how their reactions are understandable human responses to stressful and traumatic events. The second layer of therapy may involve them exploring the possibility that they may, in part, play a role in contributing to the occurrence of stressful and traumatic life events. This second layer of work—exploring the client's role as co-creator of the continuing trauma (as in PTSD)—represents an introduction to the client's potential heroic journey. There are two pathways through this second layer: (1) making meaning of incomprehensible tragic life events over which the client has no control (death, victim of violence); or (2) recognition of the client's role as co-creator of traumatic events (divorce, failure, and rejection).

Either pathway requires acceptance by clients that they may get worse before they get better. This journey is more demanding and rigorous than the symptom solution path. To make meaning of tragic life events, clients must first accept their powerlessness in the face of irrevocable loss (of loved ones, a sense of safety, innocence). Only in facing this void of meaninglessness can clients claim their roles as creators of meaning. Robert Neimeyer's book (2000), *Lessons of Loss: A Guide to Coping* provides a map for the many possibilities of creation that follow significant loss. As R. A. Neimeyer articulates:

> As we sift through the lessons of loss, we come to approach life
> with renewed priorities, with a clearer sense of what is impor-

tant, and what is not worthy of concern. As we revise the
philosophies by which we live, we also "re-vision" ourselves,
perhaps opening ourselves to possibilities that once seemed
foreclosed, developing skills and interests that previously have
lain dormant within us, or cultivating relationships with others
that previously had been neglected or unexplored. In this sense,
while loss diminishes us, it can also lead to our renewal. (p. 47).

In other cases, the client may have played a role in creating
the traumas and tragic life events. A woman who exhibits passive-
aggressive behavior finds herself facing a series of professional failures. A narcissistic man finds himself alone and facing a long series
of failed relationships. In these cases, long-standing fundamental
approaches to the world contribute to suffering from life events that
are tragic, but that ultimately the client is, in part, responsible for
creating. This work will require of the client a willingness to take
responsibility, to stop blaming others, and to give up the comfort of
seeing oneself only as a victim.

Many clients are not interested in this second layer of the
journey. They come to therapy to get rid of their pain, not to embark
on a hero's journey. Ultimately, it is the client who must accept this
new leg of the journey, but it is the therapist who, through story, may
open the possibility to the client that the solution to the immediate
problem is not the end of his or her concerns, but rather the beginning. It is at this critical juncture that stories may be most useful in
facilitating the client's journey along the path to not only overcoming presenting problems, but making meaning of them in ways that
will effect long-standing changes in the way the client construes the
world.

One story that evokes the importance of this journey for the
client is in the well-worn tale about the gatekeeper guarding the
entrance into a small town. When travelers would inquire about what
the town and its people were like the guard would respond with a
question "What was it like where you are coming from?" No matter
what the traveler replied, the guard's response was always the same
"That's what it is like here." This story is only one example of stories
about boundaries that might proffer encouragement and motivation
to a client to undertake the hero's journey of self-exploration that
begins after immediate symptoms have abated. Clients may attempt
to solve relationship problems by ending relationships, or solve
work-related difficulties by changing positions. Social phobic clients
might expand the circumferences of their worlds by diligently practicing graded exposure homework assignments. However, underly-

ing these temporary solutions are long-standing ways of construct-ing the world and making meaning of events that will lead to more of the same if these constructs are not examined. The therapist's vig-ilance in recognizing when the boundary between problem solution and the hero's journey of seeing the self as co-creator has been reached, along with an apt boundary-spanning story, can provide the client valuable hope for the journey that lies ahead.

WHY THERAPISTS RESIST STORYTELLING

Given the healing power of stories and their use throughout time as potent interventions, why might therapists be resistant to telling stories in psychotherapy? Storytelling predates the written word as a tool of healers. Why has this time-honored traditional healing method fallen into disuse? There are several potential expla-nations for therapists' resistance to using stories as a psychotherapy intervention.

The art of telling stories may be inconsistent with the grow-ing vision of psychotherapy as a science and specific interventions as a "technology of change." The metaphor of therapist as technician has replaced the metaphor of therapist as artist or creative healer. The vision of psychotherapy as a creative process is fast being replaced by the vision of psychotherapy as guided by manuals that have been demonstrated to be effective in randomized controlled clinical trials. Many training institutions endorse this latter vision of therapy, mak-ing anything as individualized, creative, and artistic as telling stories particularly discordant with therapists' training and understanding of clinical work.

Like any intervention with which one has little experience, therapists may be personally threatened by the prospect of telling stories. Therapists require specific training and experience with the art of telling stories. The only exposure to storytelling to which ther-apists-in-training may have been exposed is as one method for inducing hypnotic states (Erickson, Rossi, & Rossi, 1976). However, it is a rare graduate program in which training in hypnosis is core.

Therapists may also be resistant to telling stories in psy-chotherapy because of distaste for indirectness. It may seem to ther-apists that telling stories is manipulative or deceptive in that, if the therapist wants to encourage a certain behavior or reframing of an event, a direct advisement or intervention would be more appropri-ate. We argue that telling stories is more client-centered (rather than less client-centered), in that it allows clients to interpret stories in ways consonant with their own growing edges. This valuable indirectness mitigates the power of therapists by allowing clients to interpret stories in ways that fit their own predilections for change. Research has documented the potentially negative impacts of client deference on therapeutic progress (Rennie, 1994). Stories allow therapists to implement persuasive interventions that, because of their indirectness and openness to multiple meanings, allow clients to be exposed to the persuasive message without the power implications of persuasive response modes implemented by therapists.

A final, and perhaps most intense, deterrent to therapists telling stories in psychotherapy is a personal aversion to primary process that many therapists may experience. Telling stories induces a hypnotic-like trance in both storyteller and listener. Therapists who are threatened by this apparent loss of control may be less likely to implement storytelling interventions. Not only do personality traits of a high need for control increase the threat posed by primary process, but the role demands associated with the therapist's interpersonal position also impose constraints on the therapist's perceived freedom. To the extent that therapists are guided by the metaphor that they should be expert technicians—in control and responsible for providing prescribed doses of empirically supported therapeutic active ingredients—the more difficult will be the selection of an intervention likely to induce primary process in both the client and the therapist. The therapist may be daunted by the prospect of handling both the client's and his or her own trance-like state of consciousness.

CONCLUSIONS

Storytelling can be a healing tool for therapists to use in psychotherapy. While traditional narrative solutions in therapy rely upon coaching clients to re-story their past and future lives (e.g., Eron & Lund, 1996; Gardner, 1993; White & Epston, 1990), we have offered a different use of both storytelling and story listening. Consonant with current trends toward psychotherapy integration, we have suggested specific ways in which fictional stories external to the client's life can be incorporated into a wide array of theoretical orientations: personal construct, feminist, cognitive, behavioral, emotion-focused, existential, psychodynamic and family systems approaches. In reviewing the container model (Honos-Webb et al., 2001) as a basis for understanding how stories heal, we elaborated mechanisms of change that are not consonant with some current trends in psychotherapy. The container model suggests that clients heal not by eliminating pain, but by increasing their capacity to tolerate emotional suffering and tragic life events. This is not to encourage the increased experience of painful feelings, but rather that in the face of the inevitable "slings and arrows of outrageous fortune," a lack of human responsiveness may itself be pathological. According to this model, the ideal of psychological health encompasses the importance of human sensitivity and emotional responsiveness. By this account, the freedom from pain (a detached, numbed response) may not be a symptom solution but rather itself a pathological reaction. Leitner (1985) elaborates this point in his emphasis on the emptiness that is found in the safety of retreat from intimate relationships.

Telling stories may also facilitate clients' abilities to contain multiple and contradictory aspects of their selves. Postmodern constructivist approaches have articulated the fundamentally multiple and permeable nature of the self (Honos-Webb, Surko, Stiles & Greenberg, 1998; Honos-Webb & Stiles, 1998; R. A. Neimeyer, 2000). The polyphonic nature of stories mirrors the postmodern construction of the self as inherently multivoiced. A client may be helped not only by identifying with one story character, but by identifying with the conflict among multiple characters in helping elucidate an internal conflict, which is substantially different than traditional narrative therapeutic approaches (e.g., Eron & Lund, 1996; White & Epston, 1990). Recent psychotherapy research findings suggest that recovery from depression might be understood in terms of increasing one's interior complexity by assimilating new voices into one's self (Honos-Webb, Stiles, & Greenberg, 2003).

This alternative reconstruction of the aims of psychotherapy also suggests that a re-emplotment of the story of psychotherapeutic healing, such that a transformation that requires a descent into previously avoided pain, encompasses the client's own heroic journey. Indeed the journey to solve one's problem and eliminate pain is a significant one. It is that "less traveled path" to get to the source of chronic dysphoric life patterns and the attendant willingness to explore one's personal role in creating life events that constitute a hero's journey. As clients often do not come to therapy with the vision of a quest of heroic proportions, it may be that the therapist can bring to bear persuasive interventions and support to instill hope and courage for this therapeutic task. We have suggested that stories are particularly appropriate for facilitating this therapeutic transition. Stories balance the dialectical tensions of the therapist's requirement to be both validating of current experience and facilitating of change. Stories can be persuasive in that they offer an alternative construction on clients' dilemmas. Furthermore, as a displaced form of intervention, evoking distant lands and times long ago, clients are free to make their own meaning of the stories told by therapists. Finally, we acknowledged that telling stories in psychotherapy might promote a heroic journey by the therapist as well. Telling stories requires a great deal of the therapist: in part intuition (to match the right story to the right client) and in part performance (as the presentation evokes as much healing properties as does the content of stories). Telling stories in psychotherapy clearly requires therapists to construe their therapeutic role as creative, artistic healers rather than technicians.

> In West Africa, when a person in the village becomes sick, the healer will ask, "When was the last time that you sang? When was the last time that you danced? When was the last time that someone told you a story?"

REFERENCES

American Psychiatric Association. (2000). *Diagnostic and statistical manual of mental disorders* (4th edition, text revision). Washington, DC: Author.

Avis, J. M. (1992). Where are all the family therapists? Abuse and violence within families and family therapy's response. *Journal of Martial and Family Therapy, 18*, 225-232.

Bandura, A. (1977). *Social learning theory.* Englewood Cliffs, NJ: Prentice-Hall.

Beck, A. T. (1976). *Cognitive therapy and the emotional disorders.* New York: International Universities Press.

Beck, A. T. (1991). Cognitive therapy: A 30-year retrospective. *American Psychologist, 46*, 368-375.

Beck, A. T., & Weishaar, M. (1989). *Cognitive therapy.* In A. Freeman, K. M. Simon, L. E. Beutler, & H. Arkowitz (Eds.), *Comprehensive handbook of cognitive therapy* (pp. 21-36). New York: Plenum.

Bem, S. L. (1987). Gender schema theory and the romantic tradition. In P. Shaver & C. Hendrick (Eds.), *Sex and gender* (pp. 251-271). Newbury Park, CA: Sage.

Bem, S. L. (1993). *The lens of gender: Transforming the debate on sexual inequality.* New Haven, CT: Yale University Press.

Brown, L. S. (1994). *Subversive dialogues: Theory in feminist therapy.* New York: Basic Books.

Dwivedi, K. N. (Ed.) (1997). *The therapeutic use of stories.* New York: Routledge.

Dwivedi, K. N., & Gardner, D. (1997). Theoretical perspectives and clinical approaches. In K. N. Dwivedi (Ed.), *The therapeutic use of stories* (pp. 19-41). New York: Routledge.

Epting, F. R. (1984). *Personal construct counseling and psychotherapy.* Chichester: John Wiley.

Erickson, M. H. Rossi, E. L. & Rossi, S. I. (1976) *Hypnotic realities.* New York: Irvington.

Eron, J. B., & Lund, T. W. (1996). *Narrative solutions in brief therapy.* New York: Guilford.

Freedman, J., & Combs, G. (1996). *Narrative therapy: The social construction of preferred realities.* New York: W. W. Norton.

Freeman, A. (1987). Cognitive therapy: An overview. In A. Freeman & V. Greenwood (Eds.), *Cognitive therapy: Applications in psychiatric and medical settings* (pp. 19-35). New York: Human Science Press.

Gardner, R. A. (1993). *Storytelling in psychotherapy with children.* Northvale, NJ: Jason Aronson.

Gilligan, C. (1977). In a different voice: Women's conception of self and morality. *Harvard Educational Review, 47,* 481-517.

Gilligan, C. (1982). *In a different voice.* Cambridge, MA: Harvard University Press.

Goldner, V. (1985). Feminism and family therapy. *Family Process, 24,* 31-47.

Hare-Mustin, R. T., & Marecek, J. (1988). The meaning of difference: Gender theory, postmodernism and psychology. *American Psychologist, 43,* 455-464.

Harper, P. & Gray, M. (1997). Maps and meaning in life and healing. In K. N. Dwivedi (Ed.), *The therapeutic use of stories* (pp. 42-63). New York: Routledge.

Honos-Webb, L., Sunwolf, Hart, S., & Scalise, J. (2002). *A comparison of assimilation vs. accommodation based narrative approaches in the treatment of trauma symptoms following 9-11.* Paper submitted for publication.

Honos-Webb, L., Sunwolf, & Shapiro, J. L. (2001). Toward the re-enchantment of psychotherapy: Stories as container. *The Humanistic Psychologist, 29,* 70-97.

Honos-Webb, L., Stiles, W. B., & Greenberg, L. S. (2003). A method of rating assimilation in psychotherapy based on markers of change. *Journal of Counseling Psychology, 50,* 189-198.

Honos-Webb, L. & Leitner, L. M. (2001). How using the DSM causes damage: A client's report. *The Journal of Humanistic Psychology, 41,* 36-56.

Honos-Webb, L., Surko, M., Stiles, W. B., & Greenberg, L. S. (1999). Assimilation of voices in psychotherapy: The case of Jan. *Journal of Counseling Psychology, 46,* 448-460.

Honos-Webb, L., & Stiles, W. B. (1998). Reformulation of assimilation analysis in terms of voices. *Psychotherapy, 35,* 23-33.

Kantor, D., & Lehr, W. (1975) *Inside the family.* San Francisco: Jossey Bass.

Kelly, G. A. (1991a). *The psychology of personal constructs:Vol. 1. A theory of personality.* London: Routledge. (Original work published 1955)

Kelly, G. A. (1991b). *The psychology of personal constructs:Vol. 2 . Clinical diagnosis and psychotherapy.* London: Routledge. (Original work published 1955)

Krop, H., & Burgess, D. (1993). The use of covert modeling in the treatment of a sexual abuse victim. In J. R. Cautela & A. J. Kearney (Eds.), Covert conditioning casebook (pp. 153-158). Pacific Grove, CA: Brooks/Cole.

Lazarus, A. A., & Messer, S. B. (1991). Does chaos prevail? An exchange on technical eclecticism and assimilative integration. Journal of Psychotherapy Integration, 1, 143-158.

Leitner, L. M. (1985). The terrors of cognition: On the experiential validity of personal construct theory. In D. Bannister (Ed.), Issues and approaches in personal construct theory (pp. 83-103). London: Academic Press.

Leitner, L. M. (1988). Terror, risk, and reverence: Experiential personal construct psychotherapy. International Journal of Personal Construct Psychology, 1, 261-272.

Leitner, L. M., & Dill-Standiford, T. J. (1993). Resistance in experiential personal construct psychotherapy: Theoretical and technical struggles. In L. M. Leitner & N. G. M. Dunnett (Eds.), Critical issues in personal construct psychotherapy (pp. 135-155). Melbourne, FL: Krieger.

Mahoney, M. J. (2000). Core ordering and disordering processes: A constructive view of psychological development. In R. A. Neimeyer & J. D. Raskin (Eds.), Constructions of disorder: Meaning-making frameworks for psychotherapy (pp. 43-62). Washington, DC: American Psychological Association.

Meichenbaum, D. (1993). Stress inoculation training: A 20-year update. In P. M. Lehrer & R. L. Woolfolk (Eds.), Principles and practice of stress management (2nd ed., pp. 373-406). New York: Guilford.

Minuchin, S. (1974). Families and family therapy. Cambridge: Harvard University Press.

Minuchin, S., & Fishman, H. C. (1981) Family therapy techniques. Cambridge: Harvard University Press.

Neimeyer, G. J. & Rood, L. (1997). Contemporary expressions of constructivist psychotherapy. In G. J. Neimeyer & R.A. Neimeyer, Advances in personal construct psychology (Vol. 4, pp. 185-205). London: JAI press.

Neimeyer, R. A. (2000). Lessons of loss: A guide to coping. Memphis, TN: Center for the Study of Loss and Transition.

Neimeyer, R. A. (2000). Narrative disruptions in the construction of the self. In R. A. Neimeyer & J. D. Raskin (Eds.), Constructions of disorder: Meaning-making frameworks for psychotherapy (pp.207-242). Washington, DC: American Psychological Association.

Neimeyer, R. A. & Raskin, J. D. (2000). *Constructions of disorder: Meaning-making frameworks for psychotherapy.* Washington, DC: American Psychological Association.

Nichols, M. P., & Schwartz, R. C. (2001). *Family therapy: Concepts and methods* (5th ed.). Needham Heights, MA: Allyn and Bacon.

Peseschkian, N. (2000). *Positive psychotherapy: Theory & practice of a new method.* New Delhi: Sterling Publishers.

Rennie, D. L. (1994). Client deference in psychotherapy. *Journal of Counseling Psychology, 4,* 427-437.

Rinfret-Raynor, M., & Cantin, S. (1997). Feminist therapy for battered women: An assessment. In G. K. Kantor & J. L. Jasinski (Eds.), *Out of darkness: Contemporary perspectives on family violence* (pp. 219-234). Thousand Oaks, CA: Sage.

Sharf, R. S. (2000). *Theories of psychotherapy and counseling: Concepts and cases.* Belmont, CA: Brooks/Cole.

Spiegler, M. D., & Guevremont, D. C. (1998). *Contemporary behavior therapy* (3rd ed.). Pacific Grove, CA: Brooks/Cole.

Stallings, F. (1988). The web of silence: Storytelling's power to hypnotize. *The National Storytelling Journal,* Spring/Summer, 6-19.

Stampfl, T. G. (1970). Implosive therapy: An emphasis on covert stimulation. In D. J. Levis (Ed.), *Learning approaches to therapeutic behavior change* (pp. 182-204). Chicago: Aldine.

Sturm, B. W. (2000). The "storylistening" trance experience. *Journal of American Folklore, 113,* 287-304.

Sunwolf (2003). Buried in the stacks: Storied-treasures. *Healing Story, 9,* 1-2.

Sunwolf, & Frey, L. R. (2001). Storytelling: The power of narrative communication and interpretation. In W. P. Robinson & H. Giles (Eds.), *The new handbook of language and social psychology* (pp. 119-135). Sussex: John Wiley.

Thomas, A. G. (1997). *The women we become: Myths, folktales, and stories about growing older.* Rocklin, CA: Prima Publishing.

Walker, L. J. (1984). Sex differences in the development of moral reasoning: A critical review. *Child Development, 55,* 667-691.

White, M., & Epston, D. (1990). *Narrative means to therapeutic ends.* New York: Norton.

Wolpe, J. (1990). *The practice of behavior therapy* (4th ed.). New York: Pergamon.

Worell, J., & Remer, P. (1992). *Feminist perspectives in therapy: An empowerment model for women.* New York: Wiley.

CHAPTER 6

Making Meaning of Child Abuse: Personal, Social, and Narrative Processes[1]

Stephanie Lewis Harter

... people are usually ashamed of seeing what they are not supposed to see, so these are the stories that never get told (Kelly, 1969, p. 335).

This chapter provides a partial summary of personal, social, and narrative processes in making meaning of childhood abuse, in order to illustrate the potential relevance and synergy of constructivist, constructionist, and narrative approaches. The introductory section uses personal construct theory as a base to suggest that some of the apparent contradictions between constructionist and constructivist approaches may result from differing uses of language. Whereas the social constructionists may hear "personal" as a label for the contrast to "social," constructivists see personal meanings as intrinsically social, embedded within larger contexts of meaning. As the chapter continues to discuss the dialectic between personal and social meanings in the aftermath of childhood abuse, the narrative metaphor emerges as a potential bridge between the personal anticipations traditionally emphasized by the constructivists and the

[1] A version of this chapter was originally presented as part of a symposium entitled Constructivism versus Constructionism—Bridging the Gap, which was conducted at the 110th American Psychological Association Convention, Chicago, IL, August 2002.

social dialogic processes traditionally emphasized by the social constructionists.

Within personal construct psychology, "personal" is not synonymous with "individual" (Larry Leitner, 2002, oral communication). An emphasis on personal meaning processes should not be misconstrued as locating meaning within self-contained individuals. In Kelly's (1955/1991a, 1955/1991b) descriptions, personal meanings are inextricably multiplicitous and constituted within social relating, which might itself be described as a meaning process. Walker (1996) relates that Kelly considered the title "role theory" for his work, illustrating that Kelly's personal meanings were inextricably entwined within social processes. While we might be described as co-constructing the shared meanings of relationship, our relationships, in turn, come to constitute our evolving self-related constructions. These co-constructed roles can be better described as "communities of selves that [we] jostlingly live through" (Mair, 1989a, p. 74), rather than as single, essential, separate structures within individuals. Within our varying relationships, we, together with our partners in conversation, call forth our possible selves.

Efforts to make meaning of abusive experiences, exemplify that meaning making is not an abstract intellectual venture located in the head of a self-contained individual. Personal meaning making is an embodied process embedded within larger ecologies of meanings that both afford and constrain the personal meaning processes. George Kelly (1955/1991a, 1955/1991b) described a continuity of meaning processes from physiological to those more traditionally denoted as emotional, behavioral, cognitive, or interpersonal. Indeed our most core meaning processes may be largely tacit, difficult to verbalize, physiological and behavioral anticipations, including our patterns of relating to others. Similarly, from a family systems perspective, Reiss (1981) described the family construct system as maintained by behavioral rituals or "ceremonials" within the family. Thus, a focus on meaning-making processes is not necessarily cognitive or individualistic, but rather refers to the self-organizing processes of living systems, including personal, familial, and larger cultural processes (c.f., Harter, 1988; Mahoney, 1991, 2000; Prigogine & Stengers, 1984).

Rather than offering incompatible descriptions of our meaning making, constructivists and constructionists approach these processes from different positions of observation. Each position offers its own perspective that may elaborate, rather than invalidate, the other's view. Subsequent sections of this chapter will further elaborate the potentially creative tension between personal and social positions. The first section introduces efforts to understand childhood abuse as illustrative of the social embeddedness of personal constructions. The second section describes constructions of personal meanings within abusive family systems, further illustrating interdependent ecologies of relational meanings. The third section locates personal and family meanings within larger social systems, describing cultural contexts that are intrinsic to abusive experience. These cultural contexts include professional systems that may constrain efforts to transcend oppressive relationships and related personal meanings. The final section focuses on use of the narrative metaphor in therapeutic relationships with abuse survivors. Approaching meanings from a narrative position offers possibilities to disrupt oppressive stories or dialogues, transcending "ready-made" explanations of "what happened" and "what yet might be."

PERSONAL AND SOCIAL CONSTRUCTIONS OF ABUSE

My journey as a personal construct psychologist has unfolded concurrently with my work with abuse survivors. Because I began doing constructivist psychology as I was studying sexual abuse and related family relationships, I have always been positioned, or thrown, in that creative space between personal meanings and the communities of meaning within which they evolve. Later exposure to social constructionist and narrative psychologies seemed to add additional depths to my understanding of meaning making, rather than requiring a disjunctive leap from an earlier emphasis on personal processes.

I began to work in the area of child abuse by the serendipity of a research assistantship my first year of graduate school (not the assignment that I had requested). My engagement in this research, and my continued interest in working with abuse survivors, has grown from the lived experiences of personal meanings that these clinical and research relationships have afforded. As survivors share their struggle to make meaning of abusive experience, we struggle with issues that our society and profession often fail to constructively address. When I have been willing to engage with survivors in their meaning-making ventures, we reach toward the unspeakable. We bring silenced voices into a larger conversation. While my position, as psychologist, in such relationships is to co-create a healing space for the client, in doing so, my own meanings are challenged toward new possibilities. Abuse survivors offer therapists and researchers the challenge to expand the boundaries of our personal, professional, and cultural meanings.

When I began working in this area in the early 1980's, sexual abuse was just beginning to be recognized as a social problem. Even health professionals often disbelieved disclosures of sexual abuse. There was considerable controversy about the prevalence and harmfulness of sexual activities between adults and children. Thus, it seemed important to researchers to document the incidence and abusiveness of sexual activities between adults and children and the potential harmful effects of such experiences for child victims. More recently research has expanded to examine nonsexual physical and emotional abuses of adult power over children, as abuse has been increasingly conceptualized as a form of violence and oppression. Over the past twenty years, research has consistently documented that abuse of children is common; that child victims may experience abuse with distress, horror, shock, and shame, and that related distress may continue throughout the lifespan. Adult survivors of childhood abuse are at increased risk for a wide range of life difficulties, including revictimization, generalized distress, anxiety, depression, dissociation, and difficulties in social relationships (for reviews see Beitchman, Zucker, Hood, DaCosta, Akman, 1991; Beitchman et al, 1992; Briere, 1992; Browne & Finkelhor, 1986; Harter & Neimeyer, 1995; Jumper, 1995; Kendall-Tackett, Williams, & Finkelhor, 1993; Malinosky-Rummell & Hansen, 1993; Thompson & Kaplan, 1996).

Studies of sexual abuse survivors suggest that characteristics of the abuse, including paternal perpetrators, more intrusive abuse, and use of force, are related to more difficulty in long-term functioning (Beitchman et al., 1992; Briere, 1992; Browne & Finkelhor, 1986). However, the considerable variability in adult outcomes appears to be more closely related to meaning processes and to the family environments in which they occur than to objective characteristics of the abusive experiences. Emerging constructions of self and close others appear particularly vulnerable to child abuse and related family environments (Erbes & Harter, 2002; Harter, 2001; Harter & Neimeyer, 1995).

Although constructivist research initially focused on meaning making in survivors of childhood sexual abuse, more recently research has expanded findings to survivors of childhood physical and emotional abuse. Types of abuse frequently co-occur and similar meaning processes appear to occur across types of abusive experi-

118

ences. These similar processes may reflect a common core of emotional abuse, including objectification of the child for the adults' needs and invalidation of the child's own experiencing (Briere, 1992; Harter, 2001; Harter & Taylor, 2000; Harter & Vanecek, 2000).

Our personal meaning systems evolve as we anticipate experiences, most of which are interpersonal. Parents and other early caregivers play a crucial role in a child's construing. They not only differentially validate or invalidate possible constructions of experience, but more importantly validate, or invalidate, the child as an experiencing person, as a legitimate maker of meanings. Early interactions with caregivers provide an important context for our initial distinctions between "me-not me" and elaboration of those distinctions into core constructions of "self-other" (Leitner, Faidley, & Celentana, 2000). The child's evolving constructions of "self" are closely tied to bodily experience and dependence on adult caregivers. Threats to physical well-being and relationships to caregivers offer constructions of self as unworthy and weak. Sexual activities for which the child is developmentally unprepared, invasive sexual abuse, and physical violence may further contribute to constructions of self as fundamentally vulnerable, contaminated, and damaged (Harter, 2001).

While early constructions of self and others continue to evolve, they provide a sense of coherence as a person and an evolving core for our subsequent relating. Thus, we both constitute meanings of self within relationships, and in turn are constrained or contained by those meanings. While we may later reconstrue our experiences, and ourselves, available meanings are limited by alternatives offered within our personal meaning systems and the larger communities of meaning within which we participate.

OPPRESSIVE FAMILY ENVIRONMENTS

Elaboration of self-other constructs may be particularly difficult in abusive families, which invalidate the child as an experiencing person and offer a limited range of dominant, oppressive constructions of relationships. Based on extensive clinical observations, Herman (1981) describes incestuous families as isolated, secretive, and patriarchal, with roles rigidly defined by gender. Mothers are also often absent, abused, and disabled. The oldest daughter may be expected to fulfill the mother's presumed domestic and sexual duties. Large scale studies with college student populations extend these observations to survivors of other childhood sexual, physical, and emotional abuse. Abuse survivors describe their families as rigid, patriarchal, authoritarian, conflictual, and as lacking in emotional closeness, expressiveness, and openness to outside relationships (Alexander & Lupfer, 1987; Harter, Alexander, & Neimeyer, 1988; Harter & Vanecek, 2000).

Similar family environments appear related to vulnerability for abuse outside the family, regardless of whether explicit abuse occurs within the family (Alexander & Lupfer, 1987; Draucker, 1996; Nash, Hulsey, Sexton, Harralson, & Lambert, 1993). Also, even when the abuse occurs outside family relationships, such families may invalidate the child's attempts to make meaning of the abusive experience. Parents may react with disbelief and/or blame to the child's attempts to disclose the abuse. They may minimize any distress experienced by the child, or impose their own distress on the child, privileging adult constructions of the experience and its implications for relationships. Patriarchal organization of family roles may further invalidate the child as one who can make meaning of experience. Expectations that the child has been irrevocably damaged by the abuse may constrain the child's future possibilities for self-construction. The child's and family's struggles to make meaning of the abuse continue to reverberate through subsequent family relationships, continuing to offer abuse-saturated and other oppressive constructions of experience.

Studies of maltreated children and their parents illustrate the connection between relationship behaviors and evolving constructions of emotional experience, of self, and of close others. Parents of maltreated children have more difficulties responding to children's initiation of activities, understanding the child's emotional displays, and offering support or appropriate strategies for expressing emotions. Children, in turn, are less likely to display emotions to parents and are able to describe fewer effective strategies for expressing emotions. On interview, maltreated children demonstrate less emotional understanding and ability to regulate emotions in a culturally sanctioned manner. Their expressions of emotion are perceived as more extreme, bizarre, and atypical. They anticipate less support and more conflict when expressing anger and sadness to parents (Howe, Tepper, & Parke, 1998; Kavanaugh, Youngblade, Reid, & Fagot, 1988; Shipman & Zeman, 2001; Shipman, Zeman, Penza, & Champion, 2000).

Studies with adult survivors suggest continuation of difficulties in expressing emotional aspects of experience. Sexual abuse survivors use fewer constructs with emotional content, particularly those expressing anxiety, in describing themselves and important others on Kelly's Role Construct Repertory Grid (Harter, Erbes, & Hart, in press). They also generally use fewer emotional constructs, particularly those expressing anxiety or fear, in self-characterization sketches. However, those who have experienced the most invasive abuse by family members are an exception, using more constructs expressing anxiety and depression, but also more constructs expressing optimism or energy in their self-characterizations. These apparent contradictions in emotional expression may reflect affectively laden but unstable self-constructions as more severely abused survivors struggle to integrate greater emotional distress (Erbes, 2000).

Abuse survivors may deal with self-threatening emotions through fragmenting tacit, physiological meaning making from more explicit verbalized experience. A recent experimental study recording sexual abuse survivors' heart rate during a self-protective speaking task found a paradoxical discordance between survivors' physiological response to the anxiety-evoking task and their awareness of anxiety. Abused participants with the greatest increase in heart rate, reported the least awareness of somatic anxiety (Reynolds & Harter, 2002).

Emotional invalidation may be a core feature of abusive experiences. Adults, including the perpetrator and non-offending parents, have the power to label the experience. They may impose their own descriptions on the child's response, including denying, minimizing, or blaming the child for the abuse. The child's expressions of distress, resistance, or other attempts to make meaning of the experience may be ignored, actively rejected, or punished. The child may be expected to care for the emotions of adults, rather than being allowed to express his or her own needs. Children are often pressured to keep silent about abuse, further reducing opportunities to make verbal meaning of their experience. Emotional experiences that are not verbalized may be tacitly expressed through a range of psychological and physical symptoms, which may be interpreted as individual pathology, rather than as suppressed acts of meaning (Erbes & Harter, 2002; Harter, 2001).

Invalidation of the child's emotional experiencing makes it difficult for the child to negotiate a coherent, positive, efficacious construction of self and others. Narratives of maltreated children suggest less coherent constructions of self and parents, more negative constructions of self and others, and the juxtaposition of a negative and grandiose self (Fischer et al., 1997; MacFie, Cicchetti, & Toth, 2001; Shields, Ryan, & Cicchetti, 2001; Toth, Cicchetti, MacFie, Maughan, & Van Meenen, 2000). While the misuse of adults' power inherent in abuse renders experience uncontrollable and unpredictable, the child often receives contradictory messages that he or she is to blame for the abuse. This may contribute to the paradoxical constructions of the self as helpless and vulnerable and, at the same time, as responsible for powerful others.

Similar themes emerge in studies of adult abuse survivors, using a variety of methodologies. Abuse survivors are more likely to construe themselves and close others negatively. They may construe themselves as different from close others, as stigmatized, and as to blame for the abuse (Coffey, Leitenberg, Henning, Turner, & Bennett, 1996; Harter, et al., 1988; Harter, 2000; Harter & Vanecek, 2000; Hazzard, 1993; McMillen & Zuravin, 1997; Wyatt & Newcomb, 1990). They may construe their self and their body as fundamentally damaged (Nash et al., 1993). There may be a fragmentation in self constructions, including discontinuity between constructions of past, present, and future selves (Claussen, Field, Atkinson, & Spiegel, 1998). Life stories of abuse survivors tend to contain more emphasis on the past and to de-emphasize the central role of the self (Klein & Janoff-Bulman, 1996). Stories written in response to TAT cards also contain themes of powerlessness and betrayal (Liem, O'Toole, & James, 1996).

Similar to those of child victims, meaning processes of adult survivors reflect contradictory elements of experience, echoing the dilemmas offered victims by the larger culture. Adult survivors are simultaneously held responsible (blamed for their experiences, their responses to those experiences, and any continuing symptoms) and denied legitimacy as authors of their life stories. They are both marginalized by patriarchal myths of childhood, family, gender, and sexuality, and also feared as potential challengers to the bases of these assumptions.

PERSONAL MEANING MAKING WITHIN CULTURAL AND PROFESSIONAL CONTEXTS

Constructions of power and privilege within the larger culture enforce patriarchal and other authoritarian assumptions within the family of origin. This may further objectify the child victim or adult survivor, invalidate his or her attempts to make meaning of the abusive experience, and impede attempts to construct a coherent life story that acknowledges, but is not saturated by the abuse. Even after the survivor begins to resist oppressive meanings at an explicit level, it may be more difficult to resist established implicit organizations of experience, such as behavioral interactions that continue to place the survivor in an inferior and silenced position.

The helping professions are not immune to the assumptions of their larger culture. Indeed, our relative position of privilege and power within the culture may blind us to our participation in performing and maintaining oppressive dialogues. Even when well-intended, professional actions may replicate the abuse of power characteristic of child abuse and maintain the marginalization of abuse survivors. Diagnostic practices characterize survivors based on external observation of symptoms, with little reference to their meaning within the context of the person's life. This may further limit the survivor's authorship of his or her experience. Therapists' evaluations of the client's memories, whether denying the reality of abuse remembered by the client or prescribing reality to memories about which the client remains uncertain, may further invalidate the client's own meaning process. Prescriptive therapy approaches deny the client's authorship of his or her life and ignore personal efforts after meaning, variations between abusive experiences, and creative acts of resistance (Erbes & Harter, 2002; Harter, 2001; Pope & Brown, 1996).

Much more of our research literature is devoted to documenting the pathologies of abuse survivors than to identifying the strengths that have allowed them to survive, or sometimes even to flourish. Very little attention is directed to deconstructing professional practices that may reenact oppressive dialogues and to identifying liberating alternatives. While much of the initial impetus in documenting the long-term effects of abuse was to witness against abuse of power and to advocate for the rights of children and women, the resulting research documenting the potential harmful effects of abuse may be appropriated to stereotype and to further marginalize those it sought to empower. For instance, group tendencies toward continued distress and other life difficulties might be over generalized to pathologize individual survivors who are successfully resisting the oppressive effects of abuse. Other aspects of the person's life may be ignored, enforcing an abuse-saturated life narrative. Persons reporting a history of abuse may be further recruited into a limiting, pre-emptive "victim," or even "survivor," identity.

Examples of limiting discourses regarding abuse survivors can be drawn from training of students, advice to clients, and relationships to colleagues. We may assume an unwarranted expert stance in evaluating the effects of abusive experiences, in contrast to survivors who are seen as less capable in making meaning of their personal experience. In one training program, a supervisor repeatedly warned student therapists working with abuse survivors that persons who had been abused could not be effective therapists or researchers, particularly working in the areas of abuse and family relationships, because their own perceptions would inevitably be distorted. This colleague never inquired about her supervisees' abuse histories, perhaps assuming that by selecting capable students, she was eliminating any abuse survivors. Any survivors training with her would be unable to contradict her assumptions, without endangering their own professional future. Such a "don't ask, don't tell" policy created a contradictory and oppressive climate. Student therapists were being trained to work empathetically with survivor clients, to break silence about the client's abuse, but survivor therapists were pathologized and silenced. I could relate other stories, from other places (e.g., trainees warned not to reveal their abuse histories to supervisors, a gifted psychology student prescriptively redirected to some other goal when her physician became aware of her abuse history), but little systematic attention to such practices in the mainstream professional literature.

Assumptions that abuse survivors will not be competent health professionals are not grounded in empirical data. Studies suggest that mental health providers are even more likely to have a history of abuse and trauma than the general population (Elliott & Guy, 1993; Pope & Feldman-Summers, 1992). However, there is no evidence that abuse survivors are less capable as therapists or researchers than those with no abuse histories. The few attempts to identify differences in practice with abuse survivors based on therapist's history of abuse have been largely unsuccessful (Polousny & Follette, 1996; Wind, 1999). Nevertheless, psychologist survivors may find their competence and motivations challenged when they break silence and share their personal stories (Freyd, 1996). When we limit the roles to which survivors might aspire in the health professions, detaching ourselves as expert, objective observers, we also limit our profession and ourselves maintaining our own participation in oppressive dialogues.

The politics of science and of psychological practice become particularly apparent in the discourses about sexual abuse, within the professional literature and in more public arenas. As professional and popular psychological literature has begun to address experiences of abuse, there has been a corresponding backlash. Psychologists are represented on both sides of struggles between those seeking to better meet the needs of children and abuse survivors and those advocating for family and parental rights, including an advocacy organization founded by accused parents. This organization has reportedly disseminated inaccurate information and supported aggressive harassment of disclosing survivors, therapists, researchers, and their associates, while at the same time criticizing the motivations and science of abuse therapists and researchers. Tactics such as suing therapists working with abuse survivors, picketing therapists offices, photographing client license plates, and violating the privacy of clients have made it more difficult for abuse survivors to seek appropriate treatment and intimidated therapists working with them. The authority of science has been invoked to legitimate these political efforts to silence disclosures of abuse (Brown, 1998; Calof, 1998; Cheit, 1998; Freyd, 1996, 1998; Hoult, 1998; Pope & Brown, 1996; Salter, 1998). An implicit assumption behind these activities by and on the behalf of accused parents is that parents have a right to control the lives of their adult offspring, to dictate a relationship to those offspring, and to define the reality of the adult child's childhood experience.

NARRATIVES OF POSSIBILITY

A constructive therapy relationship may provide an important context for a qualitatively different relational dialogue, providing a witness to previously unvoiced meanings, legitimating the client as an experiencing person, as a meaning maker, as an author of future possibilities. Both personal construct and social constructionist approaches privilege the client as the expert in his or her own life. Kelly (1955/1991a, 1955/1991b) described this as a "credulous" approach and social constructionists have described it as a "not-knowing" stance (Anderson, 1997).

Drawing from social constructionist theories, recent narrative approaches explicitly challenge disempowering "abuse-dominated" life stories, identify creative resistance, and privilege more self-validating stories. Validating audiences are recruited to support the client's emerging story (Adams-Westcott & Dobbins, 1997;

125

Harker, 1997). Personal constructivists have also been increasingly attracted to narrative approaches to foster self-re-creation in the aftermath of trauma (e.g., Neimeyer, 2000; Sewell & Williams, 2002). The client may be assisted in constructing a coherent narrative of the abuse and locating that narrative within a life story that provides a sense of authorship and future possibilities. As in constructionist approaches, the therapist and client identify opportunities to enact the preferred story outside the therapy room. Similar to constructionist approaches, constructivist narrative strategies include acknowledgement of multiple alternative meanings, instead of viewing therapy as correction of a singular narrative of events.

Rather than offering a prescriptive set of techniques, narrative therapy, consonant with constructivist and constructionist approaches, is best characterized by its attitude towards the client's and therapist's struggle for meaning. Therapist and client alike live in a storied world, inhabited by the stories of their families, communities, cultures, and professions. These stories permeate the personal meanings that locate our ongoing experience within a meaningful world. Harker (1997) describes narrative therapy with male sexual abuse survivors as a process of deconstruction. "Deconstruction is the process of taking apart or looking beyond the taken-for-granted meanings and commonsense explanations related in male survivors' stories, to locate their origins in the social context" (p. 195). This includes identifying dominating, oppressive stories that contribute to and maintain abusive experiences, such as cultural narratives of masculinity. Similar ideas might also be applied to female survivors and to cultural narratives of femininity. Harker also describes therapeutic deconstruction as actively seeking unique moments that offer alternative stories. Paradoxically, identifying the not-so-silent and often oppressive co-authors of abusive life stories may also free the survivor to experience and enact his or her own authorship of experience.

Harker (1997) notes that isolation of men from each other's lived experience maintains the oppressive power of prescribed masculine narratives. Conversely, sharing narratives of personal experience can powerfully challenge seemingly impermeable constructions. This was most apparent to me in working with two men on an inpatient unit. I initially was very concerned that these men would not be able to work together in the therapy group to which they had been assigned. Both were admitted with severe, suicidal depression and angry outbursts. The younger man, in his late twenties, struggled with self-hatred and anger following his family's rejection of him in response to his disclosure that he was homosexual. In individual therapy he requested to use the group therapy to "come out" as a homosexual man more fully and publicly than he had in previous social contexts. The older man, in his mid-fifties, was struggling to adjust to increasing physical problems that prevented him from continuing to work as a longshoreman. In individual therapy, he disclosed his hatred of homosexuals and acknowledged a past history of joining group assaults on gay men. Deconstruction of meanings of masculinity and homosexuality motivating these assaults, resulted in his disclosure that he was violently raped by "two homosexual men" when he was ten years old.

For both clients, individual therapy provided a context to construct and deconstruct stories that they might share in the group and their anticipations of the group response. It also provided opportunities to construct roles they might play in the "safe context" for sharing personal experience, which the therapy group worked to construct. Disclosing personal aspects of their experience in the group, both men were able to identify experiences of oppression that connected their seemingly incompatible experiences. Both felt painfully unable to live the cultural expectations for men: the younger man because of his homosexuality and estrangement from his family, the older because of his physical disability and history of rape. As he performed his homosexual identity in the group and in his developing friendship to the older man on the unit, the younger man became less concerned with convincing his family to accept his sexual orientation and more focused on exploring his own preferences for several impending life choices. The older man also became more comfortable in his own masculinity as he reconstrued his abuse experience as a crime of violence and abuse of power, rather than as a sexual perversion. This allowed him to differentiate men who have consensual sex with other men from men who violate children. The friendship with a gay man allowed him to enact a masculine identity that did not depend upon physical strength and participation in violence. For each, openness to the other's experience seemed to facilitate a new self-acceptance.

Participation of female survivors of childhood and adult abuse in the group further facilitated deconstructions of power, violence, and cultural prescriptions for masculinity and femininity. As in other successful mixed groups, members with no explicit history of childhood abuse or adult assault were also able to acknowledge the

127

relevance of helplessness, rejection, and oppression in their own life experiences, if only in living with the threat of victimization.

Although these descriptions of narrative themes may seem abstract, they emerge from deeply personal sharing of lived experience, not from more distanced, intellectual discussion. Such relating of personal stories offers unique opportunities to transcend the positions that often separate people and polarize relationships.

Mair (1988) suggested extending Kelly's (1955/1991a) original metaphor of personal science to a metaphor of storytelling. The storytelling metaphor conveys the complexity of our experience as it unfolds across time within communities of meaning. It also conveys our effort to express non-explicit behavioral and affective dimensions of experience through language or other shared meaning systems. It conveys our struggle to transcend the myths of our families, cultural, and political systems, to speak the unspeakable, to conjure new roles and new possibilities (Harter, 1995).

Discussing personal construct psychology as an essentially storytelling discipline, Mair (1988, 1989ab) argues that the stories of our families and culture *tell* us, as much as we *tell* them. In speaking of psychological practice, he cautions

> Almost everything speaks of the story that lives us. Almost nothing speaks of freedom. Hints of new degrees of freedom are bought only at a price. The speaker of a new word, a different story, has to leave the warmth of the tribal fires to live as an outsider, beyond the pale, isolated, often invalidated. There is a terrible passion that is involved in coming to know what is beyond the story of our tribe. There is waiting and the necessity of being given over to feeling, a willingness to speak into being what has not yet been said. It is a matter of returning again and again to a place of beginning, to be a learner and not an expert. (1988, p. 135)

The quote from Mair could well describe our struggle to wrest personal meaning out of dominant social assumptions, discourses, and practices. More specifically, it could also describe constructivist practice with abuse survivors. Both therapist and client, or researcher and participant, come to such encounters as learners. Both struggle to co-construct roles that transcend those enacted in the survivor's family of origin. In doing so, they struggle with myths within the larger society, reflected in roles within the family, roles often also unwittingly enacted in helping relationships.

Although increasingly aware of the co-authorship of culture, family, and important others in my own and others' lives, I have remained a "personal construct psychologist." Not because I disregard the communities of meaning that both allow and contain our personal meaning efforts, but because I am still listening for those sparkling exceptions, for those moments when we are able to transcend the given. To me those moments are both deeply connected and deeply personal.

REFERENCES

Adams-Westcott, J., & Dobbins, C. (1997). Listening with your "heart ears" and other ways young people can escape the effects of sexual abuse. In C. Smith & D. Nylund (Eds.), *Narrative therapies with children and adolescents* (pp. 195-220). New York: Guilford.

Alexander, P. C., & Lupfer, S. L. (1987). Family characteristics and long-term consequences associated with sexual abuse. *Archives of Sexual Behavior, 16,* 235-245.

Anderson, H. (1997). *Conversation, language, and possibilities: A postmodern approach to therapy.* New York: Basic Books.

Beitchman, J. H., Zucker, K. J., Hood, J. E., DaCosta, G. A., & Akman, D. (1991). A review of the short-term effects of child sexual abuse. *Child Abuse and Neglect, 15,* 537-556.

Beitchman, J. H., Zucker, K. J., Hood, J. E., DaCosta, B. A., Akman, D., & Cassavia, E. (1992). A review of the long-term effects of child sexual abuse. *Child Abuse and Neglect, 16,* 101-118.

Briere, J. (1992). *Child abuse trauma: Theory and treatment of the lasting effects.* Newberry Park, CA: Sage.

Brown, L. S. (1998). The prices of resisting silence: Comments on Calof, Cheit, Freyd, Hoult, and Salter. *Ethics and Behavior, 8,* 198-193.

Browne, A., & Finkelhor, D. (1986). Impact of child sexual abuse: A review of the research. *Psychological Bulletin, 99,* 66-77.

Calof, D. L. (1998). Notes from a practice under siege: Harassment, defamation, and intimidation in the name of science. *Ethics and Behavior, 8,* 101-187.

Cheit, R. E. (1998). Consider this, skeptics of recovered memory. *Ethics and Behavior, 8,* 141-160.

Claussen, C., Field, N. P., Atkinson, A., & Spiegel, D. (1998). Representations of self in women sexually abused in childhood. *Child Abuse and Neglect, 22,* 997-1004.

Coffey, P., Leitenberg, H., Henning, K., Turner, T., & Bennett, R. T. (1996). Mediators of the long-term impact of child sexual abuse: Perceived stigma, betrayal, powerlessness, and self-blame. *Child Abuse and Neglect, 20,* 447-455.

Draucker, C. B. (1996). Family-of-origin variables and adult female survivors of childhood sexual abuse: A review of the research. *Journal of Child Sexual Abuse, 5,* 35-63.

Elliott, D. M., & Guy, J. D. (1993). Mental health professionals versus non-mental-health professionals: Childhood trauma and adult functioning. *Professional Psychology: Research and Practice, 24,* 83-90.

Erbes, C. R. (2000). *Child sexual abuse and the self: Affect and differentiation* (Doctoral dissertation, Texas Tech University, 2000). Dissertation Abstracts International, 61 (6-B), 3274.

Erbes, C. R., & Harter, S. L. (2002). Constructions of abuse: Understanding the effects of child sexual abuse. In J. D. Raskin & S. K. Bridges (Eds.), *Studies in meaning: Exploring constructivist psychology* (pp. 27-48). New York: Pace University Press.

Fischer, K. W., Ayoub, C., Singh, I., Noam, G., Maraganore, H., & Raya, P. (1997). Psychopathology as adaptive development along distinctive pathways. *Development and Psychopathology, 9,* 749-779.

Freyd, J. J. (1996). *Betrayal trauma: The logic of forgetting childhood abuse.* Cambridge, MA: Harvard University Press.

Freyd, J. J. (1998). Science in the memory debate. *Ethics and Behavior, 8,* 101-113.

Harker, T. (1997). Therapy with male sexual abuse survivors: Contesting oppressive life stories. In G. Monk, J. Winslade, K. Cricket, & D. Epston (Eds.), *Narrative therapy in practice: The archaeology of hope* (pp. 193-214). San Francisco: Jossey-Bass.

Harter, S. L. (1988). Psychotherapy as a reconstructive process: Implications of integrative theories for outcome research. *International Journal of Personal Construct Psychology, 1,* 349-367.

Harter, S. L. (1995). Construing on the edge: Clinical mythology in working with borderline processes. In R. A. Neimeyer & M. J. Mahoney (Eds.), *Constructivism in psychotherapy* (pp. 371-383). Washington, DC: American Psychological Association.

Harter, S. L. (2000). Quantitative measures of construing in child abuse survivors. *Journal of Constructivist Psychology, 13,* 103-116.

Harter, S. L. (2001). Constructivist psychology of child abuse and implications for psychotherapy. *Humanistic Psychologist, 29,* 40-69.

Harter, S. L., Alexander, P. C., & Neimeyer, R. A. (1988). Long-term effects of incestuous child abuse in college women: Social adjustment, social cognition, and family characteristics. *Journal of Consulting and Clinical Psychology, 56,* 5-8.

Harter, S. L., Erbes, C. R., & Hart, C. C. (in press). Content analysis of the personal constructs of female sexual abuse survivors elicited through Repertory Grid technique. *Journal of Constructivist Psychology*.

Harter, S. L., & Neimeyer, R. A. (1995). Long term effects of child sexual abuse: Toward a constructivist theory of trauma and its treatment. In R. A. Neimeyer & G. J. Neimeyer (Eds.), *Advances in personal construct psychology* (Vol. 3, pp. 229-269). Greenwich, CT: JAI.

Harter, S. L., & Taylor, T. L. (2000). Parental alcoholism, child abuse, and adult adjustment. *Journal of Substance Abuse, 11*, 31-44.

Harter, S. L., & Vanecek, J. (2000). Cognitive assumptions and long-term distress in survivors of childhood abuse, parental alcoholism, and dysfunctional family environments. *Cognitive Therapy and Research, 24*, 445-472.

Hazzard, A. (1993). Trauma-related beliefs as mediators of sexual abuse impact in adult women survivors: A pilot study. *Journal of Child Sexual Abuse, 2*, 55-69.

Herman, J. L. (1981). *Father-daughter incest*. Cambridge, MA: Harvard University Press.

Hoult, J. (1998). Silencing the victim: The politics of discrediting child abuse survivors. *Ethics and Behavior, 8*, 125-140.

Howe, T. R., Tepper, F. L., & Parke, R. D. (1998). The emotional understanding and peer relations of abused children in residential treatment. *Residential Treatment for Children and Youth, 15*, 69-82.

Jumper, S. A. (1995) A meta-analysis of the relationship of child sexual abuse to adult psychological adjustment. *Child Abuse and Neglect, 19*, 715-728.

Kavanaugh, K. A., Youngblade, L., Reid, J. B., & Fagot, B. I. (1988). Interactions between children and abusive versus control parents. *Journal of Clinical Child Psychology, 17*, 137-142.

Kelly, G. A. (1969). Epilogue: Don Juan. In B. Maher (Ed.), *Clinical psychology and personality: The selected papers of George Kelly* (pp. 333-351). New York: John Wiley.

Kelly, G. A. (1991a). *The psychology of personal constructs: Vol. 1. A theory of personality*. London: Routledge. (Original work published 1955)

Kelly, G. A. (1991b). *The psychology of personal constructs: Vol. 2. Clinical diagnosis and psychotherapy*. London: Routledge. (Original work published 1955)

Kendall-Tackett, K. A., Williams, L. M., & Finkelhor, D. (1993). Impact of sexual abuse on children: A review and synthesis of recent empirical studies. *Psychological Bulletin, 113,* 164-180.

Klein, K., & Janoff-Bulman, J. (1996). Trauma history and personal narratives: Some clues to coping among survivors of child abuse. *Child Abuse and Neglect, 20,* 45-54.

Leitner, L. M., Faidley, A. J., & Celentana, M. A. (2000). Diagnosing human meaning making: An experiential constructivist approach. In R. A. Neimeyer & J. D. Raskin (Eds.), *Constructions of disorder: Meaning-making frameworks for psychotherapy* (pp. 175-203). Washington, DC: American Psychological Association.

Liem, J. H., O'Toole, J. G., & James, J. B. (1996). Themes of power and betrayal in sexual abuse survivors' characterizations of inter personal relationships. *Journal of Traumatic Stress, 9,* 745-761.

MacFie, J., Cicchetti, D., & Toth, S. L. (2001). The development of dissociation in maltreated preschool-aged children. *Development and Psychopathology, 13,* 233-254.

McMillen, C., & Zuravin, S. (1997). Attributions of blame and responsibility for child sexual abuse and adult adjustment. *Journal of Interpersonal Violence, 12,* 30-48.

Mahoney, M. J. (1991). *Human change processes: The scientific foundations of psychotherapy.* New York: Basic Books.

Mahoney, M. J. (2000). Core ordering and disordering processes: A constructive view of psychological development. In R. A. Neimeyer & J. D. Raskin (Eds.), *Constructions of disorder: Meaning-making frameworks for psychotherapy* (pp. 43-62). Washington, DC: American Psychological Association.

Mair, M. (1988). Psychology as storytelling. *International Journal of Personal Construct Psychology, 1,* 125-137.

Mair, M. (1989a). *Between psychology and psychotherapy: A poetics of experience.* New York: Routledge.

Mair, M. (1989b). Kelly, Bannister, and a story-telling psychology. *International Journal of Personal Construct Psychology, 2,* 1-14.

Malinosky-Rummell, R., & Hansen, K. J. (1993). Long-term consequences of childhood physical abuse. *Psychological Bulletin, 114,* 68-79.

Nash, M. R., Hulsey, T. L., Sexton, M. C., Harralson, T. L., & Lambert, W. (1993). Long-term sequelae of childhood sexual abuse: Perceived family environment, psychopathology, and dissociation. *Journal of Consulting and Clinical Psychology, 61,* 276-283.

133

Neimeyer, R. A. (2000). Narrative disruptions in the constructions of the self. In R. A. Neimeyer & J. D. Raskin (Eds.), *Constructions of disorder: Meaning-making frameworks for psychotherapy* (pp. 207-242). Washington, DC: American Psychological Association.

Polousny, M. A., & Follette, V. M. (1996). Remembering childhood sexual abuse; A national survey of psychologists' clinical practices, beliefs, and personal experiences. *Professional Psychology: Research and Practice, 27,* 41-52.

Pope, K. S., & Brown, L. S. (1996). *Recovered memories of abuse: Assessment, therapy, forensics.* Washington, DC: American Psychological Association.

Pope, K. S., & Feldman-Summers, S. (1992). National survey of psychologists' sexual and physical abuse history and their evaluation of training and competence in these areas. *Professional Psychology: Research and Practice, 23,* 353-361.

Prigogine, I., & Stengers, I. (1984). *Order out of chaos: Man's new dialogue with nature.* New York: Bantam.

Reiss, D. (1981). *The family's construction of reality.* Cambridge, MA: Harvard University Press.

Reynolds, L. L., & Harter, S. L. (August, 2002). Triple response anxiety and dissociation in child sexual abuse survivors. Paper presented at the 110th Annual Convention of the American Psychological Association, Chicago, IL.

Salter, A. C. (1998). Confessions of a whistle-blower: Lessons learned. *Ethics and Behavior, 8,* 115-124.

Sewell, K. W., & Williams, A. M. (2002). Broken narratives: Trauma, metaconstructive gaps and the audience of psychotherapy. *Journal of Constructivist Psychology, 15,* 205-218.

Shields, A., Ryan, R. M., & Cicchetti, D. (2001). Narrative representations of caregivers and emotional dysregulation as predictors of maltreated children's rejection by peers. *Developmental Psychology, 37,* 321-337.

Shipman, K. L., & Zeman, J. (2001). Socialization of children's emotion regulation in mother-child dyads: A developmental psychopathology perspective. *Development and Psychopathology, 13,* 317-336.

Shipman, K., Zeman, J., Penza, S., & Champion, K. (2000). Emotion management skills in sexually maltreated and nonmaltreated girls: A developmental psychopathology perspective. *Development and Psychopathology, 12,* 47-62.

Thompson, A. E., & Kaplan, C. A. (1996). Childhood emotional abuse. British Journal of Psychiatry, 168, 143-148.

Toth, L., Cicchetti, D., MacFie, J., Maughan, A., & van Meenen, K. (2000). Narrative representations of caregivers and self in maltreated pre-schoolers. Attachment and Human Development, 2, 271-305.

Walker, B. M. (1996). A psychology for adventurers: An introduction to personal construct psychology from a social perspective. In D. Kalekin-Fishman & B. M. Walker (Eds.), The construction of group realities: Culture, society, and personal construct theory (pp. 7-26). Malabar, FL: Krieger.

Wind, P. J. (1999). Use of memory techniques with survivors of child sexual abuse: A national survey of psychotherapists (Doctoral dissertation, Texas Tech University, 1999). Dissertation Abstracts International, 60 (8-B), 4260.

Wyatt, G. E., & Newcomb, M. (1990). Internal and external mediators of women's sexual abuse in childhood. Journal of Consulting and Clinical Psychology, 58, 758-767.

CHAPTER 7

The Search for Emotional Meaning and Self-Coherence in the Face of Traumatic Loss in Childhood: A Narrative Process Perspective[1]

Lynne Angus and Beverley Bouffard

This chapter presents findings from the intensive case analysis of one good outcome, brief process-experiential therapy dyad drawn from the York "Unfinished Business" study, Toronto, Canada. The client, named Alex for the purpose of this chapter, brings to life the previously untold story of the traumatic loss of his mother by suicide in his childhood, and together with his therapist, re-authors a new account of the broken story that has plagued him for more than twenty years. The chapter begins by outlining a comprehensive narrative process model of therapeutic change that draws on the work of Jerome Bruner (1986) and is coherent with the fundamental assumptions of experiential approaches generally, and Process-experiential psychotherapy in particular (Greenberg 2002, Greenberg, Rice, & Elliott 1993). In order to illuminate three stages of narrative change entailed in the successful resolution of trauma-based "Unfinished Business," key episodes are drawn from the transcribed therapy sessions and analyzed for narrative process mode shifts. The chapter concludes with clinical implications for working with narrative in the context of experiential psychotherapy for "Unfinished Business."

[1] A version of this paper was presented at the Tenth Biennial Conference of the North American Personal Construct Network, Vancouver, BC, July 2002. Segments have previously appeared in the Spanish journal *Revista Psicoterapia*. See Angus, L. & Bouffard- Bowes, B. (2002) "No lo entiendo": La busqueda de sentido emocional y coherencia personalante una perdida traumatica durante la infancia. *Revista Psicoterapia*. Vol. XII, 49, 25-46. The research analyses reported in this chapter were generously funded by the Canadian Social Sciences and Humanities Research Council, Standard Grant Programme.

OVERVIEW

For experiential therapists, "Unfinished Business" represents that subset of client concerns that develop as a result of conflictual and/or traumatic interactions with significant others. A defining characteristic of trauma-based "Unfinished Business" is the feeling of being trapped in an emotionally exhausting, un-resolvable dilemma. On the one hand, there is an urgent desire to rid the self completely of the traumatic memory and to not allow oneself to be vulnerable to the painful emotions that are connected to the experience. On the other hand, an array of ordinary everyday experiences inexplicably cue memories of the trauma and/or unbidden distressing emotions of fear, rage, sadness and anger are evoked in the context of current relationships.

Additionally, there is often a nagging awareness that in order to achieve closure, the circumstances of the traumatic situation must be re-engaged in such a way that an understandable, emotionally coherent and livable account of both the event, and its aftermath, can be constructed and integrated into the sense of self and life-story. It is this quest for coherence and understanding that propels trauma survivors to tell and re-tell their stories, over and over again, to anyone who will listen. The emergence of a coherent trauma narrative enables the trauma survivor to reflexively "look back upon" the trauma experience and from this new vantage point, begin to construct a more comprehensive and personally coherent understanding of what happened and what it means, in terms of views of self and others. And finally, the telling of trauma tales also elicits the support and concern of others and reinstates a sense of personal safety and connection with caring others.

Conversely, when there is no community of support, or the trauma stories are forbidden to be re-told—as is sometimes the situation in cases of sexual assault and parental suicide in childhood—the trauma experiences remain "raw," unintegrated, and are disruptively active in the person's ongoing life. From a narrative perspective, trauma-related "Unfinished Business" represents the definitive "broken story" or narrative incoherence in which the client's thoughts and feelings about the traumatic event have remained fragmented, disconnected and "not understood." It is in this manner that traumatic memories of loss resist assimilation to pre-existing views of self and others in the world. Not surprisingly, childhood experiences of early separation, abandonment, trauma, abuse and loss are often associated with "Unfinished Business" in later life and unresolved grief (Greenberg & Foerster, 1996).

THE NARRATIVE PROCESS MODEL AND TRAUMATIC LOSS IN CHILDHOOD

The Narrative Process Model (Angus, Levitt, & Hardtke 1999) is predicated on the key assumption that we negotiate our senses of self through our contact and experiences with others. In this model, personal identity is understood as being comprised of emotionally significant, autobiographical memory narratives, which represent core beliefs about self and others. In turn, the salient emotional tone of the autobiographical memory narrative—anger, sadness, joy, or fear—acts as an associative connection that links one memory with another. Accordingly, implicit emotion schemes, as well as the memories they contain, become the lens through which we classify, story, and make meaning of our new interpersonal experiences with others in the world.

While personally significant memories are marked by the expression and evocation of emotions, the personal significance of emotions are "understood" when organized within a narrative framework that identifies what is felt, about whom, in relation to what personal need, wish, intention, purpose, or value. In order to generate a coherent memory narrative of a lived experience, there must be a match between the emotions felt and the intentions attributed to actions undertaken in a situation. In the case of trauma-related memories, the overpowering, and at times contradictory emotions experienced in relation to the devastating events resist assimilation to pre-existing emotion schemes and story structures.

For instance, when a child suffers the suicidal death of a parent, the question of who is responsible for the horrific loss is of paramount importance. The motivations and actions of self and others are called into question. Basic attachment needs for safe and trustworthy care are shattered and a sense of deep betrayal, as well as profound grief and loss, may persist for years after the loss of the significant other. Emotional memories of the trauma scene are disjunctive with pre-existing attachment-related emotion schemes and exert a disorganizing influence on the sense of self, pre and post trauma. It is as if a sudden disconnect occurs between the child who existed prior to the suicide and the person who emerges from the devastating loss and has to find a way to go on living.

Accordingly, in the context of working with clients experiencing "Unfinished Business" in response to sudden traumatic loss, it is not only the trauma memory but also the lifelong emotional impact of that loss which must be acknowledged, storied, and understood. Long standing feelings of resentment, bitterness, anger and shame may permeate the stories told about the deceased parent and reflect the deep sense of betrayal felt by the survivor self.

From a narrative process model (Angus, Levitt, & Hardtke, 1999) perspective, accessing and articulating the client's world of emotions, beliefs, expectations, needs, and goals—what Jerome Bruner (1986, 1990, 2002) has termed the landscape of consciousness—is critical for the resolution of trauma-based "Unfinished Business". The reflexive de-centering from, and then re-engagement with, the traumatic experience from different relational vantage points facilitates the articulation of new understandings about the self in relation to others. It is the reflexive processing of emotions, beliefs, hopes, needs, motives, intentions and goals—and their inclusion in the events of the trauma narrative—which enables the experience to be fully understood and accepted as part of the lifestory. In essence, it is the integration of the landscape of action (a description of the sequential, linear unfolding of an event which answers the question of what happened) with the landscape of consciousness (the internal responses of self and others which addresses the question of what was felt and what does it mean) that enables the construction of a coherent and meaning-filled narrative account of our interpersonal experiences with others in the world.

In order to facilitate a coherent account of the traumatic events surrounding the loss of a parent, it is essential that clients elaborate and differentiate emotional meanings and personal understandings (the landscape of consciousness) in the context of a detailed narrative account of the traumatic events and their impact on the client's life (the landscape of action). Both client and therapist achieve this goal by collaboratively engaging in three distinct modes of inquiry: (1) *External Narrative Mode*, which entails the description and elaboration of the traumatic autobiographical memories in which the question of what happened is addressed; (2) *Internal Narrative Mode*, which entails the description and elaboration of painful emotions and bodily experience connected with the traumatic memory and addresses the question of what was felt during the episode as well as what is felt now in the person's life and/or the therapy session in response to remembering the experience; and finally (3) *Reflexive Narrative Mode,* which entails the reflexive analyses of issues attendant to what happened in the event (external) and what was felt (internal) in which the question of what does it mean is addressed and contribute to the articulation of the landscape of consciousness. In essence, the narrative process modes are viewed as essential components of a distinctive mode of human meaning making which creates, maintains and, when needed, revises our sense of self in the world.

A systematic method for the identification of therapy-discourse parameters associated with narrative-processing modes was developed (Angus & Hardtke, 1994; Angus, Levitt, & Hardtke, 1999) in order to conduct an empirical investigation of narrative processes in psychotherapy. The Narrative Processes Coding System (NPCS) and revised manual (Angus, Hardtke, & Levitt, 1996) has evolved from the intensive analyses of psychotherapy transcripts and provides researchers with a rational, systematic method of unitizing therapy transcripts, regardless of therapeutic modality. The NPCS is a two-step process that enables the researcher to (1) reliably subdivide and characterize therapy session transcripts into topic segments according to content shifts in verbal dialogue; and (2) further subdivide and characterize these topic segments in terms of one of three narrative-process mode types:

> i. *External Narrative Process Sequences* that include description of events (past, present, and/or future; actual or imagined)

> ii. *Internal Narrative Process Sequences* that include a subjective/experiential description of experience

> iii. *Reflexive Narrative Process Sequences* that entail recursive questioning and meaning making processes in relation to beliefs, actions and emotions represented in current, past and/or future events.

It is recommended that each identified narrative sequence contain at least 4 transcript lines of client/therapist discourse, in order to provide an adequate sampling for the application of standardized psychotherapy process measures. The Narrative Process Coding System has demonstrated construct validity and good levels of inter-rater agreement in a series of recent psychotherapy process studies (Goncalves, Machado, Korman, & Angus in press; Angus & Bouffard 2002; Hardtke, Levitt, & Angus 2002; Levitt, Korman, & Angus, 2000; Goncalves, Korman, & Angus 2000; Levitt & Angus 2000; Angus, Levitt, & Hardtke 1999; Levitt, Korman, Angus, &

141

Hardtke 1997; Angus & Hardtke 1994). For the purposes of this chapter, however, a more fine-grained, intensive case analytic approach (Latilla, Altonen, Wahlstrom, & Angus, 2001) was adopted for the assessment of client and therapist narrative mode shifts identified in the context of one good outcome, brief process-experiential therapy dyad involved in an "Unfinished Business" research study (Paivio & Greenberg 1995) at York University in Toronto, Canada. In order to illuminate the stages of narrative change entailed in the successful resolution of trauma-based "Unfinished Business," key episodes were drawn from the transcribed therapy sessions and then analyzed for narrative process mode shifts.

The client, who is called Alexander for the purposes of this chapter, was twelve years old when his mother killed herself by means of a drug overdose. A suicide note made it clear that the overdose had been a deliberate act, but gave no specific reason for her decision to take her life. Alexander was the first person to discover his mother at the time of her suicide and exhibited symptoms of Post-Traumatic Stress Disorder at pre-treatment assessment. The client was thirty-five years old when he presented for treatment and stated that he "would like to find a better way of accepting myself and being okay with myself." He reported chronic feelings of anxiety, insecurity and shame, despite a successful business career and stable marriage. Alex also reported strong feelings of anger and resentment towards his mother—20 years after her death—and as such met criteria for "Unfinished Business". He stated that he found it difficult to live with the shameful secret of his mother's suicide and that he was unable to tell others about the circumstances of her death. He completed 15 sessions of brief experiential therapy and all sessions were transcribed as part of a process-outcome study (Paivio & Greenberg, 1995).

At post-treatment assessment, Alex's pre treatment Symptom Checklist-90-Revised (SCL-90-R; Derogatis, 1983) score of 81 had dropped to 35. He identified himself as having experienced significant change in relation to his key concerns on post-session self-report measures and, at therapy termination, stated that he had achieved a sense of resolution in his relationship with his mother. The therapist who worked with Alex was an advanced clinical psychology doctoral student, in her late thirties, who had three years of clinical experience and one year of supervised training in process-experiential therapy.

This chapter next examines how the goals of narrative re-construction and emotional-meaning making were addressed in the context of Alexander's courageous struggle to understand and accept the traumatic loss of his mother, in the context of brief process-experiential therapy for "Unfinished Business."

PROCESS-EXPERIENTIAL PSYCHOTHERPAY , UNFINISHED BUSINESS AND NARRATIVE CHANGE

Process-experiential psychotherapy is an emotion-focused, constructivist therapy approach rooted in an integration of both Gestalt and client-centered therapies. As such, it shares a common faith in humanity's innate capacity for self-reflective awareness and push toward positive growth and self-development (Greenberg, Rice, & Elliott, 1993). While the Gestalt approach provides a set of interventions designed to evoke problematic thoughts, feelings and behaviors, the client-centered approach is anchored in an empathic, prizing, and genuine attunement to the client's emotionally salient experiences.

The process of resolving "Unfinished Business" using empty chair dialogue has been rigorously modeled (Greenberg et al., 1993) and empirically verified (Paivio & Greenberg, 1995). A key compo-nent of process-experiential therapy is empty-chair dialogue, a ther-apeutic technique that originated in Gestalt therapy (Perls, Hefferline, & Goodman, 1951). Empty chair dialogue is a specific intervention designed to transform the difficulty in processing affec-tive information by helping the client confront the "significant other" in imagination and find new ways to come to terms with, and in some instances construct a new story of, the unresolved situation.

In using this intervention, therapists follow an empathic style and, having established an alliance, introduce an empty-chair dia-logue when they detect a marker of "Unfinished Business." Such markers typically involve the client giving expression to lingering unresolved feelings towards a significant other or statements of painful childhood memories. Interrupted or restricted expressions of anger over past treatment, and/or non-verbal behavior, such as sti-fling tears or holding one's breath, often accompany these moments in therapy sessions. A vital element in this process of engaging in lively contact with the imagined other is that creative adjustment is facilitated by the re-storying of the person's emotional memories and the emergence of new views of self and significant others. Emotional arousal (Greenberg & Korman, 1994) is viewed as a key mechanism in evoking salient memories and accessing self-other schematic structures.

The use of empty chair and two chair interventions in process-experiential therapy facilitates the client's re-engagement in emotions evoked in the context of his memory of the traumatic event, and the negative life consequences that followed, in three important ways. First, the therapist supports clients and encourages them to tell their stories of loss and trauma in a safe, secure, and caring relationship. The therapist's capacity to empathically attend to the client's key concerns is essential for the development of a strong therapeutic alliance and basic trust in the person of the therapist.

Next, the client is helped to story the unique emotions experienced in the context of the traumatic memory of the suicide event and to differentiate those emotional responses from the emotions experienced in relation to the devastating losses that ensued following the parent's self-inflicted death. Specifically, the therapist helps the client to story his experiences of trauma and loss by initiating process shifts to (a) the external narrative mode to more fully articulate the landscape of action and elaborate "what happened" and (b) to the internal and reflexive narrative modes to elaborate the landscape of consciousness and facilitate emotional meaning-making and new perspectives on self and others in the world. In turn, the differentiation and narrative organization of painful emotion enables the client to reflexively explore and symbolize emergent meanings of the trauma and loss, from a variety of relational vantage points.

The first vantage point that emerged in Alex's therapy sessions was the perspective and story of the "traumatized child." It was the twelve-year-old Alex who was the first to discover his dead mother's body at the time of her suicide. The second vantage point addressed in the therapy sessions was that of the adult "survivor self," who managed to find a way to live in the landscape of loss that emerged after his mother's death. The voice and story of the "survivor self" has been addressed in a recent publication (Angus & Bouffard, 2002). In response to telling his story, the vantage point of the lost mother then emerged and became a focus within the therapy sessions. Alex, the client, was encouraged to place an imaginal representation of his mother in the empty chair and to voice her response to his stories of loss and unrelenting emotional pain. This stage represented the emergence of the mother's story, and her affirmation of her enduring love for her children and her profound remorse and regret for the impact that her suicide had on her children. In this dialogue the client also voiced the mother's suicide story and explored her possible intentions and beliefs, at the time of the suicide. For the purposes of this chapter, the roles of story-telling, emotional expression and meaning-making in the context of the vantage point of the traumatized child and the lost mother will be elaborated and clinical examples of the three narrative process modes provided.

Stage One: Telling the Story

First of all, the process-experiential therapist supports the client to describe his fragmented experiences of the trauma event and to detail the legacy of loss and devastation that ensued from the death of his mother. In terms of the therapist's tasks, the process-experiential therapist is an empathic, supportive and trustworthy listener who encourages the client to express and story painful emotions and validates the importance of the client's quest for understanding, self-acceptance and where possible, forgiveness.

For Alex, the opportunity to tell his story was particularly important, as he and his siblings had been advised by extended family members to not talk about her death with each other or friends. His mother's death was experienced as a painful, shameful family secret that was best left untold. During the third therapy session, addressing his mother in the empty chair, Alex discloses the following generic memory:

> CLIENT: We never talked about you after you died. It was just kind of...it was just there. Dad never talked about you, although he missed you very much. It was very painful for me to listen to him crying for you in his sleep and crying for you and crying because he felt so bad that you did what you did.
>
> THERAPIST: Hmm.
>
> CLIENT: He didn't, I don't know if he knew why you did what you did . . . he never talked about it. I don't think he knew. He went on a road to, on a road of self-destruction to kill himself. It took him ten years after you died for him to do it, but he did finally accomplish that too.

When his therapist acknowledged the enormity of the loss of both his mother and father, Alex disclosed "I don't think I've ever had the privilege of even being able to accept that, even within my family, the loss. It was just supposed to be that things went on merrily after." His confirmation that he has never had an opportunity to tell his story of trauma and loss lays the ground for the intensive exploration of the trauma event and the description of both what happened and how Alex experienced it.

Stage Two: The Suicide Scene and the Child's Story of Horror and Disbelief

The suicide of a parent is a highly traumatizing experience, especially during childhood. In order to construct a meaningful, coherent understanding of "what happened," Alex first needed to story the horrifying childhood experience of discovering his dead mother's body and to distinguish that experience from the devastating emotional impact that ensued after her suicide. With the sudden and unexpected death of a parent, children experience overwhelming feelings of grief and sadness, fears of abandonment, and a profound breach of trust or betrayal of the safety, fairness, and goodness of the world. Moreover, childhood survivors of suicide are left to question why the parent chose to abandon them.

In session three, Alex begins to disclose his memories of finding his mother shortly after she had committed suicide in the family home. In the following sequences the therapist empathically supports the client to (a) to describe a detailed unfolding of the sequence of events that frame the suicide scene (Landscape of Action; External Narrative Sequences) and (b) to differentiate emotions, intentions, appraisals experienced in the context of the scene (Landscape of Consciousness/ Internal and Reflexive Narrative Sequence shifts) and (c) construct new emotional meanings, in the context of empty chair dialogues in the therapy sessions. It is the integration of the landscape of action and consciousness that facilitates the construction of a coherent memory narrative.

Session Three

CLIENT: I just can't you know, because the images of certain things like that are so clear in my mind and it was so long ago (*shift to external narrative mode and the description of a single event memory*). And I said that to my sister yesterday, that night is so clear to me.

THERAPIST: The night she died

CLIENT: The night she killed herself. It's so clear, I can remember everything.

THERAPIST: Just like it happened yesterday.

CLIENT: And I remember (*shift to memory of childhood*) and it sort of came into clear focus of me as a kid, and I hate it, I mean I hate it (*shift to internal/emotional differentiation*). I remember the night that my mother died, that's what it was like. (Emergence of single event memory of suicide scene and external shift/Landscape of action.) I was walking and my brother and sister—my sister was supposed to be babysitting my brother in the house—and, um, it was quiet and I thought they were waiting to jump out and go "boo!" You know? Kid's stuff.

THERAPIST: Mm-hmm.

CLIENT: So I tiptoe, tiptoe up the sidewalk and open the front door very carefully and listen, still nothing, just the sound in my eardrums (shift to internal/landscape of consciousness).

THERAPIST: This deafening silence. (Therapist evocative reflection of internal experience.)

CLIENT: So quiet, and I'm thinking (shift to reflexive/landscape of consciousness) this is really berserk, really crazy, because usually by now they've jumped out and scared the living daylights out of me and we've all laughed.

THERAPIST: Mm.

CLIENT:…and punched each other, or whatever kids do. And I remember walking in (shift to external) and still nothing, and thinking this is really funny (shift to reflexive/landscape of consciousness), and I took my boots off and I went creeping down into kitchen and I saw my mother's foot first and (shift to internal) I was in absolute shock and not knowing what to do.

THERAPIST: And your heart almost stopped. (Therapist evocative elaboration of client internal experiencing.)

CLIENT: (Shift to external narrative mode) and I started shouting because I thought my sister was supposed to be there and I started screaming for my sister and then I noticed that on the table there was a note saying that she was over at my aunt's and uncle's at a new year's party and they had put my little brother to bed there and (Reflexive shift/landscape of consciousness) that was really, because of all the turmoil as a child, too, I was frightened to call anybody because you know your own business stays within the four walls of your house so…

THERAPIST: Sure, sure.

CLIENT:…it felt like ten hours. I'm sure it was a minute, but it seemed like ten hours.

THERAPIST: So then you walked in and saw what had actually happened. (*Therapist invites a return to the differentiation of the suicide scene and shift to external /landscape of action.*)

CLIENT: I tried waking her up. I thought she might just have, you know...

THERAPIST: Who knows as a child?

CLIENT:...and I'm just shaking her and shaking her and trying to wake her up and thinking (*Shift to reflexive/landscape of consciousness*) you know, oh god, what do I do, who do I call, what do I do?

THERAPIST: Mm.

CLIENT: So the first thing I did (*Shift back to external/landscape of action*), I called my uncle and he came over with my sister because of course I said—I don't know what I said, I have no idea—and of course when he came in (*Shift to reflexive/landscape of consciousness*) my heart also goes out to him because I can't imagine an adult, myself, now walking in on a situation like that— with your family.

THERAPIST: Yeah.

In this sequence, both the client and therapist collaborate in a detailed unfolding of the trauma scene in the context of a narrative framework with a clear beginning, middle and end. Additionally, a clear scene and setting is provided along with the internal experiences of both the protagonist (Alex) and significant others (the Uncle) involved in the event. For the first time, a coherent narrative of the trauma memory begins to take shape for Alex. Additionally, a continual interplay between external and internal/reflexive narrative shifts seamlessly interweaves the unfolding narrative scene with the emotions, intentions, and expectations that Alex experienced at the time of his mother's suicide.

Session Seven

The following example of an empty chair intervention in session seven demonstrates the important role that the therapist's empathic reflections, selective questions, and suggestions play in helping Alex to further articulate the landscape of consciousness— emotions and meanings—in relation to the loss of his mother. In this sequence, the therapist first invites a shift to an external narrative mode (to describe the trauma scene) followed by an encouragement to elaborate felt emotions (an internal narrative mode). The client, in turns, moves back and forth between describing the remembered suicidal scene and describing his felt emotions in response to these terrifying images. In this therapeutic dance, the therapist empathically follows the client's lead and facilitates the expression of painful emotions and deep fears. Finally, the client shifts to a reflexive questioning mode at the end of the sequence in an attempt to bring understanding to this trauma experience,

THERAPIST: Tell her what you remember about the things, about the memories. (*Therapist invites shift to external narrative mode.*)

CLIENT: The horror and the terror (tears). (*Client focuses on felt emotions—internal narrative mode—experienced in response to internalized image of mother at the suicide scene.*)

THERAPIST: Let it go. (*Therapist stays with the client focus on felt emotions in the internal mode and differentiates fear, horror, and terror.*) Tell her about your fear (client takes a Kleenex), the horror, and the terror (seven second pause). Stay with it, you're doing well. What do you remember? Tell her what it's like for you. It's important.

CLIENT: (crying) I feel these memories are absolutely horrific and things I never should have seen.

THERAPIST: Tell her.

CLIENT: It's etched so deeply in my mind I can't erase it. When I think of you I can't even think of you because I just remember you . . .

THERAPIST: Tell her what you see. (*Therapist invites a shift to external narrative mode to elaborate image of the trauma scene.*)

CLIENT: All I see is just you laying there. I can't believe it and you're not waking up (Shift to *reflexive and elaboration of appraisals unfolding in the suicide scene*).

THERAPIST: Not waking up. What's it like for you? (Therapist invites a shift to internal narrative mode.)

CLIENT: I'm just so afraid (*client shift to internal/emotional differentiation*).

THERAPIST: I feel terrified (*therapist empathic reflection and emotional differentiation*). That's good, keep breathing. I feel terrified. What's going on? (*Therapist's question invites the client to elaborate internal experiencing.*)

CLIENT: And absolute disbelief. (*Client shifts to reflexive mode.*) How could you? How could you?

THERAPIST: So how could you do this? (*Therapist invites client to confront his mother directly with his reflexive questions in a search for understanding and meaning.*) Tell her this.

CLIENT: I don't really understand why you did it

THERAPIST: Stay with those memories. And what do you want to say? (15 second pause.) What are you feeling now? (*Therapist invites client to elaborate felt emotions and a shift to internal narrative mode.*)

CLIENT: (15 second pause) (*Client continues in reflexive narrative mode.*) I'm thinking that, um, how can I . . . how can something that happened so long ago control me so much now?

It is important to note that after this disclosure of his trauma in session three, Alex returned to the suicide scene on several other occasions, in later sessions. It was as if his vantage point on the suicide scene shifted and changed over time, with new meanings emerging in each re-telling. In particular, the back and forth movement between the vantage point of the traumatized child—caught in the unfolding suicide scenario—and the adult "survivor self" who is resentful and bitter about his mother's actions, seemed to be an important aspect of articulating and integrating the meaning of emotions, appraisals and beliefs across time and settings.

Stage Three: A Mother's Story of Love and Remorse

Having developed a differentiated, emotionally coherent narrative account of his mother's suicide, Alex can now reflexively distance himself from the emotional pain of the hurt child and enter into the world of the distressed other, his mother. For the first time, Alex is able to imaginatively enter into his mother's "landscape of consciousness" and begin to articulate her probable motives, emotions, beliefs, thoughts, and intentions at the time of the suicide. The reflexive re-processing of emotion-laden traumatic memories, as seen through the eyes of the other, facilitates the creation of new meanings and a more emotionally coherent account of the traumatic loss that addresses the dual perspectives of Alex and his mother, in relation to her suicidal death.

Mother, role-played by Alex in the context of empty chair dialogues, now has an opportunity to (a) provide an account of personal responsibility for the suicide and clarify her intentions for committing suicide; (b) acknowledge responsibility for the landscape of loss and devastation that ensued after her death and to express deep regret for the unforeseen and unintended impact on her children's lives and most importantly; and (c) affirm her love for the client. In the following empty chair dialogue, all three critical issues are powerfully addressed in the context of the client's expression of puzzlement regarding his mother's reasons for committing suicide. In the position of his mother, in the empty chair, Alex gives voice to the following account in which she provides a differentiated account of her suicidal intentions and motives and asks her son for forgiveness:

Session Nine

CLIENT (as mother): Yes, I wasn't well and I didn't mean to hurt you children (Shift to reflexive mode and the elaboration of the meaning of the mother's suicidal intentions and motives.) I didn't know the kind of impact it would have on you. I obviously didn't think about it very much. I should have gone for help, you're right. I should have gone to my...I had, I have a large family. I should have gone to my brothers and sisters for help. I should have made sure you kids were taken care of. I should have done a lot of things that I didn't do.

THERAPIST: So I made a terrible mistake (Continuing in the reflexive voice of the mother, the therapist takes her regrets about actions not taken in her life and suggests that her decision to commit suicide was a terrible mistake.)

CLIENT: I made a terrible mistake. (The client, role-playing the mother, restates the mother's new admission that the suicide was a mistake—an error in judgement that she wishes she had not made—and elaborates the meaning of this new realisation in terms of the unintended impact that her suicide had on her family and her son.) On account of I never should have done what I did. And I realize now that I've hurt you. I realize now how I hurt your sister and your brother. And I realize how I've hurt your father. I can't undo it.

THERAPIST: Sounds like I'm sorry (shift to internal mode and the underlying emotional experience).

CLIENT: I can't undo it and I'm very sorry for hurting you. (From his mother's perspective, the client articulates his mother's regrets about the hurtful impact of her suicide on him)

THERAPIST: Can you say that again?

CLIENT: I'm very, very sorry for hurting you. I'm not there now and I'm really sorry for the things that you feel that I've done to you. (In the reflexive mode, a new perspective on the mother's caring for her children emerges in the context of her personal account of the circumstances or reasons why she made a terrible mistake and committed suicide.) Wasn't about you kids at all. You're probably the reason that I stayed as long as I did stay. It wasn't about you children. It was about a life that I just thought there was no hope and a sense of hopelessness.

This affirmation of enduring love from his mother sets the stage for Alex to address the question of his mother's intentions at the time of the suicide. This inquiry is undertaken from the perspective of a loved child who is trying to understand how—and under what conditions—a caring mother can commit such a tragic mistake without knowing that it will have devastating emotional outcomes for family and loved ones. It is important that the mother provide a compelling account that not only includes the circumstances that led to her suicide and her motivation and intentions for doing so, but also expresses her deep remorse for her actions and her recognition of and responsibility for the devastating impact it had on others.

Additionally, the process-experiential model suggests that in the context of "Unfinished Business," a client's repetitive expression of needing to know "why" a hurtful action was undertaken is almost always a marker of underlying feelings of resentment and hurt. From this perspective, it is argued that negative feelings need to be openly expressed and responded to, by the significant other, in order that successful problem resolution—and a positive emotional shift—can take place. Later in the same session, a significant shift occurs when Alex, role-playing his mother in the empty chair, articulates a new account of the mother's suicide story in which she now acknowledges that her suicide was based on a mistaken belief, expresses her deep regret for her actions and affirms her continuing love for her children.

Session Nine

CLIENT (as mother): I am so very, very sorry that I did what I did to you. And you're right, I didn't realize the ripple effect of what I did to your father and to your brother, your sister, my own sisters and my own parents even. I...I saw the pain. There was no turning back at that point. I had already done what I had done. And I never realized for a moment, until the aftermath, that there was so many people that cared about me as much as they did care about me. And I did have alternatives and I did have places to go.

THERAPIST: Mmm.

CLIENT: I didn't exercise those options. I don't know why I didn't exercise them, but it was too late to exercise them.

THERAPIST: Mmm.

CLIENT: I need you to forgive. I'm sorry for what I did.

THERAPIST: I need you to forgive me.

CLIENT: I cared about you children more than anything in the whole world. I can't make an excuse for what I did. I've no...I don't know why, it just was there. But I should not have left you children. I love you more than anything in the world and it's been very difficult for the three of you all of these years

THERAPIST: Hmm.

CLIENT: And I never should have left you.

THERAPIST: Hmm.

The question of whether a mother who loves her children can commit suicide is re-engaged from a new perspective in which the parent has now shared profound regrets regarding her selfish actions, wished to undo her actions if she could, and expressed enduring love for her children. This invites a compassionate understanding of the mother's distress from the perspective of both the traumatized child and opens up the possibility of forgiveness.

The final stage of story reconstruction lies beyond the scope of the present chapter. This important step entails the client's shift to forgiveness and is marked by the emergence of positive memories of the loving mother and a re-experiencing of her warmth and love. The integration of the memories, stories, and perspectives of the traumatized child with those of the survivor self, in relation to a distressed but loving mother, lead to the creation of a coherent life narrative.

DISCUSSION

In the foregoing excerpts, we have tried to demonstrate how Alex and his therapist undertook the important, but difficult, experiential work of disentangling and differentiating emotions and events of the suicide trauma so that a coherent narrative organization of the landscapes of action and consciousness might be constructed. In particular, the narrative organization of painful emotions occurring before, during, and after his mother's suicide allowed the client to reflexively explore the emotional meaning of these experiences from new relational vantage points. Of particular importance was the emergence of the perspective of the loving mother, via empty-chair role-plays in the therapy sessions, which led to the co-construction of a new account of her suicide story.

The therapist helped facilitate this process of narrative reconstruction by initiating narrative process shifts to (a) the external narrative mode, to more fully articulate and coherently organize the landscape of action and elaborate "what happened;" (b) to the internal narrative mode, to more fully differentiate and symbolize painful emotions and feelings; and (c) to the reflexive narrative mode, in order to articulate intentions, expectations, and appraisals that populated the client's landscape of consciousness. This dialectical movement between external, internal, and narrative modes facilitates the articulation and integration of the dual landscapes of action and consciousness (Bruner, 1990) in Alex's stories of trauma and loss.

In particular, it appears that shifts to internal (emotional differentiation) and reflexive (meaning-making) modes are key to the emergence of new, more satisfying, and coherent ways of understanding old stories. The narrative organization of distressing emotional responses and states facilitates a reflexive processing of emotional memories, which can then be explored from different relational vantage points or perspectives. In turn, emotion shifts and new meanings emerge for clients while engaged in the movement from one relational vantage point to another. Greenberg (2002) has argued that effective process-experiential therapists operate as emotion coaches for their clients. On the basis of the current analysis, it would appear that the therapist shifts to both emotional differentiation (Internal) and reflexive meaning-making are essential for productive therapy. In this regard, the Narrative Process model would seem to hold promise as an effective framework for therapists to adopt when working with clients who present with "Unfinished Business."

Additionally, the mother's validation of Alex's painful stories of terror, shame, sadness and resentment, enacted by Alex via the empty-chair, allowed him to empathically enter the imagined intrapersonal world of her felt emotions, intentions, beliefs and concerns, at the time of her suicide. For the first time in his life, Alex constructs and accepts a coherent, compelling account of how a loving mother makes a terrible mistake and commits suicide. The emergence of a new understanding of the loving basis of his relationship with his mother results in the creation of an emotionally coherent, comprehensive and integrative account of Alex's life story.

REFERENCES

Angus, L., & Bouffard-Bowes, B. (2002). "No lo entiendo:" La busqueda de sentido emocional y coherencia personalante una perdida traumatica durante la infancia. *Revista Psicoterapia*, 12, 25-46.

Angus, L., & Korman, Y. (2002). Coherence, conflict and change in brief therapy: A metaphor theme analysis. In S. Fussell (Ed.), *The verbal communication of emotions: Interdisciplinary perspectives* (pp. 151-165). Lawrence Erlbaum.

Angus, L., Levitt, H., & Hardtke, K. (1999). Narrative processes and psychotherapeutic change: An integrative approach to psychotherapy research and practice. *Journal of Clinical Psychology*, 55, 1255-1270.

Angus, L., Hardtke, K., & Levitt, H. (1996). *An expanded rating manual for the narrative processing coding system.* Unpublished manuscript.

Angus, L., & Hardtke, K. (1994). Narrative processes in psychotherapy. *Canadian Psychology*, 35, 190-203.

Bouffard, B. A. (2002). *Reworking the past: The role of autobiographical memories and emotion in the resolution of unfinished business.* Paper presented at the Ontario Psychological Association Convention, Toronto, Canada.

Bruner, J. (2002). *Making stories: Law, literature, life.* New York: Farrar, Strauss, & Giroux.

Bruner, J. (1990). *Acts of meaning.* Cambridge, MA: Harvard University Press.

Bruner, J. (1986). *Actual minds, possible worlds.* Cambridge, MA: Harvard University Press.

Gonçalves, O., Machado, P., Korman, Y. & Angus, L. (in press). Assessing psychopathology: A narrative approach. In L. Beutler (Ed.), *Alternatives to the DSM.* Washington, DC: American Psychological Association Press.

Gonçalves, O., Korman, Y., & Angus, L. E. (2000). Disorder as metaphor in cognitive narrative psychotherapy. In R. A. Neimeyer & J. D. Raskin (Eds.), *Constructions of disorder: Meaning-making frameworks for psychotherapy* (pp. 265-284). Washington, DC: American Psychological Association Press.

Greenberg, L. (2002). *Emotion-focused therapy : Coaching clients to work through feelings.* Washington, DC: American Psychological Association Press.

Greenberg. L. S., & Foerster, F. S. (1996). Task analysis exemplified: The process of resolving unfinished business. *Journal of Consulting and Clinical Psychology, 64*, 439-446.

Greenberg, L., & Korman, L. (1994). Assimilating emotion in psychotherapy integrations. *Journal of Psychotherapy Integration, 3*, 249-264.

Greenberg, L.S., Rice, L., & Elliott, R. (1993). *Facilitating emotional change: The moment by moment process.* New York: Guilford Press.

Hardtke, K., Levitt, H., & Angus, L. (in press). Investigating narrative processes in psychotherapy discourse: The Narrative Processes Coding System. *Zeitschrift fuer qualitative Bildungs-,Beratungs- und Sozialforschung.*

Laitilla, A., Altonen, J., Wahlstrom, J., & Angus,L. (2001). Narrative Process Coding System in marital and family therapy: An intensive case analysis of the formation of a therapeutic system. *Contemporary Family Therapy, 23*, 309-322.

Levitt, H., Korman, Y., & Angus, L. (2000). A metaphor analysis in the treatment of depression: Metaphor as a marker of change. *Counseling Psychology Quarterly,13*, 23-36.

Levitt, H., & Angus, L. (2000). Psychotherapy process measure research and the evaluation of psychotherapy orientation: A narrative analysis. *Psychotherapy Integration, 9*, 279-300.

Levitt, H., Korman, Y., Angus, L., & Hardtke, K. (1997). Metaphor analyses in good and poor outcome psychotherapy: Unloading a burden vs. being burdened. *Psicologia:Teoria, Investigao e Practica, 2*, 329-346.

Paivio, S. & Greenberg, L. (1995). Resolving "Unfinished Business": Efficacy of experiential therapy using empty-chair dialogue. *Journal of Consulting and Clinical Psychology, 63*, 419-425.

Perls, F., Hefferline, R., & Goodman, P. (1951). *Gestalt therapy.* New York: Delta.

CHAPTER 8

Looking Through the Mask: Transforming Trauma by Restorying the Self Through Action[1]

Patrice Keats and Marla J. Arvay

Over the last decade the treatment of trauma has evolved from conceptualizations of traumatic stress that are based on models of "disease" and "disorder" to new approaches that move the focus of treatment from a solely intrapyschic phenomenon to both intra- and interpsychic realms of human existence. As constructivists, our interests pertain to those treatments that emphasize a dialogical, embodied approach.

According to van der Kolk (2002), there are two critical issues in the treatment of trauma. First, the therapist needs to provide the client with an experience that contains elements that are sufficiently similar to the trauma event that will activate a trauma response. Second, the therapist needs to ensure that the experience contains aspects that are incompatible enough with the event to change it. For example, as the client tells or enacts a stressful trauma story, the therapist may provide an experience of safety or social support that was not present at the time of the trauma. We see this process as a re-storying of the trauma experience through the action of contextually situated language in action. Further, we believe that the therapy model called Therapeutic Enactment (Westwood, Black, & McLean, 2002; Westwood, Keats, & Wilensky, 2003), meets van der Kolk's criteria. However, we extend Westwood's Therapeutic Enactment model and reconfigure it within a narrative-constructivist approach by reconceptualizing this treatment of traumatic stress as a language centered, contextually situated, and embodied experience. The focus of our understanding is on the meaning reconstruction

---

[1] Originally presented at the Tenth Biennial Conference of the North American Personal Construct Network, Vancouver, BC, July 2002.

processes (Neimeyer, 2001) within the trauma story, and our approach to trauma repair is multidimensional, dialogical, participatory, and embodied.

After a brief review of narrative therapy concepts and the Therapeutic Enactment model, we offer an in-depth case illustration. Here, we will explicate meaning reconstruction in a clinical context through the use of the Therapeutic Enactment process.

NARRATIVE THERAPY CONCEPTS

From a narrative perspective, the self is constituted through language practices (Arvay, 2002). Through storytelling, the narrative functions as a means of self-construction. Story construction is a way of coming to know oneself and one's world; it is through new scripts or storylines that change becomes possible. The reconstruction of meaning in a story through the telling and re-telling in participation with others, allows changes in identity to occur. It is in this performance of languaging the self forth into the world that a person fashions, challenges, and reconstitutes identity at both intrapersonal and interpersonal levels of self-construction (Neimeyer & Arvay, 2003).

In narrative therapy, the therapist privileges a person's lived experience in a changing world where subjective implicit meaning, reflexive thought, and multiple perspectives are the norm in co-constructed storing between therapist and client (White & Epston, 1990). Examples of the effective use of storying in the treatment of trauma include Pennebaker (1997), Neimeyer (2000), and Sewell (1998). Pennebaker has done extensive studies on effectiveness of therapeutic journaling about trauma and other painful life experiences. His studies suggest that writing and re-writing in detail about the trauma story has a profound positive impact on both physical and emotional health. Further, Neimeyer's (2000) narrative-constructivist approach to the reconstruction of disrupted narratives of the self has been effective in helping clients integrate experiences of traumatic loss. He uses narrative techniques such as "symptom deprivation" (p. 221) to promote an ongoing reconstruction of self through articulating, elaborating, and negotiating meaning so that clients may organize their experience and actions in light of traumatic loss. Finally, Sewell, Baldwin, and Williams (1998) have applied a narrative-constructivist approach using the Multiple Self Awareness model to a personal growth therapy group for women. Using autobiographical monologues and role-plays, the participants

158

reported positive results in terms of self-awareness and personal growth.

In working through their trauma narrative, clients tell stories about fragmented experiences such as embodied (or disembodied) suffering, shattered beliefs, and emotional devastation. Often, clients are unable to develop a narrative that includes a continuous tale about the trauma experience and are thus left with a fragmented sense of self and a discontinuity in life. We believe that through the action of storying the fragments of a trauma experience during a re-enactment of the trauma story, clients are able to re-envision and reconstruct a more cohesive and integrated self-narrative.

THERAPEUTIC ENACTMENT

Therapeutic enactment is a combined individual and group-based treatment approach created by Marvin Westwood in his work with traumatized veterans and peacekeeping soldiers (Westwood, Black, & McLean, 2002). Westwood has also employed therapeutic enactment with clients experiencing a variety of clinical concerns such as complicated bereavement, traumatic loss, sexual assault, homicide, suicide, and childhood physical, emotional, and sexual abuse. Although therapeutic enactment has its roots in psychodrama, therapeutic enactment is a pre-planned, structured experience that is action oriented and narratively based. Westwood et al. (2002) contend "more recent work has emphasized that the reliving through physical action is central to the facilitation of the participant's experience of change" (p. 226). Therapeutic enactment is an embodied story in action.

Westwood's therapeutic enactment is a treatment approach that is multifaceted and integrative. It begins with a therapist/group leader and co-facilitator who are highly trained in trauma therapy, group work, and Therapeutic Enactment facilitation. These professionals interview the storyteller to assess current psychological and emotional functioning a few weeks before the enactment. At this time, the therapist/group leader and the client carefully script the story to be enacted. Additionally, the leaders help the storyteller ascertain various personal and social resources that might be used during the enactment. Examples of personal resources include artifacts that are symbolic representations of secure support (e.g., family photographs, crystals), or social supports including important people to the storyteller (e.g., friends, therapist). In the case illustration below, the first author designed and created a variety of masks

159

that she used during her enactment based on her expertise in this modality (see Keats, 2000, 2003). The preparation and use of masks is not a part of the standard form of the therapeutic enactment of trauma in Westwood's model.

Once the preparation of the enactment story is complete, a date is set for the enactment to take place within a group context. Westwood's witness groups often consist of other health care providers (e.g., doctors, nurses, massage therapists) and mental health professionals (i.e., psychologists, clergy, counselors). The group is prepared in the typical fashion for building group cohesion and confidentiality before the enactment begins, as it provides a safe container in which the enactment may unfold. In the process, members of the group create a shared story through the act of witnessing the storyteller's experience. Once the enactment is complete, the witnesses are given time to express their personal reactions to the story, and thereby, hearing, seeing, and validating the storyteller's experience. This safe social environment supports storytellers to reintegrate their new story, reconstitute their identity, and restructure shattered beliefs. Finally, because this therapy model requires extensive training, the authors caution other professional in using this modality without proper education and experience in trauma therapy, group work, and the skills related to the Therapeutic Enactment model.

Extending Westwood's view of the change process occurring within this intervention, we believe that physically moving through the trauma story is linked to the psychophysiology of trauma—the impact of trauma on the body and the phenomenon of somatic memory. We know that the somatic memory, embedded during a traumatic event, becomes one's personal history. Rothschild (2000), in her book on the psychophysiology of trauma, states:

> [T]he goals of trauma should be: (1) to unite implicit and explicit memories into a comprehensive narrative of events and aftermath of the traumatic incident. This includes making sense of body sensations and behaviors within that context; (2) to eliminate symptoms of hyperarousal in connection with those memories, and (3) to relegate the traumatic event to the past." (p. 150)

Given Rothchild's perspective on the physiology of trauma, a strictly narrative approach that operates solely at a cognitive level may be inadequate because traumatic memory presents itself in both somatic and narrative forms. Therapeutic enactment provides an opportunity to restory the trauma, re-experience somatic memory, and reconstitute the self, all of which unfold within the safe community of the group.

The following narratives begin with a trauma story written by the first author before the enactment process. The second narrative includes verbatim transcript excerpts from the first author's experience of her therapeutic enactment including a reflexive voice that illustrates the complexity of the experience and the multiple perspectives inherent in the narrative process.

PATRICE'S TRAUMA NARRATIVE

My back is aching. I am four months pregnant and I am still adjusting to sharing my body with this hidden miracle called "baby." I have just cleaned up from eating my supper, and it is dark outside now. I am living in solitude, moving through my baby's growth and all of the daily routines and preparations alone. The "father" fled the country at the joyous news of the baby's coming. I hope he is having a good time; maybe he is even growing up a little on the Eurorail track. I pull my mind back from emerging imaginations about him and wonder what to do about this ache in my back. Maybe a short walk might help. I have heard that walking helps to change the baby's position. It is worth a try. I look out the window. I can see the near full moon on this crisp February evening. I glance at the clock— almost nine. I had better get going. I pull my coat down off the hanger. It's a beautiful coat, a gift that I had given my mother several years ago. An elderly aboriginal woman had hand-sewn the coat with much care. I can feel a sense of protection as I run my hands over the embroidered-appliquéd flowers along the bottom. It is thick emerald green wool with an outer shell of gray. I zip up each layer—it will not be long before I cannot zip it up over my thickening belly.

It is dark, but I have no fear. It has always been my belief that I can protect myself. Although I am pregnant, I am strong, fit, and healthy. I know this city so well—I have not lived anywhere else in the last twenty-three years. It is a safe place to me. I walk out the door of my apartment and lock it behind me with confidence and determination. I walk down the three flights of stairs to the front door and out onto the street. I notice right away how odd the air feels as I turn the corner to walk uphill along the faintly lit road. I look up to see the still clear moon. I wonder about her clairvoyant tendency as she watches me walking. I think about her near fullness; it is like me. I think about the myth that the full moon creates human lunacy. I falter for a moment—maybe it is not a good night to be on the street. It just doesn't feel right out here. I decide to walk to the end of the street. I am good at setting goals. I will not go too far.

As I walk, I feel a tension rising inside me. I am struggling between my feelings and my thoughts. I cannot discount the undeniable feeling of foreboding; I try to ignore it and rationalize to myself that it is just a short distance to walk. To what part of myself should I listen—feelings or thoughts? My feelings become a louder voice—almost shouting "Go Home!" My mind, a logical analyst, calmly speaks "Just a little further! You have a goal!" (As if that was a signal for safety to abate my feelings of unease.) I cannot give in to either, so I give in to my will. I walk despite the debate. I notice that my legs are getting heavy. I concentrate on fighting to move each foot forward towards my objective. The pain in my back is still there. I walk. I fight. I walk. I see the last block—my decided goal. I will get there and then walk home—maybe I will even run home. That feels like a good logical decision!

Wait! I see something moving in the bushes where the lane divides the block. A man? Yes! He is coming out putting on a pair of plain black gloves. Those gloves are a signal; this is serious trouble. He looks over at me as I walk; I quickly avert my eyes. This is not like me. What is this newfound apprehension? Is it because of the moon? An effect of pregnancy? He is walking towards me and against my will I continue to walk as if I am drawn forward. It is like an automatic response. I know I am in danger! Does the devil possess me? My heart is beating out of control. I cannot catch my breath! As he closes in, I fight to keep the air flowing into my frantic lungs. He approaches me slowly, watching me. I have lost control of myself. He smells my fear like an animal—I can tell by the look in his face. His gloves are on. All in the flow of a seemingly normal movement, we meet and, closely, he passes by. I hear his voice. "Hi." My God! He passed me by! What an imagination I have. I am safe. It was a friendly gesture after all! He is not going to harm me. I feel relieved. I smile to myself and walk a little easier now.

I take a deep breath in—then, shock! Like a magician, he is beside me. I startle and jump onto the street. He matches my movements—now he stands in front of me, blocks my way—too close. I have to look at him; I cannot take my eyes off him. He traps me in his gaze. He has my breath, my life. I experience giving over to him all my power, every cell of energy. I hand it over willingly in hopes of compassion. My baby draws my attention. What can I do? He

162

speaks again, asking directions. I can't think of the answer; I can't think! I fumble; some words come out, something meaningless and confused. I recognize that I am buying time. I suffer from the hate in his eyes. I begin to hate myself. How could I have been so stupid to put my baby and myself in this danger? I must deserve this punishment for my lack of common sense. Who do I think I am being out on this dark street at night? I find myself wishing that he would have mercy on my foolishness, and that he will forgive me, and let me go. He has all the power. Don't move—he may notice your panic. The look in his eye has become a look of disgust. His repulsion pierces into me like a knife. It makes me loathe myself. He is reaching for the collar of my coat. His gloves are to protect his hand from my hideousness. He has a metal pipe tucked in his belt; he pulls it out, grasps it forcefully and tests it for balance. What is he going to do? All I think about is my baby. In a desperate plea, I tell him that I am pregnant. He falters, hesitates—is he human after all? NO! There is no compassion in evil. He pulls me along into the lane. He moves quickly, I am off balance and I can hardly keep up. I trip! What power can stop this? All I have left is God. I shout to God! Out of my peripheral vision, I see the man reaching up to strike me, and then the earth smashes me in the face.

I dream I have no body. The echo of my voice sounds through infinite space.

I am here again. He sits in front of me. He has his naked hand between my legs. I feel it. I see the greed in his eyes. He reaches his hand towards my breast.

I dream I have no body. I am free. I am held in a field of infinite peace and compassion. Is it angels that I hear? We talk about living and dying. I chose life. They point me towards the light.

Suddenly—a door. I can barely see it. I pound on the screen. Someone is there. "My baby, my baby!" They bring me in. I cannot understand their words. I cannot speak. There is blood—so much blood dripping into my eyes. I am sitting inside now. What are they saying to me? Hang on. Hold on—the ambulance is coming…it is coming…it will be here soon.

PATRICE'S THERAPEUTIC ENACTMENT:
THE RE-CONSTRUCTION OF THE TRAUMA NARRATIVE

It is a secluded place—little cabins scattered in a group within the trees. The cabins are where we go, as individuals to contemplate and sleep with the stories that we see. As a group, we meet in

163

the staff lodge, the largest building "on the hill." A stone fireplace keeps us warm and heavy logs walls keep us contained. There are windows to look out of when the enacted story is too hard to watch—thank God for the windows. It is the night of my therapeutic enactment. We are sitting in a tight circle—twenty-nine of us. I look at everyone in the circle. Will I be safe? Can I trust them? I am afraid. I'm not sure why, but it is hard to breathe, even though the doors are open and fresh air is in the room. Tonight, I am wearing the mask of the protagonist, the star, the storyteller. No one can see it, but I can feel it under my skin. I hope I have prepared enough to go back in time—back to the perpetrator. We will turn the clock back eighteen years for me for this one night. I am prepared and ready to go.

I am called to come into the center of the circle. T is with me; he will be the perpetrator. My box of masks and paraphernalia is waiting in the middle of the circle for me. The circle of people around me is tight, warm, and seemingly safe. We are purified; we are prepared to go on a journey of remembering. T leaves my side and sits in the circle. Marv, the director, is with me now; he is my guide tonight. I feel attached, dependent, and safe with him. I have tested him long and hard looking for that trust that I know will keep me safe. I am sure that he can help me over the threshold of my fear. He begins.[2]

> M: (*He speaks to the group*) First Patrice is going to explain what we have here and how we are going to set up. Your role is to be the witnesses only. We don't want anyone to come up because it will be very focused and clear. She has asked that you just be witnesses so that this will be carried by all of us. (*He speaks to me*) You're ready...and it's been a long time coming hasn't it?

> P: (*I am nervous, cautious, and trying to stay present and in control of myself*) Yes.

> M: Would you like to start by telling us how long it's been in getting here...or what you want us to do? What would you like to do? It's yours.

> P: I was 25 years old at the time...and pregnant...with my first child. So it's been a long time.

> M: (*He notices that I am nervous*) Do you want to walk? It's easier that way.

---

[2] Ellipses in this text denote pauses due to thought processing and the storyteller's attempts to catch her breath.

FIGURE 1. MASKS

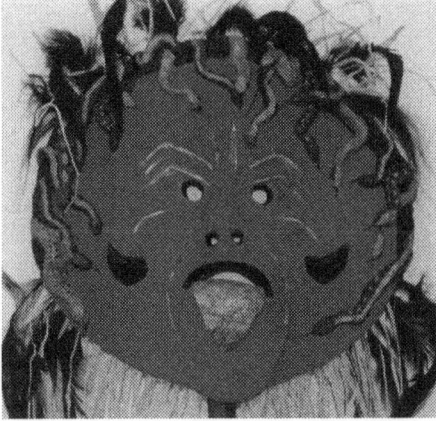

Mask of Medusa (sculpture)

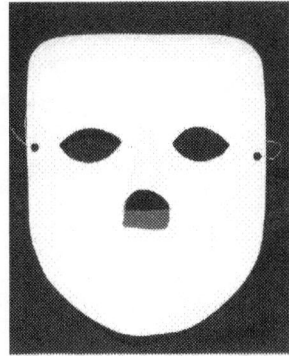

Neutral Mask

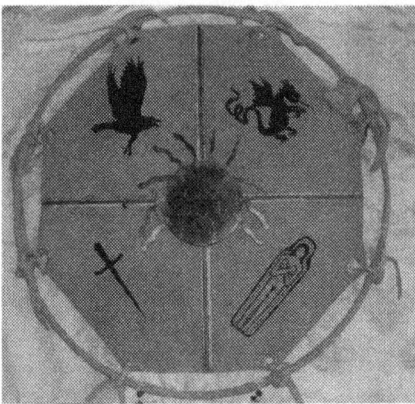

Aegis or Shield (sculpture)

And so we walk. I tell the group about how I decided to do a therapeutic enact-
ment and the preparation that I did before I came. I tell them about the masks that I
have made and brought with me to portray characters and the importance of the masks
that each one will wear so that I remain safe and free of judgment as the enactment
takes place.

P: Somewhere along the line...I connected with Medusa. When anyone met Medusa...if they looked at her they would freeze into stone. This is what happened to me the night I was assault-ed. I froze. Since then, that has been my reaction to everything that scares me. I freeze.

M: From that one night?

P: Yes. (*I stop in front of the mask. It is a wild red gorgon face that I built onto a long, straight branch. The branch is hidden with long strands of raffia that dan-gled off Medusa's chin.*) This is the Medusa mask.

M: This is Medusa. Tonight she will be shown directly to you— maybe freeze you.

P: That's...(I hesitate—could that be true?) I don't know if she will freeze me...I will probably freeze myself! (I did not know how or what Medusa would do during the enactment. I just knew she was a key figure and would play a key role.)

M: You will probably freeze yourself, but we will thaw you every time you freeze. We will thaw you. That's the whole point of doing this enactment, isn't it?[3]

P: Yes.

M: You may freeze, but that's the purpose of Medusa.

P: She represents to me...that frozen moment in the assault...I want to be able to use that freezing consciously...not uncon-sciously. That is why I put her copper image in the center of my shield...because when she was beheaded...Perseus used her head...her eye...her power to freeze or make people turn to stone...to do good.

M: To do good. Tonight you want to take that back.

P: Yes...to have the good of it...I need her...to speak to me. (*I give her to D, one of the witnesses who will carry her behind the perpetrator*)

---

[3] In trauma theory the actual moment of trauma results in a psychophysiological response of freezing (Rothschild, 2000). The storyteller is experiencing a somatic memory.

M: What's happening right now? Take a deep breath—rub your hands! Let's feel your hands—cold! Not frozen, just cool right? Remember when we talked you knew that this is all a part of how it will go.

P: Yes. (*I am anxious and somewhat self-conscious in front of the group. I am struggling to breathe calmly and naturally.*) So...shall we just get on with it? (*I was anxious and wanting to get it over with.*) Can we just do it now?

M: I think we should just do it now. Know that as we go through it, we will just stop-start-stop-start and we will just move through the whole thing. You will signal to me when you are ready to move on and I'll stop and check in with you.[4]

The group sits all around me. I can hardly stay in touch with myself. I am dissociating. I notice that I reach to touch Marv often; it helps me stay connected. I want to breathe normally, but it is just not happening. Maybe just moving on will help me calm down. I need to do something; it distracts me from my feelings. I worry about being crazy with feelings that are out of control. And so I place the other masks in the hands of the players.

First, I give T, who plays my perpetrator, a black Zorro-type mask, black toque, a pair of black gloves, a heavy brown leather jacket, and a heavy metal pipe that is about twenty inches long and two inches in diameter. Next, I give each of the witnesses a neutral mask. I cut these masks from plain beige cardpaper. They each have eyeholes and an inset nose but no mouth. Neutral holds everything, but also holds nothing. It is absolute balance. The neutral place is the nonjudgmental place from which I wanted my trauma witnessed. Last, I gave an angel mask to H, who would act as my intuition, the wise part of me that tried to warn me of danger.

P: (*I speak to H the angel.*) You will be wearing a mask of my face.

M: Is that actually a copy of your face?

P: Yes...I made it out of fine white silk...I hope it is not too hard for you to wear...I also have this white silk garment, too. (*I put the silk cloth over her head and shoulders and Marv helped her put the mask on her face. As I looked on, it was as if the mask fused onto her face. Shocked, I found myself looking at my own image. It surprised me; emotion surged within me.*)

---

[4] In TE it is important to reassure the storyteller that she has control over the pace, content, intensity, and length of each aspect of the enactment story. The facilitator needs to be conscious of all aspects of trauma response during the enactment, so as not to overwhelm the storyteller. He accomplishes this by keeping the storyteller grounded through breathing, physical touch, movement, and bringing her awareness to the witnesses in the outer circle and their presence in the current context.

M: This is getting very serious. It is more and more to the core isn't it?

P: Yes...yes. *(I felt hesitant. I was not expecting this.)* I will just tie it on. *(I look carefully at her again. As I looked, I was overcome with grief. I fall into her arms crying.)* I am so sorry...I'm sorry...I didn't listen to you *(Tears of regret, guilt, and sorrow pour out of me. Marv moves around and holds me, too. We stay there for a few minutes.)*

H: I am always inside you.

P: I know...you never punished me for that. It didn't matter. You stayed beside me always...

H: I always do love you. *(I did not know that I had carried so much shame about having ignored my inner voice. It was as if I had the opportunity to actually speak the words to my spirit-self. It was a very powerful moment for me.)*[5]

M: Keep breathing—in and out—in and out. Coming back to that really upset you didn't it?

P: Hmm *(I let her go after a few moments. I feel relieved somehow. She follows behind me without touching me. The spirit is there, but not physical anymore; it was only for that moment. I just needed to know she was there. She remained behind me for the duration of the enactment. We continued on).* Okay.

M: Are you wearing a mask?

P: No...I'm not wearing a mask.

M: You are not wearing a mask at all. It's just you and me then.

P: You and me

M: You and me. Before the witnesses put their masks on, do you want to explain what we are doing? Do you want to talk as we go along? Do you want to set a context?

P: *(I needed a moment to breathe in deeply. I am not in contact with myself.)* Maybe we should just be quiet...before they put the masks on.

M: Before they put the masks on. Then you and I will tell the story. *(Marv speaks to the group.)* OK, so we would like you to be quiet and when you feel ready, then put your mask on. *(There is a short pause. It is quiet and still. All the witnesses now don their masks.)* Just take a look around. What are you aware of?

---

[5] In trauma repair, the therapeutic work often involves a restorying of the role of shame in the trauma experience. Survivors' self-blame is a common experience in trauma.

P: (*I am amazed! There is no judgment—no expression. I feel free.*) They really look neutral.

M: Yes, they look neutral. I didn't realize that it would be like
this. It is great actually.

P: Yes…it is…I don't feel like I have anything to worry about
with them.[6]

M: No, they are there behind the masks. These masks make this
pure, actually. (*We look at the group together for a moment. Marv turns to
me and takes my hands.*) My covenant to you is this: we will go
through this event as accurately as it really was, so that when we
come out the other end you'll be whole again. It will be seen by
all of us so that it will no longer be so much inside of you.[7] (*I
take a deep breath and try to relax. I know this story so well. Why do I worry
so?*) Now—we are ready. Do you want to set the tone by walk-
ing? Will that be easier?

I describe some of the facts about my living conditions at the time of the
assault including where the apartment was, how pregnant I was, how my boyfriend left
me when he found out that I was pregnant. I describe why I went out for a walk. As I
spoke, it was as if it was happening again. My legs were heavy and I had trouble moving forward. I remember the way the night felt and the feeling of the moon. I felt confused—as if I was in two worlds. My body was remembering, responding—yet, at the
same time, I was aware that I was in the cabin with Marv and all the witnesses. In this
state of multiple worlds, I described the fight I had with myself as to whether I should
go home or keep walking.

P: It is strong… it's warning me. (*I am remembering the inner struggle.*) Fear is finding its way up through my breath—I am getting
very upset. My breathing is labored, strained.

M: It's warning me that…

P: …I should…go home… (*I cannot hold back my tears. Marv stops and
holds me for a moment.*)

---

[6] Neutrality is a release from the shame and judgement about being a trauma victim, a sexual assault survivor—an actual example of the storyteller knowing how
to construct a safe container in order to confront the horror.

[7] Having the trauma witnessed is a key aspect to this healing process; it moves the
trauma story from the individual to the communal.

M: (*Marv speaks softly*) Something bad might happen. (*His voice is soothing me. I try to gather myself. I am able to walk again. I struggle to get my legs to move*).[8]

P: It's hard to walk. It's hard to lift my legs even. Big warning. Big…big warning. (*I cry and through my tears, reach for my breath. Marv comforts me as we walk. I hold on to his arm; it is grounding.*)

M: Big warning—you keep going.

P: I keep going…anyway.

M: Take a pause—take a deep breath. Just glance around and see the witnesses. They are listening and watching. You were just going for a walk.

P: Just a walk. (*I feel like I am pleading. Pleading for it to have been different that night. Pleading to myself to have listened.*) That's all I wanted to do.

M: We don't have to talk. Walking is a way to come back to your center.

M: (*We stop for a moment.*) You see someone now—coming towards you.

P: I notice somebody.

M: What do you notice?

P: I notice there are some bushes…there is a lane way. (*I am looking into my mind's eye as I remember. It is as if the pictures are stored in my mind and the memories are stored in my body—I am trying to breathe—just breathe.*)

M: There is a lane way there.

P: I notice there's a man…and he's coming out from…behind the bushes. He's putting…on…(*It is hard to bear the memory that comes into my mind and into my body.*)

M: He's putting on…

P: He's putting on…black gloves. (*I have to force out the words with the last of my breath.*) On his hands (*I cry uncontrollably. Marv holds me.*) I know I'm in trouble.

M: (*His voice is calm and reassuring.*) We're here. You know you're in trouble now. I'm in trouble now; it's too late.

P: I'm just trying…to catch my breath as I'm walking.

---

[8] The somatic memory is being re-experienced in the TE, but within a safe container.

170

M: Shall we go around one more time? We saw him, didn't we? Breathe. Walk. Breathe. Walk. Breathe.

P: (*As we walk, I feel like I can go on although I still struggle to breathe.*) I say...I'm in trouble...but then I ...kind of say...it's OK. I'm just going to go to the end of the block. (*I am trying to reassure myself; I feel sad, yet compassionate for myself in that moment.*)[9]

M: You say, "It's OK; I'm going to the end of the block. I've seen him. He's coming towards me. I know I'm in trouble, but I'm going to be OK."

P: (*I am triggered. I cry out*) I don't know if I'm going to be OK, Marv! I don't know...if I'm going to be OK...I don't know.

M: I know. I know (*He holds me as I cry*) I convinced myself again, right? Do you want to stop now? We are going to stay here for just as long as you need to stay here. We are just stopping, so you know we are still here. The witnesses are still here. We are all still here. You are not alone. That's the difference tonight. The terror is inside of you, but we are here. There's no rush. Remember we are going to go forward when you want to—every step of the way. That is the control that you are taking back tonight—that you didn't have—that was taken away from you. You felt like you didn't have control. You said, "I'm in trouble." Here, tonight, you can say "I'm terrified but safe. I'm safe." There's the difference. "I'm terrified and I'm not in trouble tonight." This is now. The controls are present tonight. That's what we are honoring here. The power of remembering is so strong it's overwhelming. The only way to release it is to take control of it. You can even say, "I want to go a little ways further" or you might just want to stand here and say you're not ready to see him there. We'll stop if you want.

I had waited a long time to see him again. I had a relationship with this per-petrator—even though he was a stranger to me. I had given myself over to him. You see,

---

[9] A reflexive moment—standing outside of self. The storyteller demonstrates the multiple perspectives of the self that are made available through therapeutic enactment. These reflective moments are not necessarily contained in the present time—the protagonist's experience of reality shifts from current time/space to other dimensions of time. In a single sentence, she moves from here-and-now to previous somatic experiences that place her in another time dimension. These shifts occur rapidly and unpredictably. The director works to keep her grounded in the here-and-now.

he violently forced himself into my life that night—infiltrating into my thoughts, my feelings, and my cells completely. He was every strange man that I saw, every man that was on the street. I saw his face everywhere—the mask of the perpetrator—all men wore it. The fact was that he had not been apprehended—the police let him slip through their fingers. I knew he was out there somewhere. I knew there was a possibility that I might run into him someday. In the beginning, I looked for him all the time. I looked around corners, in parking lots, in crowds—any crowd, in the grocery store, in my car, in the forest, behind every bush. I had to be on the alert, hypervigilant. It became a habit. It became a way of life. The police had let him get away, so I had to do the searching. Knowing his whereabouts was the only way I could be safe because I did not want to be surprised again. But I could never find him—until tonight.

P: (I experience the control that Marv speaks of and I decide to go on.) I think he can come out now.

M: He can come out. We want to do this in slow steps. (Marv gives instruction to the perpetrator.) First, he turns around. (T turns slowly, but not completely, around.) He's turned around now.

P: (I look at T.) He must have…seen me walking.

M: He must have seen you. Sometimes it works better if you tell him what to do. "I'm ready to see you."

P: (I take a breath. I speak to T.) I'm ready to see you now.

M: (To T.) Turn around. You tell him when to stop—just look at him (I look.)

I examine him with my eyes and with my heart. The mask over his face intensifies his anonymity. It creates a reality for me. It was a frightening moment eighteen years ago and I experience that now. Even though I can see through the mask and my eyes tell me that this is not the perpetrator that I had met on the street so many years ago, my body tells me differently. My inner experience is, without exception, exactly the same as all those years ago. In fact, it is even more intensified. This night, as I tell the story, I am more present than I could have been during the first experience. It is a slow arduous process of working through my body's memory, moment to moment, as I take each step along the way. Now, he has come out of the lane. He will put on a pair of black gloves. I try to believe that I have some control, but my inner being is in chaos and I struggle with every moment to remain present.

M: Don't tell him to start until you are ready. It's your move.

P: OK. (I cannot stand the tension. I just want to have it over with. I speak to T.) Go!

M: He will only come as far as the circle (The perpetrator puts on gloves slowly, very slowly. I am frozen, watching in fear.) Then he will stop. Then we have to…

P: (*I am breaking apart—I gasp for breath. The terror overwhelms me*) NO!

M: It is the gloves, isn't it? These are the gloves that hurt you, right? You saw the figure before, now you see the gloves. It took you back there, didn't it?

P: (*After a moment, I look up. It is a long-standing trigger in my life.*) Every time people put gloves on...no matter who they are...I see that. (*I feel the frustration I have experienced, all these years, trying to rid myself of this sight.*)

M: You know we have to watch this. You know what's happening as you control this. Who's maintaining the control here?

P: (*I believe I had some control for the first time. However, it was not control over the perpetrator, but it was control over myself. I am able to breathe a little better.*) I am...I have it.

M: Yes, that's right. You could even say, "I know you're putting on gloves. I see you."

P: I know what you're doing (*I sense this different feeling in me—an emerging anger.*)

M: And what you're doing is...

P: What you're doing is...putting those gloves on your hands.

M: Yes, and you don't want to get you hands bloodied or dirty, right?

P: Yes...he did it...so slowly. He wanted me to see that.

M: That's the attack. It feels like an attack right now. Doesn't it?

P: It does...already.

M: It does. It's like we already started. We are already there; it's started. But tonight, when he walks towards you, it's you who's going to move us towards him when you're ready. As a matter of fact, he is going to pass us the first time.

P: Yes he is. He's going to trick me.

M: He's going to...

P: Trick me! It's a surprise...

M: Oh, that is even more sinister isn't it?

P: Yes...it is...(*I can sense the anger rising; I can't let this out, I might kill him. It is very strong.*)

M: Evil—isn't he?

173

P: It is so…damn evil. (*I start to get very upset. I shout out to the witnesses.*) Can you see what he is doing to me! No one should…ever have had this…done to them.

It is an important moment as I address the witnesses. I call on them to be responsible, to parent their children with love, and to step in and raise their voices against oppression and abuse. At that moment, I believe that it is the community's response to this atrocity that may bring me resolution.[10] Their moral stance and acknowledgement of the violation may bring me a sense of order and justice. It brings me out of my sense of isolation into a place of acceptance and compassion. Within the context of acceptance, I am able to meet the perpetrator face to face.

M: He is very evil. He tricks you by passing you by. And then…

P: He comes…quickly…in front of my face. (*I am dissociated—caught in the rush and panic of the moment. I am talking quickly—moving into the scene—being hasty. I know what is going to happen. I want this moment. I am willing to die for healing.*)

M: (*Marv talks directly to T*) Come quickly in front of her face.

P: (*My body is moving of its own accord.*) I jump over here.

M: Over here onto the street.

P: Because…it scares me…onto the street. (*I am looking inwardly—dreaming, following myself.*) He comes quickly in front of me. He follows me exactly…exactly what I am doing he follows me…and he comes in front of me…and right close to me. (*I look up for the first time and I meet his eyes. I am transfixed. The inner evil has me now. I gasp—gasp—gasp—my breath is—gone. I am standing on the edge of the abyss.*) I…can't…breathe.

M: Breathe.

P: (*I am struggling to get the words out.*) I …can't …breathe…now.

M: I can't breathe.

P: I'm…absolutely…terrified. (*My panic is rising—I am almost hysterical.*)

M: OK, I'm holding you. I'm right here! (*Fraught with panic—struggling—attempting—grasping for breath*)

P: (*I scream*) I'M ABSOLUTELY TERRIFIED! (*gasp*) TERRIFIED! (*gasp*) I'M TERRIFIED! I CAN'T BREATHE! (*gasp*) I'm so

[10] This acknowledgement by the storyteller demonstrates knowledge reconstruction at the communal level. From a constructivist-narrative perspective, healing is an embodied, relational, and communal experience.

scared...I can't breathe...(*gasp*) I can't even take a breath...I have...NO... (*gasp*) LIFE...I have no...life...

M: I have no life.

P: I...have...(*gasp*) no life...I have...no . . .

M: No...

P: ...Breath...

M: No breath. (*Time stands still. I feel like I am dying—strangled with my own terror. Marv steps between the perpetrator and me. I am saved!*) Your breath is coming—now it's coming . . .

P: (*Whispering with a small captured breath—surprised and relieved.*) Oh, it feels good to say that.

M: Say it again. I have no...

P: (*Struggling to breath my words are strained, weak.*) Life... it is my breath...it has been...stolen.

M: It has been stolen. I haven't been alive since that night. (*I am struggling to get myself under control again.*) What are you doing now?

P: (*I am fighting to find words—to speak*) I'm trying to breath...he asked me a question. (*I am in the trauma. I am in the story.*)

M: A question. And when you are ready to hear the question—then you answer it don't you?

P: Hmm...

The most difficult moment has passed. I looked at him face-on. I experienced the terror of the original moment, as if it had just happened. From there, I was able to look at him again and again, each time gaining control of myself more and more quickly. Through re-enacting, I was able to reconstruct the story in minor detail, looking at each second and filling in the gaps of my experience. I articulated the moment of terror, the sensation of feeling frozen, and the injustice that was done. In the process, I recognized the genius of my body's response and how it was meant to save me. I was able to name the evil and experience having a voice in the moment of my greatest fear. I recognized that this perpetrator was disconnected to me, my essence, my Self. I came closer to safety with the guidance of the director/therapist and my own control of re-storying the past. At one point, the director drew my attention to the Medusa mask that was behind the perpetrator.

M: When you looked at him this time, did you see the mask behind him?

P: No...(*I was so captured in the eyes of the perpetrator, I could see nothing else.*)

M: It was there—the mask. Do you want him to step aside and let the mask be there for a second?

P: Yes...I think so. (*A brilliant idea. I needed her to speak to me—something was there in that mask for me. Knowing that she would be visible brought me back to myself.*)

M: When you lift up your eyes the Medusa mask will be there. You created this mask to help you, right? You need to speak to the mask. (*The perpetrator and the Medusa trade places in front of me.*) The mask should be right here where he was. So, when you open your eyes you will see her. When you're ready—you can look up. The mask will be there. (*I looked up. She is familiar but this time she has eyes and moves in front of me. I am enchanted. It was as if I had not seen her before.*) What do you see?[11]

P: (*A different aspect is visible to me.*) She is female power...

M: Female power and—

P: She's what's going to help me live...(*I am watching carefully—waiting for the message that I need to hear.*)

M: Would you like to hold that mask—touch it for a second? You could put it in your hands—then give it back because this guy is going to reappear again and she could help you.

P: No...(*This doesn't seem the right thing to do. I am waiting, looking—I know it will come to me. I watch; she's speaking but I cannot hear her.*)

M: You're feeling her power and need her to be what?

P: In me...(*I hesitate—is that right? In me? What needs to be in me?*)

M: In me—and if I can have her in me then what?

P: (*What do I need to hear Medusa? What do you need to tell me?*) She can give me (*Yes—I know now!*)...her head.

M: She can give you her head because then you would be able to—

P: I would be able to have...that strength...on me. (*Yes—not in me but on me—on my body!*)

M: On you—rather than inside of you. (*Marv hesitates and then decides to change the alignment back. He speaks to Medusa.*) OK, will you

---

[11] The director is resourcing the protagonist by using her own hand-made mask as a tool to restory the trauma story.

switch back now? (*Medusa does not move. We are engaged, communicating something. Wait . . . I am watching. Wait! Wait! There's something I am forgetting! Marv speaks to me.*) You are still looking—closely.

P: (*Yes! I hear her—her silent voice shouts clearly to me! It is her head—her copper head that I need on me! I can hardly force the words out of my mouth.*) I want . . . the aegis . . . I want the aegis now (*Medusa hands me the aegis—her head made of engraved copper. It was a pivotal moment.*)

M: Oh, you want that.

P: Yes.

Oh! The ecstasy! Medusa is in my hands! I close my eyes and put her to my lips. I feel her as a vehicle of communication, a means to accommodate an understanding that I could not receive in any other way. A symbol that is translucent in my mind—the light of her genius shining through. She moves me through the veil from the Netherworld. I feel it materialize behind me, now close to my stepping back in—I am reborn. I stand in a new world. I hold her there for a few moments. I have to steady myself. This feeling of separation between myself and the world is new and untried. I sense a skin, a shield, an armor! I am safe at last!

Joseph Campbell asks: What is the hero's ultimate and most difficult task?

How render back into light-world language the speech-defying pronouncements of the dark? How represent on a two-dimensional surface a three-dimensional meaning? How translate into terms of "yes" and "no" revelations that shatter into meaninglessness every attempt to define the pairs of opposites? How communicate to people who insist on the exclusive evidence of their senses—the message of the all-generating void? (Campbell, 1949/1973, p. 218)

How does one explain the moment of change?

M: When your assailant looks at you again what is going to happen? (*He trusted me now; he recognized that I would know what to do.*)

P: (*I answer as if I had thought it all through, but I had not. I was just listening to some silent voice inside of me repeating in words what Medusa was saying in silence.*) I will turn the copper aegis . . . like this. (*I take the aegis and turn it so that Medusa's face is looking at the perpetrator.*) That's what I am going to do . . . yes . . . yes.

M: Shall we try it?

P: (*I am in a state of rapture! It is divine. I can breath again.*) Yes . . . yes.

M: So you hold that. (*With my eyes still closed, I put the aegis to my chest. I am crying; it is such a relief.*) This feels pretty good doesn't it?

P: Feels good. (*It is hard to leave the feeling to speak.*)

177

M: You are drinking it in. (*I hold the aegis for a few moments—then open my eyes. The feelings of separation and safety are firmly within me now. It is like a miracle took place; fear is far way.*)

With the copper representation of Medusa's head (aegis) in my hands, I had a weapon that I never knew existed before this moment. I took the aegis and turned it around so Medusa's face was looking at the perpetrator. I noticed a reflected light from the ceiling lamp shining on his jacket. I moved the aegis until the reflected light shone from her face onto his. It was like the moon reflecting the light of the sun; shining brightly in the dark night. His face was now full of light.

P: (To T.) Now…you can see yourself…in me. (*I felt completely separate from him—totally detached. My voice feels strong and firm.*)

M: (*Marv observes the light as it shines in the perpetrators face.*) Hmmm—yes. Great! How do you feel now? You don't seem to be slipping.

P: I feel good…I feel really good!

M: I know! I feel good because there's light in his eyes—it's blinding him, isn't it? Are you sure you want to do this?

P: Yes, I do! (*Everyone laughs. His eyes are no longer the eyes of a psychopath—the dark evil is gone. I hold the light there and I look at his enlightened eyes for a few moments. I want to fuse this memory into my mind and into my heart.*)

M: Because as long as I can reflect this light…

P: As long as I can do that…I am safe…he is not able to absorb me…into his evil…it is reflected back…I have Medusa with me now…I'm going to put her on me. (*Once again, I am following an inner impulse—there is no plan. It just seemed like the right thing to do. I attach the aegis onto my necklace. It sits almost exactly over my heart.*) And with this on… I will remember that it will help me.

M: It will help me with what I have to do now. I will be reflecting back the evil.

P: Yes.

M: You can attack me but you won't get…what?

P: You are not going to get into my heart.

The enactment continues. I face the perpetrator head on. I feel in total control of everything that is happening. Even though, I know that he will beat me and sexually assault me, I clearly recognize and experience safety.

M: And even though you can physically damage me—

P: You can't hurt…me…you can't hurt my baby…my spirit self…my power…you can't hurt that.

178

M: You can't.

P: You can't...you don't even know where to go to get it...you can't touch that.

M: You can't know.

P: You can't.

M: Before we go on, be aware of what you just did. Recall what you feel right now. Describe your body and your breathing.[12]

P: I'm tingling (*I feel really present for the first time. I can really feel my body and respond to Marv's question about it.*)

M: What have you just done?

P: I am putting up the shield...that I need...that I've needed all these years...I put up the shield tonight. (*It is a miracle!*)

M: You've put the shield up in the worst situation. The worst thing that you could possibly imagine is what we are looking at right now, isn't it? Amazing!

P: Yes...yes...that's so amazing...that is so amazing. (*We are overwhelmed with wonderment. We hold our amazement for a moment, basking in its radiance. There is magic in the air.*)

M: (*He looks over to the perpetrator.*) What do you think of the power of his look now?

P: You can harm me outwardly...but you can't hurt me and my baby now. You may overpower my body...but I am here...and I am going to protect my baby. I'm clear, I'm really clear...so you can go ahead and do whatever you want.

M: I'm safe.

P: I'm safe...my baby is safe. (*I close my eyes, gently touching the copper aegis; I am overcome by this deep, true feeling of safety.*)

M: Yes! Oh God, Patrice, we've come this far.

P: Because I am...I really am safe. (*He is overcome with the miracle of what we have done; tears come into his eyes.*)

M: Say again what has changed. What's changed now?[13]

---

[12] The director is asking the protagonist to reflect on the experience in order to recognize the change in her body.

[13] The facilitator anchors the experience of change by drawing the storyteller's attention to the new reconstituted self, and embodied self. The trauma-focused self is now an integrated present-centred self—a transformative experience has taken place.

P: You can't harm me...you can't touch my spirit...my soul...nor my baby's soul. You can't get to who I am...who I really am is absolutely safe...completely safe...

M: My body's not safe, it can be broken.

P: It's my body...my temple...but it's not me.

M: It's my temple—my arms, my legs, but it's not me. What about his power over you?

P: It's gone. It really is...it's really gone. He doesn't get either of us.

Ready and sure of my inner safety for the first time in eighteen years, we re-enact the beating and sexual assault in slow motion. The feeling of protection never leaves me. I know myself to be more than a body and have no fear of possible death. During most of the actual assault, I was unconscious because of the severity of the injuries. This night, I felt totally free of the trauma and the perpetrator. The relief was indescribable. At the end of the enactment, Marv invited me to sit among the witnesses, so that they might have a chance to talk about their experience of being with me through this re-enacted story. As I sat down, it began to rain. A witness spoke, "One of the things that are interesting is that generally, quite often after ceremonies like this—like a Sundance—it rains. The rain takes all the horror and washes it away—all the disease and the evil are gone. It's just like you said when it started to rain, in the spiritual path that I follow, the fact that it rained is very significant. So the evil is washed away; you are purged and clean. The earth has taken it away for you."

CONCLUSION

In this chapter, our aim was to illustrate a narrative-constructivist approach to trauma repair using therapeutic enactment, a group-based trauma intervention. Having been involved in many therapeutic enactments as co-facilitators and witnesses, we have come to understand the complexity underlying this narrative-constructivist intervention. Therapeutic enactment addresses trauma from multiple vantage points. First, therapeutic enactment provides the survivor an opportunity to reconstruct the trauma story in a safe environment. The skill of the director to resource the storyteller, to move slowly through the enactment, checking the storyteller's physical, emotional and cognitive experiences is essential to the storyteller's sense of safety and control over the traumatic event. By restorying the traumatic event with the guide of a skilled facilitator, the storyteller can gain mastery over the trauma story. In essence, the storyteller restories the previously traumatized self and in doing so, reconstitutes a "post-trauma" self.

Second, the restorying also involves a re-experiencing of the somatic memory. However, in this scenario the storyteller has control over the trauma experience, an experience that was not possible during the original traumatic event. This is a crucial aspect to therapeutic enactment. The somatic memory must be experienced in the present in order to unfreeze the body from the terror of the past and restory the body into the present by physically moving the body through the trauma. The director must ensure that the resources that the storyteller has brought to the enactment be brought into play in a metaphorically significant way. The pacing is very important so as not to overwhelm the storyteller. The director is always checking to make sure that the resources, physical, emotional, and social are holding. Often, the director will have the storyteller focus on the witness group to bring awareness back into the here-and-now. It is important that the storyteller has direct access to somatic memory, making sense of the body's sensations and behaviors within the context of the moment of terror. Restorying the experience gives words to the unspeakable, fills in the cognitive gaps and names the experience. In doing so, the storyteller reconstitutes new beliefs and a new sense of self emerges.

Finally, therapeutic enactment is a collective story. At the end of the enactment, every one has the opportunity to speak into the circle or directly to the storyteller. First the individuals who played a part in the enactment derole and speak about their experience of taking on their part in the enactment. Then the witnesses in the outer circle speak about their experience as witness. Often this communal acknowledgement is experienced as a sense of integration for the storyteller. There is now a collective story being told—a story to which we all connect. This is a significant part of the healing process.

We believe that therapeutic enactment, as a narrative-constructivist practice, has the potential to transform trauma and in doing so, offers our clients a new story, a new sense of self in their meaning-making efforts.

REFERENCES

Arvay, M. J. (2002). Talk as action: A narrative approach to action theory. *Canadian Journal of Counselling, 36*(2), 113-120.

Campbell, J. (1949/1973). *The hero with a thousand faces.* Princeton, NJ: Princeton University.

Keats, P. (2000). *Using masks for trauma recovery: A self-narrative.* Unpublished masters thesis. University of British Columbia, Vancouver, BC, Canada.

Keats, P. A. (in press). Constructing masks of the self in therapy. *Constructivism in the Human Sciences, 8*(1).

Neimeyer, R. A. (2000). Narrative disruptions in the construction of the self. In R. A. Neimeyer & J. D. Raskin (Eds.), *Constructions of disorder: Meaning-making frameworks for psychotherapy* (pp. 207-242). Washington, DC: American Psychological Association.

Neimeyer, R. A. (Ed.). (2001). *Meaning reconstruction and the experience of loss.* Washington, DC: American Psychological Association.

Neimeyer, R. A., & Arvay, M. J. (in press). Performing the self. In H. J. M. Hermans & G. Dimaggio (Eds.), *The dialogical self in psychology.* East Sussex, UK: Brunner-Routledge Publishers.

Pennebaker, J. (1997). *Opening up.* New York: Guilford.

Sewell, K. W., Baldwin, C. L., & Williams, A. M. (1998). Multiple Self Awareness Group: Format and application to a personal growth experience. *Journal of Constructivist Psychology, 11*, 59-78.

Rothschild, B. (2000). *The body remembers: The psychophysiology of trauma and trauma treatment.* New York: W. W. Norton.

van der Kolk, B. (2002). *The assessment and treatment of complex PTSD.* Retrieved May 14, 2003, from www.traumacenter.og/van_der_Kolk_complex_PTSD.pdf

Westwood, M. J., Black, T. G., & McLean, H. B. (2002). A re-entry program for peacekeeping soldiers: Promoting personal and career transition. *Canadian Journal of Counselling, 36*, 221-232.

Westwood, M., Keats, P., & Wilensky, P. (in press). Therapeutic enactment: Integrating individual and group counselling models for change. *Journal for Specialists in Group Work.*

White, M., & Epston, D. (1990). *Narrative means to therapeutic ends.* New York: W. W. Norton.

PART III

THE PERSONAL AND SOCIAL IN RESEARCH

CHAPTER 9

The Zen of Social Phobia: A Context-Centered Group Treatment[1]

Jay S. Efran and Sanjay R. Nath

In 1997, a group of us at Temple University formed a research team to develop and evaluate a context-centered group treatment for social phobia. The approach was to be based on contextualist and constructivist principles (Efran, Lukens, and Lukens, 1990). Although many family and systems-oriented clinicians were already embracing such ideas, individual and group psychotherapists were less prone to incorporate them into their practices. Therefore, it seemed useful to show that these methods were applicable to common clinical problems such as social phobia. Moreover, because research trials on contextualist therapies had been limited, we were interested in gathering formal data on the effectiveness of a context-centered method.

The project convinced us that context-centered treatment is indeed a viable approach—at least as effective as many traditional methods and potentially more efficient for the treatment of social phobia. In this chapter, we first outline the theory on which this form of context-centered treatment is based. Then, we describe the contractual elements, didactic materials, and semi-structured exercises that constitute the major components of our group method.

THE THEORY OF CONTEXT-CENTERED PSYCHOTHERAPY

All psychotherapies focus on one or more of three levels of analysis—content, process, or context. At the content level, counselors and therapists typically offer clients practical advice or provide them with objective information. For example, a person suffering

[1] Originally presented at the Tenth Biennial Conference of the North American Personal Construct Network, Vancouver, BC, July 2002.

from insomnia might be instructed to drink a glass of warm milk before going to bed, to get more physical exercise, or to list troubling thoughts on a piece of paper before attempting to fall asleep. In part, the content domain on which a therapist concentrates depends on his or her theoretical allegiance. For example, a psychodynamic therapist is likely to explore the details of a patient's childhood history, whereas a cognitive-behavioral therapist is more apt to concentrate on the client's current array of maladaptive thoughts.

By contrast, therapists working at the process level usually focus on interpersonal or relationship factors. For instance, in our insomnia example, the process-oriented therapist might work to resolve the marital tensions that lead to sleepless nights rather than on providing specific suggestions for falling asleep. Because process concerns are at a level higher than content issues, relationship-focused approaches are potentially more efficient than content-centered methods. For example, concentrating on a couple's relationship issues might be expected to ameliorate a range of symptoms rather than just reducing sleeplessness.

The change in emphasis from content to process characterized the relationship therapies of the 1960s, including Rogers' client-centered counseling and Fritz Perls' Gestalt approach. Client-centered therapists were specifically trained to avoid giving direct advice, dispensing objective information, or making value judgments. Instead, they worked to establish a therapeutic milieu that emphasized unconditional positive regard. Rogerian theory held that the client's problems would be transformed as a function of this special, nonjudgmental relationship.

A decade later, with the emergence of family, marital, and systems approaches, therapists increased their attention to recurrent family patterns, such as husbands who repeatedly sided with their children instead of their spouses, or wives who seemed excessively protective of a particular son or daughter. From a family systems perspective, straightening out family boundaries was considered more critical than refereeing particular conflicts, such as who should take out the garbage or do the dishes.

In the last twenty-five years, cognitive-behavioral therapists also redirected their attention from content to process, concentrating more on generalized schemas rather than specific thoughts (e.g., Layden, Newman, Freeman, & Morse, 1993). Similarly, psychodynamic therapists expanded their concerns from the initial narrow focus on transference to a more inclusive investigation of the here-and-now relationship (Meissner, 2002; Shapiro, 2002).

The third level of analysis—context—represents the most recent theoretical development. Just as process determines content, context—still another rung up the ladder of abstraction—determines process. Context refers to the envelope or framework within which processes occur and from which content derives. By establishing the boundaries of an event, contexts circumscribe meanings and shape perceptions. Getting married is an example of a context shift. Marriage tends to alter the interpretation of every event in the person's life—past, present, and future. By establishing new templates for experience, marriage modifies virtually everything the person says, does, and is.

When people marry, even though various aspects of their lives may appear outwardly similar, there are subtle and profound changes in the meaning of events. For example, after getting married a husband may look forward to an occasional "night out with the boys." Prior to marriage, he may have gotten together with those same individuals. However, now that he has tied the knot, their time together takes on added significance, perhaps providing a welcome respite from the duties of the marital state.

It should be noted that unlike process events, shifts in context occur instantaneously. In other words, the moment an individual says "I do," the context of marriage is invoked/created and its ramifications begin to take hold. Similarly, parenthood is a transformative context that begins with the birth of a child and automatically turns the two adults into parents.

Paradoxically, shifts in context both create new opportunities and foreclose others. For instance, when a couple has a child, they acquire new roles in the larger family. At the same time, they are prohibited from spending a romantic evening alone unless they first call a babysitter. Although a couple can plan their wedding day or shop for baby furniture, the full implications of context shifts such as marriage and parenthood can rarely be anticipated. Moreover, such shifts are binary events—just as you cannot be partially pregnant, you cannot be partially married or partially a parent. The all-or-nothing (digital) nature of contextual change contrasts sharply with the time-dependent and gradual (analogic) nature of process changes.

Therapists should note that problems and symptoms can appear and disappear as contexts shift. For instance, when couples decide to marry, some of their relationship issues may simply evap-

187

orate. Alternatively, marriage can usher in a whole new set of difficulties that were not foreseen during courtship. Because problems are embedded in contexts, the job of the context-centered therapist is to help clients identify and move beyond problem-saturated contexts. From our perspective, working at the level of context is more powerful than working at either of the two lower levels—process or content. In other words, working from the top down is usually preferable to working from the bottom up. As epistemologists Humberto Maturana and Francesco Varela point out, effective solutions to problems generally require "changing the nature of the question, to embrace a broader context" (1987, p. 135).

Our particular version of context-centered psychotherapy has roots in Gregory Bateson's (1979) writings on cybernetics and systems thinking, Paul Watzlawick's explorations of second-order change (e.g., Watzlawick, Bevin, & Jackson, 1969; Watzlawick, Weakland, & Fisch, 1974), and Humberto Maturana's theory of structure determinism (e.g., Maturana & Varela, 1987). In addition, as an acceptance-based treatment, it draws heavily upon Eastern philosophy, including Zen, Taoist, and Buddhist teachings (see, e.g., Gregson & Efran, 2001).

Acceptance-based approaches emphasize the virtue of being true to oneself rather than struggling to be someone else. Paradoxically, surrendering fully to one's basic nature can be the fastest route to change. We have noticed that many of the roadblocks that socially phobic individuals experience derive, not from their shyness but from their frantic attempts to become more outgoing. Therefore, in our groups, we continually highlight the virtues of "riding the horse in the direction it is going."

Acceptance-based approaches are an alternative to the deficiency orientation that characterizes much of psychiatry (Goldiamond, 1972). Deficiency approaches are usually pathologizing—they focus on weaknesses and abnormalities. It is assumed, for example, that socially phobic individuals lack basic social skills. Yet, in our experience, these individuals already possess the skills they need, although they do not always make optimal use of them. For example, they may be appropriately assertive with their children, but more passive with a job supervisor. Unfortunately, therapies based on a deficiency orientation can intensify the feelings of inadequacy and shame that shy individuals already have. These well-intended treatment strategies can inadvertently reinforce the very context from which such introverted individuals need to escape.

Before discussing the details of our acceptance-based method, we will take a few moments to review social phobia as a psychiatric disorder and will list some of the other treatments that have been proposed.

SOCIAL PHOBIA AND PAST APPROACHES

Epidemiological studies report that 73 percent of the population has been troubled by social inhibition at some point in their lives. The group treatment program we designed focuses on the most severe 3 to 13 percent of this group—those diagnosable as socially phobic (American Psychiatric Association, 2000, [DSM IV-TR]). Socially phobic individuals are often unable to socialize successfully, date, make friends, marry, or hold jobs that require public speaking or sustained social interchange. Also called social anxiety, social phobia was added to psychiatry's official diagnostic compendium in 1980. Some socially phobia individuals fear a wide variety of social circumstances. Others may have problems only in particular situations, such as those that involve public speaking, attending parties, or dealing with authority figures.

Most cases of social phobia develop through a complex interaction of biological temperament and environmental factors. Harvard developmental psychologist Jerome Kagan reports that about 20 percent of infants have a reactive temperament that results in their becoming easily and repeatedly aroused and distressed (Kagan, Snidman, Arcus, & Reznick, 1994). Despite the fact that most of them were raised by loving parents, many of these infants become fearful, cautious children, and a substantial subset of that group grow up to be socially phobic adults. In fact, most of the members of our workshops appear to have that kind of background—they report having been socially reticent their entire lives, beginning in early childhood. The heritability of the inhibited temperament that is at the root of social phobia is moderate to high—it is estimated to be about 40 percent on the basis of recent twin and adoption studies (e.g., Kagan et al., 1994).

Existing approaches for treating social phobia include behavioral, cognitive-behavioral, and pharmacological methods. Three methods appear on the American Psychological Association Division 12 Task Force list of "probably efficacious" empirically supported treatments (APA Division 12 Task Force, 1995, p. 9). These include (a) cognitive behavioral therapy (Heimberg et al., 1990), (b) exposure treatments (Feske & Chambless, 1995), and (c) systematic

189

desensitization (Paul, 1967; Paul & Shannon, 1966; Woy & Efran, 1972). Most investigators have studied group formats, but individual approaches have also been used. The popular methods incorporate techniques such as role-playing, cognitive restructuring, simulated or in vivo exposure, homework assignments, relaxation training, and rational self-talk. Treatments may also include assertiveness and social skills training modules (e.g., Turner & Beidel, 1994). In the research studies, treatment length varies from 6 to 16 sessions, with an average length of 8.55 meetings (Feske & Chambless, 1995).

As we indicated earlier, a common feature of these methods is the belief that phobic individuals lack crucial skills or are plagued by maladaptive cognitions. Often, such deficits are simply assumed to exist and, as we have indicated, this wholesale assumption has the disadvantage of reinforcing pre-existing self-critical tendencies. Shy individuals have been told repeatedly that to succeed in life they must conquer their fears and become more assertive. Because they have difficulty following such advice, they come to think of themselves as weak-willed and cowardly.

When socially phobic individuals seek professional help, the message they hear often replicates the "just do it" suggestions they heard at home. The research evidence suggests that being urged to be more outgoing can indeed result in increased social activity, at least temporarily. However, many who have been exposed to such treatments complain that they continue to feel uncomfortable in social situations. They feel as if their new-found assertiveness is a false front that may cease to fool people at any moment. By contrast, our context-centered approach stresses being oneself. We demonstrate to clients that they can be successful without mastering an entirely new social vocabulary. In our groups, we remind participants that the world has room for both Woody Allen and Robin Williams.

TREATMENT PROTOCOL

We have used two meeting formats: (a) two seven-hour sessions held on successive Saturdays, or (b) four three-and-a-half-hour evenings spaced over a two-week period. In an early phase of the project, we experimented with a more traditional series of weekly hour-and-a-half group meetings. However, we found that weekly sessions were too short and too widely spaced to generate the necessary momentum. Furthermore, because of occasional absences, we felt obliged to spend part of each session reviewing the previous week's accomplishments. Often, by the time the group the group was up to speed, it was time to adjourn.

The two marathon formats allow for high levels of involvement and still give participants an opportunity between sessions to think about what has transpired and to test new perspectives in the "real world." The four-evening format was developed to accommodate participants who were unavailable on weekends. We found it best to schedule such meetings, two per week, on either Monday and Wednesday evenings or Tuesday and Thursday evenings. In our experience, the weekend and weeknight formats operate similarly. Therefore, in describing the protocol, we will present only the four-night version (sessions 1-4).

Because we were working with socially phobic individuals, we found it essential to meet individually with every participant prior to the first group meeting. Before we instituted these pre-group sessions, we found that our "no show" rate for the first group session was unacceptably high. Shy individuals, it turns out, routinely get cold feet just before participating in a group—especially if they have to travel to an unfamiliar site and have not already formed a relationship with a member of the staff. Thus, in addition to providing an opportunity for screening and orientation, the pre-meetings helped insure that participants would actually arrive the night of the group.

Participants were solicited through advertisements in community newspapers. The ads described a workshop for individuals who were shy or who had difficulty "speaking up, socializing, or presenting to groups." We labeled the program a "workshop" rather than psychotherapy to decrease any stigma associated with seeking treatment and to emphasize that these were time-limited, semi-structured experiences rather than process groups. The ad stated that there would be a one-time charge of $50.00 for the two weekend (or four weeknight) sessions. This low fee was made possible by a grant-in-aid from Temple University. We wanted the workshop to be affordable even for participants with few financial resources. Unlike in some research projects, there were no exclusion criteria except age—everyone over 18 who answered the ad was considered eligible to participate.

The workshop consists of three intertwined components: (a) the presentation and discussion of basic principles, (b) the use of demonstrations and exercises to bring those principles to life, and (c) the provision of opportunities for participants to raise questions, share reactions, and report experiences. Some exercises have been invented specifically for the workshop. Others have been adapted from human relations exercises, large-scale awareness training techniques, and Zen meditation methods (see, e.g., Erhard & Gioscia, 1977; Pfeiffer & Jones, 1970-1971; Rhinehart, 1976). An overarching principle of the workshop is the Zen principle that "whatever you resist, persists." In other words, most attempts to avoid awkwardness and social anxiety backfire and lead to more discomfort rather than less.

THE FIRST SESSION

When the group convenes for the first time, the leader and co-therapist introduce themselves and invite participants to do the same. In our experience, the opening moments of these groups are extraordinarily awkward. Usually, group members say nothing to one another. They fidget in their seats, look at the floor, and avoid eye contact. The tension in the room becomes almost unbearable. When the leader says "hello," the group reacts with silence. The atmosphere is so punitive that even the leaders wish they could be somewhere else. According to their subsequent reports, participants may feel so nervous that they wonder if they will be able to pronounce their names. One group member—having just arrived—whispered an apology to the co-therapist, indicating that he would have to leave soon; he suddenly realized he had something important to do at home!

The Contract

After initial introductions, the leaders provide a brief history of the project—its purposes, rationale, and methods. Providing this background information gives participants a sense of what is ahead, and it also helps take the "heat" off the group members—they can simply sit back and listen. Next, the co-therapists hand out copies of the workshop contract (Appendix A). It states that participants are never required to say or do anything in the group. If they like, they can remain silent throughout the entire process. Moreover, they can simply say "pass" any time they wish to decline participating in a task or discussion. However, signing the contract indicates that they will attend each of the scheduled sessions and are willing to remain in the room and pay attention to the proceedings, except during breaks. The actual signing of contracts takes place while the group takes a break, so that anyone wishing to leave can do so unobtrusively, without having to explain or justify the decision. Of course, people who choose to leave at this point will have their fee refunded. We suggest that anyone who leaves complete a brief "non-participation form" on the way out, but even this step is entirely optional.

We regard the signing of the contract as an important aspect of the workshop design. By making it easy for people to leave, we know that those who stay are making an informed choice to participate in the workshop. An additional clause of the contract warns participants to expect moments of doubt, confusion, boredom, discomfort, and so on. Furthermore, we emphasize that participants are apt to disagree with some of the material presented. We remind them that confusion and disagreement can be positive developments—an indication that longstanding beliefs are being challenged. As they say in the East, "Confusion is a very high state of mind."

When we began this work we fully anticipated having a substantial number of dropouts. Yet, in the entire history of the project, no one has declined to participate. Every individual who came to a first session signed the contract and completed the workshop.[2] We credit this lack of attrition to the clarity of the contractual negotiation. Elements of choice are so clearly built into the workshop design that there is little motivation to flee.

Prior to the contract-signing, the leaders briefly explain the workshop philosophy and provide a sampling of the kinds of exercises to expect. First, we state our belief that inhibition and hypersensitivity have strong inherited components. Just as some individuals are extraverted and gregarious, others happen to fall at the introverted end of the temperament continuum. Our emphasis on behavior genetics is new to most participants. Those who have previously seen mental health professionals have usually been encouraged to seek environmental explanations of their difficulties. They have searched their backgrounds for evidence of traumatic childhood incidents or blamed their problems on unsympathetic teachers, cruel peers, bullying siblings, or harsh parents. In contrast, we argue that social reticence is a legitimate personality configuration for which no one is necessarily "to blame."

To augment this point, the senior author—who was shy as a child—mentions some of the misguided beliefs he harbored while growing up. His story usually brings nods of recognition from group

---

[2] Two individuals missed a single session each—one was very ill with stomach flu and the second had to respond to a last-minute work-schedule change. Both individuals telephoned and were able to rejoin the group for the remaining meetings.

members, who are relieved to discover that one of the group leaders has had first-hand experience with problems similar to their own. Since he obviously survived such experiences and has gone on to lead groups, they are intrigued to find out what he has learned about social phobia over the years. As part of this general introduction, the leaders reiterate that the workshop emphasizes a shift in perspective, not the learning of new skills. It is sufficiency-based, not deficiency-oriented.

At this point we introduce the two sample exercises. The first involves several popular expressions that have been written on the blackboard before the group arrived. The sayings we use are "Paris in the Spring," "Pop Goes the Weasel," and "Peas in a Pod." Each phrase is enclosed in a triangle and contains an extra word (see Figure 1). The members of the group are instructed to read the phrases to

FIGURE 1. BLACKBOARD ILLUSIONS

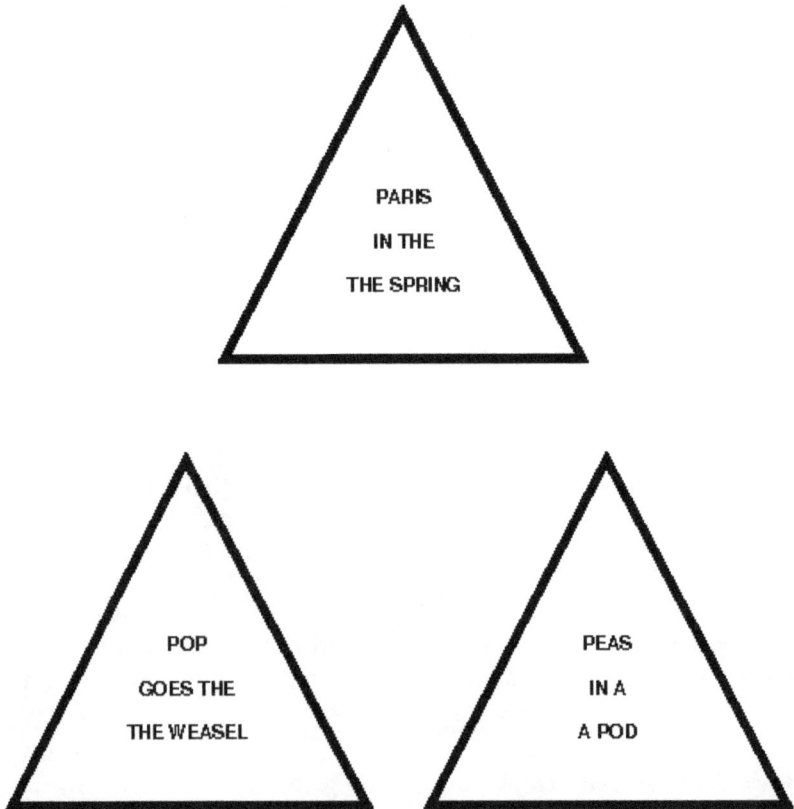

themselves and to raise their hands if they believe that the writing on the board says "Paris in the Spring," "Pop Goes the Weasel," and "Peas in a Pod." Except for those who have seen this demonstration before, everyone raises his or her hand. We then announce that they have not read the expressions correctly. Even with this warning, most participants continue to miss the redundant word. Eventually, by having someone read the phrases aloud, word-by-word, the deception is revealed. Group members are astonished that they could have repeatedly missed seeing a word that was printed in such large letters.

This exercise serves a dual purpose. Because it has nothing directly to do with personal problems or shyness, it lightens the atmosphere. At the same time, it underscores the power of contexts to shape even rudimentary perceptions. It demonstrates that people continually filter reality through their own expectations, and usually without knowing it. Until the filter is brought to their attention, they firmly believe that they are seeing the world rightly. The exercise is a good example of novelist Anaïs Nin's point that "we don't see things as they are, we see them as we are" (Anaïs Nin Quotations, n. d.).

The leaders can now draw an analogy between this demonstration and the goals of the workshop—in both cases, the intent is to challenge suppositions that are ordinarily invisible. With this exercise as the backdrop, the leaders now move into the second pre-contract task. Each group member is asked to say a few words about his or her personal goals for the workshop. Most members are willing to contribute to this discussion, having been primed for the topic during the pre-group interviews. Furthermore, they are relieved to discover commonalities between their experience and the experiences of others. Thus, a group that began in utter silence now finds itself engaged in conversation and showing the initial signs of group cohesion (Yalom, 1975). At this point, we take a break, during which participants can sign their contracts or choose to leave. Those who return from the break—and, as we have said, this has thus far included everyone—are ready to begin.

Conversations with Self

After the break, the co-leaders introduce several brief, conceptually connected exercises. The first calls attention to the internal running dialogue that dominates our lives. We arrange for a few minutes of silence, during which group members are invited to listen to their self-conversation (for a written description of an exercise of this sort, see Gregson & Efran, 2001, p. 28-30). After the silence, group members are asked to share their experiences. Frankly, some participants are confused. They couldn't identify any self-conversation. From their perspective, they were just sitting quietly, waiting for the group to resume. However, it is an easy matter for the leaders to point out that while these individuals were ostensibly doing nothing, they were actually having a succession of thoughts such as "I'm not talking to myself—I'm just waiting," or "I don't know what kind of dialogue these leaders are talking about." Of course, this is exactly the kind of internal commentary being highlighted. Even when apparently listening to others, people talk to themselves. Like ventriloquists, they silently repeat what others say, adding their own evaluations and judgments: "I suppose she's right." "This is boring." "How is this going to help me?" "He's kinda cute." It would not be farfetched to argue that our lives consist largely of this ongoing conversation with self.

Unlike cognitive therapists, we are not suggesting that group members change what they say to themselves. In fact, we do not believe they are capable of directly making such changes. The current exercise is aimed only at allowing individuals to notice the ubiquity of their internal commentary. This insight is augmented by the next exercise, in which participants are instructed to close their eyes (to avoid distractions) and focus their internal dialogue on the topics of shyness and social caution. What are their responses to questions such as the following: "What do you say to yourself about asking someone out?" "What do you tell yourself about going to a party?" "What do you say to yourself about expressing your opinions?" "What do you say to yourself about a scheduled meeting with the boss?" Whereas the first exercise was neutral with regard to content, the second zeroes in on issues related to social phobia. Predictably, participants find that their self-conversation in this domain is unremittingly negative.

This discovery usually prompts group members to ask how they might change or get rid of these negative self-perceptions. We suggest that getting rid of them is the wrong approach—it is the strategy that has been unsuccessful for them. Instead, we recommend the Eastern approach based on two Zen aphorisms: "Whatever you resist, persists," and "Whatever you let be, lets you be." Attempts to avoid negativity produce more negativity. Attempts to stay calm can produce more nervousness. On the ski slope, the fear of falling can make falling more probable. Trying to eliminate self-criticism can result in becoming self-critical about being self-critical. For the moment, we suggest simply noticing negative thoughts and allowing them to be. Perhaps, if you don't bother them, they won't bother you.

To illustrate the fluidity of self-conversation, we next ask group members to close their eyes and listen as we describe the location of their tongues in their mouths: We suggest that each person's tongue is quite large compared to the area (between the teeth) where it is forced to reside. There is simply not enough room in there for the tongue to rest comfortably without the danger of getting caught between the teeth on one side or the other. As we amplify this train of thought, group members find themselves becoming increasingly self-conscious about the position of their tongues—an anatomical arrangement that, under other circumstances, presents no problem. The more they think about it, the worse the situation becomes. It begins to seem as if protecting one's tongue is going to become a lifetime pursuit.

At that point, the leaders shift the conversation to people's feet, which are described as being confined "against their will" in a pair of hot, tight-fitting shoes. People's feet are pressed against the floor all day, forced to deal with the strain of supporting the body. As participants shift their attention to their feet, new "problems" arise and supplant those that concerned the tongue. By shifting the conversation to a succession of body parts, the leaders demonstrate how problems come and go as a person's internal conversation ebbs and flows. Also, they show how getting stuck on a particular theme can turn a minor annoyance into a major preoccupation.

Eyes-Closed Exercise: Changing a Liquid

The next task is also an eyes-closed exercise. Group members are asked to visualize a succession of images, beginning with a glass or pitcher. They are then asked to imagine that their container is filled with a liquid. In a series of steps, participants are asked to change the color of the liquid and also to experiment with its opacity and viscosity. For instance, if they began with a clear fluid such as water they could then change it to something more opaque, such as milk. They can also try making thin fluids thicker and vice versa. In the last section of the exercise, they are instructed to bring the liquid back to its original condition and, finally, to get rid of it by pouring half of it down the sink and "vanishing" the rest. After this imaginal adventure, group members open their eyes and compare notes about their experiences.

Because of the impersonal nature of the material, most members share their experiences freely and the leaders take the opportunity to point out some interesting commonalities in their reports. First, participants typically describe their imagery in the third person. For instance, they report that "the liquid changed from bright orange to a kind of muddy brown," or that "it started out as grape juice and than became automobile oil." The wording suggests that participants observe these images as they arise—they do not have full control over them. In fact, group members will explicitly say, "I wanted it to be orange juice, but it refused." "I don't know why it insisted on turning blue at that point." "I was expecting green, but not that shade." "It wouldn't go back to its original color." or "I could pour it down the sink but I had trouble making the rest disappear." Such statements accurately reflect how our thoughts drift in and out without permission. We like to believe that we think our thoughts, but—as Martin Heidegger and other philosophers have argued—it would more accurate to say that our thoughts think us. Tunes pop into our heads uninvited and frequently overstay their welcome. The solutions to problems arrive at the oddest moments. Unexpected, fearful images keep us awake at night and then may disappear as suddenly as they arrived. The "liquids" exercise helps group members understand how the mind operates and why direct attempts to control unwanted thoughts can be frustrating.

To bring the first meeting to a close, we give group members a between-session assignment: We ask them to notice—but not change—bits and pieces of their conversation with themselves.

THE SECOND SESSION

When the group reconvenes, participants often report that they experienced an increase in energy following the first session, although they are not sure why. Often, they are both intrigued and confused by the events that transpired at the first meeting. At the start of this session, we remind participants about the between-session task and open the floor for questions and reactions. Before we turn to the main agenda, we also provide a quick review of the previous session.

Mind and Self

The theme of the second session is the distinction between "mind" and "self." We use the definitions of these terms provided by psychiatrist Ron Smothermon (1979). In his model, "mind" stands for the person's vast array of defense mechanisms and survival maneuvers. By contrast, the term "self" signifies the person's sense of connection to the larger universe. The operations of the mind are egoistic and fear-driven; the perspective of the self is loving and holistic.

The mind's single agenda is to win, dominate, and be right. When those goals cannot be met, it shifts to its secondary priorities—to avoid losing, resist being dominated, and circumvent being made wrong. From the perspective of the mind, withdrawing from a task altogether is often preferable to risking failure; reporting in sick is a better alternative than looking foolish. The framework of mind epitomizes our concern with personal and psychological safety. In its relentless preoccupation with survival, it is willing to sacrifice participation, satisfaction, communication, and growth. Being broader in scope, the self includes the mind (as a subset of concerns), but the reverse is not true. In other words, for the self, survival issues make up only a small part of the package—for the mind, they are the whole show.

As the leaders discuss mind vs. self, group members immediately recognize how much of their existence has been dominated by survival fears. Their modus operandi has been to maintain a low profile and avoid risk. We recall one member who reported working the night shift at a local supermarket in order to avoid interacting with other employees. Each night, he would arrive after the store had officially closed, restock the shelves, and drive off before dawn. The job was not gratifying, but it was safe. Other members have recalled dropping courses or changing majors in order to avoid the possibility of giving a classroom presentation.

We illustrate the power of the mind by asking for a volunteer without explaining what that individual will be asked to do. This immediately raises the threat level in the room, and typically no one volunteers. The absence of a volunteer completes the experiential aspect of the exercise. The discussion that follows explores the mind's fear-driven and avoidant strategies, such as "Let someone else go first," or "If I look away, I won't get called on." Following this discussion, we again ask for a volunteer—implying that this time there will be an actual task to be done. Once more, the fear in the room rises and each individual's need for safety trumps his or her desire to participate. In some groups, we eventually do find a lone volunteer—usually someone who has decided to get the worst over with as quickly as possible. Again, there is no actual task. The leaders encourage a second discussion about the powerful grip of the mind, even in the face of rational argument about the minimal nature of the threat. From our perspective, noticing the power of the mind is the first step to undoing the pervasiveness of its influence.

Finding a Space

We now move to a lighter group experience called "Finding a Space." Participants are instructed to walk about the room, looking for a comfortable place to sit or stand. This task works best if participants do not preselect the spot on which they will settle and do not necessarily choose the first place they explore. Soon, everyone has found a suitable space and has a chance to examine the internal dialogue that guided—or at least accompanied—their search. Some realize that their main motive was to locate a spot far away from the others. Even in this simple exercise, some group members go to extremes of self-protection, hiding in a corner, crawling under a piece of furniture, or ducking out of sight of the leaders.

After locations have been found, the co-leaders introduce the next phase of the task: Several group members are designated to invite others to join them in the spot they selected. This creates a whole new set of mind concerns: Who will receive an invitation? Who will be left out? Do I have to leave my safe haven? How will it feel to be physically closer to another human being? Interestingly, despite the artificial nature of the task, it evokes the same concerns that dominate the rest of their lives. This is, after all, a group in which some members have never had a cup of coffee with a co-worker and may never have initiated a conversation with the person who works in the next cubicle. They typically eat alone and go to the movies by themselves. They may spend an inordinate amount of time rehearsing what they will say on the telephone before they pick up the receiver to dial.

In the final phase of the "Finding a Space" exercise, the co-leaders request that each "pod" of two individuals pay a visit to another pod. This process is repeated until the entire group re-coalesces into a single unit. Then they all return to their seats to process the reactions that have occurred. In the ensuing discussion, the leaders speculate about how the experience of "Finding a Space" might have been different for a person operating from self rather than coming from mind.

Conclusion of Second Session

The second session concludes with two tasks that are more demanding than anything that has come before. For the first, group members are asked to stand alone—silently—in front of the group. Being in the limelight for even a short period of time is agonizing for members of this population. Those willing to try the task find themselves fidgeting, apologizing for how they look, not knowing what to do with their hands, giggling, and so forth. Group members are encouraged to repeat the task a number of times in order to notice whether or not the mind eventually quiets down. As an analogy, we describe the strategy of horseback riders who learn to "sit through the trot" (which is uncomfortable) in order to help the horse shift into a canter (a more comfortable gait). Similarly, allowing the mind to have its say—while continuing with the assigned task—can be a useful strategy. We argue that sooner or later the mind's protests will have been exhausted and will recede into the background. In fact, as the person moves from the context of mind to the context of self, he or she may discover that standing in front of a group is no more difficult than being at home by oneself. As Stewart Emery (1977) notes in the title of his book: *You don't have to rehearse to be yourself.*

If time permits, the leaders introduce a second performance task—imitating a turtle. The suggested scenario is that a turtle is munching food, hears a frightening noise, retreats to the safety of his shell, waits for the coast to clear, and finally ventures forth again to continue eating. Of course, pantomiming a turtle requires no special acting skills and no special knowledge about the animal kingdom. Furthermore, the fact that turtles are silent makes imitating them easier. In most groups, participants spontaneously recognize and enjoy the metaphorical significance of our having picked a threatened turtle as the animal for them to imitate.

Like the "standing" exercise, imitating a turtle can be easy or difficult, depending on context. If you are trying to look good (i.e., coming from mind) it is hard; if you are willing to just be a turtle (i.e., coming from self), it is easy. Nursery school children have fun with this task because, unlike adults, they do not worry about looking foolish. As with the "standing" exercise, we encourage individuals to try the exercise several times, noticing when and if their human concerns fall away and they "become" the turtle. Those who manage the transition find that at that point any embarrassment they were experiencing disappears. After all, turtles are not embarrassed

201

being turtles. Invariably, the experience of embarrassment is trace-able to an incomplete commitment to the task at hand.

At the close of session two, we give participants another between-session assignment. They are asked to observe their minds at work. If they have trouble doing so, they can at least observe other people's minds at work. (Sometimes it is easier to first notice the defensive maneuvering of others before one identifies similar machinations in oneself.) As they leave the session, participants are given a handout (Appendix B) that summarizes the themes of the first two sessions.

THE THIRD SESSION

Like the second session, the third begins with an opportuni-ty for sharing and questions. We have found that this is a good time to remind group members of those first horribly awkward moments when the group initially convened. Of course, their initial stiffness has long since disappeared and participants are now contributing freely, often playfully. The co-leaders share how difficult it was for them to keep going during those first few moments of non-respon-siveness. We point this out to help group members gain insight into their considerable impact on others. For instance, many do not real-ize how often others interpret their silence as haughtiness or anger, disinterest or disaffection. They may turn down a party invitation because of their fear of interaction. However, the host or hostess may interpret it as a slight.

Levels of Mastery

A major chunk of the third session is devoted to a discussion of "levels of mastery." The chart we present (Figure 2) is intended to be read from the bottom up. The first word, "avoidance," signifies the mind's most primitive reaction. As conservative organisms, our first impulse is always to steer clear of anything new or unknown. Why taste a berry that might turn out to be poisonous, if you can continue eating something familiar? One step up from avoidance is right and wrong. This represents a slightly more nuanced strategy, where the novel input is at least recognized, although it is immedi-ately disparaged: "Raw fish can't be good for you." "Okay, I'll try it, but I am sure I won't like it." Next comes entitlement, where the attention shifts to complaints about the person's overall predicament: "Why am I being made to put up with this?" "I can't be expected to change my habits at this age." Above entitlement is observation. The

FIGURE 2. LEVELS OF MASTERY

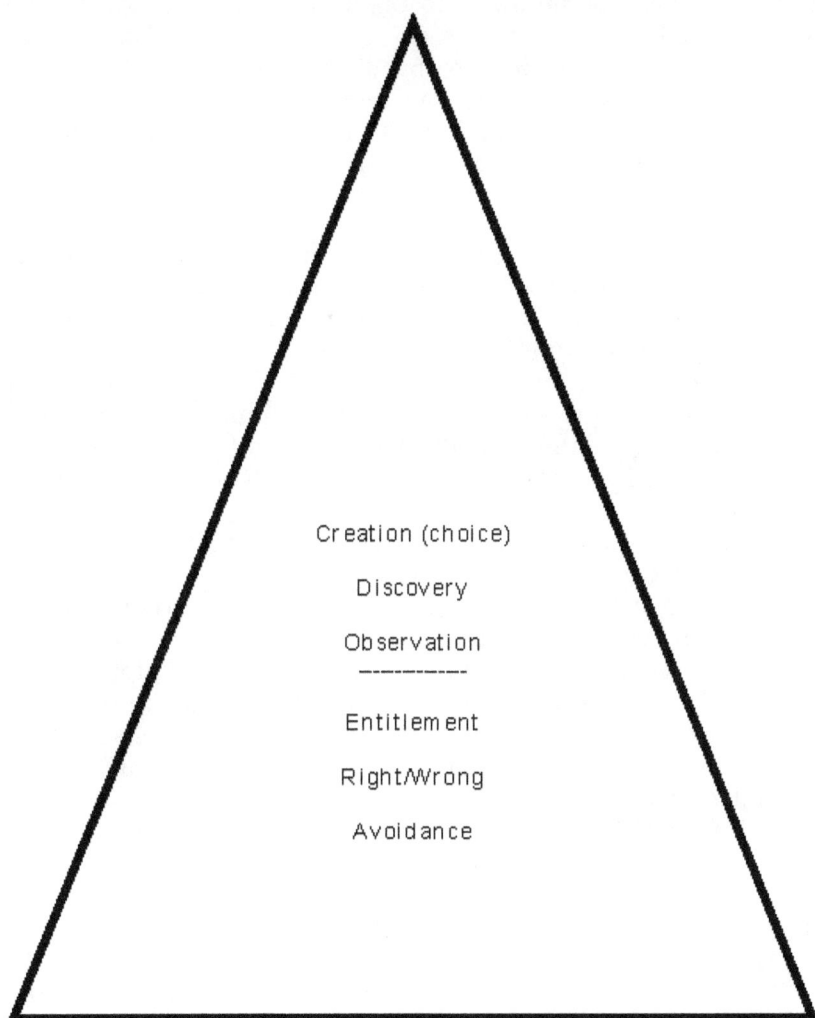

Creation (choice)

Discovery

Observation

- - - - - - - -

Entitlement

Right/Wrong

Avoidance

line on the chart indicates that this represents the first point at which resistance gives way to genuine openness—prejudgment gives way to curiosity: "This is a crunchy texture." Observation paves the way for discovery, which, in turn, energizes creation. The chef who has discovered the rewards of sushi may soon be inventing new recipes.

The initial steps of the mastery chart can be considered mind-dominated. Beginning with observation, the self comes into play. The paradox is that after reaching the top of the chart, people revert to the bottom in order to handle the next threat. Hopefully, with increased enlightenment, the excursion from top to bottom picks up speed—mastery is achieved more quickly, and the probability of getting stuck at the lower levels decreases.

Keeping Secrets

As might be expected, the group operates with more spontaneity during the third and fourth sessions, and there is less need for structured exercises. However, there are still a number of principles we find it useful to introduce. First, we do an eyes-closed exercise about secrets. We invite participants to think of something they have been unwilling to share with others, including the other members of the group. Is this something they find difficult to accept? If so, what makes it unacceptable? What would happen if this secret was known?

In the ensuing discussion, group members have an opportunity to appraise the costs and benefits of keeping secrets and withholding information. Even though they are unwilling to disclose the secret, they are often able to talk about how they think group members would react if they did. Ultimately, many decide simply to spill the beans. They are usually relieved to discover that the information they have worked so hard to withhold creates much less of a stir than they had imagined. In fact, others in the group often admit to having similar issues.

During the progression of the workshop, we highlight distinctions between various terms. For example, we point out that "reasons" are often mind operations used to justify, excuse, or defend behavior: "The reason I was late is that the alarm clock didn't go off." "The reason I was fired is because my boss is prejudiced." On the other hand, the term "considerations" is more neutral. It does not imply righteousness or entitlement. A person may have personal considerations about attending a party, but these do not constitute an indictment of the party. A consideration is a recognition of a particular thought, opinion, feeling, or belief—nothing more. Therefore, a person can have considerations about going back to college but decide to return anyway. Considerations do not shift responsibility to others and events, as reasons often do.

Similarly, we distinguish between "trying" and "doing." As Yoda says in *Star Wars*: "Try not. Do. Or do not. There is no try." A person "trying to quit smoking" usually continues to smoke. In similar ways, we also distinguish between "wanting" and "intending," "evaluating" and "experiencing," "obligations" and "gifts," "entrapments" and "invitations." In all these instances, the first term reflects the mind at work and the second represents self.

Gift Giving

After defining these terms, we usually do a special two-part exercise on gift-giving. In round one, each participant offers every other member of the group a gift in the form of a verbal compliment. These can be fanciful or realistic—trivial or more profound. The job of the recipient is to hear the compliment and say "thank you," indicating that it has been received. This simple acknowledgement contrasts with the urge of group members to protest or nullify the gift—arguing, for example, that it is undeserved.

In the second round, each person receives a series of gifts in a less recognizable form—as criticisms. Again, the appropriate response is "thank you." Gifts, by definition, do not require agreement or disagreement. We should add that when we began running these groups, we expected participants to enjoy compliments and have trouble accepting criticisms. We have learned that, for this population, being complimented can be as troublesome as being criticized.

We next turn our attention to the subject of invitations. Group members think of invitations as grand gestures. Coming from mind, they worry that an invitation will be rejected. Coming from self, we favor issuing many casual invitations and worrying less about how many are accepted. Invitations of the sort we envision include the following: "I'm going downstairs for a sandwich. Can I bring back something for you?" "I want to see the new movie at the Ritz tomorrow night—care to join me?" "I have to get my report copied at Kinko's. While I'm there, I might as well do yours as well."

From feedback about our workshops we know that one of the concrete outcomes is a general increase in invitations. Partly tongue-in-cheek, we tell group members that most of them are not living up to their public duty to provide others with opportunities to reject them. How are others supposed to feel superior if they have no one to reject? The point is that extraverted individuals need not have a monopoly on invitations. Moreover, coming from self, many more invitations are likely to elicit a positive response than the mind imagines.

Pantomime Elephants

Toward the end of the third session, we suggest a second animal pantomime—this time, an elephant. Elephants are more difficult than turtles because they trumpet and take up more space. However, because the group is now at a more advanced stage of development, they are ready for the challenge. First, we give group members an opportunity to try the exercise individually. Then we invite everyone to join in, including those who may have initially declined participating. The entire group becomes a herd of elephants, roaming the room, waving their "trunks," trumpeting, and bumping into one another. This playful adventure involves more physical contact than the previous experiences. However, the light-hearted context renders the increased intimacy acceptable.

The session ends with a new assignment—participants are instructed to issue a series of invitations to co-workers and others. As an alternative, they can at least dream up invitations that they might have extended. They are also to notice any considerations this assignment elicits.

THE FOURTH SESSION

By the fourth session, most of the didactic content has been presented. Group members have bonded well and are listening empathically to each other's concerns. One of the few structured exercises used in this final session concerns the handling of thoughts and feelings. The topic is approached through an eyes-closed task. Participants are asked to imagine a small table directly in front of them—perhaps a night table or kitchen table. They are instructed to conjure up a piece of fruit or a vegetable and to place it on the table. Next, they are to imagine two side tables, one on their left and one on their right. They are then asked to remove the orange, carrot, celery stalk, or what-have-you from the center table and to "park" it on the table to the left or right. This provides room for another object to be imagined and placed in the middle. Participants keep imagining items of produce, first putting them in the center and then moving them off to the left or to the right to clear the way for whatever comes next. As the pace of the exercise quickens, they get used to tossing their imaginary objects around, continually clearing enough space—center stage—for the next creation.

What has distributing imaginary produce got to do with handling thoughts and feelings? The answer is that this exercise provides a model for how thoughts and feelings can be allowed to register in consciousness without becoming obstacles. This relaxed Eastern approach is the opposite of our Western attempts to banish or change thoughts and reactions. A favorite saying of Japan's Morita therapists is that "feelings are as changeable as the Japanese sky." In other words, feelings that are simply allowed to be felt may quickly melt away and be replaced by others. Lightly accepting thoughts and feelings is the Eastern secret to change.

Touch

In some groups, we next introduce an experiential exercise that involves light touching. This exercise provides an opportunity for group members to air their considerations about touching, intimacy, and sexuality. Of course, this is a big topic that could constitute the focus of a separate workshop. However, our goal is to at least touch on the subject—no pun intended. After all, some of our group members have had few opportunities to engage in the kinds of casual physical contact the rest of us take for granted.

For the exercise, each participant is assigned a partner. One person stands in front of the other and they both face in the same direction. The person in the back then lightly pats the person in front, beginning at the top of his or her head and working down the side of the person's body until they reach the feet. This is a series of rapid, repetitive light taps as the person's hands move from top to bottom—no rubbing is allowed. The leaders always demonstrate the method before group members attempt it. During the patting process, participants notice their "considerations." How does it feel to be patted this way? What is it like to do the patting? Afterward, roles are reversed—the person patting becoming the "pattee" and vice versa. Participants are then re-paired so that everyone has an opportunity to try the exercise with a person of the same sex as well as a person of the opposite sex.

Many of our participants have found this exercise challenging and powerful. It helps dispel their fear of touching another human being. It provides an opportunity to distinguish between the alarmist messages of the mind and the self's desire to connect. Because participants interact with men and women, the exercise opens the door to a consideration of sexuality. Although some might consider the exercise controversial, it seems to work well in this safe group setting.

Life Is Not Personal

In some groups, we introduce the "advanced" notion that life is not personal. The mind continually deludes us into exaggerating our own self-importance—a condition Eastern thinkers call maya. A corrective to the mind's distortions is the notion that "it doesn't matter and it doesn't matter that it doesn't matter." From the perspective of the universe, life is fleeting and our heavy investment in our own ego is often self-defeating. On the other hand, participating and contributing to something larger than oneself is, at the same time, self-enhancing.

Concluding the Group

At the end of the fourth session participants are provided with a second handout (Appendix C) and reminded that they will be contacted in three weeks to provide follow-up information. In the closing moments of the workshop we suggest that participants simply allow the material to percolate—they are not required to draw any hard and fast conclusions. In fact, the effectiveness of the workshop does not seem to hinge on their recalling particular bits of content or struggling to apply what they may have learned. Before concluding, we express our deep appreciation for everyone's willingness to share their experiences and to place their trust in the group leaders and each other.

We generally end with a parting ritual. Sometimes the group elects to repeat their award-winning impersonation of an elephant herd—usually with more abandon than in their previous performances. Sometimes, they end by making up a group story to which everyone in the room contributes. We begin such a story with the phrase "Once upon a time" to indicate that this is to be a light, fantasy creation. Sometimes, they simply end by saying goodbye to us and to one another.

OUTCOME DATA

Having presented the treatment protocol, we now turn our attention to describing the outcome data we collected. In this section we discuss the subjects' characteristics, the measures we used, the pre-post comparisons, and the follow-up data. Then, we cite a few participant reactions—solicited and unsolicited.

Subjects

We collected formal data for 46 socially phobic individuals (20 women and 26 men), ranging in age from 20 to 53 (mean age = 34).[3] All participants met DSM-*IV* criteria for social phobia, using the Anxiety Disorders Interview Schedule-IV (ADIS-IV; Brown, DiNardo, & Barlow, 1994). Our only exclusion criterion was age—participants were required to be 18 or older. We included participants currently on medication as well as those who had co-morbid diagnoses or had been in other forms of psychotherapy. Five participants (11%) had taken or were currently taking psychopharmacological medication, five participants (11%) had previously been involved in psychotherapy, and 15 participants (33%) had a history of both medication and psychotherapy.

Measures

In addition to the ADIS-IV interview, the study used three self-report measures—the Fear of Negative Evaluation Scale (FNE; Watson & Friend, 1969), the Symptom Checklist-90-Revised (SCL-90-R; Derogatis, 1992), and the Beck Depression Inventory (BDI; Beck & Steer, 1987). These are standard instruments with excellent psychometric properties, including high reliability and good construct validity. Each of these instruments has been used in many of the published studies of social phobia treatment outcomes. An informal measure calling for open-ended reactions and responses to several Likert-type items was administered at the 18-month follow-up evaluation.

Procedure

Workshop groups varied in size from 3 to 10, with a mean of 6.6 participants. All workshops were led by the first author, an experienced group facilitator; advanced graduate students in clinical psychology served as co-therapists. At the pre-group meeting, participants signed an informed consent form and then completed the ADIS-IV interview for social phobia. They then completed the FNE, the BDI, and the SCL-90-R and had an opportunity to have their questions about the project answered. Three weeks after the workshop sessions, all participants completed a measurement packet that again included the FNE, the BDI, and the SCL-90-R. The same self-

[3] There were some additional groups for which there is only informal data. These were run for purposes other than formal data collection, such as staff development and training.

209

report measures were mailed to them six months following treatment. Finally, the informal response form was sent to participants 18 months after the group treatment. They were provided with stamped, addressed envelopes in which to return their materials. If they did not respond, they received telephone reminders and—if necessary— were sent duplicate sets of materials.

Results

The three-week follow-up assessment (n = 46) demonstrated significant decreases on the FNE (t = 5.70, df = 45, p < .0001, d = 1.70), the BDI (t = 5.11, df = 45, p < .0001, d = 1.52), and— as predicted—several indices on the SCL-90-R. These included the Interpersonal Sensitivity scale (t = 8.25, df = 45, p < .0001, d = 2.46), the Positive Symptom Distress Index (t = 5.43, df = 45, p < .0001, d = 2.46), the Phobic Anxiety scale (t = 4.53, df = 45, p < .0001, d = 1.35), and the Global Severity Index (t = 7.62, df = 45, p < .0001, d = 2.27). These treatment gains were maintained at the six-month follow-up (n = 34).[4] These results are summarized in Table 1 and depicted in Figure 3. The effect sizes for these comparisons are large and are at least comparable to published effect sizes for previous studies of social phobia that utilized similar outcome measures.

Eighteen-month follow-up data was available for 21 participants.[5] On a four-point Likert-type scale measuring the extent to which important principles from the workshop were remembered (1 = not at all, 4 = fairly clearly), the average rating was 2.9. When asked to what extent the workshop helped with the problems that led individuals to attend the group, the average rating was 3.0 on a four-point scale (1 = it seemed to make things worse, 4 = it helped a great deal). The majority of participants recalled specific principles from the workshops and gave examples of how they had been applied in their lives since attending the workshop.

Discussion of Formal Outcomes

Based on the very large effect sizes associated with our results (Cohen's d ranges from 1.35 to 2.46), the context-centered approach

---

[4] Of 46 subjects, only 38 could be contacted. Some had left the area, changed their home address, or found new employment. Four of those contacted did not complete the materials.

[5] Of 46 subjects, only 25 could be contacted. Of those, 21 completed the materials.

FIGURE 3. TREATMENT OUTCOMES

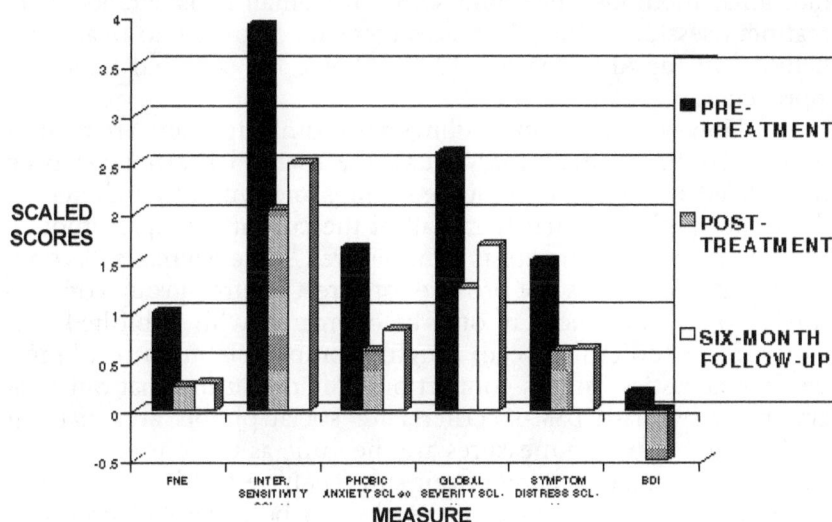

TABLE 1.

PRE- AND POST-TREATMENT MEANS AND STANDARD DEVIATIONS FOR
SOCIAL PHOBIA WORKSHOPS

Measure	Pre-treatment (n=46)	3-weeks post (n=46)	6-months post (n=34)	t (pre vs. 3-wk.)	t (pre vs. 6-mos.)
FNE	24.02 (6.03)	17.66 (7.78)	17.82 (7.44)	5.70**	5.78**
BDI	12.33 (8.59)	6.83 (5.61)	-------- [a]	5.11**	--------
SCL-90 Inter. Sens.	1.81 (0.84)	1.08 (0.79)	1.26 (0.82)	8.25**	4.91**
SCL-90 Symp. Distress	1.96 (0.48)	1.57 (0.53)	1.58 (0.46)	5.43**	5.99**
SCL-90 Phobic Anxiety	0.64 (0.64)	0.32 (0.51)	0.38 (0.51)	4.53**	4.36*
SCL-90 Global Severity	1.12 (0.55)	0.69 (0.53)	0.83 (0.49)	7.62**	4.21*

Note. [a] Measure not included in 6-month follow-up.

*$p < .001$. **$p < .0001$.

to the treatment of social phobia appears to be at least as effective as traditional methods, including some that entail considerably more treatment sessions. Our effect sizes compare favorably to treatments included in the APA Division 12 Task Force list of "gold standard" approaches.

However, while our findings are promising, there are reasons to consider them preliminary. First, the method has not yet been manualized and tested in multiple settings and with other clinicians. The senior author primarily ran all of the current groups, although graduate student co-therapists administered some exercises. Second, the current study does not provide for direct control-group comparisons. Project outcomes can only be compared with published outcomes from studies that seem roughly comparable in terms of sample characteristics. In this connection, it is reassuring that our subjects meet standard DSM-IV criteria for social phobia and that our standardized outcome measures are the same as those used in other studies. Also, because many of our subjects have had long treatment histories, it is unlikely that our results can be attributed simply to spontaneous remission, generalized treatment factors, or placebo effects. Third, although it would have been useful to repeat the ADIS assessments at post-treatment, staffing considerations prevented the inclusion of a second round of diagnostic interviews. Fourth, in the absence of a dismantling design, it is impossible to say which elements of the current approach are essential and which may be superfluous.

An advantage of the current study is the absence of exclusion criteria, such as co-morbidity or medication use. Other research endeavors often use rarefied samples that do not correspond to the realities of clinical practice. In addition, we intentionally postponed measuring outcomes until three weeks and six months following the last group session. After a group experience, immediate feedback is notoriously unstable. Some group members tend to be overly enthusiastic after having formed positive bonds with the other members and the group leadership. Others may initially underestimate the impact of the experience because they have not had enough time to explore the possibilities of functioning in a different context.

Participant reactions

For us, the informal reactions of participants are as important as the formal data. We have gathered together a sampling of their comments, some of which were obtained as part of the feedback procedures and some as unsolicited responses delivered later by mail or e-mail. We should add that not all of the participants were as positive about the outcomes as this selection of reactions suggests. A small minority expressed the view that although the workshop was an interesting experience, it had not solved their everyday problems. On the other hand, none of them claimed that the workshop caused them any harm or caused their circumstances to worsen. Furthermore, virtually all participants indicated that they had no regrets about having chosen to participate and would recommend the experience to others.

Here, in no particular order, are a few of the most interesting reactions. We have changed the names of the contributors to protect their identities:

- I've turned my life around from a state of deep depression to the happiest I've been in years. I've made many new friends and am beginning a relationship with a beautiful woman. (Mike)

- I don't feel pressure to meet someone. It's almost like being in a new place and seeing things for the first time, a realization of how much was going on that I hadn't noticed before. (Jack)

- It was great to find out what actually helps, rather than always focusing on what's wrong with us. I feel better about taking chances job-wise, and discovered that I'm actually better at meeting people than I thought I was. Despite my fear, I took a chance and decided to participate in life. (Sophia)

- I was amazed by the amount of energy I had at the end of each workshop, a desire to be around people and a clearness of mind. Things in everyday life don't appear to be life or death struggles anymore. (Serena)

- A few weeks ago I overheard someone I work with mentioning that he needed a ride home. I didn't know him too well and so I probably would not have offered him a ride home if I did not attend the workshop, but instead of dwelling on whether or not he would like me, I offered him a ride, and wound up getting along with him really well. We're now pretty good friends. (Jeffrey)

- The "art of elephant impersonation" taught me that most foolishness is in the foolish eye of the observer. (Gary)

213

- I imagine [that] doing the elephant among grown men and women is a memory that will remain vivid into my declining years. It reminded me of how much I enjoy acting silly and how few opportunities there are for it in my "adult" world. (Mark)

- I did some presentations after the workshop [where] I knew what I wanted to say and I said it. I didn't worry what others might think. (Adam)

- The second part of my life really began when I finally accepted that I was shy and withdrawn and it was a waste of time to pretend otherwise (Kenny).

For us, Kenny's appraisal epitomizes the shift in perspective that we believe context-centered approaches can achieve.

CONCLUSION

Many questions about our protocol remain to be answered. For example, can leaders in other settings obtain similar results? To what degree are the results dependent on specific exercises and procedures? Can an effective treatment manual be produced? In the meantime, because of the promising nature of the results, we are pleased to be able to share this description of the treatment with other clinicians and researchers. In contrast to other approaches, the workshop is not designed to teach particular skills. It does not provide group members with specific training in giving talks, making dates, or carrying on conversations. It does not even encourage participants to adopt a more outgoing style. Instead, the design is intended to help participants distinguish between two contexts— mind and self—and to recognize the ramifications of each of these experiential frameworks. Judging from formal and informal reactions, we believe that the protocol succeeds in making these distinctions real for participants, providing them with an alternative perspective on their difficulties.

REFERENCES

American Psychiatric Association. (2000). Diagnostic and statistical manual of mental disorders (4th edition, text revision). Washington, DC: Author.

Anaïs Nin Quotations. (n.d.). Retrieved January 11, 2003, from http://www.geocities.com/Paris/Bistro/2187/main.html/

Bateson, G. (1979). Mind and nature: A necessary unity. New York: E. P. Dutton.

Beck, A. T., & Steer, R. A. (1987). Beck Depression Inventory manual. New York: Harcourt Brace Jovanovic.

Brown, T. A., DiNardo, P. A., & Barlow, D. H. (1994). Anxiety disorders interview schedule for DSM-IV. Albany, NY: Graywind Publications.

Derogatis, L. R. (1992). SCL-90-R administration, scoring, and procedures manual. Towson, MD: Clinical Psychometric Research.

Efran, J. S., Lukens, M. D., & Lukens, R. J. (1990). Language, structure, and change: Frameworks of meaning in psychotherapy. New York: W. W. Norton.

Emery, S. (1977). Actualizations: You don't have to rehearse to be yourself. Garden City, NY: Doubleday & Co.

Erhard, W., & Gioscia, V. (1977). The est standard training. Biosciences Communications, 3, 104-122.

Feske, U., & Chambless, D. L. (1995). Cognitive behavioral versus exposure only treatment for social phobia: A meta-analysis. Behavior Therapy, 26, 695-720.

Goldiamond, I. (1972). Toward a constructional approach to social problems: Ethical and constitutional issues raised by applied behavioral analysis. Behaviorism, 2, 1-84.

Gregson, D., & Efran, J. S. (2002). The tao of sobriety: Helping you recover from alcohol and drug addiction. New York: St. Martin's Press.

Heimberg, R. G., Dodge, C. S., Hope, D. A., Kennedy, C. R., & Zollo, L. J. (1990). Cognitive behavioral group treatment for social phobia: Comparison with a credible placebo control. Cognitive Therapy and Research, 14, 1-23.

Kagan, J., Snidman, N., Arcus, D., & Reznick, J. S. (1994). Galen's prophecy: Temperament in human nature. New York: Basic Books.

Layden, M. A., Newman, C. F., Freeman, A., & Morse, S. B. (1993). Cognitive therapy of borderline personality disorder. New York: Allyn & Bacon.

Maturana, H. R., & Varela, F. J. (1987). The tree of knowledge: The biological roots of human understanding. Boston: Shambhala.

Meissner, W. W. (2002). The problem of self-disclosure in psycho analysis. *Journal of the American Psychoanalytic Association, 50*(3), 827-867.

Paul, G. L. (1967). Insight vs. desensitization in psychotherapy two years after termination. *Journal of Consulting Psychology, 31*, 333-348.

Paul, G. L., & Shannon, D. T. (1966). Treatment of anxiety through systematic desensitization in therapy groups. *Journal of Abnormal Psychology, 71*, 123-135.

Pfeiffer, J. W., & Jones, J. E. (1970-1971). *A handbook of structured experiences for human relations training* (Revised ed., Vols. 1-3). Iowa City, Iowa: University Associates Press.

Rhinehart, L. (1976). *The book of est.* New York: Holt, Rinehart and Winston.

Shapiro, T. (2002). From monologue to dialogue: A transition in psychoanalytic practice. *Journal of the American Psychoanalytic Association, 50*(1), 199-219.

Smothermon, R. (1979). *Winning through enlightenment.* San Francisco: Context Publications.

Task Force on Promotion and Dissemination of Psychological Procedures. (1995). Training in and dissemination of empirically validated treatments: Report and recommendations. *The Clinical Psychologist, 48*(1), 3-23.

Turner, S. M., & Beidel, D. C. (1994). A multicomponent behavioral treatment for social phobia: Social effectiveness therapy. *Behaviour Research and Therapy, 32*(4), 381-390.

Watson, D., & Friend, R. (1969). Measurement of social-evaluative anxiety. *Journal of Consulting and Clinical Psychology, 33*, 448-457.

Watzlawick, P., Beavin, J. H., & Jackson, D. D. (1967). *The pragmatics of human communication.* New York: W. W. Norton.

Watzlawick, P., Weakland, J. H., & Fisch, R. (1974). *Change: Principles of problem formation and problem resolution.* New York: W. W. Norton.

Woy, R. J., & Efran, J. S. (1972). Systematic densensitization and expectancy in the treatment of speaking anxiety. *Behaviour Research and Therapy, 10*, 43-49.

Yalom, I. D. (1975). *The theory and practice of group psychotherapy* (2nd ed.). New York: Basic Books.

APPENDIX A. WORKSHOP CONTRACT

By participating in this workshop, I agree to the following conditions:

1. To remain in room except during announced breaks.

2. To anticipate that aspects of the process will be confusing, boring, and uncomfortable—perhaps very unlike what I was expecting.

3. To attend all four sessions, even if I have already concluded that the experience is worthless.

4. To complete the feedback forms even if my opinions about the experience are wholly negative.

Moreover, by participating, I indicate my understanding that:

5. The workshop is complete in itself. No additional participation is required.

6. There will be three types of activities: First, the provision of "data"—information about how aspects of life operate. Second, opportunities to share experiences, ask questions, express reactions, state considerations, and so on. Third, voluntary opportunities to participate in exercises and demonstrations that illustrate the principles of the workshop.

7. There will be many opportunities to share reactions, but no obligation to do so.

If all of your questions have been answered and you accept these agreements, indicate your willingness to participate by signing below. If you are not choosing to continue, you are invited to complete the optional non-participation form you were given.

Signed_____Date_____

APPENDIX B. SESSION 2 HANDOUT

The mind's agenda is SURVIVAL. Its three sub-goals are:
- Win, or at least avoid losing.
- Be right, or at least avoid being wrong.
- Dominate, or at least avoid being dominated.

Although you have a mind, you are not your mind. Although you have feelings and reactions, you are not your feelings and reactions. Although you have positions and considerations, you are not your positions and considerations.

Anything you resist, persists. Anything you let be, lets you be.

Common Forms of Resisting:
Evaluating, judging, regretting, changing, avoiding, hoping.

Common Forms of Experiencing:
Allowing, observing, noticing, accepting, acknowledging, owning, participating.

Withholding: When you withhold, others frequently conclude that they have done something wrong. They think that perhaps you do not like them or are not interested in them. Sometimes they decide that you must be haughty or that they do not measure up to your standards.

APPENDIX C. SESSION 4 HANDOUT

1. You have feelings and you are not your feelings. You have a mind and you are not your mind. You have considerations and you are not your considerations.

2. The mind is interested only in your physical survival or the survival of your position (i.e., being right, avoiding being wrong; winning, avoiding losing; dominating, avoiding being dominated).

3. Whatever you resist, persists. Whatever you let be, lets you be.

4. There are reasons and there are results.

5. In your conversation with yourself, what you say is so, is so; what you say is not so, is not so; what you say might be so, might be so.

6. Don't pretend it is otherwise.

7. Do not confuse protection with participation.

8. Life is not personal. The universe doesn't care.

9. You are already whole, complete, and sufficient.

10. It doesn't matter and it doesn't matter that it doesn't matter.

CHAPTER 10

Reconstructing Sociality After Bereavement[1]

Kenneth W. Sewell and Louis A. Gamino

The death of a loved one requires adjustments at a variety of levels: psychological, physical, familial, functional, and emotional, among others. In particular, intrapersonal and interpersonal negotiations in the realm of "sociality" are necessitated by bereavement, if the bereaved person is to establish an effective post-loss adaptation. This chapter discusses preliminary findings from a program of research evaluating bereaved persons in the south-central United States. Findings, both quantitative and qualitative, show the extent to which a breach of sociality via loss relates meaningfully to functioning in the areas of psychological symptoms, social connectedness, and meaning-making. The therapeutic implications of these findings are explored, such that therapists working with bereaved persons can orient their interventions in theoretically and empirically consistent ways.

Adjusting to the death of a loved one poses many challenges. Clearly, the bereaved person faces challenges in how to view the self, physical existence, familial and other social relationships, emotions, and even daily functioning. Debate has emerged in recent decades regarding the relative importance of understanding constructions at the personal level (Mancuso, 1998) versus the social level (Stam, 1998). The dichotomies implied by the "personal versus social construction" debate are defied by the psychosocial challenges presented by the loss of a loved one. The role-loss represented by bereavement reveals the inextricable link between personal meaning-making and social inter-relatedness. Clearly, the bereaved person's meaning-

[1] A version of this paper was presented at the Tenth Biennial Conference of the North American Personal Construct Network, Vancouver, BC, July 2002.

making system prior to the loved one's death included, at least in part, the presence of the role relationship and the shared meanings negotiated therein. After the loss, the bereaved person must adapt to a new realm of construing in which the loved one (and many of the shared anticipated contexts) no longer exists in the same forms as before.

In his personal construct psychology (Kelly, 1955/1991, 1955/1991b), George Kelly defined "sociality" as the prerequisite for one person engaging another in a social process, specifically via the construction and enactment of a role. Paraphrasing, the sociality corollary (Kelly, 1955/1991a, p. 95/66) asserted that to the extent that Person "A" construes the construction processes of Person "B," Person "A" could play a role in a social process with Person "B." Thus, the extent to which a person can meaningfully relate to others in social contexts depends upon her/his engagement in the process of construing others' construction processes.

The death of a loved one often results in a paralysis of sociality as the person grieves the loss of the valued other. The bereaved person can still engage in a sort of memorial sociality—engaging the lost loved one at the level of remembering her or his values, words, actions, intentions. However, sociality as it relates to defining the social self (Sewell, 1995) is oriented toward anticipation (cf. fundamental postulate, Kelly, 1955/1991a) rather than retrospection. The adaptational task for the bereaved person thus involves placing the remembrances of the lost loved one into a framework for anticipating future relationships, functioning, and existence.

Over the past decade, we have been studying the bereavement process via a series of research projects (Easterling, Gamino, Sewell, & Stirman, 2000; Gamino, Hogan, & Sewell, 2002; Gamino, Sewell, & Easterling, 1998; Gamino, Sewell, & Easterling, 2000a; Gamino, Sewell, & Easterling, 2000b; Williams, Gamino, Sewell, Easterling, & Stirman, 1998) assessing and interviewing bereaved persons in the south-central United States. The earliest of these efforts (Gamino, Sewell, & Easterling, 1998) evaluated the viability of a "risk factor" model of complicated bereavement. Although elements of the model seemed to garner empirical support, its practical utility was judged to be limited, given that many of the so-called risk-factors were static variables—aspects of the mourner, of the decedent, or of the death that were associated with negative outcomes but that were not amenable to intervention. It was concluded that more attention must be devoted to understanding how people adapt following a loss, rather than simply finding actuarial ways to predict who will experience adaptational difficulties.

Having noticed the depth and richness of information generated in conversations with bereaved persons, Williams, Gamino, Sewell, Easterling, and Stirman (1998) undertook a content analysis of the constructs represented in participants' responses to structured questions (a semi-structured interview and a repertory grid). This investigation revealed useful relations between post-loss adjustment and anger toward others, anger toward God, denial of the death's impact, and social support. Nearly all of these variables are at least ostensibly amenable to psychological intervention.

We further elaborated on the extent to which fluid ways of construing of loss-related events can impact functioning by examining how adverse occurrences in funeral services are related to functioning and perceived comfort derived from the funeral. Participating in funeral rituals appears to be a powerful method of reducing negative grief affect. Only custom and convention dictates that such participation is restricted to the days following a death. Psychotherapy can often provide a context to explore creative ways to participate in memorial experiences long after a loss that can help the mourner place the loss in her or his life story.

This push toward a model of grieving that could lead to useful therapeutic implications prompted the second phase of our collaborative efforts. With a new cohort of bereaved individuals, we evaluated an "adaptive model of grief" that used only plastic/fluid variables to predict levels of grief-related distress as well as post-loss growth (Gamino, Sewell, & Easterling, 2000a). This model not only yielded useful therapeutic implications (e.g., how a bereaved person can reconstruct an experience of leave-taking, or "saying goodbye" to the loved one; how a bereaved person can come to identify aspects of the death that had positive outcomes; how therapy might aid a person in gaining perspective on the loss in reference to other life experiences), but also demonstrated greater empirical coherence than the pathological model (as studied previously and as replicated in the Gamino, Sewell, & Easterling, 2000a study). Most recently, we have evaluated this latter sample of bereaved persons to examine, among other things, the extent to which a breach of sociality via loss relates meaningfully to functioning in the areas of psychological symptoms, social connectedness, and meaning-making. We derived both quantitative findings (Gamino, Sewell, & Easterling, 2000a) and qualitative findings (Gamino, Hogan, & Sewell, 2002), and ultimately have attempted to integrate these levels of analysis. The following section of this chapter briefly describes these findings, specifically as they relate to the breach and reconstruction of sociality. Following the discussion of the research findings, we will conclude with an elaboration of the therapeutic implications of these findings and the associated theoretical concepts supported by them.

METHODS

Participants

Data were collected from 85 individuals grieving the death of a significant person. The composition of this sample, described in detail in an earlier report on this cohort (Gamino, Sewell, & Easterling, 2000), was recruited from both non-psychiatric and psychiatric sources. A total of 45 individuals were connected to a major medical-surgical teaching hospital by way of recently experiencing the loss of a loved one. Most were individuals contacted by the chaplain service after a loved one died in the hospital; others were participants from self-help grief support groups or volunteers who learned of the study from one of the investigators. The remaining 40 participants included outpatients from the medical school's psychiatry clinic who had been referred to the study. All of these outpatients had experienced a significant loss; however, the loss was not necessarily the focus of their outpatient treatment. Quantitative tests of variance homogeneity showed no significant differences between these non-patient and outpatient groups; therefore, they were considered a single cohort for purposes of data analysis (Gamino et al., 2000).

The sample consisted of 77.6% women with an average age of 50.9 years (SD = 13.6) and an average of 15.1 years of education (SD = 3.2). The majority of participants were white (89.4%), reflecting the demographic composition of the region (central Texas). Hispanics (4.7%), African-Americans (2.4%) and other races (3.6%) were represented to a lesser extent. Marital status varied among participants with 43.5% married, 38.8% widowed, 10.6% separated/divorced, and 7.1% never married.

Causes of death of the participants' loved ones included illness (n = 64; 75.3%), accidents (n = 12; 14.1%), suicides (n = 8; 9.4%), and homicides (n = 1; 1.2%). Decedent types included spouses (n = 36; 42.3%), parents (n = 31; 36.5%), children (n = 10; 11.8%), and others (n = 8; 9.4%) such as siblings, grandparents or friends. Most of the participants (n = 75; 88.2%) had lost their loved one within three years of the study; the median number of months since the death was 8. Time since death was not found to be a significant covariate for participants' scores on quantitative measures of bereavement (Gamino et al., 2000).

Instruments

Narrative task . Participants were given a sheet of paper asking them to write an answer to the question, "What does the death of your loved one mean to you?" They could take as much time as they needed and write as much or as little as they wanted (extra paper was available). They were encouraged simply to express themselves in their own words.

Semi-structured interview . A semi-structured interview, derived from that used in prior studies of grieving (Gamino, Sewell, & Easterling, 1998, 2000a) was used to obtain loss-related data, demographic data, and data identified as potential risk and protective factors (derived from literature, theory, and previous studies by the authors). This interview requires approximately 45 minutes to administer, and is available from the authors upon request.

Grief symptomatology . Two instruments were used in this study to quantify the various dimensions of grief: the Grief Experiences Inventory (GEI; Sanders, Mauger, & Strong, 1985) and the Hogan Grief Reaction Checklist (HGRC; Hogan, Greenfield, & Schmidt, 2001). The GEI is a 135-item true-false self-report test with nine scales measuring different grief-related affect states: despair, anger/hostility, guilt, social isolation, loss of control, rumination, depersonalization, somatization, and death anxiety. The measure has demonstrated reliability and has shown evidence of incremental and criterion validity (Sanders et al., 1985). The HGRC is 61-item self-report, Likert-style questionnaire that sorts items into five scales of grief misery: despair, panic behavior, blame/anger, detachment, and disorganization. In addition, the HGRC contains a sixth scale measuring personal growth following bereavement. The HGRC has demonstrated internal consistency reliability as well as validity data to show that the instrument is sensitive to affect changes in grievers over the course of mourning (Hogan et al., 2001).

Intrinsic spirituality . To quantify the extent to which participants intrinsically invest belief and emotional energy towards a sense of spirituality, the INSPIRIT scale (Kass, Friedman, Leserman, Zuttermeister, & Benson, 1991) was administered. From six multiple choice items and 13 Likert-style ratings of various spiritual beliefs and experiences, a single mean score is derived that shows high reliability (Cronbach's Alpha coefficient = .90) and demonstrated concurrent validity (Kass et al. 1991).

Procedures

A nurse investigator who was trained by the authors collected all data. After obtaining informed consent, participants were asked to complete the narrative task. Then the semi-structured interview was conducted. Finally, the psychometric self-report instruments were administered. Participants were debriefed and thanked with a token gift (a book on bereavement recovery) to conclude their participation.

Data coding/scoring . The semi-structured interviews were coded, consistent with their use in previous studies, to reflect variables thought to represent potential risk and protective factors. These variables served as estimates of the social and functional status of the participants. Quantitative instruments were scored according to standard protocols for each instrument. Participants' narratives were coded and analyzed using procedures designed to make useful inferences from open-ended questions in survey research (Weber, 1985). The analysis assumed that the structure of a participant's meaning related to the loss experiences was inherent in her/his written narrative. The role of the researcher was to identify, describe and classify these embedded meanings. Thus, we attempted to represent authentically the "voices" of the participants *as we heard them* in the essays. Narratives were coded by the researchers while being masked to any other data collected on these individuals except for age, gender and relationship to the decedent (for identification purposes).

First, narratives were broken down into units of discrete thoughts or sentiments and classified under a content category. Participants' own words were used to label the categories if possible. Additional categories were generated via iterative comparison between participants' narrative descriptions and those categories already identified. In other words, each datum was compared to all others in order to assign its content category or identify a new category. No limits were imposed on the number of categories to be discovered and there were over 50 by the completion of this initial coding process.

In the second step, the multiple initial categories were reviewed systematically for potential overlap and/or hierarchical organization. This process yielded a total set of nine major categories of meaning. These broader categories were crosschecked against each other to minimize overlap and to insure the uniqueness of each. Again, this was accomplished by consensus among the researchers, while remaining masked to the participants' quantitative data or to the statistical relations between the qualitative and quantitative data.

Next the basic properties of each category were defined and made explicit. Each single descriptive phrase or sentiment expressed in the narrative was evaluated as a possible instance of an identified category. Thus, any one participant's narrative might contain instances of one or several of the primary categories. These data (presence vs. absence or the nine categories, as well as theoretically chosen combinations of these indices) functioned as the criterion variables against which the remaining quantitative data could be compared.

RESULTS

The nine major meaning constructs that emerged from the content analysis (Gamino, Hogan, & Sewell, 2002) were named: *Feeling the Absence, Experiencing Relief, Disbelieving the Death, Changing Relationships, Focusing on Negativity, Experiencing Meaninglessness, Continuing the Connection, Invoking an Afterlife, Going on with Life.* The majority of participants exhibited more than one of the nine major meaning constructs in their essays.

The content categories that form the basis of the present discussion (i.e., those seen as directly related to sociality) are defined and then elaborated below using the raw data provided by participants to illustrate the nuances of meaning they expressed. Then, the empirical trends are described for how each category related to the quantitative data. Given the level of data (presence vs. absence of a content category as it relates to ordinal and interval variables) and the high frequency of binary imbalance (more "absent" than "present" in most cases, but sometimes vice versa), robust statistical effects would be unlikely at best. Furthermore, the modest sample size of 85 precludes many sophisticated multivariate methods. Rather than manipulate the data in ways that would make interpretation dif-

227

ficult, we have decided to compute straightforward point-biserial correlations and report the trends somewhat liberally (reporting one-tailed tests, and considering alpha levels below .05 as significant and those below .10 as trends). Caution is applied in interpreting relations that are not firmly supported by theory.

Feeling the absence . Fundamentally, Feeling the Absence meant missing the deceased person's physical presence, his/her involvement in the survivor's life as well as roles he/she played in the family (including prospective future roles). Thus, the mourner is left with a sense of loss, void or emptiness, including a loss of part of self. Feeling the Absence seemed to be evident at multiple levels and in multiple ways. We identified six distinct facets or subcategories, which revealed some key aspects of the central theme of Feeling the Absence. These included: yearning, companionship, lost dreams, void, depersonalization, and finality. Two of these, companionship and depersonalization, are relevant to sociality.

At an interpersonal level, the everyday presence and companionship of the decedent—that sense of "we-ness"—is missing after the loved one's death. Participants missed the essence of day-to-day living with the decedent; their anticipation of a shared life together now was gone. In addition, for some mourners, it was also the family roles performed (or anticipated to be performed) by the decedent that determined how his or her absence was felt.

- "It means we will never hold hands again or share each other physically." (50-year-old widow)

- "She was my everyday companion, friend and shopping buddy. We done and went everywhere together…When mom got sick it was more than I could take." (52-year-old bereaved daughter)

- "The loss of a companion—after 42 years—the loneless (sic) of sharing the memories we had and the shared jokes. The fun and games we had each day—and his teaching the parrot more words." (58-year-old widow)

- "Loss! Loss of a partner of 40 years; loss of a beloved and loving spouse, father of our children, anchor, friend, cook, fixer-upper and breadwinner." (65-year-old widow)

Table 1 shows the statistical trends and relations identified between loss of companionship and other study variables. Participants who noted loss of companionship as a fundamental meaning of the death also tended to view the death as unpreventable, report a more positive relationship with the decedent, show higher levels of ruminative mourning, depersonalization, and somatization, show higher levels of despair and disorganization, mention few "silver linings" to the loss, and note religion/God as a source of help. *Loss of Companionship* was noticed more frequently in older, less educated participants. This configuration was informally termed the "widow's profile," given its predominance among women who had lost spouses.

TABLE 1. CORRELATIONS WITH FEELING THE ABSENCE:
LOSS OF COMPANIONSHIP.

Variable	Correlation	Significance
Preventability	.21	< .05
Relationship Quality	.37	< .001
Rumination[§]	.19	< .05
Depersonalization[§]	.22	< .05
Somatization[§]	.28	< .01
Despair[¥]	.17	.06[ε]
Disorganization[¥]	.27	< .01
Age	.26	< .01
Education	-.17	.06[ε]
Silver Linings	-.22	< .05
Religious Coping	.16	.08[ε]

Note: [§] GEI indices; [¥] HGRC indices; [ε] marginal trends.

For some mourners, the disturbance related to *Feeling the Absence* was so fundamental and profound as to alter or threaten their very sense of self, as in feelings of incompleteness and depersonalization. It was as if they lost part of their vital spirit when their loved one died. For these individuals, the loss seemed to include a loss of part of self.

• "I lost my soul mate when I lost my husband. He was the other half of me." (59-year-old widow)

• "I find myself looking through the eyes of an empty person since his death." (35-year-old widow)

• "Without him I am nothing and no one." (49-year-old widow)

Construal of the self is requisite to construing other in relation to the self (i.e., sociality). Depersonalization seems to reflect a

229

breach in such self-construal. Table 2 shows the relations between depersonalization and other study variables. Participants who related such depersonalization also showed less post-loss growth, showed higher levels of despair, mentioned few "silver linings" to the loss, noted social support as a source of help, and tended not to note religion/God as a source of help.

TABLE 2. CORRELATIONS WITH FEELING THE ABSENCE: DEPERSONALIZATION.

Variable	Correlation	Significance
Despair[§]	.16	.07[ᶜ]
Despair[¥]	.18	< .05
Growth[¥]	-.16	.07[ᶜ]
Silver Linings	.23	< .05
Social Coping	.17	.06[ᶜ]
Religious Coping	-.16	.07[ᶜ]

Note: [§] GEI indices; [¥] HGRC indices; [ᶜ] marginal trends.

Changing relationships . Changing Relationships refers to recognition of an alteration in the mourner's social position with the salient persons in her/his life given the departure of the decedent; movement could be to cohere more closely or to disengage from others.

- "I have experienced 'caregiving' from others in a way I never before have. Being a 'professional' caregiver, the meaning of this has been profound." (45-year-old bereaved daughter)

- "It has also drawn three of us—me and 2 sisters—closer to share our grief process." (51-year-old bereaved son)

- "It also means a breakdown in my family. She was the magnet in our family—the one who pulled us together...I already feel us pulling apart—going our own separate ways." (40-year-old bereaved daughter)

- "Our family isn't quite the same since he's been gone. It's been 10 years. The only picture we have of all of us together was taken the (S)unday before he died...that was the last time we were all together again." (40-year-old bereaved daughter)

Expressions of *Changing Relationships* are reflective of a sociality "demand" as perceived by the construer. The person sees that she/he must rearrange the social domain and come to construe a social world that is different from the one preceding the loss. Table 3 shows

230

the statistical relations between *Changing Relationships* and other indices. Participants who mentioned *Changing Relationships* in their essays also reported a more positive relationship with the decedent, showed lower levels of ruminative mourning and guilt, and showed lower levels of panic. Although they tended not to note religion/God or positive memories as sources of help, they did identify multiple sources of help, and indicated a willingness to consider a grief support group.

TABLE 3. CORRELATIONS WITH *CHANGING RELATIONSHIP.*

Variable	Correlation	Significance
Relationship Quality	.17	.06[e]
Rumination[§]	-.17	.06[e]
Guilt[§]	-.24	< .05
Panic[¥]	-.17	.06[e]
Silver Linings	-.22	< .05
Coping Resources	.28	< .01
Consider Group	.18	.06[e]
Memory Coping	-.21	< .05
Religious Coping	-.17	.06[e]

Note: [§] GEI indices; [¥] HGRC indices; [e] marginal trends.

Continuing the connection . *Continuing the Connection* meant maintaining a sense of the decedent's presence in one's life through an inner bond comprised of positive memories, emotions, or a spiritual type of presence. This continuing attachment seemed to indicate an attempted solution to the griever's dilemma of how to go on loving someone who is physically gone from life but who remains a reference point and an object of affection. Developing a new way of remaining connected to the deceased appeared to have a reassuring effect on those who referenced such efforts.

• "Sometimes I feel he's close by or there's a presence watching over me. . . . I do visit the gravesite to talk to my spouse occasionally." (49-year-old widow)

• "I still feel an inner connection (difficult to explain) to him. Now that he's gone, that connection is still present to an extent . . . you can't simply stop loving someone that you once had such strong feeling for." (35-year-old mourning ex-husband)

• "I still start to say something to him as we talked a lot. I am

231

lonesome—but I feel that he is still with me." (68-year-old widow)

- "I believe that if you remember the person (both good & bad) then a part of that person continues to live. . . . I still feel her presence." (35-year-old bereaved daughter)

Table 4 lists the empirical associations to Continuing the Connection. Those who mentioned Continuing the Connection as part of their meaning-making also reported a more positive relationship with the decedent, showed lower levels of blaming and despair, tended to have negative mental health treatment history, mentioned few "silver linings" to the loss, were not interested in a support group, and tended to view the funeral as a source of comfort. Those utilizing Continuing the Connection also tended to be more educated that other participants.

TABLE 4. CORRELATIONS WITH CONTINUING THE CONNECTION.

Variable	Correlation	Significance
Relationship Quality	.19	< .05
Blame[¥]	-.19	< .05
Despair[¥]	.16	.07[e]
Consider Group	-.16	.08[e]
Education	.19	< .05
Mental Health History	-.16	.07[e]
Silver Linings	-.15	.08[e]
Funeral Comfort	.16	.07[e]

Note: [¥] HGRC indices; [e] marginal trends.

Invoking an afterlife. Invoking an Afterlife meant utilizing the metaphysical concept of a life or location beyond earth, often "heaven", in which to place the deceased loved one and, possibly, anticipate reunion.

- "I know that while he would have wanted to live with me he is in a happier place with God." (64-year-old widow)

- "I feel she completed her work on earth and that God rewarded her by taking her to heaven. . . . She is in a better place." (42-year-old bereaved daughter)

- "I do believe he is our guardian angel, on the other side watching over us." (39-year-old mother bereaved over intrauterine death of one twin son)

- "I'm looking forward to being with him again in a much better & brighter world." (72-year-old widow)
- "I look forward to someday seeing his sweet little face in heaven." (31-year-old bereaved father of premature son)

Much like *Continuing the Connection*, the strategy of *Invoking an Afterlife* allows the mourner to salvage some continuity from this drastic change that has occurred. Table 5 lists the empirical associations to *Invoking an Afterlife*. Persons *Invoking an Afterlife* in their essays also showed lower levels of ruminative mourning and somatization, showed less post-loss growth, tended to note positive memories as sources of help, were able to find "silver linings" to the loss, and tended to have experienced the loss very recently.

TABLE 5. CORRELATIONS WITH INVOKING AN AFTERLIFE.

Variable	Correlation	Significance
Rumination[§]	-.24	< .05
Somatization[§]	-.21	< .05
Growth[¥]	.15	.09[ε]
Silver Linings	.22	< .05
Memory Coping	.16	< .07[ε]
Time Since Loss	-.15	.09[ε]

Note: [§] GEI indices; [¥] HGRC indices; [ε] marginal trends.

Intercorrelation of categories. Notably, the five categories of meaning-making discussed here are not substantially intercorrelated. Thus, a person who included content in their essays reflecting any one of these categories was neither more nor less likely to include content reflecting the other categories.

DISCUSSION

The present discussion focuses on the applied implications of the research described above. However, caution must be exercised in interpreting the relations between the contents of meaning-making and functional outcome variables (such as symptoms, growth, etc.). It is theoretically consistent to hypothesize that the movement toward meanings that are associated with better functioning might portend such positive outcomes. However, the cross-sectional nature of the research conducted thus far allows the possibility that the content is driven by the functioning, rather than vice versa. That being acknowledged, clinicians are encouraged to consider and tentatively

233

experiment with the possibility that assertively elaborating certain meanings of loss might aid mourners in their pursuit of post-loss adaptation.

Clearly, bereaved persons struggle to reconstruct a sense of self in the face of breached sociality. This can lead to straightforward depersonalization experiences associated with feeling "stuck" and in despair. Even so, persons who note depersonalization experiences also express the opinion that social supports have been helpful in the wake of the loss. Thus, there is a tacit (if not overt) recognition that the path to the reconstruction of selfhood is via sociality. Clinicians should be alert to the griever's depersonalization experiences and guide her/him toward connection with others, even if that connection is temporary and superficial (at least at first). Sociality establishes role investment, the absence of which can be frightening and disorienting.

One way in which personal identity constructions can be elaborated in the face of loss involves therapeutic exploration of the ways in which the bereaved person felt that he could "be himself" with the loved one. Then, the therapist can assist the client in identifying situations, times, or role-relationships in which this specific sense of selfhood is experienced (even if to a lesser extent) after the loss.

In the "widow's profile," the bereaved person has a focus on the loss of companionship incurred with the loved one's death. This is clearly a content focus that is associated with more negative emotional outcomes. It is likely that the loss represented a loss of sociality in its most prized form (i.e., a primary companion). Even though the bereaved person treasures the positive relationship she/he had with the decedent, there is a tendency to view the loss as an unpreventable complete tragedy. Often, only God is a possible source of support for this griever. Thus, the transformation or transfer of sociality efforts toward other conceptions of the lost loved one or toward other relationships seems preempted.

Rather than belaboring the difficulties associated with focusing on the loss of companionship, it is likely more fruitful for the clinician to guide the mourner toward transferring sociality to other valued social connections. This involves focusing on positive memories of the relationship while at the same time identifying and being willing to utilize multiple sources of support. Thus, the griever focuses on the often-stressful yet adaptive ramifications of the loss in its demand for *Changing Relationships*. The griever can come to value the memory of the loved one in the context of developing sociality in the living world.

The therapist must be willing to utilize the therapeutic relationship as the "laboratory" for the client's initial experiments in social reconnectedness. Sewell (2002) argued that the therapeutic relationship offers traumatized and bereaved clients a particular kind of "healing love" when post-loss functioning has been compromised: "Thus, love—by way of its dual connection with the sense of personal agency as well as with social belongingness—works directly in opposition to the disruptions that traumatic experiences create" (p.25). Then, as the client begins to feel bolstered by the relationship with the caring therapist, she will be more likely to experiment socially beyond the therapeutic setting.

Likewise, making room for a Continuing Connection with the decedent represents yet another adaptive way to transform the sociality of the griever from an external to an internal focus. This emphasis on continuing/transforming the psychological relationship with the deceased person, so eloquently described by Klass, Silverman, and Nickman (1996) in their work on continuing bonds, is contrary to traditional concepts of grief (i.e., that the person must "decathect" from attachment to the deceased). Placing the relationship with the deceased person into the psychological "ecology" of the bereaved person's new and changing social environment creates a shift away from the concept of "getting over" the loss, and allows a focus on positive movement, growth, and adaptation.

Finding ways to ritualize and/or memorialize the on-going psychological relationship can be important components of this focus. These rituals and memorials need not be limited to culturally prescribed and supported activities such as funerals, memorial services, obituaries, and memorial funds/scholarships/charities. Many clients find it immensely useful to carry on active communication with the spirit of the decedent. Celebrating anniversaries of significant experiences shared with the loved one, perhaps by structuring time to review photographs or other memorabilia as part of the celebration, can punctuate the post-loss existence—giving appropriate honor and significance to the relationship without foregoing continued functioning.

Although not compatible with every griever's values, rituals and beliefs, Invoking an Afterlife as a way to understand or cope with loss seems to be associated with fewer negative mental health ramifications. By Invoking an Afterlife, some grievers seem to effectively combine

235

the *Changing Relationships* and *Continuing Connection* concepts. Therapists working with bereaved persons must become comfortable with religious and spiritual explorations in order to allow clients to fully explore the meanings of the loss, and to allow clients to fully utilize what appears to be a powerful coping strategy (i.e., placing the deceased loved one in a religiously/spiritually validated eternal place of rest and peace where the bereaved can someday rejoin the decedent).

In our study, *Invoking an Afterlife* was also associated with the ability to find "silver linings" in the loved one's death (i.e., ways in which the death had resulted in some good, or had some secondary positive effect). There are likely varieties of ways (other than *Invoking an Afterlife*) to help a bereaved client explore possible "positives" to a loss. Of course, timing is important in such an inquiry. Asking too soon about possible "good results" realized from the death of a loved one can be disrespectful of a mourner, particularly early in the grieving process. Frantz et al. (2001) have suggesting asking the question this way, "Despite the tragedy of the death, is there anything positive or good that has come about as a result of the death?" For example, one bereaved adult son stated, "My father not only taught me how to live; he taught me how to die." Although this statement does not focus on some happy memory or relationship quality, it clearly identifies a positive personal effect of the deceased life and death. Such identification and focus appears to be important for post-loss adaptation.

These ideas are preliminary and represent only a few of the potential clinical implications from this on-going work. Clinicians are encouraged to pursue idiosyncratic and novel ways to help bereaved clients make their losses meaningful and make their lives adaptive, productive, and vital.

REFERENCES

Easterling, L. W., Gamino, L. A., Sewell, K. W., & Stirman, L. S. (2000). Spiritual experience, church attendance, and bereavement. *Journal of Pastoral Care, 54,* 263-276.

Frantz, T. T., Farrell, M. M., & Trolley, B. C. (2001). Positive outcomes of losing a loved one. In R. A. Neimeyer (Ed.), *Meaning reconstruction and the experience of loss* (pp. 191-209). Washington, DC: American Psychological Association.

Gamino, L. A., Hogan, N. S., & Sewell, K. W. (2002). Feeling the absence: A content analysis from the Scott & White grief study. *Death Studies, 26,* 793-813.

Gamino, L. A., Sewell, K. W., & Easterling, L. W. (1998). Scott & White grief study: An empirical test of predictors of intensified mourning. *Death Studies, 22,* 333-355.

Gamino, L. A., Sewell, K. W., & Easterling, L. W. (2000a). Scott & White grief study--Phase 2: Toward an adaptive model of grief. *Death Studies, 24,* 633-660.

Gamino, L. A., Sewell, K. W., & Easterling, L. A. (2000b). Grief adjustment as influenced by funeral participation and occurrence of adverse funeral events. *Omega, 41,* 79-92.

Hogan, N. S., Greenfield, D. B., & Schmidt, L. A. (2001). Development and validation of the Hogan Grief Reaction Checklist. *Death Studies, 25,* 1-32.

Kass, J. D., Friedman, R., Leserman, J., Zuttermeister, P. C., & Benson, H. (1991). Health outcomes and a new index of spiritual experience. *Journal for the Scientific Study of Religion, 30,* 203-211.

Klass, D., Silverman, P. R., & Nickman, S. L. (Eds.). (1996). *Continuing bonds: New understandings of grief.* Washington, DC: Taylor & Francis.

Kelly, G. A. (1991a). *The psychology of personal constructs: Vol. 1. A theory of personality.* London: Routledge. (Original work published 1955)

Kelly, G. A. (1991b). *The psychology of personal constructs: Vol. 2 . Clinical diagnosis and psychotherapy.* London: Routledge. (Original work published 1955)

Mancuso, J. (1998). Can an avowed adherent of personal construct psychology be counted as a social constructionist? *Journal of Constructivist Psychology, 11,* 205-219.

Sanders, C. M., Mauger, P. A., & Strong, P. N., Jr. (1985). *A manual for the Grief Experience Inventory.* Palo Alto, CA: Consulting Psychologists Press.

Sewell, K. W. (2002). Psicoterapia con clients traumatizados y en duelo: Un marco constructivista para el amor y la curacion [Psychotherapy with bereaved and traumatized clients: A constructivist framework for love and healing]. *Revista de Psicoterapia, 12*, 123-132.

Sewell, K. W. (1995). Sociality lost: The schizophrenic's neurocognitive dilemma. [Review of the book *The cognitive neuropsychology of schizophrenia*]. *Journal of Constructivist Psychology, 8*, 163-167.

Stam, H. (1998). Personal construct theory and social constuctionism: Difference and dialogue. *Journal of Constructivist Psychology, 11*, 187-203.

Weber, R. P. (1985). *Basic content analysis*. Beverly Hills, CA: Sage.

Williams, A. M., Gamino, L. A., Sewell, K. W., Easterling, L. W., & Stirman, L. S. (1998). A content and comparative analysis of loss in adaptive and maladaptive grievers. *Journal of Personal and Interpersonal Loss, 3*, 349-368.

CHAPTER 11

Constructivist Stances for Promoting Justice in Spirituality Research[1]

Derrick Klaassen, Marvin McDonald, and Matthew Graham

> "How can we determine the hour of dawn, when the night ends and the day begins?"
>
> "When from a distance you can distinguish between a dog and a sheep?" suggested one of the students.
>
> "No," was the answer of the rabbi.
>
> "Is it when one can distinguish between a figtree and a grapevine?" asked a second student.
>
> "No."
>
> "Please tell us the answer then," said the students.
>
> "It is then," said the wise teacher, "when you can look into the face of a human being and you have enough light to recognize in him your brother. Up until then it is night and the darkness is still with us."
>
> Hasidic tale (e.g., in Kunz, 1998, p. v)

Echoes of the falling World Trade towers continue to resound across the globe. In the ensuing years since September 2001, a certain intensity has emerged from an insistent international and interdisciplinary focus on global violence, war, and terrorism. Now culture and religion are frequently acknowledged as matters of urgent global concern. For scholars in psychology an intense focus on ideologically grounded violence resonates with longstanding sensibilities of social responsibility. Scholars promoting social responsibility

---

[1] A version of this paper was presented at the Tenth Biennial Conference of the North American Personal Construct Network, Vancouver, BC, July 2002.

can ill-afford to ignore traditional worldviews in the name of intellectual superiority or to fragment inquiry incessantly along cultural and political lines. The widespread concern for current tragedies can help us take an honest look at our own commitments as they are embodied in our research practices. In this chapter, then, we examine strategies for determining whether researchers in religious studies are doing "just research" or are simply "just" doing research. Do we as members of academic and professional communities promote practices that contribute to enlarging of the humanity of others? Or might our ideals of justice become compromised by institutional demands or academic discourse? Moreover, how can we confront violence in scholarship and the world at large as scholars without merely reproducing it?

In this essay, we want to frame research on spirituality in the context of the "big questions" of existential and political concern. We draw inspiration from George Kelly's willingness to address large social issues with constructivist openness. In like spirit, we invite the reader on a wide-ranging journey. First, we critically examine ideological interests camouflaged in the concrete procedures and practices of research. We are interested in exploring ways that research practices can explicitly embody aspirations for promoting justice while also advancing concrete investigations. After setting the academic stage, this exploration is grounded in an unfolding research project of our own. Following this case study of justice-promoting research, we draw on the insights of one who addresses violence by summarizing Miroslav Volf's stance for confronting violence justly. We then extend his strategy into a viable constructivist ethic for researchers who promote justice—in the lives of the study participants, in the practices of researchers, and in debates with other scholars. We situate "just research on spirituality" within practices that (a) embody a basic respect for others, (b) facilitate critical challenges of one another's worldviews, and (c) mediate triadic reflexivity in investigations of spiritual experience. We formulate triadic reflexivity as an inclusive orientation toward conflicting voices and stakeholders in research practices. It is not sufficient, in our view, to ignore or dismiss those with whom we disagree, nor is a rhetorical insistence on common ground an adequate basis for confronting ideological differences.

Constructivist psychology is fertile ground for nurturing our vision because authors in the field have readily focused on renovations in the epistemology and methodology of science, including the political and moral dimensions of such transformations. Human science researchers widely acknowledge the responsibility to engage in ethically sound research practices; in fact, concerns for equality and justice between investigators and participants are prime motivations for the promotion of qualitative research methodologies. However, research that confronts ideological violence and conflict demands greater resources than professional codes or methods protocols. Advancing the project of promoting justice in spirituality research, then, entails proactive, reflective engagement with ideologically opposed positions and a capacity to confront violence amidst conflicting worldviews (cf. Hadjistavropoulos & Smythe, 2001; Renner, Alksnis, & Park, 1997; Rouse, 2002; Smythe & Murray, 2000; Tjeltveit, 1999). To help orient this research project, we begin with a brief look at current literature on religious orientations and health.

SPIRITUALITY AND HUMAN WELL-BEING: FRAMING AN ACADEMIC PROJECT

A growing body of evidence in the well-being and mental health literature points to substantial relationships between spirituality, religion, and health (e.g., Koenig, McCullough & Larson, 2001). Some researchers argue further that existential growth and spiritual fulfillment are empirically distinguishable from personal happiness and satisfaction (e.g., Compton, 2001; Keyes, Shmotkin & Ryff, 2002). Evidence and theory for a distinguishable but correlated construct of other-directed spirituality is emerging (cf. Compton, 2001; Hill et al., 2000; Klaassen & McDonald, 2002).

As the implications of these developments are pursued, Koenig and his colleagues (2001) point out that improving the quality of empirical assessments of religion and spirituality is critical. However, the nomothetic research paradigms dominating this research provide little opportunity for research participants to supplement or correct investigators' research practices or interpretations. Idiographic and qualitative approaches can more readily provide substantive correctives, especially as key constructs in the psychology of religion are elaborated (cf. Graham, 2001; Klaassen & McDonald, 2002; Watson et al., 1998). One such construct is the religious orientation termed "quest."

A CASE STUDY: RELIGION-AS-QUEST

Psychologists of religion have spent decades investigating different spiritual orientations in investigations of spiritual maturity.

One thread of discussion examines the work of Daniel Batson and his colleagues on the construct of Religion-as-Quest (Batson, 1976; Batson & Schoenrade, 1991a, 1991b; Batson, Schoenrade & Ventis, 1993). In supplement to Allport's (Allport & Ross, 1967) early conceptualizations of religiousness as either Intrinsic (internalized, mature, lived religion) or Extrinsic (immature religion or religion as social convention), the Quest dimension of religiosity is characterized by a continuous and never-ending search. Indeed the process of questioning has become the master motive of the "quester," while finding answers, conclusions, and certainty remains secondary (Batson et al., 1993; Donahue, 1985). Accordingly, Batson and his colleagues (Batson et al., 1993), define Quest as

> facing existential questions in all their complexity, while at the same time resisting clear-cut, pat answers. An individual who approaches religion in this way recognizes that he or she does not know, and probably will never know, the final truth about such matters. Still, the questions are deemed important, and however tentative and subject to change, answers are sought. There may or may not be a clear belief in a transcendent reality, but there is a transcendent, religious aspect to the individual's life. We call this open-ended, questioning approach religion as quest. (p. 166, italics in original)

Batson, Schoenrade and Ventis (1993) argue that the Quest construct incorporates three basic components of mature religion, previously neglected by Allport in his formulation of Intrinsic religion. They are "(1) a readiness to face existential issues without reducing their complexity, (2) self-criticism and perception of religious doubt as positive, and (3) openness to change" (p. 181). Batson and his associates (Batson & Schoenrade, 1991a; Batson et al., 1993) also claim that the construct of Quest is not determined or limited by one's age, gender, or religious affiliation, but rather spans the breadth of the population. Since the publication of the Religious Life Inventory in 1976, Quest as a construct and an instrument has spawned a flurry of activity, including critiques and extensions of method and conceptualization in multiple research centres (e.g., Benson, Donahue, & Erickson, 1993; Burris, Jackson, Tarpley, & Smith, 1996; Donahue, 1985; Kojetin et al., 1987; Sanders, 1998; Ventis, 1995; Watson, Morris & Hood, 1989; Watson, Morris & Hood, 1992; Watson, Morris, Hood, Milliron & Stutz, 1998).

The empirical evidence on the relationship between the Quest scale and a variety of socially desirable and undesirable measures has yielded mixed results thus far (Batson et al., 1993). On the positive side, Altemeyer and Hunsberger (1992) reported that Quest correlated negatively with religious fundamentalism and racial and sexual prejudice. Fulton, Gorsuch, and Maynard (1999) also found weak, negative relationships between Quest and some of their measures of intolerance toward gays. A variety of studies describe questers as open-minded, flexible individuals with a strong sense of self. On the negative side, Kojetin, McIntosh, Bridges and Spilka (1987) reported that the Quest orientation was positively correlated with anxiety and religious conflict. Genia (1996) reported that higher Quest scores were indicative of greater levels of personal distress and lower spiritual well-being.

Batson originally construed quest as an open-ended, authentic, and mature approach to religion, but its critics have viewed the construct quite differently. Donahue (1985; Benson et al., 1993), for example, challenged the assumption of an entirely constructive quest and identified at least one possible version of existential searching as sophomoric, inauthentic, and immature questioning.

> In what other area of human endeavour is [questing in Batson's sense] considered appropriate or mature? Someone who from month to month is a Marxist, a Green, a Tory, and a Fascist would not be lauded for their "quest" anymore than someone who is gay, then straight, then, bi, then monogamous, then promiscuous. . . . If it's not mature in politics or sex, why should it be considered mature in religion? (M. Donahue, September 22, 1999, personal communication)

Watson, Hood, and Morris (e.g., Watson et al., 1992; Watson et al., 1998) have also challenged Batson's version of an authentic and mature Quest. They see the construct and measurement of Quest as biased against fundamentalist or faith-affirming beliefs. In particular, they claim that the controversy over the concept and measurement of Quest can be attributed, at least in part, to divergent ontological and epistemological assumptions of researchers. Watson and his colleagues provided evidence for different interpretations of Quest items when they asked the participants in their study to rate the items of the Quest scale. Some idiographic ratings identified certain items as antireligious.

A variety of researchers have sought to defend Quest as originally conceived, that is, as a conceptually and empirically valid dimension of religious orientation which highlights important facets of religion omitted by other orientations (e.g., Burris, Jackson, Tarpley, & Smith, 1996). Unfortunately, however, the main response to ideological and theoretical critiques has been reassertion of the paradigm and the gathering of more nomothetically defined data. For example, Batson and his colleagues (1993) countered the claim that Quest is contrary to some of the beliefs of orthodox or conservative Christians with the assertion that Protestant seminarians have scored high on the scale. Such responses are incomplete at best, evading the force of ideological critique by redefining such questions as entirely resolvable through more research conducted within an empiricist philosophy of science. By failing to acknowledge the underdetermination of theory by empirical data, Batson and his colleague presume their methodological and conceptual predilections to be privileged with respect to alternative paradigms. Furthermore, some writers have accused proponents of Intrinsic dimensions of spiritual maturing of being biased against Quest and allowing their scientific judgment to be clouded by ideology (e.g., Ventis, 1995), presumably implying that proponents of Quest were able rise above their metaphysical commitments and survey the debate from a value-neutral point of view.

In short, a central theoretical focus of scientific debate for more than 20 years hinges on the definitions of religious or spiritual maturity. Is Quest an indicator of religious maturity? Is mature religion what correlates with health and well-being? Does Quest tap more into facets of spiritual life associated with distress and social dysfunction? Is Quest's emphasis on ambiguity and uncertainty a sign of existential courage or is it simply a bias against traditional formulations of organized religion and of Christianity in particular? Quest is seen, then, as (a) an authentic, open stance that acknowledges the fundamental, irreducible complexity of life and religion; or as (b) an immature, developmental stage of life that sophomorically rejects any form of spiritual commitment; or as (c) some combination of these factors and other confounds. Intrinsic religiosity, on the other hand, is spun as either an authentic, engaged, and vital spirituality or as a rigid orthodoxy that forfeits meaningful spiritual engagement to sustain a preoccupation with conformity and correctness. Even an extrinsic orientation, originally formulated by Allport as immature, conventional religious orientation has been interpreted to pick up on a legitimate function of religion as solace—a source of personal and social support in times of need. These differences in judgment, we propose, rest less upon consistent patterns of empirical evidence than they do upon divergent (and sometimes unacknowledged) worldview commitments and philosophies of science. Advances in the scientific study of religious and spiritual maturity have gained little ground in the last 25 to 30 years. In our estimation it is time to entertain the possibility slow advance in the field may be due, at least in part, to a nearly exclusively on countering divergent claims with further data gathering within a narrow paradigmatic mould rather than engaging reflexive examination of personal worldview commitments embedded in research practices.

RE-EXAMINING QUEST AND EXISTENTIAL SEARCH

As members of a research team studying spiritual health and well-being, we are conducting a series of studies examining ways that Intrinsic and Quest religious orientations capture dimensions of mature spirituality. Klaassen and McDonald (2002) explored questions about Quest as developmental process or as stable religious orientation. The results indicated that Quest religiosity is nomothetically distinguishable from identity development as formulated by James Marcia's (Marcia, Waterman, Matteson, Archer, & Orlofsky, 1993) theory of identity status. However, the study also suggested that Quest fails to sustain meaning seeking or engagement with purpose in life (Wong, 1998). Thus, the anti-authoritarian facets of Quest seem to distract attention from a dialectical synthesis of commitment and search that informs the life journeys of some seekers. As one way of coming to grips with this apparent complexity, we proposed that existential searching may well encompass multiple idiographic pathways that only partially trace the lines of emphasized Quest constructs.

Further explorations by McDonald, Klaassen, Gallant, and Graham (2002) and Gallant (2001) identified additional features of spiritual and existential seeking. Nearly 400 university students from public and private universities were administered measures of religious orientation, personal meaning, existential courage, and hope. Consistent with previous research, an Intrinsic orientation was strongly associated with existential factors such as level of personal meaning and hope. Quest demonstrated only weak, negative associations with two sources of personal meaning but it did seem to reflect an active pursuit of existential questions for some respondents. These results thus support the first study and its theoretical emphasis on developing a theory of spiritual maturity that reflects the multiplicity of spiritual and existential modes of engagement.

To elaborate the idiographic richness behind the nomothetic analyses of the larger study, Graham (2001; McDonald et al., 2002) focused on qualitative aspects of spiritual searching for 16 people scoring relatively high on the Quest scale. Open-ended interviews explored the fit between these questers' experience of seeking and the definitions of Batson and his colleagues. The questers' descriptions supported key features of the definition of Religion-as-Quest while also qualifying other facets of the model. Religion-as-Quest seems to take the form of different psychological pathways for different people and this diversity of forms is directly relevant to psychological models of spiritual maturity. A central quality to spiritual journeys for these participants was a desire to ask profound and difficult questions. The shared themes emerging from the discussions also highlighted psychological and spiritual costs to spiritual seeking and the creative tensions among critique, community, and commitment.

The themes of existential journey and seeking were implicit, however, for many of those interviewed. Participants readily welcomed the dialogical, open-ended mode of engagement promoted in the interviews, but "seeking" as an explicit self-characterization emerged spontaneously for only three of sixteen people. As the interviewer and participants explored spiritual life, their desires to address existential questions were often situated in the context of specific events or situations, not as an intentional effort brought to everyday activities. Although these co-researchers clearly recognized themselves in descriptions of seeking, they often experienced the recognition as a surprising or novel formulation of a familiar but preverbal awareness. These results suggest that the conversational engagement of the interviews provoked respondents to articulate core patterns of construal that frequently remain implicit until notable situations kindle existential explorations. Nevertheless, daily life is often not engaged in these modes. The questions of the Quest scale may help elicit some of these construals. But because interviews were not conducted with people scoring low on the Quest scale, it is not clear how widely this kind of implied openness might emerge.

Given the implicitness of many core construal processes described here, research investigating spiritual journeying needs to foster diverse strategies that are sensitive to the positioning of speakers in existential conversations. For instance, people in these interviews were engaged as co-researchers, actively positioning them as collaborators in the formulation of accounts about seeking and exploring challenges in life. The widely shared account of situating existential engagement to events and actual contexts undermines traditional treatments of religious orientations as "stable dispositions" to organize behavior independent of events or relationships. Perhaps some people quest in relationships while orienting intrinsically to prayer and extrinsically to worship. Or perhaps people cycle through various orientations in the same spiritual practices over time. Nevertheless, reading patterns of questionnaire responses idiographically as shared patterns of meaning fits well with the descriptions offered by the questers who shared their stories with us. And the issue of "fit" here is not merely "validity" as a value-neutral, cognitive standard of correspondence between statistical associations and conceptual propositions. We want to highlight the accessibility of shared meanings among various stakeholders and to assert a priority for the familiar, recognizable meanings highlighted by qualitative interviewing. These research practices are formulated, in part, to embody just relationships and to position respondents as voices of integrity in the research process. In this manner, the egalitarian ethic embedded in personal construct psychology facilitates the recognition of spiritual journeying lived as situated modes of engagement. As constructive alternativist formulations, however, these constructions are presumed to reflect but one set of commitments for informing spirituality research in this field.

In summary, as our investigations of Quest progressed, we became increasingly convinced that a core of theoretical debate, whether or not ideological commitment is a sign of spiritual maturity, remained largely untouched by nearly three decades of empirical investigation. The reason for this, we purport, is that ideological commitments of researchers often remain implicit and beyond the reach of traditional, nomothetic research. This may not be surprising for a field like the psychology of religion, which struggled over the years with ways to address theological and ideological bias. A flight to neutrality is understandable in retrospect. However, researchers' commitments about the nature of spiritual maturity are eminently relevant to its investigation and continue to enter into the practice of research, whether acknowledged explicitly or not. But how can different, even conflicting, ideological commitments explicitly shape research practices while simultaneously maintaining empirical adequacy and theoretical import of these projects? We propose here a positioning approach built on a tri-fold strategy of mutual respect, mutual critique, and a stance of triadic reflexivity for addressing ideological conflicts amidst research practices investigating spiritual maturity. To begin, it is crucial to address the possibility of violence amidst ideological conflict.

ENGAGING THE VIOLENT OTHER:
MICROSLAV VOLF'S THEOLOGY OF EMBRACE

Constructivist psychologists can readily adopt strategies for justice promotion from other scholars who engage these issues directly, especially when they confront violence through work in other disciplines of religious studies. One such colleague can be found in the Croatian theologian Miroslav Volf (1996, 2001). In his inspiring work, Exclusion and Embrace, Volf develops a theology of embrace in response to a colleague's challenging question: How could he, a Croatian theologian, committed to following spiritual principles of reconciliation and forgiveness, embrace a "czetnik" (or Serbian terrorist, an ultimate, violent Other for him)? The relevance of this challenge for researchers of spiritual maturity is direct and poignant. To offer one's embrace to the Other, the enemy, transcends traditional definitions of just conduct and enters into the realms of sacrificial love for those with whom one passionately disagrees, whether in politics or in spirituality research. As we "listen" to Volf, we can seek clues for ways psychologists of religion can address spiritual maturity that furthers empirical and theoretical understanding while genuinely advancing justice.

Volf (1996) takes up his challenge elegantly, striving for an alternative to interminable oscillations between foundationalist and anti-foundationalist ethics. The stakes of his project are, however, dramatically different than those in a debate pursued largely through the institutions of academic publication. For Volf the issues of debate and the consequences of decisions and actions may have direct and dire consequences for people's lives because he speaks as one who has lived in a war zone. After all, in war the Other may not decide to "play" nicely or argue in a civil manner.

Volf argues first of all for the capacity to make strong, even "objective," judgments when encountering a violent Other. Speaking to Rorty and Derrida as proponents of anti-foundationalist ethics, Volf declares that "there are incommensurable perspectives that stubbornly refuse to be dissolved in a peaceful synthesis; there are evil deeds that cannot be tolerated. The practice of 'judgement' cannot be given up" (p. 52). Irony and play are inadequate responses to the rape and murder of innocent human beings. Demanding responses to evil deeds is ethically necessary even though others may not concur with our perspective. While anti-foundationalist stances may seem less insufficient when resituated to academic debate, Volf contends that such tactics are ineffective in resolving ideological disputes even in scholarly domains.

> Vilify all boundaries, pronounce every discrete identity oppressive, put the tag of 'exclusion' on every stable difference—and you will have aimless drifting instead of clear-sighted agency, haphazard activity instead of moral engagement and accountability and, in the long run, a torpor of death instead of a dance of freedom. (Volf, 1996, pp. 64-65)

Anti-foundationalist approaches lead, paradoxically, to exclusion when freedom has gone astray. If no jointly intelligible and mutually accessible ways of bridging incommensurate worldviews can be set up in the face of actual violent events, then disagreements, in war or in research, can readily generate exclusion, whether it takes the form of academic isolation, deliberate omission, or unrestrained violence (cf. House, 1994).

Volf moves on to make a categorical distinction between embrace and exclusion. Exclusion is a process of creating space between oneself and the Other, and is marked by a profound disengagement from the process of authentic dialogue. The excluded one is positioned beyond the pale of civilized dialogue. In academia this exclusion often takes the form of ignoring, deliberate omission, and other forms of silencing. Exclusion can, however, be replaced by "differentiation," which consists of both "separating-and-binding." The dialectical process of separation and binding combines the power of evaluation or critique with the "soft edge" of binding or engagement. Volf notes, "By itself, separation would result in self-enclosed, isolated and self-identical beings. Feminist thinkers have rightly rejected separation as an ideal" (p. 65). Moreover, critique is not detached judgment, but is rather a judgment of justice that is dialogical, situated, and contextualized by a profound appreciation for the other and humility about one's own fallacy and limitations. Judgment, in other words, becomes open to critique (and therefore mutual) without undermining the force of judgment that promotes justice.

Embrace, in contrast, is defined by the movement toward the Other regardless of the Other's commitment to reciprocity. Volf notes that embrace is "guided by the indestructible love which makes space in the self for others in their alterity, which invites the others who have transgressed to return, which creates hospitable conditions for the confession, and rejoices over their presence" (p. 165). Echoing themes of feminist research, Volf (1996) calls for the primacy of embrace over judgment, even judgment in the mode of differentiation. He notes first that embracing involves risk-taking and courage. Embracing rests on a willingness to gamble, on a faith sufficient to open oneself to the potentially destructive arms of the other even while maintaining the demand for justice. Positioning oneself first in this vulnerable courage, embrace becomes a guiding metaphor for action that shapes our practices through four distinct moments—opening, waiting, closing and finally opening again.

Opening is the first moment of embrace. In the case of spirituality research, openness is towards the ideological Other of academic colleagues and research participants, as well as the Other of adherents to diverse worldviews and faith traditions. Openness is an invitation that expresses our genuine will to learn, our dissatisfaction with our self-enclosed identity, our ultimate insufficiency without the Other, and our invitation to grow, expand, and learn together while promoting justice with integrity. Secondly, we wait. Participation in embrace is voluntary for all parties. The wait signals to the Other that we respect his or her freedom to reject the embrace; our invitation is tentative, not invasive. Waiting costs us as we offer time and space for the Other to give voice. In academic work, the costs of giving one another space are substantial but necessary. The third moment is the closing—the moment that signifies mutual commitment, joint risk and goodwill toward the Other. The embrace remains gentle—leaving room for the other, empowering her to remove herself from this activity should it move beyond the pale. In actual instances of scholarly embrace, jointly shaped academic activities provide opportunities for a mutual gentleness that nurtures respect and understanding. Finally, embrace ends with an opening of the arms. The goal of engagement is not assimilation or rigid binding as an absolute state of affairs. Rather, release signifies the finite, local nature of the relationship and the opportunity to start the cycle of engagement anew. Temporary joining for academic exchange does not imply continuous interaction, but it does invite a reassessment of ideological conflicts in light of jointly shaped activities.

Volf's theology of embrace presents a compelling, ethical model for engaging the Other. Embrace as ethical strategy is compelling not only because it is grounded in the lived-experience of a theologian "at war," but also because it provides a vision for ideological disagreement that can be constructive and radical without surrendering to foundationalist or anti-foundationalist extremes. His vision reiterates the primacy of action and engagement; we are compelled to deal with the Other precisely because he or she is there. Ignoring or avoiding the issues at stake, or the person, is not an option. Yet any parties to the engagement cannot coerce the vulnerable courage of embrace. Violence can be risked, justice can be addressed, but silencing of one another is undermined at the outset. It is this refusal to silence the demand for justice or ideological conflict that commends Volf's guidance to scholars daring to address spiritual maturity and spirituality in a globally situated era.

CONSTRUCTIVIST ETHICS:
RESPECT, CRITIQUE, AND TRIADIC REFLEXIVITY

Current dangers of violence, of ideological conflict feeding into unremitting strife, of ideologically amplified exploitation generating conditions for violence—these social and political challenges contextualize research on spirituality whether or not individual researchers privilege such concerns. Such themes are not novel. Constructivists, and many others, are gradually working out and disseminating transformational practices for ethical, political, and moral action as an academic mode of participation in social responsibility (cf. Dreyfus & Dreyfus, 1999; Hadjistavropoulos & Smythe, 2001; Harré & Gillette, 1994; Kunz, 1998; Taylor, 1995). In the academic case study described above we highlighted practices for strengthening the voice of research participants, but Volf's challenge underscores the moral significance of keeping ideological conflict in focus as well. The reflexive moment in embrace provides the decisive move here. Embrace of the (potentially) violent other is grounded in a demand for justice, but the vulnerable stance of embrace positions us as (potentially) complicit in violence, and therefore equally subject to the demand for justice. Personal construct theory can help us further articulate this reflexive strand in the stance of embrace.

George Kelly's work and many wide-ranging elaborations of personal construct psychology provide opportunities for nurturing reflexively coherent positions. The reflexivity of "person as scientist" has been most widely employed to highlight the epistemological centrality of human agency in both "scientist" and "subject." Kelly's legacy also includes effective synergies among qualitative and quantitative modes of inquiry, strengthening of idiographic dimensions of research, and a seamless integration of research and therapy as mutually enriching practices in psychology and the human sciences. What is more, constructivist innovations in fields like psychometrics (e.g., Fransella & Bannister, 1977) are well-established developments in specific domains of disciplinary practice. Both ethical standards and reflexive insights are repeatedly brought forward in this literature. We offer here a dialogue between Kelly and Volf to help articulate a justice-provoking research ethic sufficient to play a part in spirituality research.

Constructive alternativism, like embrace, is radically open to alterity and the moral dimensions of inquiry (Kelly, 1965; cf. Harré & Gillette, 1994). Strategies for nurturing politically effective pluralism in psychology can no longer rely on polarities between public justice and private morality to sustain social discourse, nor can we presume a "common ground" of civility to sustain public debate in the face of violence. Today's pluralisms are pluralisms of normativity and so are better served by embrace, by direct engagement with profoundly different others in the promotion of peace and justice. As Kelly (1965) proposed nearly forty years ago, facing aggression and the political challenges of our age requires audacity and initiative in the face of uncertainty and the threat of imminent change to our most cherished aspirations. Kelly's legacy of contextual inquiry helps us reconstrue the Other and ourselves as interlocutors even in the face of hostility. We elaborate this possibility as three moments of respect, mutual critique, and triadic reflexivity in the constitution of a justice-provoking research ethic.

Mutual respect readily appears in Volf (as above), in Kelly, and personal construct psychology (PCP) more broadly, naturally following from constructive alternativism and the reflexivity of "person as scientist." Respect for research participants can be shown in the "credulous stance" of asking people how they understand spirituality, for instance. In the quest projects, qualitative methods widened range of respect in the project. Respect for ourselves as researchers and for other scholars in the field can readily take the shape of acknowledging and valuing different notions of spiritual maturity explicitly identified in the literature. Minimally in quest research, this involves acknowledgement of the visions of spiritual maturing informing the work of Allport, Bateson, Watson, and others.

Mutual Critique may not seem quite as transparent, although constructive alternativism clearly evokes a certain openness to reconstrual even as we adopt the position of critic. And Kelly's reminder that hostility is rooted in attempts to extort confirmation for precious construals of life can wedge open the door of reconsideration a bit further. It may become easier to situate ourselves as (potentially) complicit in violence, even as we demand justice, by addressing the other's core patterns of construal. Kelly's notion of aggression as audacity helps move another step into the mutual critique of embrace. What Kelly recognizes as existential courage and initiative in the face of uncertainty and the threat of impending change in one's core, Volf promotes as love for the violent Other that brooks no compromise in the demand for justice. Both authors highlight the risk of failure in the process of engagement and Volf's compelling compassion comes through especially vividly within the specific situations of human violence he calls us to address.

Volf and Kelly together provide a gripping account of ways to address ideological conflicts in spirituality research. The courageous vulnerability that meets tragedy and violence head-on can also nurture research practices that audaciously acknowledge conflicting ideological commitments as they shape empirical projects. As researchers and critics, we have the opportunity to open ourselves to critique of other researchers as well as that of our participants. Aggressive pursuit of our interests as scholars—including demands for justice—positions us to acknowledge ideological criticism as having legitimate voice in our research projects. The place of ideological critiques within research is not merely a rhetorical straw target to motivate pre-emptive rebuttal. Volf calls us to embrace the ideological other as a genuine voice central to our research projects. Even hostility might find a place in ideologically motivated critique.

In the literature on religion-as-quest, it is not difficult to make out ideological tensions in the visions of justice being promoted. Criticisms of intrinsic orientations as overly conventional and authoritarian can easily reflect concerns about the abuses of religious authority, whether by clergy or others. Similarly, disparagement of extrinsic orientations arises from associations with prejudice, presumably reflecting a kind of privilege accorded to in-group status. And criticisms of relativist bias in quest orientations can likewise reflect concerns about abuses of political authority to the disadvantage of traditional worldviews. Recognizing the range of religious diversity easily encompasses a wide range of visions of justice to be addressed by spirituality researchers.

Openness to a mutuality of critique can still, however, hold certain privileges in reserve. "Fair-mindedness" to a violent other in research might not legitimate discussion of the worth of one's research project per se. Adopting the promotion of justice as intrinsic to research on spirituality moves openness to another level

253

because the research enterprise itself is subject to a standard of justice. Ideological critique may legitimately address more than methods and theory. When the very worth and nature of research itself as situated by specific investigators, settings, procedures, and theories can be critiqued legitimately in relation to actual conduct of the project, then the demand for social justice becomes internal to and explicit within research practices instead of being isolated to circumscribed moments such as ethical review or peer review of research reports. Accountability for the promotion of justice becomes, in this approach, a principle for shaping the ongoing practices of conducting research, much like the rigor of detachment for experimental social psychology, the discipline of bracketing for phenomenology, or the faithfulness of immediacy in hermeneutic investigation. We describe this moment in the promotion of justice in research as "triadic reflexivity."

Triadic reflexivity as strategic research practice emerges, then, as an aspiration to embody as fully as possible a diversity of ideological commitments in the practices of investigation. In spirituality research, triadic reflexivity is called for as we envision follow-up investigations to the existential search studies summarized above. Figure 1 diagrams aspects of triadic reflexivity as a process-oriented research strategy. Widely disseminated principles of human-science research help researchers design methods and formulate theories that are informed by the lived experience of research participants as our "co-researchers" (1-2 link). And traditional literature reviews obligate scholars to consider available methods and theories as alternatives to any specific proposal. In spirituality research, we recommend that this accountability to scholarly standards be expanded in practice to include divergent research paradigms and, even more unusual, to incorporate mutual ideological critique as it arises in the literature (1-3 link). Furthermore, other scholars might have insights on our research participants, either as empirical investigators or as stakeholders familiar with life contexts of import to participants in our studies (2-3 link). For instance, scholars with broad experience in comparative religious studies can frequently enrich the research of psychologists of religion. These and other dyadic collaborations provide incremental enhancements for research. In common practice, however, the sheer quantity of such cumulative enhancements prevents radical impact for any but the most longstanding research programs. Volf and Kelly are not, however, offering yet one more item to some exaggerated wish list of research quality. They are both crystal

254

clear that "business as usual" is what is put at risk in aggressive, audacious pursuits, such as the research strategies suggested above. The challenge of triadic reflexivity is to embody justice promotion as basic research practice instead of compartmentalizing this responsibility into "extra" processes of interpretation or application.

The mutual critique of embrace facilitates another level of reflexive demand for justice into our research practices. When mere-

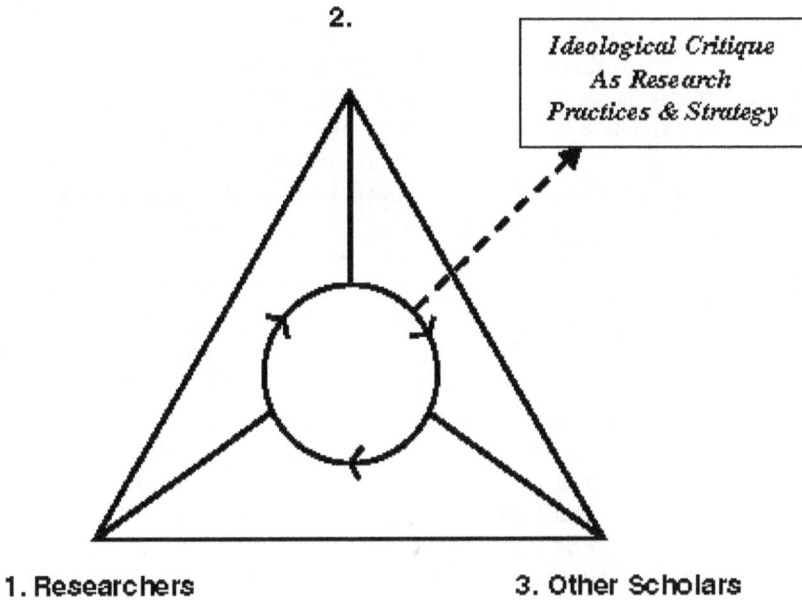

Figure 1. Triadic reflexivity embodying three-way conversations

ly passive openness to ideological critique (link 1-3) becomes a responsibility for proactive, reflexive incorporation of the ideological Other in the practices of any research, another synergy emerges. Not only are the core premises of a project vulnerable and accountable to the lives of research participants and our reading of the literature, but the study design and procedures are incomplete until place is made for the ideological critic and their position becomes visible in ongoing practices as well as post hoc interpretation. Justice-promotion risks research practices in their entirety. The circle at the cen-

255

ter of Figure 1 is intended to suggest the way that our research practices can accommodate peer consultation (as ideological Other) as an
explicit requirement of ethics review, for instance, rather than waiting until a study report is complete. And perhaps the position of ideological Other could be taken up by articulate participants in a religious tradition who are critical of perspectives offered by research
participants, of research practices per se, or both. The key element is
to make justice-promotion internal to research practices and to
proactively solicit and incorporate stakeholders who can reflect voice
of ideological critique.

One implication of triadic reflexivity in empirical investigation in religious studies may require particular adjustment in disciplinary practices. Psychological investigations often presume a single, unitary conceptual framework as sufficient for entire programs
of investigation and employ conceptual coherence as a criterion for
scientific adequacy. In comparative religious study, however, a certain
openness to fundamental incommensurability among theories is
often required to do justice to the various worldviews engaged in
particular projects. When the acknowledgement of diverse worldviews becomes internal to the research enterprise, investigating
adherents to various worldviews no longer becomes a simple matter
of sample generalizability. For instance, in our quest research, the
conceptualization of religious orientations as stable dispositions
across multiple life domains becomes problematic. We have adopted
the rubric of "existential pathways" to help increase the permeability of conceptual tools available as we investigate religious maturity as
lived by participants in our projects. Perhaps researchers on spiritual
maturity need to ask how often pathways for existential search take
the shape of stable predispositions, superordinate life motives, or
temporary projects second to more superordinate narrative structures. Varying patterns of this kind may require substantial permeability of research method and theory as investigators trace the
threads of spiritual maturity in various communities and traditions.
In such manners, the prioritizing of justice promotion in research
may well have substantive implications for the science taking shape
in these domains.

IMPLICATIONS

Nowhere in the academy is the promotion of just research
practices more directly germane than in the investigation of spirituality and faith. While some scholars have chosen to engage the inves-

tigation of passionate, perhaps even violent disagreement directly with appropriate accommodation in the scholarly enterprise (e.g., Newbigin, 1996; Peterson, 1999; Volf, 1996, 2001), much of the research literature in the psychology of religion remains enamored with uncritical traditions in the nomothetic paradigms of individual differences and experimental social psychology. Such work in North America is often isolated from broader, multidisciplinary dimensions of religious studies and continues to strive for misleadingly "objective" descriptions. To move forward by dealing with fundamental questions surrounding the nature of religious or spiritual maturity (cf. Hill et al., 2000), psychologists of religion need to acknowledge ideology in research through innovations in theory, method, and paradigm in interfaith contexts (cf. Moore, 2002). Our invitation for justice-promoting research strategies requires disciplinary projects to be vulnerable to the projects of the Other—whether research participant, disciplinary other, cultural other, or ideological opponent. Promoting justice as constructivist psychologists necessitates the framing and dissemination of disciplinary practices that bolster core permeability among scholars as well as among research participants. A viable strategy for enhancing one's own core permeability is to proactively incorporate ideological critique as internal to the research enterprise. We have illustrated some possibilities arising with our invitation through a project the investigation of existential search and spiritual maturity.

At times, scholars of spirituality have trivialized justice as an intellectual standard—sometimes through neglect, sometimes through ideological presumption, and sometimes through uncritical assumptions about the viability of consensus. Disagreements among scholars are not polite parlor games, nor are they disembodied contemplations of abstract relations among propositions. Serious political disagreements can be much more than arbitrary prejudices that reproduce current power structures. Embrace emerges powerfully in encounters between people. Core permeability is lived out in audacious experiments in life that are socially impactful. Scholarship embodies forms of life that vigorously defies violence as well as providing flesh for our dearest, most heartfelt aspirations. Intellectual visions are likely no more important in human communities than are political purposes or personal aspirations, but they can also be no less consequential than other strivings that shape human life. Acknowledging responsibility to one another in the academy and to other communities in which we are situated, then, as scholars we are caught up in human projects being worked out in community life. Constructivist ethics provides resources for engaging such responsibilities and for holding one another accountable in the process without presuming our personal political ideology as the final arbiter of all matters of import.

Spirituality research instantiates these challenges in especially poignant ways. Religious studies as an academic enterprise has struggled with ways to legitimately acknowledge commitments at the heart of scholarship. Furthermore, growing globalization can magnify contacts among adherents of diverse worldviews, leading both to polarization and to mutual understanding. Advocating for justice in spirituality research while engaging competing visions for justice requires reflexive elaboration of standards for intellectual adequacy. Advocacy in a pluralist mode may require the risk of all that we hold dear—as constructivists, as adherents to our own worldviews, or as scholars. The empirical projects briefly described here could be read merely as an elaboration and corrective of Batson's Quest theory and as an endorsement of Watson's ideological critique. If that is all that our work can accomplish, we fail to promote justice in the practices psychology. Our studies can support critique in preliminary ways through practices of data gathering, analysis, and interpretation. To embrace justice more fully as intrinsic to research on spirituality, we must engage—as internal to the project of empirical investigation—our participants, adherents of other worldviews, scholars who reject our positions, and proponents of alternative visions for justice.

For our part, we propose a constructivist ethic of embrace that can situate research and writing in a face-to-face encounter with an Other who is enemy. This proposal is an invitation, striving to provide orients among alternative research practices. By centering a mode of ethics in ways to address adversaries, we do not exclude consensus with colleagues or others of like mind, nor do we privilege offensiveness as higher quality scholarship. Adversarial conflict is no more or less central to intellectual integrity than is consensus. Rather, the stance promoted here strives to avoid impotent alternatives like (a) a self-effacing vulnerability that minimizes or displaces responsibility, or (b) a narrow dogmatism that remains impermeable to the demands of justice embodied in the presence of the other. Refusing to address conflicts among worldviews, on the other hand, banishes the passions of commitment to a netherworld of "privatized values"—the legacy of a bankrupt liberalism. While searching for commonality and shared values remains strategically worthwhile, an ethic of embrace requires direct engagement, whether or not common ground is clear.

Kelly (1965) reminded humanists and constructivists alike that aggression is critical for the fully alive human—scholars included! Commitment to ideals of justice can and must be audaciously pursued in scholarship and in the general conduct of psychology, notwithstanding the ample risks of failure. Volf (1996, 2001) showed us an additional route for attaining justice in a world shaped by violence—scholars included! By demanding vulnerability even in the face of a violent adversary and by situating that vulnerability in the demand for justice, Volf invites us as constructivists to embrace all Others. Moreover, this invitation demands of us the mobilization of constructivist paradigms to promote justice in psychology, even when the demand and our paradigms are excluded! If Volf can accept the challenge to love an enemy in the face of war, can we aspire to any less courage when faced with violence emerging from academic politics, ideological struggle, or oppression in our own communities? If constructivist celebrations of pluralism undermine commitment or eschew embrace, we must step aside from the challenge of addressing today's world, a world in which violence sometimes shapes the lives of people.

We invite constructivists to continue elaborating these projects and to engage criticism even when embrace is required among stakeholders. Spirituality research is in the midst of exciting transformations. Clinical practice is likewise addressing spirituality with greater intensity in recent years. Multicultural perspectives, spirituality-health research, and Volf's prophetic call to social justice can all help elaborate constructivist ethics as a transformational project. As many different scholars undertake such transformations we hope that diversity will strengthen as a multi-voiced chorus singing justice in and through the practices of psychology. This aggressive, justice-promoting psychology can help sustain courage and hope like that offered by the rabbi in the oft-quoted Hasidic tale.

REFERENCES

Allport, G. W., & Ross, J. M. (1967). Personal religious orientation and prejudice. *Journal of Personality and Social Psychology, 5*, 432-43.

Altemeyer, B., & Hunsberger, B. (1994). Authoritarianism, religious fundamentalism, quest, and prejudice. *The International Journal for the Psychology of Religion, 2*, 113-133.

Batson, C. D., & Schoenrade, P. A. (1991a). Measuring religion as quest: (1) Validity concerns. *Journal for the Scientific Study of Religion, 30*, 416-429.

Batson, C. D., & Schoenrade, P. A. (1991b). Measuring religion as quest: (2) Reliability concerns. *Journal for the Scientific Study of Religion, 30*, 430-447.

Batson, C. D., Schoenrade, P. A., & Ventis, W. L. (1993). *Religion and the individual: A social-psychological perspective.* New York: Oxford University Press.

Benson, P. L., Donahue, M. J., & Erickson, J. A., (1993). The faith maturing scale: Conceptualization, measurement, and empirical validation. *Research in the Social Scientific Study of Religion, 5*, 1-26.

Burris, C. T., Jackson, L. M., Tarpley, W. R., & Smith, G. J. (1996). Religion as quest: The self-directed pursuit of meaning. *Personality and Social Psychology Bulletin, 22*, 1068-1076.

Compton, W. C. (2001). Toward a tri-partite factor structure of mental health: Subjective well-being, personal growth and religiosity. *The Journal of Psychology, 135*(5), 486-500.

Danziger, K. (1997). *Naming the mind: How psychology found its language.* Thousand Oaks, CA: Sage.

Donahue, M. J. (1985). Intrinsic and extrinsic religiousness: Review and meta-analysis. *Journal of Personality and Social Psychology, 48*, 400-419.

Dreyfus, H., & Dreyfus, S. (1999). *What is moral maturity? A phenomenological account of the development of ethical expertise.* Retrieved from http://ist-socrates.berkeley.edu/~hdreyfus/24-1_s02/pdf/moral_maturity.pdf.

Fransella, F., & Bannister, D. (1977). *A manual for repertory grid technique.* New York: Academic Press.

Fulton, A. S., Gorsuch, R. L., & Maynard, E. A. (1999). Religious orientation, antihomosexual sentiment, and fundamentalism among Christians. *Journal for the Scientific Study of Religion, 38*, 14-22.

Genia, V. (1996). I, E, quest, and fundamentalism as predictors of psychological and spiritual well-being. *Journal for the Scientific Study of Religion*, 35, 56-64.

Gallant, C. M. (2001). *Existential expeditions: Religious orientation and personal meaning.* Unpublished masters thesis, Trinity Western University, Langley, British Columbia.

Graham, M. D. (2001). *A phenomenological study of Quest-oriented religion.* Unpublished masters thesis, Trinity Western University, Langley, British Columbia.

Hadjistavropoulos, T., & Smythe, W. E. (2001). Elements of risk in qualitative research. *Ethics & Behavior*, 11, 163-174.

Harré, R., & Gillette, G. (1994). *The discursive mind.* Thousand Oaks, CA: Sage.

Hill, P., Pargament, K., Hood, Jr., R., McCullough, M., Swyers, J. P., Larson, D., & Zinnbauer, B. (2000). Conceptualizing religion and spirituality: Points of commonality, points of depature. *Journal for the Theory of Social Behavior*, 30, 51-77.

House, D. V. (1994). *Without God or his doubles: Realism, relativism, and Rorty.* Boston, MA: Brill.

Keyes, C. L. M., Shmotkin, D., & Ryff, C. (2002). Optimizing well-being: The empirical encounter of two traditions. *Journal of Personality and Social Psychology*, 82(6), 1007-1022.

Kelly, G. A. (1965). The threat of aggression. *The Journal of Humanistic Psychology*, 5(2), 195–201.

Klaassen, D. W., & McDonald, M. J. (2002). Quest & identity development: Re-examining pathways for existential search. *International Journal for the Psychology of Religion*, 12(3), 189-200.

Koenig, H. G., McCullough, M. E., & Larson, D. B. (2001). *Handbook of religion and health.* New York: Oxford University Press.

Kojetin, B. A., McIntosh, D. N., Bridges, R. A., & Spilka, B. (1987). Quest: Constructive search or religious conflict? *Journal for the Scientific Study of Religion*, 26, 111-115.

Kunz, G. (1998). *The paradox of power and weakness: Levinas and an alternative paradigm for psychology.* Albany, NY: SUNY Press.

Marcia, J. E., Waterman, A. S., Matteson, D. R., Archer, S. L., & Orlofsky, J. L. (1993). *Ego identity: A handbook for psychosocial research.* New York: Springer.

261

McDonald, M. J., Klaassen, D. W., Gallant, C., & Graham, M. (2002, May). *Existential distinctives among Quest, Intrinsic, and Extrinsic religious orientations*. Poster presented at the annual meeting of the Canadian Psychological Association, Vancouver, British Columbia.

Moore, J. F. (2002). Interfaith dialogue and the science-and-religion discussion. *Zygon, 37*, 37-43.

Newbigin, L. (1995). *Proper confidence*. Grand Rapids, MI: Eerdmans.

Parke, R. D. (2001). Introduction to the special section on families and religion: A call for a recommitment by researchers, practitioners, and policymakers. *Journal of Family Psychology, 15*, 555-558.

Peterson, J. B. (1999). *Maps of meaning: The architecture of belief*. New York: Routledge.

Renner, K. E., Alksnis, C., & Park, L. (1997). The standard of social justice as a research process. *Canadian Psychology, 38*, 91-102.

Richards, P. S., & Bergin, A. E. (Ed.) (2000). *Handbook of psychotherapy and religious diversity*. Washington, DC: American Psychological Association.

Rouse, J. (2002). *How scientific practices matter: Reclaiming philosophical naturalism*. Chicago: University of Chicago Press.

Sanders, J. L. (1998). Religious ego identity and its relationship to faith maturity. *Journal of Psychology Interdisciplinary & Applied, 132*, 653-659.

Smythe, W. E., & Murray, M. J. (2000). Owning the story: Ethical considerations in narrative research. *Ethics & Behavior, 10*, 311-336.

Taylor, C. (1995). *Philosophical arguments*. Cambridge, MA: Harvard University Press.

Tjeltveit, A. C. (1999). *Ethics and values in psychotherapy*. London: Routledge.

Ventis, W. L. (1995). The relationships between religion and mental health. *Journal of Social Issues, 51*, 33-48.

Volf, M. (1996). *Exclusion and embrace: A theological exploration of identity, otherness, and reconciliation*. Nashville, TN: Abingdon Press.

Volf, M. (2001, February). *Forgiveness, reconciliation and justice*. Annual Capps Lecture in Christian Theology presented at the University of Virginia, Charlottesville, February 8. Retrieved from http://livedtheology.org/pdfs/Volf.pdf.

Watson, P. J., Morris, R. J., & Hood, Jr., R. W. (1989). Interactional factor correlations with means and end religiousness. *Journal for the Scientific Study of Religion, 28,* 337- 47.

Watson, P. J., Morris, R. J., & Hood, Jr., R. W. (1992). Quest and identity within a religious ideological surround. *Journal of Psychology and Theology, 20,* 376-388.

Watson, P. J., Morris, R. J., Hood, Jr., R. W., Milliron, J. T., & Stutz, N. L. (1998). Religious orientation, identity, and the quest for meaning in ethics within an ideological surround. *International Journal for the Psychology of Religion, 8,* 149-164.

Wong, P. T. P. (1998). Implicit theories of meaningful life and the development of the Personal Meaning Profile (PMP). In P. T. P. Wong & P. Fry (Eds.), *Handbook of personal meaning: Theory, research, and practice* (pp. 111-140). Mahwah, NJ: Lawrence Erlbaum.

Part IV

Dialogue, Reflection, and Anticipation: Future Directions

CHAPTER 12

Adlerian Psychology and Psychotherapy: A Relational Constructivist Approach[1]

Richard E. Watts and Kati A. Phillips

Akin to ideas expressed by Botella and Herrero (2000) and R. A. Neimeyer (2000), we see Relational Constructivism as a dialogic bridge between cognitive constructivist and social constructionist perspectives. Adlerian psychology and psychotherapy situates within this dialogic space in a flexible, integrative manner. Thus, Adlerian theory and therapy—explicitly and implicitly—share these assumptions of relational constructionism and may be rightly understood as a relational constructivist approach. The purpose of this chapter is to demonstrate the plausibility of this proposition.

To begin, it is important to note that Adler's theory has remained obscure and is often misunderstood and misrepresented. There are several potential reasons that may account for this situation.

1. *Alfred Adler was not an academician.* Adler was a mediocre and unsystematic writer and was more interested in helping people than becoming well known. "Adler once proclaimed that he was more concerned that his theories survive than that people remembered to associate his theories with his name. His wish was apparently granted" (Mosak, 1995, p. 55).

2. *"Power as Knowledge."* In the history of psychology, we see numerous examples of the "Power as Knowledge" political phenomenon that social constructionists have borrowed from Michel Foucault. Common wisdom says, "Knowledge is power." Foucault suggested that instead, "Power is knowledge." In other words, whoever has the power determines what is worth knowing, what is *true*

---

[1] A version of this paper was presented at the Tenth Biennial Conference of the North American Personal Construct Network, Vancouver, BC, July 2002. Portions are adapted from Watts (2003) and Watts and Shulman (2003).

or right. For a long time, psychoanalysts and radical behaviorists controlled both the academy and therapy training institutions. Whereas they had the "power," they determined what "knowledges" were worth knowing. Psychoanalysts either ignored Adler or misrepresented him—i.e., a minor neo-Freudian—because Adler was a dissident who rejected classical psychoanalysis. Behaviorists ignored Adler because he was "unscientific." Consequently, students at that time—who subsequently created their own theories of psychotherapy—were not honestly introduced to Adler, and consequently presented ideas that sounded remarkably like Adler's but with little or no acknowledgement of him. This same phenomenon may have occurred with George Kelly and Personal Construct Theory at the beginning of the cognitive revolution. Bruner (1990) states that when the cognitive revolution began, it originally had a constructionist orientation (e.g., George Kelly's Personal Construct Theory). Whereas this perspective did not fit with the dominant "logical positivist" zeitgeist in psychology (like Adler earlier in the century), it was circumvented by a more "scientific" view: the information-processing model, a computational perspective of cognition that views the mind as a computer.

3. *Adler's theory is often poorly presented in the literature.* Many "secondary source" textbooks and journal literature have provided inadequate and erroneous presentations of Adlerian Psychology and Psychotherapy. For example, Adler's theory often has been erroneously described as "neo-Freudian" and placed alongside discussions of other Psychoanalytic theories. While it is true that the neo-Freudians were strongly influenced by Adler (Ellenberger, 1970), it is not true that Individual Psychology was merely the first neo-Freudian position:

> When Maslow introduced his "third force," subsequently named "humanistic psychology," he listed Adlerians first among the groups included and the *Journal of Individual Psychology* among the five journals where these groups are most likely to publish. He also invited [H.L. Ansbacher], as representing Adlerian psychology, to become a founding sponsor of the Association for Humanistic Psychology and member of the editorial board of the *Journal of Humanistic Psychology*. (Ansbacher, 1990, p. 46)

ADLERIAN THERAPY AS A RELATIONAL CONSTRUCTIVIST
APPROACH : THEORETICAL CONSIDERATIONS

Adlerian theory and therapy contains many ideas that resonate with ones from both cognitive constructivist and social constructionist theories and therapies. The Adlerian approach affirms
with social constructionism the sociocultural origins of human psychological development. In addition, the Adlerian perspective agrees
with cognitive constructivism's emphasis on the importance of
humans as active agents creatively involved in the co-construction of
their own psychology: "Although humans exist in a sociocultural
world of persons, a distinguishing characteristic of personhood is
the possession of an individual agentic consciousness" (Martin &
Sugarman, 1997, p. 377). Some constructive theorists and theories
eschew individualism and declare the inescapability of being situated in some relational matrix. However, if there is no self-reflective
individual and situatedness is indeed inescapable, then it is a spuri-
ous notion to think that we can engage in the "emacipatory potential of discourse analysis, that is, inquiry which causes us to reflect
critically and creatively on our own forms of life" (Gergen, 1999, p.
80). The conviction that "all that is meaningful stems from relationship" has no particular utility for the situation you happen to be in,
because "the constraints of that situation will not be relaxed by that
knowledge" (Stanley Fish, as quoted in Korobov, 2000, p. 368).

In agreement with Martin and Sugarman (1997), a relational constructivist understanding of Adlerian therapy affirms that the
individual is understood to arise from the social but is not the same
as, nor reducible to, the social (Martin & Sugarman, 1997, p. 377).
Adlerian theory is a holistic perspective, one that eschews viewing
humans in a reductionistic manner. It views knowledge as socially
embedded and relationally distributed, but does not empty the self.
Rather than a forced "either/or" position between individualism and
constructionism, the Adlerian/relationally constructivist position
embraces a "both/and" one, accounting for and affirming that
knowledge and experience is a co-construction of self and others in
a socially embedded matrix.

According to R. A. Neimeyer (1995a), constructivist
approaches share a common or similar epistemology and may by
distinguished by their "operative assumptions about the nature of
personal knowledge and its social embeddedness" (p. 5). Mahoney
(1995b) notes that constructivism is essentially "a family of theories
and therapies that emphasize at least three interrelated principles of

human experience." (p. 44). These three central features of constructive metatheory include:

> (a) humans are proactive (and not passively reactive) partici-
> pants in their own experience--that is, in all perception, mem-
> ory and knowing; (b) the vast majority of ordering processes
> organizing human lives operate at tacit (un- or super-con-
> scious) levels of awareness; and (c) human experience and per-
> sonal psychological development reflect the ongoing operation
> of individualized, self-organizing processes that tend to favor
> the maintenance (over the modification) of experiential pat-
> terns. Although uniquely individual, these organizing processes
> always reflect and influence social systems. (Mahoney, 1995b,
> pp. 44-45)

R. A. Neimeyer and Mahoney mention four areas that resonate with
fundamental tenets of Adlerian psychology and psychotherapy:
philosophical roots, human agency, knowledge structures, and social
embeddedness.

Philosophical Roots

Adlerian and constructive theories clearly share common
ground regarding their philosophical roots. Like constructivism, the
epistemological roots of Adlerian theory are largely found in the critical philosophy of Immanuel Kant and the "as if" philosophy of
Hans Vaihinger (Ansbacher & Ansbacher, 1956; Ellenberger, 1970;
Shulman, 1985; Watts, 1999). In fact, Jones (1995) and Mahoney
(1991), both constructivists, have acknowledged Kant and Vaihinger
as common precursors for both Adler and constructivism. Both Kant
and Vaihinger emphasized the proactive, form-giving, and fictional
character of human cognition and its role in constructing the "realities" we know and to which we respond. Adlerian theory asserts that
humans construct, manufacture, or *narratize* ways of looking at and
experiencing the world and then they take these *fictions* for truth
(Ansbacher & Ansbacher, 1956; Ellenberger, 1970; Master, 1991;
Shulman & Watts, 1997; Watts, 1999; Watts, 2003; Watts & Critelli,
1997; Watts & Pietrzak, 2000; Watts & Shulman, 2003).

In addition, Adler acknowledged the influence of Karl Marx
and Friedrich Nietzsche on his theory (Ansbacher, 1983; Ansbacher
& Ansbacher, 1956, 1979; Ellenberger, 1970). From Marx and
Nietzsche, Adler gleaned ideas such as the socially embedded and fictional nature of human knowledge, the abilities and creativity of
human beings, the necessity of egalitarian relationships and equal
rights for all persons, and the socially useful and socially useless

270

political and power issues involved in human relationships. Social constructionist therapies, via the writings of post-structural/post-modern theorists such as Derrida and Foucault, also have roots in the philosophies of Marx and Nietzsche (Gergen, 1994, 1999; Hoyt, 1996, 1998; R. A. Neimeyer & Raskin, 2000; Raskin & Bridges, 2002; White & Epston, 1990). Consequently, many ideas Adler gleaned from Marx and Nietzsche are among the prevalent themes discussed in social constructionist therapies (Watts, 2003; Watts & Pietrzak, 2000; Watts & Shulman, 2003).

Human Agency

The common ground between Adlerians and constructivists regarding human agency is noteworthy. According to Mahoney (1988, 1991, 1995a), constructivist theory espouses a proactive (vs. reactive and representational) view of cognition and organism.

> What might well be considered the cardinal feature of constructivism is its assertion that *human knowing* is active, anticipatory, and literally 'constructive' (form-giving)...In one sense, then, constructivism argues that humans are literal co-creators of the 'realities' to which they respond (Mahoney, Miller, & Arciero, 1995, p. 104).

The description of active, creative behavior in the organism sounds like what Adler called the *creative power of the self* or the *creative self*. In discussing human agency, Adler stated:

> Do not forget the most important fact that not heredity and not environment are determining factors. Both are giving only the frame and the influences which are answered by the individual in regard to his styled creative power (p. xxiv)...The individual is both the picture and the artist. He is the artist of his own personality. (Ansbacher & Ansbacher, 1956, p. 177)

Because of this creative power, humans function like actors writing their own scripts, directing their own actions, and forming their own personalities (Shulman, 1985). According to Adler (1931/1992):

> Human beings live in the realm of *meanings*. We do not experience things in the abstract; we always experience them in human terms. Even at its source our experience is qualified by our human perspective...Anyone who tried to consider circumstances, to the exclusion of meanings, would be very unfortunate: he would isolate himself from others and his actions would be useless to himself or to anyone else; in a word, they would be meaningless. But no human being can escape mean-

ings. We experience reality only through the meaning we
ascribe to it: not as a thing in itself, but as something interpreted. (p. 15)

The realization that individuals co-construct the reality in which they
live and are also able to "question, deconstruct, or reconstruct reality for themselves" is a fundamental tenet "not only of Adlerian psychotherapy but also of other constructivist psychotherapies"
(Carlson & Sperry, (1998, p. 68).

R. A. Neimeyer and Mahoney (1995) noted that Maturana
introduced a word in biology and other fields that describes the
proactive, creative, and participatory nature of organisms described
by constructivism. Maturana called it autopoiesis. Interestingly, the
Greek word literally means "self" (auto) and "creative power or construction" (poiesis) (R. A. Neimeyer & Mahoney, 1995, p. 401). The
nomenclature is remarkably similar to Adler's "creative power (or
construction) of the self."

Knowledge Structures

There is much common ground between Adlerian and constructive theories regarding knowledge structures. In this section, we
will address (a) general descriptions of knowledge structures, (b)
knowledge structures and unconscious processes, and (c) the unity
of knowledge structures and resultant selective attention.

General Descriptions of Knowledge Structures

As Disque and Bitter (1998) note, we live "storied" lives.

As humans, we not only experience life directly through our
senses, but we also transform it in an effort to make meaning
out of what we experience. We live constantly with other human
beings, and as such, we frame all that we do in the context of
social relationships. The ordering of the meaning we experience
in our lives with others most often takes the form of a story or
narrative about who we are; who others are; what we are worth
to ourselves, others, and the world; and what conclusions, convictions, and ethical codes will guide us...Adler was one of the
first to recognize this process in human development. He called
the ordering of our experiences into a teleological narrative our
lifestyle, our unique way of being, of coping, and of moving
through (and approaching the tasks of life). (p. 431)

What we know is influenced by the frames through which we view
events. Everything we know depends on how we interpret and assign
meanings (Guidano, 1995a, 1995b; R. A. Neimeyer, 1995b). As
Nelson Goodman notes, "If I ask about the world, you can offer to

tell me how it is under one or more frames of reference, but if I insist that you tell me how it is apart from all frames, what can you say? (as quoted in Gergen, 2001, p. 11). Knowledge is derived from looking at the world from some perspective or the other, and is in the service of some interests rather than others.

It is important to note that social constructionists disdain the structural language used by cognitive constructivists, and the individualist implications, thereof. They instead use literary metaphors like "narratives" or "stories." Regardless of the language used by cognitive constructivists or social constructionists, both are nevertheless addressing how persons give—or construct—*meaning* to their experiences.

Constructive descriptions of knowledge structures as "personal construct systems," "personal meaning organizations," "core ordering processes," "narratives," or "stories" are reminiscent of Adler's *style of life* or *lifestyle*, the superordinate rule or personal metanarrative for apprehending and responding to events and pressures. Mahoney (1988) acknowledged the similarity.

> Although the presence of organization in human experience may not be controversial, the nature and power of that organization take one into realms of less consensus. Few psychologists would challenge the notion that humans develop individually patterned lifestyles, for example, but many would hesitate to embrace the concept of *lifestyle* as it was originally intended by Alfred Adler. Drawing on his familiarity with Vaihinger's philosophy of fictions, Adler viewed the lifestyle as an abstract organizing principle or construct that formatively influenced the contents and process of experience. (p. 7)

The *style of life*, unique to each individual, is in Kelly's (1955/1991a, 1955/1991b) language a *personal construct system*, containing *core constructs*. It is created by the person, begins as a rule of thumb for action in the world, and becomes progressively refined. Shulman (1973) and Shulman and Mosak (1988) describe the functions of the style of life: it organizes and simplifies coping with the world by assigning rules and values; it selects, predicts, anticipates; its perceptions are guided by its own "private logic"; it selects what information it allows to enter, what it will attend to, what affects will be aroused and what its response will be. According to Shulman (1985), the lifestyle contains certain key elements. These include "a set of constructs about the self, the world, and the relationship between the two; a construct about what the relationship should be; an image of the ideal self; and a plan of action" (p. 246). All of these elements are

273

attitudes, values, and meanings that the individual has creatively constructed within a socially-embedded context.

Narrative therapists Parry and Doan (1994) note that recent neurobiological research indicates that one of the brain's primary functions is to create a "model" of the world, an internal blueprint or roadmap. This model is established early in life and becomes "reality," serves as a guide for subsequent life experiences, and selectively attends to—through modification or rejection—only that incoming data that fits with its "program." The brain's function of creating an internal blueprint or roadmap is fundamentally similar to both constructive perspectives and the Adlerian idea of the relationally co-created style of life.

Knowledge Structures and Unconscious Processes

According to constructivism, the knowledge structures or "core ordering processes" by which humans organize and construct meaning for "reality" are largely nonconscious.

> From a constructivist perspective, tacit (unconscious) processes of mental activity are deep structure ordering rules that organize ongoing experience and anticipate imminent experience. This means that abstract tacit processes operate passively in our experience, and yet, as the words *abstract* and *tacit* imply, their operations are well beyond our conscious awareness. (Guidano, 1995a, p.92)

The above quote could correctly be used to describe the Adlerian position regarding an individual's style of life. Mosak (1995) explains, "although the life-style is the instrument for coping with experience, it is very largely nonconscious" (p. 63). Humans are not typically aware of the convictions that guide their lives. Whereas the style of life is the blueprint or map for coping with experience, it nevertheless remains largely out of one's awareness—Adler's process understanding of unconscious. Thus, both the construction of the individual's unique style of life and the goals and core convictions contained therein are also essentially unconscious (Allen, 1971; Mosak, 1979; Shulman, 1985).

Unity of Knowledge Structures and Selective Attention

According to constructivist theory, knowledge structures of the human organism are unified in their processes and, therefore, selectively attend to those aspects of reality that confirm and support their maintenance.

274

The search for consistency (maintenance processes) is the basic procedure for structuring and stabilizing available levels of self-identity and self-awareness...change processes derive from attempts to convert emergent core schemata into beliefs and thought procedures and are regulated and modeled, step by step, by maintenance processes aimed at preserving the functional continuity and the sense of oneness inherent in selfhood structures (Guidano, 1995a, p. 97).

Adlerian theory sees the unity of personality and concomitant perceptual selectivity of the human organism in very similar ways. According to Adlerian theory, "personality (lifestyle) is a unity, an organized and integrated whole" (Forgus & Shulman, 1979, p. 107). The lifestyle organizes and maintains the whole perceptual system of the individual, resulting in selective perceptual processing of all incoming information. Thus, the organism looks for information confirming the core convictions of the lifestyle, "selectively perceiving information from events so that it proves to itself what it already suspects" (Shulman, 1985, p. 246). The great majority of cognitive functions (e.g., memory, learning, expectancy, fantasy, symbol creation) are influenced by perceptual selectivity. "One result of the (lifestyle) is thus a private frame of reference by which the individual orients himself (or herself) and arranges his (or her) coping strategies in the world-as-perceived" (Shulman, 1985, p. 247).

Social Embeddedness

The common ground between Adlerian and constructive theories regarding social embeddedness is especially striking. As mentioned earlier, R. A. Neimeyer (1995b) comments that one of the distinguishing marks of constructivism is its "operative assumptions about the structure of personal knowledge and its social embeddedness" (p. 15). Constructivists affirm that humans are undeniably social beings and that "any knowledge of oneself and the world is always dependent on and relative to knowledge of others" (Guidano, 1995b, p. 96). Regarding early family and developmental history, Guidano (1995b) affirms that constructivists find utility in John Bowlby's Attachment Theory.

> Within an intersubjective reality, attachment exerts an organizational role in the development of a sense of self both as subject and as object...Through regularities drawn from caregivers' behaviors and affective messages, the infant can begin to construct basic feelings that are inseparable from early perceptions, actions, and memories. (p. 97)

The constructive view of social embeddedness echoes the position taken by Adler (Ansbacher & Ansbacher, 1956, 1979) and subsequent Adlerians. *Adlerian psychology is a relational psychology.* Adler noted that humans are socially embedded and cannot be understood apart from their relational context. The cardinal tenet of Adlerian Psychology is social interest.

> [Adler's] placement of social interest at the pinnacle of his value theory is in the tradition of those religions that stress people's responsibility for each other (p. 59)...If we regard ourselves as fellow human beings with fellow feeling, we are socially contributive people interested in the common welfare, and by Adler's pragmatic definition of *normality*, mentally healthy. (Mosak, 1995, p. 53)

Manaster and Corsini (1982) state that the human personality or lifestyle "evolves from a biological being in a social context creating a sense of self in the world in which he (or she) acts" (p. 77). This social context of the child includes both the cultural values of the child's culture of origin and his or her experiences within his or her *family constellation*, Adler's phrase for the operative influences of the family structure, values, and dynamics (Shulman, 1985). Thus, "the child sees the world in general as paralleling his (or her) home environment and eventually the wider world on the basis of his (or her) initial perceptions" (Manaster & Corsini, 1982, p. 91). Peluso, White, and Kern (2001) discuss the similarity between essential elements of attachment theory and Adlerian psychology: "The major areas of convergence between the two theories are that both include a coherent and stable view of self and the world, and both acknowledge the importance of social interaction for the expression of these patterns" (p. 4). As Peluso et al. (2001) indicate, the parallels between the development of attachment theory's "internal working model" and Adler's "style of life" are remarkable indeed. They note that the lifestyle, like the internal working model of self and others, is an internalized subjective creation based on relationships with early primary caregivers and family members: "Therefore, both the internal working model of self and others, and the lifestyle are important because they have a lasting impact on an individual's work relationships, friendships, and selection of a partner" (Peluso et al., 2001, p.12).

> The cardinal tenet of Adler's theory, *social interest*, is obviously a social-contextual one. The tendency of human beings to form attachments (social feelings) was considered by Adler to be a fact of life. The striving of the human is always in some way

> connected with human bonding. Social interest is the expression
> of this tendency in a way that promotes human welfare. Some
> aspects of social interest are innate as in the infant's tendency to
> bond with its mother. However, social interest is a potential that
> must be developed through training in cooperation with pro-
> ductive endeavor. (Shulman, 1985, p. 248)

Interestingly, the development of the attachment motive in attachment theory appears to parallel the development of Adler's social
interest. Both are innate, both have to be developed in interaction
with primary caregivers, and the degree to which both are present
in an individual's life impacts the degree to which that person moves
toward or against/away from fellow human beings (Ansbacher &
Ansbacher, 1979; Ainsworth, 1964; Bowlby, 1982; Forgus &
Shulman, 1979; Peluso et al, 2001; Watts, 2003; Watts & Shulman,
2003). According to Mosak and Maniacci (1999):

> [Many] constructionists believe that through early bonding
> interactions, individuals learn to encode and process informa-
> tion in such a way as to feel secure. This becomes the basis of
> later attempts to bond with others; hence, if early attachment
> was disturbed or in any significant way disordered, as adults, we
> may continue the inappropriate attempts at bonding in much
> the same manner as we did as children. In fact, [many] con-
> structionists believe that psychopathology is itself a disordered
> attempt at bonding. This is Adler's and Dreikurs' opinion as well.
> Adlerians believe that psychopathology is a discouraged attempt
> at belonging. (p. 169).

Peluso et al. (2001) also address the parallels between attachment
styles and social interest. Adlerian psychology views social interest as
the measure of mental health. Social interest, like attachment style, is
developed from the earliest social relationships, primarily the family. Peluso et al indicate that persons described as "securely attached"
according to attachment theory manifest behaviors descriptive of
persons with elevated social interest. Conversely, persons with "anxious" or "ambivalent" attachment exhibit behaviors descriptive of
lower levels of social interest. Thus, securely attached children with
an elevated level of social interest are more likely to engage life opti-
mistically and courageously. Thus, both attachment and social interest address the mental health of individuals.

ADLERIAN THERAPY AS A RELATIONAL CONSTRUCTIVIST
APPROACH : CLINICAL / PRACTICAL CONSIDERATIONS

Hoyt (1994) states that, although the constructive approaches certainly have their differences, they share the following clinical-practical characteristics: They place strong emphasis on developing a respectful therapeutic relationship, they emphasize strengths and resources, and they are optimistic and future-oriented. Again, this statement by Hoyt is equally descriptive of Adlerian therapy. Given the aforementioned areas of common ground between Adlerians and constructive approaches, it is not surprising to find much common ground regarding the process of therapy. For the sake of brevity, however, we will address only four: perspective on maladjustment, client reluctance to change, the client-therapist relationship, and facilitating change.

Perspective on Maladjustment

Constructive descriptions of motivation for therapy parallel the Adlerian position. Both eschew the "medical model" perspective and embrace a nonpathological perspective. They both agree that clients are not sick (as in having a disease) and thus are not identified or "labeled" by their diagnoses (de Shazer, 1991; Disque & Bitter, 1998; Hoyt, 1994, 1996, 1998; Littrell, 1998; Manaster & Corsini, 1982; Mosak, 1995; R. A. Neimeyer & Raskin, 2000; Raskin & Bridges, 2002; Parry & Doan, 1994; Schneider & Stone, 1998; Walter & Peller, 1992; Watts, 1999; Watts, 2003; Watts & Pietrzak, 2000; Watts & Shulman, 2003; White & Epston, 1990). According to Parry and Doan (1994):

> The experiences that bring individuals or families to therapy represent, in our view, a "wake up call"—a message that the stories that have formed them and shaped their emotional reactions have reached their limit. Although these stories made sense to children dependent upon adults, they are no longer adequate to help individuals handle present challenges effectively. It is now time for them to question the beliefs and assumptions that their stories have coded, in order to free themselves from the constraints upon capacities that maturity and responsibility have since made available to them. (p. 42)

Littrell (1998) states that clients present for counseling because they are "demoralized" or "discouraged," not because they are sick and in need of a cure. Clients "lack hope...One of our tasks as counselors is to assist in the process of restoring patterns of hope" (p. 63).

The constructive position on maladjustment soundly resonates with the Adlerian model. Adlerians agree that early existential decisions about self and the world—decisions made within and in relation to the first sociological environment, the family—form the core convictions of a client's lifestyle or his or her "story of my life" (Adler, 1931/1992). Adlerians agree that many of the early-formed convictions may have been useful for a child to belong and survive in his or her early environment but later prove to no longer be useful for productive living. In addition, a crucial goal of Adlerian therapy is to help clients challenge and modify or replace growth-inhibiting life themes with ones that are growth enhancing. The ultimate goal is the development or enhancement of clients' social interest.

Because they do not see clients as sick, Adlerians are not about "curing" anything. Rather, in agreement with constructive approaches, therapy is "a process of encouragement" (Manaster & Corsini, 1982, p. 160). Dreikurs (1967) noted the essential necessity of encouragement in counseling. He stated that presenting problems are "based on discouragement" and without "encouragement, without having faith in himself restored, (the client) cannot see the possibility of doing or functioning better" (p. 62). Adler once asked a client what he thought made the difference in his successful experience in therapy. The client replied: "That's quite simple. I had lost all courage to live. In our consultations I found it again" (Ansbacher & Ansbacher, 1956, p. 342).

Because Adlerians view clients as discouraged rather than sick, they thus view client symptoms from a proactive rather than merely reactive perspective. According to Mosak and Maniacci (1999), symptoms are selected and chosen because they are perceived as facilitating movement toward a desired goal. In other words, symptoms are not merely reactions to situations but rather attempted solutions.

Client Reluctance to Change

According to Mahoney, Miller, and Arciero (1995), constructivists believe that the core ordering processes of human beings are less accessible and amenable to change. Furthermore, when these core ordering processes are challenged or threatened in therapy, clients will manifest self-protective mechanisms in order to preserve the integrity of their core meaning system (G. J. Neimeyer, 1995).

279

According to Liotti, "A cognitive structure that attributes meaning and casual relationships to an important class of emotional experiences will be quite resistant to change if the individual does not develop alternative meaning structures" (as quoted in G. J. Neimeyer, 1995, p. 116). G. J. Neimeyer (1995) comments that this self-protective view is common to many constructive approaches.

Adlerians also espouse a "self-protective" view of client reluctance to change. According to Shulman (1985), the core constructs of Adlerian theory's lifestyle are essentially unconscious and are also less accessible and amenable to change. When these core lifestyle convictions are challenged (in life or in therapy), the client often responds by use of "compensation." According to Mosak (1995), Adler used the word compensation as an umbrella to cover all the problem-solving devices the client uses to "safeguard" his or her self-esteem, reputation, and physical self. As in the constructivist perspective, Adlerians view client reluctance to change in terms of the client "self-protecting" or "safeguarding" his or her sense of "self" (Shulman, 1985).

Client-Therapist Relationship

Watts and Pietrzak (2000) note that constructive therapies describe the client-counselor relationship using words such as "cooperative," "collaborative," "egalitarian," "mutual," "optimistic," "respectful," and "shared." In developing the relationship, constructive therapists focus on developing a strong therapeutic alliance, trusting the client, and exploring clients' competencies. Most of the basic skills used in building this relationship are not unique to constructive approaches. In addition, Littrell (1998) states, "strategies and techniques are ineffectual if the facilitative conditions of warmth, genuineness, and empathy do not permeate the counseling process" (p. 8).

Of the many areas of common ground shared between Adlerian theory and constructive approaches, the view of the therapeutic relationship may well be the most similar. All the words used in the constructive therapy literature to describe the counselor-client relationship are also used in the Adlerian literature (e.g., Ansbacher & Ansbacher, 1956; Dreikurs, 1967; Dinkmeyer et al., 1987; Mosak, 1979; Sweeney, 1998; Watts, 1999; Watts, 2003; Watts & Pietrzak, 2000; Watts & Shulman, 2003). For Adlerians, a strong counselor-client relationship is usually developed when counselors model social interest. Watts (1998) noted that Adler's descriptions of therapist-modeled social interest look very similar to Rogers's descriptions of the core facilitative conditions of client change: congruence, unconditional positive regard, and empathic understanding. Furthermore, Mosak (1979) discusses the counselor-client relationship in terms of "faith, hope, and love" (p. 63); that is, expressing faith in clients and helping them develop faith in themselves, instilling hope in clients, and helping clients experience a relationship with an individual who truly cares. The basic skills necessary to build the therapeutic alliance discussed in the Adlerian literature (e.g., Dinkmeyer et al., 1987; Mosak, 1979) are, in the main, the same ones mentioned in constructive therapy literature (e.g., DeJong & Berg, 1998; Littrell, 1998).

Adlerian therapy typically is viewed as consisting of four phases (Mosak, 1995). The first and, for most Adlerians, most important phase is entitled "relationship." The Adlerian approach is a relational psychology and a relational psychotherapy. Because psychotherapy occurs in a relational context, Adlerian therapists focus on developing a respectful, collaborative, and egalitarian therapeutic alliance with clients. Therapeutic efficacy in other phases of Adlerian therapy—analysis, insight, and reorientation—is predicated upon the development and continuation of a strong therapeutic relationship (Watts, 1998, Watts, 2000; Watts, 2003; Watts & Pietrzak, 2000; Watts & Shulman, 2003).

Facilitating Change

Constructive therapists seek to help clients change clients' behaviors and attitudes from a problem/failure focus to a focus on solutions/successes and discover and/or develop latent assets, resources, and strengths that may have been overlooked as clients have focused primarily on "problems" and "limitations" (Watts & Pietrzak, 2000). According to O'Hanlon and Weiner-Davis (1989), counselors using this approach are trying to do three things:

1. Change the "doing" of the situation that is perceived as problematic (p. 126). By helping clients change their present actions and interactions, they become free to "use other, atypical actions that are more likely to resolve their situations than repeating unsuccessful patterns" (p. 126).

2. Change the "viewing" of the situation that is perceived as problematic (p. 126). Facilitating changes in clients' frames of reference—both in and out of counseling—may produce changes in behavior and/or elicit untapped strengths and abilities.

3. *Evoke resources, solutions and strengths to bring to the situation that is perceived as problematic* (pp. 126-127). Reminding clients of their abilities, resources, and strengths may create changes in behaviors or perceptions.

Littrell (1998) adds:

> As counselors we help clients find and/or create patterns of thoughts, feelings, actions, and meaning. We code these patterns with names like "resources" or "abilities" or "inner strengths." Some patterns we rediscover from clients' pasts; some are currently being used but clients have not yet recognized them as such. We can also co-create new patterns that do not yet exist in clients' repertoire or we can modify current ones. (pp. 63-64)

Again, the similarity between constructive therapies and Adlerian therapy is remarkable. As stated earlier, Hoyt (1994) identified three clinical-practical characteristics that constructive approaches share. These characteristics essentially mirror what Adlerians have historically called *encouragement*, or the therapeutic modeling of social interest. For Adlerians, encouragement is both an attitude and a way of being with clients in therapy (Watts, 1999). According to Watts and Pietrzak (2000), Adler and subsequent Adlerians consider encouragement a crucial aspect of human growth and development. This is especially true in the field of counseling. Stressing the importance of encouragement in therapy, Adler stated: "Altogether, in every step of the treatment, we must not deviate from the path of encouragement" (Ansbacher & Ansbacher, 1956, p. 342). Dreikurs (1967) agreed: "What is most important in every treatment is encouragement" (p. 35). In addition, Dreikurs (1967) stated that therapeutic success was largely dependent upon "(the therapist's) ability to provide encouragement" and failure generally occurred "due to the inability of the therapist to encourage" (pp. 12-13).

> Encouragement focuses on helping counselees become aware of their worth. By encouraging them, you help your counselees recognize their own strengths and assets, so they become aware of the power they have to make decisions and choices…Encouragement focuses on beliefs and self-perceptions. It searches intensely for assets and processes feedback so the client will become of aware of her (or his) strengths. In a mistake-centered culture like ours, this approach violates norms by ignoring deficits and stressing assets. The counselor is concerned with changing the client's negative self concept and anticipations. (Dinkmeyer et al., 1987, p. 124)

Encouragement skills include: demonstrating concern for clients through active listening and empathy; communicating respect for and confidence in clients; focusing on clients' strengths, assets, and resources; helping clients generate perceptual alternatives for discouraging fictional beliefs, focusing on efforts and progress; and helping clients see the humor in life experiences (Ansbacher & Ansbacher, 1956; Carlson & Slavik, 1997; Dinkmeyer, 1972; Dinkmeyer & Losoncy, 1980; Dinkmeyer, Dinkmeyer, & Sperry, 1987; Dreikurs, 1967; Mosak, 1979; Mosak & Maniacci, 1998; Neuer, 1936; Sweeney, 1998; Watts, 1999; Watts, 2003; Watts & Pietrzak, 2000; Watts & Shulman, 2003).

In agreement with constructive approaches, Adlerians are *technical eclectics* (Manaster & Corsini, 1982). The interventions specific to constructive therapies are either similar to or congruent with ones commonly used in Adlerian therapy. Thus, as part of the encouragement process, Adlerians use a variety of procedures to demonstrate concern for clients through active listening and empathy; communicate respect for and confidence in clients; help clients uncover the "hidden texts" in their life story (style of life); identify and combat oppressive and discouraging beliefs or "scripts"; create new patterns of behavior; develop more encouraging perceptions; focus on efforts, not merely outcomes; and focus on assets, resources, and strengths. The assumptions, characteristics, and methods of encouragement help to create an optimistic, empowering, and growth-enhancing environment for clients—a place where they feel en-abled rather dis-abled (Adler, 1929; Ansbacher & Ansbacher, 1956; Carlson & Slavik, 1997; Dinkmeyer, 1972; Dinkmeyer & Losoncy, 1980; Dinkmeyer et al., 1987; Dreikurs, 1967; Mosak, 1979, 1995; Mosak & Maniacci, 1998; Neuer, 1936; Sweeney, 1998; Watts, 1999; Watts, 2003; Watts & Pietrzak, 2000; Watts & Shulman, 2003).

CONCLUSION

Botella and Herrero (2000) and R. A. Neimeyer (2000) suggest that an integrative bridge between cognitive constructivist and social constructionist perspectives might be usefully labeled "relational constructivism." As noted throughout this presentation, the Adlerian theory and system is a relational and constructive psychology and psychotherapy.

> For Adler, persons must be ultimately understood in social context; it is in relationships that humans have their meaning…Psychological theories tend to be either individualis-

tic or collectivistic—in the former community disappears; in
the latter, the individual disappears. Adler's views, on the other
hand, are a healthy balance of the individual rooted in relationships. (Jones & Butman, 1991, p. 237)

Whereas Adlerian psychology and psychotherapy clearly resonate
with many foundational ideas in both cognitive constructivist and
social constructionist approaches, we believe the Adlerian model
meets the criteria for designation as a relational constructivist
approach.

REFERENCES

Adler, A. (1929). *Problems of neurosis*. (P. Mairet, Ed.). London: Kegan Paul, Trench, Trubner, & Co, LTD.

Adler, A. (1931/1992). *What life could mean to you* (C. Brett, Trans.). Oxford, UK: Oneworld Publications.

Ainsworth, M. D. (1964). Patterns of attachment behavior shown by the infant in interactions with his mother. *Merrill Palmer Quarterly, 10,* 51-58.

Allen, T. W. (1971). A life style. *The Counseling Psychologist, 3,* 25-29.

Ansbacher, H. L. (1983). Individual Psychology. In R. J. Corsini & A. J. Marsella (Eds.), *Personality theories, research, & assessment* (pp. 69-123). Itasca, IL: Peacock.

Ansbacher, H. L. (1990). Alfred Adler's influence on the three leading cofounders of humanistic psychology. *Journal of Humanistic Psychology, 30,* 45-53.

Ansbacher, H. L., & Ansbacher, R. R. (Eds.) (1956). *The Individual Psychology of Alfred Adler*. New York: Harper Torchbooks.

Ansbacher, H. L., & Ansbacher, R. R. (Eds.) (1978). *Cooperation between the sexes: Writings on women, love, and marriage*. New York: Norton.

Ansbacher, H. L., & Ansbacher, R. R. (Eds.) (1979). *Superiority and social interest* (3rd ed). New York: Norton.

Botella, L., & Herrero, O. (2000). A relational constructivist approach to narrative therapy. *European Journal of Psychotherapy, Counselling, and Health, 3,* 407-418.

Bowlby, J. (1982). *Attachment and loss: Vol. I: Attachment* (2nd ed.). New York: Basic Books.

Bruner, J. (1990). *Acts of meaning*. Cambridge, MS: Harvard University Press.

Carlson, J., & Slavik, S. (Eds.) (1997). *Techniques in Adlerian psychology*. Washington, DC: Accelerated Development.

Carlson, J., & Sperry, L. (1998). Adlerian psychotherapy as a constructivist psychotherapy. In M. F. Hoyt (Ed.), *The handbook of constructive therapies: Innovative approaches from leading practitioners* (pp. 68-82). San Francisco: Jossey-Bass.

de Shazer, S. (1991). *Putting differences to work*. New York: Norton.

DeJong, P., & Berg, I. K. (1998). *Interviewing for solutions*. Pacific Grove, CA: Brooks/Cole.

Dinkmeyer, D. (1972). Use of the encouragement process in Adlerian counseling. *Personnel & Guidance Journal, 51,* 177-181.

Dinkmeyer, D. C., Dinkmeyer, D. C., Jr., & Sperry, L. (1987). *Adlerian counseling and psychotherapy* (2nd ed.). Columbus, OH: Merrill.

Dinkmeyer, D., & Losoncy, L. E. (1980). *The encouragement book.* Englewood Cliffs, NJ: Prentice-Hall.

Disque, J. G., & Bitter, J. R. (1998). Integrating narrative therapy with Adlerian lifestyle assessment: A case study. *Journal of Individual Psychology, 54,* 431-450.

Dreikurs, R. (1967). *Psychodynamics, psychotherapy, and counseling.* Chicago, IL: Alfred Adler Institute of Chicago.

Ellenberger, H. F. (1970). *The discovery of the unconscious.* New York: Basic Books.

Forgus, R., & Shulman, B. H. (1979). *Personality: A cognitive view.* Englewood Cliffs, NJ: Prentice-Hall.

Gergen, K. J. (1994). *Realities and relationships: Soundings in social construction.* Cambridge, MA: Harvard.

Gergen, K. J. (1999). *An invitation to social construction.* Thousand Oaks, CA: Sage.

Gergen, K. J. (2001). *Social construction in context.* Thousand Oaks, CA: Sage.

Guidano, V. F. (1995a). A constructivist outline of human knowing processes. In M. J. Mahoney (Ed.), *Cognitive and constructive psychotherapies: Theory, research, and practice* (pp. 89-102). New York: Springer.

Guidano, V. F. (1995b). Constructivist psychotherapy: A theoretical framework. In R. A. Neimeyer & M. J. Mahoney (Eds.), *Constructivism in psychotherapy* (pp. 93-110). Washington, DC: American Psychological Association.

Hoyt, M. F. (Ed.) (1994). *Constructive therapies.* New York: Guilford.

Hoyt, M. F. (Ed.) (1996). *Constructive therapies.Vol. 2.* New York: Guilford.

Hoyt, M. F. (Ed.) (1998). *The handbook of constructive therapies: Innovative approaches from leading practitioners.* San Francisco: Jossey-Bass.

Jones, J. V., Jr. (1995). Constructivism and individual psychology: Common ground for dialogue. *Individual Psychology, 51,* 231-243.

Jones, S. L., & Butman, R. E. (1991). *Modern psychotherapies: A comprehensive Christian appraisal.* Downers Grove, IL: InterVarsity Press.

Kelly, G. A. (1991a). *The psychology of personal constructs:Vol. 1. A theory of personality.* London: Routledge. (Original work published 1955)

Kelly, G. A. (1991b). *The psychology of personal constructs:Vol. 2 . Clinical diagnosis and psychotherapy*. London: Routledge. (Original work published 1955)

Korobov, N. (2000). Social constructionist "theory hope": The impasse from theory to practice. *Culture and Psychology, 6*, 365-373.

Littrell, J. M (1998). *Brief counseling in action*. New York: Norton.

Mahoney, M. J. (1988). Constructive metatheory: Basic features and historical foundations. *International Journal of Personal Construct Psychology, 1*, 1-35.

Mahoney, M. J. (1991). *Human change processes*. New York: Basic Books.

Mahoney, M. J. (1995a). Theoretical developments in cognitive and constructive psychotherapies. In M. J. Mahoney (Ed.), *Cognitive and constructive psychotherapies: Theory, research, and practice* (pp. 2-19). New York: Springer.

Mahoney, M. J. (1995b). Continuing evolution of the cognitive sciences and psychotherapies. In R. A. Neimeyer & M. J. Mahoney (Eds.), *Constructivism in psychotherapy* (pp. 39-68). Washington, DC: American Psychological Association.

Mahoney, M. J., Miller, H. M., & Arciero, G. (1995). Constructive metatheory and the nature of mental representation. In M. J. Mahoney (Ed.), *Cognitive and constructive psychotherapies: Theory, research, and practice* (pp. 103-120). New York: Springer.

Manaster, G. J., & Corsini, R. J. (1982). *Individual psychology: Theory and practice*. Itasca, IL: Peacock.

Martin, J., & Sugarman, J. (1997). The social-cognitive construction of psychotherapeutic change: Bridging social constructionism and cognitive constructivism. *Review of General Psychology, 1*, 375-378.

Master, S. B. (1991). Constructivism and the creative power of the self. *Individual Psychology, 47*, 447-455.

Mosak, H. H. (1979). Adlerian psychotherapy. In R. J. Corsini (Ed.), *Current psychotherapies* (2nd ed., pp. 44-94). Itasca, IL: Peacock.

Mosak, H. H. (1995). Adlerian psychotherapy. In R. J. Corsini & D. Wedding (Eds.), *Current psychotherapies* (5th ed., pp. 51-94). Itasca, IL: Peacock.

Mosak, H. H., & Maniacci, M. P. (1998). *Tactics in counseling and psychotherapy*. Itasca, IL: Peacock.

Mosak, H. H., & Maniacci, M. (1999). *A primer of Adlerian psychology: The analytic-behavioral-cognitive psychology of Alfred Adler*. Philadelphia: Accelerated Development/Taylor and Francis.

Neimeyer, G. J. (1995). The challenge of change. In R. A. Neimeyer & M. J. Mahoney (Eds.), *Constructivism in psychotherapy* (pp. 111-126). Washington, DC: American Psychological Association.

Neimeyer, R. A. (1995a). An invitation to constructivist psychotherapies. In R. A. Neimeyer & M. J. Mahoney (Eds.), *Constructivism in psychotherapy* (pp. 1-10). Washington, DC: American Psychological Association.

Neimeyer, R. A. (1995b). Constructivist psychotherapies: Features, foundations, and future directions. In R. A. Neimeyer & M. J. Mahoney (Eds.), *Constructivism in psychotherapy* (pp. 11-38). Washington, DC: American Psychological Association.

Neimeyer, R. A. (2000). Narrative disruptions in the construction of the self. In R. A. Neimeyer & J. D. Raskin (Eds.), *Constructions of disorder: Meaning-making frameworks for psychotherapy* (pp. 207-242). Washington, DC: American Psychological Association.

Neimeyer, R. A., & Mahoney, M. J. (Eds.) (1995). *Constructivism in psychotherapy*. Washington, DC: American Psychological Association.

Neimeyer, R. A., & Raskin, J. D. (Eds.) (2000). *Constructions of disorder: Meaning-making frameworks for psychotherapy*. Washington, DC: American Psychological Association.

Neuer, A. (1936). Courage and discouragement. *International Journal of Individual Psychology, 2*(2), 30-50.

O'Hanlon, W. H., & Weiner-Davis, M. (1989). *In search of solutions: A new direction in psychotherapy*. New York: Norton.

Parry, A., & Doan, R. E. (1994). *Story revisions: Narrative therapy in a post modern world*. New York: Guilford.

Peluso, P. R., White, J. F., & Kern, R. M. (2001). *A comparison of attachment theory and Individual Psychology: A review of the literature.* [Manuscript submitted for publication].

Raskin, J. D., & Bridges, S. K. (Eds.) (2002). *Studies in meaning: Exploring constructivist psychology*. New York: Pace University Press.

Schneider, M. F., & Stone, M. (Eds.) (1998). Narrative therapy and Adlerian psychology [Special Issue]. *Journal of Individual Psychology, 54*(4).

Shulman, B. H. (1973). *Contributions to Individual Psychology*. Chicago: The Alfred Adler Institute.

Shulman, B. H. (1985). Cognitive therapy and the Individual Psychology of Alfred Adler. In M. J. Mahoney & A. Freeman (Eds.), *Cognition and psychotherapy* (pp. 243-258). New York: Plenum.

Shulman, B. H., & Mosak, H. H. (1988). Handbook for the life style. Muncie, IN: Accelerated Development.

Shulman, B. H., & Watts, R. E. (1997). Adlerian and constructivist psychotherapies: An Adlerian perspective. Journal of Cognitive Psychotherapy, 11, 181-193.

Sweeney, T. J. (1998). Adlerian counseling: A practitioner's approach (4th ed.). Muncie, IN: Accelerated Development.

Walter, J. L., & Peller, J. E. (1992). Becoming solution-focused in brief therapy. New York: Brunner/Mazel.

Watts, R. E. (1998). The remarkable similarity between Rogers's core conditions and Adler's social interest. Journal of Individual Psychology, 54, 4-9.

Watts, R. E. (1999). The vision of Adler: An introduction. In R. E. Watts & J. Carlson (Eds.), Interventions and strategies in counseling and psychotherapy (pp. 1-13). Philadelphia, PA: Accelerated Development/Taylor & Francis.

Watts, R. E. (2000). Entering the new millennium: Is Individual Psychology/Adlerian therapy still relevant? Journal of Individual Psychology, 56, 21-30.

Watts, R. E. (2003). Adlerian therapy as a relational constructivist approach. The Family Journal: Counseling and Therapy for Couples and Families, 11, 139-147.

Watts, R. E., & Critelli, J. W. (1997). Roots of contemporary cognitive theories in the Individual Psychology of Alfred Adler. Journal of Cognitive Psychotherapy, 11, 147-156.

Watts, R. E., & Pietrzak, D. (2000). Adlerian "encouragement" and the therapeutic process of solution-focused brief therapy. Journal of Counseling and Development 78, 442-447.

Watts, R. E., & Shulman, B. H. (2003). Integrating Adlerian and constructive therapies: An Adlerian perspective. In R. E. Watts (Ed.), Adlerian, cognitive, and constructivist psychotherapies: An integrative dialogue (pp. 9-37). New York: Springer.

White, M., & Epston, D. (1990). Narrative means to therapeutic ends. New York: Norton.

CHAPTER 13

Constructive Alternativism and the Self[1]

Spencer A. McWilliams

So one's epistemology does make a difference, whether in science or in one's personal life. (Kelly, 1964/1969c, p. 127)

From my initial exposure more than 25 years ago to the psychology of personal constructs (Kelly, 1955/1991a, 1955/1991b), the philosophy of constructive alternativism has fascinated me. In discovering Kelly's philosophy I had the sense that I had "come home" to a well-articulated perspective that meshed with my own tacit and as yet unformed way of thinking (McWilliams, 1996). Over the course of my PCP work, I have examined some of the implications of constructive alternativism: the importance of comprehensive construing, the use of anarchism and idolatry as metaphors for holding our ideas tentatively, methods of speech that require that we take personal responsibility for creating meaning, and the use of meditation to gain awareness of our personal role in construing (McWilliams, 1988a, 1988b, 1993,1996, 2000, 2003).

As I continue to explore the implications of the philosophy, I keep returning to a theme that has bedeviled me from the outset. I responded strongly to Kelly's concept of "reflexivity." He proposed that a psychological theory must "account for itself as a product of psychological processes" (Kelly, 1955/1991a, pp. 39/27). In addition, and perhaps more importantly, reflexivity encourages, or perhaps even requires, that we apply the theory to our own psychological processes. I believe that if I wish to consider a theory of personality as valid or useful, I should be able to apply the theory to my own psychological processes and see myself reflected in the theory.

---

[1] A version of this paper was presented at the Tenth Biennial Conference of the North American Personal Construct Network, Vancouver, BC, July 2002.

The concept of reflexivity and the notion that we might apply the theory to our own lives has thus always struck me as a crucial component of Personal Construct Psychology.

When I discovered in Personal Construct Psychology a well-developed theory that fit so well with my tacitly held understanding of the human situation, I saw its relevance not only to my professional role as a psychology professor but also to my personal perspective on how to understand and live my life. I perennially engaged in a struggle to actively apply the theory in my daily life. I have returned to the philosophy many times over the years and in re-reading Kelly's original writings I detect deeper and more profound implications to the philosophy. I find myself drawn toward a renewed investigation of constructive alternativism in order to seek deeper understanding of its practical implications.

This investigation occurs within the context of two other intriguing areas of inquiry that have attracted my interest. My exploration of these themes led me to Buddhist teachings and practices, and for the past twenty years I have studied and practiced with the founding teacher of the Ordinary Mind School of Zen meditation (Beck, 1993). More recently, my perspective has been enhanced through an exploration of perspectives on social constructionism (e.g., Burr, 1995; Gergen, 1994; Raskin, 2002; Shotter, 1993) and the convivial insights that this approach brings to the issues that have intrigued me for so long. This chapter focuses on the potential utility of constructive alternativism as a life-philosophy that we might apply to our way of construing our "selves," by explicating some of the general implications of constructive alternativism and their relationship to Zen teachings and social constructionism.

In welcoming you to join me on this journey, I suggest that in addition to its value as a stimulant to research and its use in psychotherapy, we may consider the potential of the philosophy of constructive alternativism as a means for facilitating human development and liberation by applying the philosophy actively to our own lives. I extend this invitation propositionally, following Kelly's spirit of adventure:

> The adventure in which I have invited you to join me for a little while does not...require you to deny anything you now believe or to destroy anything you now find useful. That is why I have said that you are free to return whenever you find the voyage discouragingly unproductive. You need not scuttle your present ships in order to embark on this one. Nor need you wait until you are discouraged before you quit my vessel for anoth-

er. (Kelly, 1969b, p. 96)

CORE CONSTRUCTION AND THE SENSE OF SELF

In considering how to practically apply constructive alternativism in the conduct of our daily lives, I would like to explore how we might gain awareness of our constructed interpretations of daily life events, particularly how we view ourselves. Applied constructive alternativism might enable us to expand our consciousness of our active role in construing events not only in the "external" environment but also in what we might regard as the "internal" environment of "self" and how we describe self, either publicly or privately.

The Kellian perspective views "self" within the context of core construing, the ways that we anticipate our own maintenance processes and our survival in the world—our identity and existence. Kelly defined "self" as a construct:

> It refers to a group of events which are alike in a certain way and, in that same way, necessarily different from other events. The way in which the events are alike is the self. That also makes the self an individual, differentiated from other individuals. The self, having been thus conceptualized, can now be used as a thing, a datum, or an item in the context of a superordinate construct (Kelly, 1955/1991a, p. 131/91).

In order to provide some stability along with flexibility, Kelly suggested that core constructs—our sense of self—should be rather comprehensive and not overly permeable.

Social constructionist perspectives also describe self as a product of human construction and emphasize how our picture of self evolves through language and our communications and interactions with others (Burr, 1995). In order to explain and account for our actions within the social context we develop a narrative account of our self, a story of the kind of person that we imagine ourselves to be, and that justifies our actions to others (Gergen, 1994). This account usually describes self in terms of an inner entity that we see as unified and responsible for our actions (Shotter, 1993).

Once we have created our sense of self as an object or a "thing," we tend to identify with beliefs about our self, and as we elaborate our narrative we develop a strong sense of the way that we must behave and have others behave toward us in order to survive, as well as to maintain a consistent narrative. Ordinary Mind Zen teachings (Bayda, 2002; Beck, 1993) describe this thought-based account in terms of core decisions that include a set of beliefs about our lives that function as a substitute for immediate living and direct experience. These beliefs might include identities, images, opinions, judgments, expectations, and requirements, all of which we tend to see as reality. Because of our strong attachment to this self-perspective, and the strong emotional reactions that accompany any threats to our self-account, we find it hard to consider alternative ways of construing our self. I believe that if we wish to apply constructive alternativism faithfully we must apply it to construing all events, whether in the "external" environment or the "internal" environment of "self," and to our descriptions of self, regardless of whether we express them publicly or privately.

Exploring the "self" from the perspective of applied constructive alternativism raises many fascinating questions about the nature of self. What do we mean when we speak about a "true" or "real" self from the perspective of constructive alternativism? Constructivism, social constructionism, and Buddhism agree that we do not comprehend reality directly and that all interpretations result from our own active construction. From these perspectives, does it make sense to think that we can "discover" or articulate a true or real self? Additionally, if what we construe as self and identity refers to events that constantly change, would we find it useful to assume a fixed and unchangeable entity of "self" in the first place, regardless of how we construe the process? What do we see in our construction of self that we would regard as the "real" self? A quote from Kelly helps to elaborate the implications of these questions.

> It might be helpful at this point to ask ourselves a question about children at Halloween. Is the little youngster who comes to your door on the night of October 30th (sic; it is actually the 31st), all dressed up in his costume and behind a mask, piping "trick or treat, trick or treat"—is that youngster *disguising* himself or is he revealing himself? Is he failing to be spontaneous? Is he *not* being himself? Who is the *real* child—the child behind the mask or the barefaced child who must stand up in front of adults and say "please" and "thank you"? (Kelly, 1964/1969a, p. 158, emphasis in original)

Although in everyday conversation we tend to talk as if we possess a "true" or "real" self, constructivism, constructionism, and Buddhism would suggest that we do not benefit from such a view but might instead better see self as a constructed narrative, a process, that should remain open to revision and embrace events that continually change. I would like to elaborate on this theme by exploring further some of the implications of the philosophy of constructive alternativism.

THE PHILOSOPHY OF CONSTRUCTIVE ALTERNATIVISM

Kelly described his philosophy by stating, *"We assume that all of our present interpretations of the universe are subject to revision or replacement"* (1955/1991a, p. 15/11, italics in original). Kelly placed this assumption in the context of his proposition that each of us invents or constructs our own way of construing or interpreting the events that we experience in our lives. Kelly believed that although we may see some ways of construing the world as more useful than others, no one had yet invented a completely accurate and universal system of constructs. Additionally, Kelly suggested that we always have some alternative way of dealing with the world rather than having our understanding determined by circumstances or our biography.

In addition to defining constructive alternativism thoroughly, Kelly discussed the theory in various ways over the course of his written work. In doing so he articulated several subordinate elements to the philosophy, which elaborate on its implications. I have identified five elements that Kelly discussed that seem particularly important to me in understanding the philosophy:

- Accumulative fragmentalism as the contrast pole for constructive alternativism

- The proposition that we do not have to disprove one interpretation in order to entertain an alternative

- The infinitely far away correspondence between our beliefs or interpretations and reality

- The subject-predicate nature of our language

- The use of active methods to embrace alternative ways of construing events

In the discussion that follows, I elaborate on the implications of each of these elements for the philosophy in general. I then explore their relevance to the concept of self and how we might apply them to our personal lives. Additionally, I raise further questions about the construing of self with the hope that these questions might stimulate further exploration of the topic.

Accumulative Fragmentalism

Kelly described construing as an inherently bi-polar activity, which includes both comparison and contrast. A complete construct includes the ways in which the construer sees some elements as similar and others as different, along the same dimension. As Kelly frequently pointed out, we cannot fully understand a construct, which is usually labeled by the emergent pole, without considering the contrast pole of the dimension. In the case of his philosophy, we would regard "constructive alternativism" as the emergent pole of the construct. How did Kelly characterize the contrast pole? Possibly with tongue in cheek, he called the contrast pole "accumulative fragmentalism."

The accumulative fragmentalist perspective represents a more conventional view of the human enterprise that suggests that knowledge progresses as we continue to add pieces of truth to the truths that we already presume to know:

> This is usually taken to mean that we discover nature a fragment at a time, that as each fragment is verified it is fitted into place—much like a piece in a jigsaw puzzle. Some day we'll get it all put together. (Kelly, 1964/1969a, p. 125)

From the accumulative fragmentalist perspective we believe in the ultimate validity of each piece of knowledge. Only the remaining fragments that we have not yet discovered stand in the way of our total and complete knowledge, and we expect to add the missing pieces in due course, by which time we will then know everything there is to know. As a major "comfort" of this perspective, accumulative fragmentalists do not expect to ever need to discard any existing knowledge, only perhaps add to it.

The accumulative fragmentalism pole of the construct dimension contrasts clearly with Kelly's constructive alternativism pole. From the constructive alternativist perspective, we assume that human beings have invented all interpretations of events and that we could construct alternative interpretations of the same events. Interpretations that seem final and clear-cut in the light of the current context may appear quite different when re-construed in a different light. Constructive alternativism also assumes that we will revise or replace each interpretation in the light of future understandings, so we have no need to assume or expect that any interpretation represents a final truth.

Social constructionist perspectives adopt a similar and convivial stance toward the differences between seeing knowledge as constructed and thus open to revision and seeing knowledge as final truth. For example, Gergen (1994) stated that "[t]here is no 'true' description of the nature of things" (p. 45) and that the terms that we use to account for the world arise as social products. Intriguingly, this characterization closely parallels the first verse of the *Tao te Ching*, a basic text of Taoism, which combined with Buddhism to create Zen: "The Tao that can be followed is not the eternal Tao. The name that can be named is not the eternal name. The nameless is the origin of heaven and earth while naming is the origin of the myriad things" (Muller, 1997). Gergen's perspective reflexively emphasizes the multiplicity of accounts that we might make about reality, and that our commitment to such accounts does not depend on their objective validity. Similarly to how Kelly described the implications of accumulative fragmentalism, Gergen described empiricism as a "zero sum game" in which the accuracy or utility of one theory demands the elimination of alternatives. Shotter (1993) eloquently described how we choose one description of a set of events among many alternatives, accept it as if it were true, develop a systematic account supporting that description, and then come to see it as existing independently of our construction processes; we inevitably must then interpret all new events in terms of this "true" descriptive statement. Through our naming, we create fixed "things" out of the infinite possibilities.

Because I espouse and support these constructivist views, I like to think of myself as a good practitioner of constructive alternativism, and I certainly would not wish to regard myself as an accumulative fragmentalist. However, as I look at how I behave in my daily life, I regret to see that I often act like an accumulative fragmentalist. I truly believe that I should hold my ideas tentatively and that I should remain willing to disengage from them in order to entertain alternatives. In fact, I often enjoy considering a wide range of alternatives long after it is time to make a decision, whether about which restaurant to go for dinner or which tires to buy for the car. On the other hand, I often continue to approach my ideas and interpretations as ultimate truths, and I sometimes find that this tendency gets me into quandaries that I might possibly avoid if I embodied constructive alternativism more fully.

This conundrum leads me to ask how we might apply the dimension of accumulative fragmentalism versus constructive alternativism to our notion of self and core construing. Do we act as though we believe that we have final knowledge of the "true" nature of the self, even if only fragments? Do we believe that a time will come when we manage to "put it all together" and have a final and complete notion of our self? We certainly see that perspective in popular ideas about forging a self-identity, in which "popular psychology" urges us to generate a firm answer to the question, "Who am I?" It certainly manifests in the kind of narrative account that we provide others, which we use to give clarity to the course of our lives and establish future expectations, particularly to the extent that we develop the skill to construct a socially acceptable narrative form (Gergen, 1994). From the constructivist and constructionist approaches, however, rather than truly capturing the essence of an individual, as an accumulative fragmentalist might believe, a sense of "self identity" only reflects the result of one particular method of inquiry or set of explanations within a specific discourse, among a range of alternative methods and explanations.

Do We Need to Disprove one Construction of Events before Considering Another?

> It is very commonly believed by people who should know better that one is obligated to disconfirm one explanation before he dares entertain seriously the possibility of any other. Scholars waste a great deal of time trying to disprove what others have claimed in order to make room for their own alternative explanations. (Kelly, 1964/1969a, p. 159)

The accumulative fragmentalist operates from the perspective that once we have verified our conclusions there is no point to further exploration of that which we have already determined to be "true." It therefore follows from this perspective that we cannot pose a new interpretation without disconfirming our previous "truth" (Kelly, 1964/1969a). By articulating the contrast pole of constructive alternativism, we can see more clearly one of the major implications of Kelly's philosophy. We do not have to disprove one hypothesis in order to entertain an alternative. If from the outset we view all of our interpretations as our inventions, designed for the purpose of helping us anticipate events, then we can consider new ways of looking at things without having to abandon or reject the convenience of our current understanding.

This perspective accords very well with the social constructionist invitation to consider a range of possible approaches to understanding, embracing variety through a multiplicity of ways to construe the world (Gergen, 1994). In our personal lives, this stance can provide us with exceptional freedom to entertain a variety of ways of looking at the world and considering our place in it. By seeing our beliefs as our inventions rather than revealed truths, we can imagine different ways of looking at and talking about things and find fresh alternatives to our persistent conundrums.

If we understand from the outset that events do not dictate or hold allegiance to the way that we talk about them, and that our understanding derives from our social interchanges, we have no need to disconfirm our current or existing sense of self in order to entertain an alternative. Once we understand our "self" as a narrative description of a phenomenon that constantly changes, we can also view our identity as a process, continuously open to change (Burr, 1995). We might consider methods for entertaining alternative core construing, alternative ways of construing "self," without disproving or abandoning the familiar constructions that we currently use to survive. Kelly's idea of fixed-role therapy (see below) certainly describes one approach to entertaining an alternative notion of self. He based this approach on a self-characterization in which the client describes him or herself in "the third person," and then applies a new role sketch temporarily so as not to require permanent abandonment of the original identity. This approach represents one vehicle for embracing a multiplicity of narrative discourses or ways of construing "self." It does not require abandoning existing identities or the methods that we rely on to maintain our survival, but rather involves trying something new just to see what happens. As Kelly (1969b, p. 96) stated in an earlier quote, "You need not scuttle your present ships in order to embark on this one." If we approach our sense of "self" using this third person method and become skilled at entertaining a variety of identities, what effect would it have on our sense of self as a fixed entity?

Correspondence Between Belief and Reality

As constructive alternativists, we assume that we have invented all of our present interpretations and that we will revise or replace them over time. From this perspective, it stands to reason that we do not benefit from regarding any existing interpretation as a final truth that directly corresponds to static reality, as accumulative fragmentalists would. Kelly carefully explicated his view of the relationship between our beliefs and the reality of the universe, from his constructive alternativist perspective. He began by stating that "[w]e presume that the universe is really existing and that man is gradually coming to understand it" (1955/1991a, p. 6/5). However, Kelly (1969b) further stated, "the discovery of an ultimate correspondence between the constructions we are able to devise and the flow of actual events is an infinitely long way off" (p. 96). He believed that we do construe a real world and that due to human audacity we continue to invent new and more effective ways of predicting that real world. Thus, he proposed that we might assume that our beliefs continue to evolve toward a closer correspondence with that real world. However, if we maintain a tentative perspective toward any current belief and disengage from one view in order to entertain another, we might avoid the arrogance of believing that we have any final truths. Kelly proposed an antidote to that arrogance through his suggestion that a correspondence between our beliefs and reality will eventually occur, but at such an infinitely distant point in the future that we can safely assume that our present interpretations have not yet attained that correspondence. Essentially, the Kellian perspective gives us permission not to concern ourselves with the ultimate truth of our interpretations and enables us to hold our ideas tentatively and revise them more easily.

How might we apply the view of "self" as a construction to Kelly's understanding that the correspondence between constructions and events will only occur at some infinite time in the future? Could we conceivably find a direct correspondence between our core constructions and the on-going flow of our personal events? How might we reconcile the single, finite lifetime of an individual with the infinitely long time frame for finding correspondence between constructions and reality? Perhaps such correspondence might never occur even within a single lifetime. Kelly once wrote that we could not understand the meaning of a person's life until it had come to an end.

The question of the correspondence between belief and reality occupies a central place in social constructionist discourse. Raskin (2002) summarized a variety of constructivist and social constructionist perspectives on the topic, emphasizing a distinction between epistemological constructivism, hermeneutic constructivism, and limited realism (Chiari & Nuzzo, 2003). These perspectives vary in their view of whether an objective reality exists independently of an observer, and whether we can come to know reality directly. Limited realists and epistemological constructivists believe that an external reality exists, while hermeneutic constructivists do not. Limited realists, perhaps including Kelly, believe in the theoretical possibility that we could come to know reality directly, while epistemological constructivists believe we can never know reality other than through our constructions of it. I suggest that regardless of whether we believe in the existence of an independent external reality, we have no direct access to a reality and can only "know" through our invented and socially mediated constructions, which we articulate through language. When we see all products of construing, including that of "self," as socially constructed narratives that cannot correspond directly to an external "reality," we might no longer ask the question of whether our sense of "self" corresponds to a "real self." Our use of terms such as "self" or "I" in our conversations, and our construction of a coherent narrative that accounts for our behavior in a consistent manner, may give us the sense of the existence of a fixed, solid entity of self. Similarly, Buddhist psychology describes our tendency to believe in the existence of a fixed entity of self, but demonstrates that by closely examining this sense of self through meditation practice, the self naturally dissolves. Together, these perspectives encourage us to take advantage of the freedom to construe self in a variety of alternative ways, without the need to assign "truth" to any of these descriptions, or searching for a correspondence between our belief about self and a real self.

Subject-Predicate Nature of Language

Our use of language presents another challenge in approaching the day-to-day world from an applied constructive alternativist perspective. Social constructionists describe how we reify the invented terms of our language and embody them with a sense of "fixedness" and truth. We construct our notion of identity and knowledge and use discourse as a way of providing a coherent representation of these ideas that take on such convincing features that we come to see them as real (Burr, 1995). Gergen (1994) described how our explanations of events gain meaning through our conversations and how cultural practices, including agreement on word usage over a long period of time, give the appearance that our words relate directly to reality, reinforcing our tendency to agree that they refer to an objective entity. Shotter (1993) likewise demonstrated how we create a sense that our words represent a fixed nature.

Kelly (1964/1969a) discussed what he called the "indicative mood" of the English language that attributes qualities to the events. He proposed an alternative, the "invitational mood," in which a speaker takes responsibility for attributing qualities to events and invites the listener to consider an interpretation of the event without precluding alternative interpretations. Casting a proposition in an invitational mood suggests that the subject remains open to a range

of possibilities. It encourages us to regard our language as hypothetical, a description of a set of dimensions of appraisal rather than as
attributes of nature, and it supports viewing our behavior as a way of
posing a question to test our hypotheses.

> Rather than assuming that qualities inhere in objects, we might
> invite the listener to regard an event in a potentially novel way
> by construing the event "as if" this particular dimension
> applies. Use of the indicative mood...perpetuates the notion
> that things exist in a fixed form and stay the same, with a prede-
> termined structure. They enable someone to say "This is the
> truth," or that an object "is what we say it is." They also enable
> us to avoid responsibility for our interpretations by using a pas-
> sive voice, as "It is well known that the earth is flat." Use of the
> invitational mood could free us from seeing events, including
> our construction of ourselves, in this fixed form. It could help
> us take responsibility for our own interpretations and attribute
> our own passive statements to ourselves, or assign others' pas-
> sive statements to a particular source. (McWilliams, 1995, pp.
> 60-61)

Within the general view of self as a socially constructed, lan-
guage-based invention, we might view the sense of self that arises
from core construing as a particular artifact of our subject-predicate
language in which we give the self a name and then forget that we
invented it. We might regard an individual's name as a label for a set
of constructs identified as "self," and explore the consequences of
such naming. Kelly particularly described the effect of a name on the
definition of self: "We recall that in various cultures the establishment of new adjustment patterns has customarily been accomplished simultaneously with the assumption of a new name" (Kelly,
1955/1991a, p. 367/273).

Once we assign a word label in the construing of self, we
tend to apply the indicative form of the verb "to be," attributing
qualities to the "self" rather than taking responsibility for the qualities as our own construction. Thus, we can see a tendency to say, for
example, that I am smart, generous, lazy, or irresponsible, attributing
these qualities to this "self" that I have created through my own act
of construction. Kelly described how we tend to do this with respect
to attributions that we make about others; I imagine an even greater
tendency for this to occur with respect to our self. If we apply the
indicative form to the label for self, and the superordinate construct
of self, we may also apply it to many of the subordinate implications.
How might our sense of self, and the way that we talk about self,
change if we fully embraced an invitational mood to language and

took personal responsibility for the use of labels of the self as a hypothetical interpretation of immediate experience?

In order to apply constructive alternativism to our speech and to actually use the invitational mood, we need a practical way to speak that regards interpretations as hypothetical and avoids attributing permanent characteristics to continually changing events (McWilliams, 1996). A general semantics technique called E-prime (Bourland & Johnston, 1991) applies the indicative mode by excluding the verb to be (is, are, was, were, am, be, been, being) from speaking and writing in English. Use of E-Prime can help us gain awareness of our tendency to project our interpretations onto events. It reduces use of the passive voice, which enables us to avoid personal responsibility for construing, and prevents us from making permanent qualities out of a particular interpretation. By using E-prime, we may more likely accept responsibility for making attributions. We see more clearly that we constructed the attributes as a process for interpreting recurrent patterns among events. E-prime helps focus on direct personal experience and helps us speak more propositionally, leaving other possibilities open. Effective use of E-prime requires a sustained acceptance of the value of questioning the indicative mood and our tendency to project fixedness onto events. It might increase awareness of our tendency to project personal constructions onto events and to help express attributions or interpretations more propositionally. More importantly for the purpose of self-awareness, E-prime can assist us to take more personal responsibility for our interpretations and to develop greater self-awareness of our tendencies to project our personal beliefs or interpretations onto the events we encounter in our lives. I do not find it necessary or convenient to speak in E-prime exclusively, but attempts to do so bring greater awareness of my tendency to project "fixedness" onto events. Most particularly, this technique can serve as a way to gain awareness of the tendency to make personal attributions of myself into fixed qualities rather than temporary interpretations.

Taking Active Steps to Entertain Alternatives

Kelly emphasized the importance of active, aggressive application of alternative construing as a key element of human behavior. He described what he referred to as human audacity, the active approaches by which people explore options and alternative ways of looking at things (Kelly, 1964/1969a), and he described how human behavior attempts to cast itself into the unknown by experimenting with possible alternative ways of understanding the universe and life experience (Kelly, 1977). At a practical level, Kelly invented fixed-role therapy as a conscious way to entertain alternative ways of behaving without abandoning existing beliefs.

> In the form of fixed role therapy described by Kelly, the client is asked to become someone other than themselves for a period of about two weeks. One aim is to enable the client to see how it is possible to create a new person; not totally new, of course, but to see that it is indeed possible to change and to do it oneself. It was Kelly's indirect way of demonstrating his philosophy in action: how we need not be hemmed in by circumstances, how there are alternatives available for us to choose between. (Fransella, 1995, p. 97)

Accounts suggest that Kelly may very well have applied this approach in his own life when he had to find a way to deal with a situation that did not fit his "normal" account of his self. The following narrative describes a story that I had heard in the late 1960s, which was also referred to by Fransella (1995).

> When George Kelly accepted a faculty position at Ohio State University in 1946, his duties included the role of directing the clinical psychology graduate program. According to the story, the program lacked records as to the status of the many graduate students enrolled in the department and particularly lacked clarity as to who belonged in the clinical program. According to the tale, Dr. Kelly initially came to his office dressed rather crudely, wearing farmers' bib overalls. He assumed a dramatically abrupt and brusque manner, calling many students into his office and promptly "counseling" them out of the clinical program, suggesting that they consider their specialty as developmental, social, experimental, etc. This process allegedly went on for a week or two, until Kelly felt he had completed the process of "cleaning up" the program. The following day he arrived at work wearing his customary suit and tie, and behaved in his characteristic cordial and polite, if somewhat formal, manner. To those familiar with Kelly's theory, the story suggests the possibility that, knowing he had some unpleasant duties to perform, he assumed a fixed role that would enable him to carry them out effectively. When he had completed these duties he then called the "real" George Kelly back from holiday. (McWilliams, 1996, p. 58)

What range of methods might we consider using to assist us to gain greater awareness of the invented nature of our core beliefs and try on alternatives as Kelly may have done? Social constructionists describe a variety of approaches that might enable us to "deconstruct" the process by which our discourse creates a sense of self as a fixed entity and gain greater awareness of our ability to embrace new views. As Shotter (1993) suggested, we can turn our attention to recognizing how we socially construct our sense of self. Likewise, Burr (1995, pp. 92-93) described how, "[b]y challenging and resisting the representations of ourselves on offer in prevailing discourses, we have the chance to construct or claim alternative identifies for ourselves." Gergen (1994) encouraged us to consider the value of alternative points of view, challenge dominant realities, and cast doubt on social constructions. We might consider applying these suggestions to the self by adopting personal practices related to Gergen's concepts of "dislodgement" and "destabilization" that can challenge and loosen the grip of conventions that we take for granted and our ways of talking about and understanding ourselves that we fail to see as our own inventions. We can take advantage of these opportunities to "see through" our current narratives of the self and to invent new narratives.

I mentioned earlier that although I embrace the constructive alternativist philosophy, I often find myself acting like an accumulative fragmentalist. I see this occurring most frequently or commonly when I gain some awareness of the conditioned nature of my own behavior. Although I would like to address each moment, each new event, or experience, with a fresh response, I tend to react to events in habitual ways. In a sense, these reactions, which do not grow out of conscious awareness, can be seen as a type of accumulative fragmentalism; I act as if this way of reacting is a piece of truth. If I want to act as a constructive alternativist, what else might I need to do?

As I have described above, I might wish to develop greater awareness of my own reactions, my thoughts, emotions, and behaviors. My experience as a student of Zen meditation over the past twenty years has provided an opportunity to practice such skills and apply them to a constructive alternativist perspective (McWilliams, 2000). Bayda (2002) described how Ordinary Mind Zen practice focuses on clarifying our tendency to believe in the "truth" of our thoughts, particularly our core beliefs about our selves, and the focusing on the direct physical experience of the present moment, including difficult emotional reactions:

> As we clarify our believed thoughts, no longer taking them as truth, and as we reside in the bodily component of our experience, we begin to see that our experience of these little holes is actually nothing more than a combination of deeply believed thoughts and a complex of subtle and not-so-subtle uncomfortable bodily sensations. Seeing this—and I mean seeing it in the

way that fosters real understanding—is a taste of freedom (p. 21).

The Ordinary Mind School of Zen practice focuses on core beliefs, comparable to Kelly's notion of core constructs (McWilliams, 2000). Core beliefs bear some similarity to the constructionist notion of the narrative story of self that we create through language except that because core beliefs originate at the pre-verbal stage of development and contain negative elements, we may not have articulated them clearly to others or ourselves. However, because we develop life strategies based on core decisions that we make early in life, "we believe that this thought-based picture of reality is who we are and what life is. The more we believe in this artificial life, the more we move away from 'life as it is'" (Bayda, 2002, p.49).

Ordinary Mind Zen emphasizes how we tend to accept as real the negative self-image that we construct around these decisions and the narratives that support it. Effective Zen practice includes learning to observe the all-pervasive nature of these decisions and the expectations and requirements of our self and others that they engender. It also emphasizes developing awareness of the strategies that we use to protect ourselves, the core role structure in Kelly's terms. Once we learn to see our core decisions and interrupt our strategies we can experience directly the emotional reactions that we avoid feeling. "Only by uncovering and entering this dreaded part of ourselves can we see through the artificial construct of our substitute life and ultimately reconnect with awareness of our basic wholeness" (Bayda, 2002, p. 54). Effective practice of this approach requires careful, disciplined self-observation, which might include watching everything that is going on "within" us and around us almost as if it was happening to another person (de Mello, 1990).

Self-observation might accomplish a similar objective to Kelly's request that his clients write a self-characterization that refers to themselves in the third person. What would happen to my sense of my interpretations about myself if I could come to see my responses, thoughts, feelings, etc., as something happening to "a character in a play," to use the terminology that Kelly used in his self-characterization exercises? What might I learn about my "self" if I actively experimented with new modes of behavior, perhaps using a "fixed-role" approach in particular situations and observing my reactions?

CLOSING COMMENTS

The personal application of constructive alternativism to daily life presents a variety of challenges along with intriguing possibilities for greater personal freedom. In particular, these notions about the sense of self may raise fascinating implications if we recognize that any construction that we have of "self" follows the same tentative, hypothetical sense as any other construction. How would we come to construe self if we could fully embody applied constructive alternativism? If we search carefully to find the self, we may find only the construing process itself taking place but "no one" there doing the construing. Perhaps if we developed the ability to acutely observe our thoughts and physical processes, and to attempt to locate the "self" who is experiencing, we might arrive, as Buddhists suggest, at a sense of "no-self."

REFERENCES

Bayda, E. (2002). *Being Zen: Bringing meditation to life*. Boston: Shambhala.

Beck, C. J. (1993). *Nothing special: Living Zen*. San Francisco: Harper & Row.

Bourland, D.D. & Johnson, P. D. (1991). *To be or not: An E-prime anthology*. San Francisco: International Society for General Semantics.

Burr, V. (1995). *An introduction to social constructionism*. New York: Routledge.

Chiari, D. & Nuzzo, M. L. (2003). Kelly's philosophy of constructive alternativism. In F. Fransella (Ed.), *Personal construct psychology: A handbook* (pp. 41-49). London: Wiley.

de Mello, A. (1990). *Awareness*. New York: Doubleday.

Fransella, F. (1995). *George Kelly*. London: Sage.

Gergen, K. J. (1994). *Realities and relationships: Soundings in social construction*. Cambridge: Harvard.

Kelly, G. A. (1969a). The language of hypothesis: Man's psychological instrument. In B. Maher (Ed.), *Clinical psychology and personality: The selected papers of George Kelly* (pp. 147-162). New York: John Wiley. (Original work published 1964)

Kelly, G. A. (1969b). A mathematical approach to psychology. In B. Maher (Ed.), *Clinical psychology and personality: The selected papers of George Kelly* (pp. 94-113). New York: John Wiley.

Kelly, G. A. (1969c). The strategy of psychological research. In B. Maher (Ed.), *Clinical psychology and personality: The selected papers of George Kelly* (pp. 114-132). New York: John Wiley. (Original work published 1964)

Kelly, G. A. (1977). The psychology of the unknown. In D. Bannister (Ed.), *New perspectives in personal construct theory* (pp. 1-19). London: Academic Press.

Kelly, G. A. (1991a). *The psychology of personal constructs: Vol. 1. A theory of personality*. London: Routledge. (Original work published 1955)

Kelly, G. A. (1991b). *The psychology of personal constructs: Vol. 2 . Clinical diagnosis and psychotherapy*. London: Routledge. (Original work published 1955)

McWilliams, S. A. (1988a). Construing comprehensively. *International Journal of Personal Construct Psychology, 1*, 219-228.

McWilliams, S. A. (1988b). On becoming a personal anarchist. In F. Fransella & L. Thomas (Eds.), *Experimenting with personal construct psychology* (pp. 17-25). London: Routledge & Kegan Paul.

McWilliams, S. A. (1993). Construct no idols. *International Journal of Personal Construct Psychology, 6,* 269-280.

McWilliams, S. A. (1996). Accepting the invitational. In B. E. Walker, J. Costigan, L. L. Viney, & B. Warren (Eds.), *Personal construct theory: A psychology for the future* (pp. 57-78). Melbourne: Australian Psychological Society (APS Imprint Books).

McWilliams, S. A. (2000). Core constructs and ordinary mind Zen. In J. W. Scheer (Ed.), *The person in society: Challenges to a constructivist theory* (pp. 261-271). Giessen, Germany: Psychosozial-Verlag.

McWilliams, S. A. (2003). Belief, attachment, and awareness. In F. Fransella (Ed.) *Personal construct psychology: A handbook* (pp. 75-82). London: Wiley.

Muller, C. (Trans.). (1997). *Tao Te Ching.* Retrieved from http://www.human.toyogakuen-u.ac.jp/~acmuller/contao/laotzu.htm.

Raskin, J. D. (2002). Constructivism in psychology: Personal construct psychology, radical constructivism, and social constructionism. *American Communication Journal, 5* (3). Retrieved from http://www.acjournal.org/holdings/vol5/iss3/special/raskin.htm.

Shotter, J. (1993). *Conversational realities: Constructing life through language.* Thousand Oaks, CA: Sage.

CHAPTER 14

Personal and Social Responses to Tragedy: A Case for "Both/And" Constructivism

Sara K. Bridges

On September 11, 2001, two airplanes piloted by suicide hijackers were flown into the twin towers of the World Trade Center in New York City, while another plane plunged into the Pentagon in Washington, DC. Shortly thereafter, a fourth plane crashed in a Pennsylvania field, unsuccessful in reaching its' target (assumed to be a high profile building in Washington, DC, however it remains unclear which one). Thirty-three passengers, 7 crewmembers and 4 hijackers died in Pennsylvania, 184 people died at the Pentagon, and 2795 lives were lost in the Twin Towers. Along with the tragic loss of life (and landmark buildings) came the loss of the assumption of peaceful coexistence and stability for many people worldwide. Additionally, the feeling that the United States was an impenetrable fortress of security was shattered, producing sweeping ramifications in the economic market, the travel industry, and in personal and professional relationships. Consequently, many were faced with the arduous tasks of either altering perceptions of what is normal, safe, and predictable in life or of somehow making sense of the tragedies in their former ways of understanding the world.

We have just recently marked the two-year anniversary of September 11, 2001. I have heard people start to remark that closure will have been reached, that the grieving will have ended and that we can finally "move on" with our lives. Yet, there are others that reject the idea of closure and the traditional timeline of the "grieving process." For these people, finding a place for the events of that day and all that have followed in their meaning making systems will be an ongoing venture. How one goes about changing or maintaining assumptions and expectations, both individually and collectively can be understood through constructivist epistemologies.

In the following chapter I will briefly explore constructivist and social constructionist epistemological approaches to the shift in meaning making and belief systems imposed by the events of September 11. In particular, I propose a "both/and" constructivist that considers both individual and relational ways of meaning making seems particularly relevant when discussing the massive shift in beliefs systems produced by these catastrophic events. Specifically, I will focus on levels of change in meaning making and how they can be approached from both an individual and a relational perspective. But first, I would like to tell my story.

MY STORY

I was in my ninth month of pregnancy and was working at my desk at home while NPR played in the background. I remember turning in my chair to face the radio as I heard Bob Edwards of Morning Edition say that a plane had hit the World Trade Center in New York. Assuming that it must have been a Cessna or some other small plane, I remember thinking that the national television news stations probably hadn't picked it up yet. Regardless I went into the bedroom, assumed the only comfortable position available to me at that time (sitting on the bed with my legs sticking out in front of me) and picked up the remote control. I stayed in that position for three hours. I saw the second plane hit. I saw both towers collapse. I heard the reporter inside the Pentagon saying that he just heard something that sounded like a bomb. I heard that a plane had crashed somewhere in Pennsylvania. They announced that all airports were being closed and all flights were being forced to land. I called my parents, my sister, my husband and my friends. I wanted them to know. I'm not sure why. I needed them to know what I was seeing, what was happening, I didn't want to experience this alone—with my son happily floating around inside me, kicking and stretching. I sat on my bed and cried, glued to the television.

SHARED STORIES

As I started to write this chapter, I felt a need to tell my story. To tell the story of how I heard, where I was, what I was doing and how I felt. When I have heard others speak about the events of that day, I have found myself wanting to talk about what was happening to me—to share with them my experiences, just as I wanted to hear theirs.

It interests me that I have not been satisfied with simply hearing that Sue was at work, or John was at home, or Steve was driving
in his car. I wanted the details: how they felt, what they were doing,
how time stood still for them (if it did). I wanted to know their personal constructions of the events as they were happening and then
the place they have made for that day in their lives since that time.
Telling the story of where you were when the attacks happened,
what your life was like at that point, can be point of commonality or
"pulling together" because of the universal or shared meanings that
were created on that day.

However, as I started to talk with more friends and family
across the U.S. in the days and months following, it appeared that
there was no "normal" reaction for any individual or even any community. Granted, the national news media and several friends and
colleagues of mine reported a surge in national pride and patriotism
across the country—United States flags flew, bumper stickers were
placed on cars, red white and blue ribbons were worn to show our
solidarity and support, and t-shirts were purchased and worn with
pride. Yet, this was not the case in my former home of Northern
California. There were some U.S. flags flown. However, it was more
common to see Peace symbols and small gatherings of people, holding candles and praying, meditating, or chanting for peace. None of
these reactions were the "right" reactions. However, they were all
appropriate for these people at that time, in their particular situations. Constructivism's ability to understand the personal meaning
making abilities of both individuals and communities, even in light
of overwhelming national tragedy places it in a theoretically ideal
position to assist in the arduous task of developing new or revised
life meanings.

CONSTRUCTIVISM AND SOCIAL CONSTRUCTIONISM

Constructivism and social constructionism share the same
"negative identity" in that they do not subscribe to an objective reality that is "out there" somewhere waiting to be uncovered and
known. Instead our realities are waiting to be created through our
personal meaning making processes and our relational interactions.
Constructivism and social constructionism are the same in what they
are not, and thusly, both have been criticized for being ultimately relativistic and one of the sources that helps to justify unthinkable
atrocities (Rothstein, 2001). The critics argue that if all realities are
acceptable because they are personally or socially constructed, then

313

how can one judge what is right or wrong, good or bad (Raskin, 2002)? It is true that people cannot judge what is right, wrong, good, or bad for one another. However, they can judge what is good and acceptable for themselves in their own reality. For example, I can understand that the perpetrators of the September 11 attacks believed that they were doing brave and noble acts within their own belief systems, but I do not have to accept that those beliefs excuse their behaviors.

Constructivism and social constructionism diverge in their "positive identity." Whereas constructivists believe that meanings are personally or internally created or construed, social constructionists assert that meanings are co-constructed through relationships, language and existing social structures (Burr, 1995; McNamee, 1996). For social constructionists, knowledge is created through language (Gergen, 1999). Thus, meaning does not exist in the minds of the individual, rather meaning is situated in and created by continuing relationships (Gergen, 1999). In other words meaning is located in the performance and not in the person (McNamee, 2002). By contrast, for constructivists meaning making is ultimately an individual process, with meanings originating in the individual rather than in the relational. However, I am proposing that a relational approach to constructivism is not entirely in opposition to the epistemological underpinnings of constructivism.

As has been noted above, constructivism is commonly criticized for being too individualized and placing meaning making only in the mind of the individual without adequate attention to the role of relational or social influences. Moreover, Kelly's (1955/1991a, 1955/1991b) analogy of "person as scientist" has been used to further the idea that constructivists hold the position that individual meaning making is private and idiographic (see McNamee, 2004 [this volume]). From this position it would seem that Kelly is proposing that individual meaning making is necessarily a very individualistic, cognitive, "scientific" endeavor. However the origins of the personal as scientists metaphor and Kelly's assertion that the therapist is a "co-experimenter" with the client in the therapy process suggests that perhaps there has been some misinterpretations in what the person as scientist metaphor means. In Kelly's "Autobiography of a Theory" (1969a), he describes how the metaphor of "person as scientist" came to life: Kelly discovered that in alternating between appointments advising students in their research and appointments counseling clients with their difficulties he was basically doing the same kind of work, or more importantly the student researchers and the clients were basically doing the same king of work. With both a graduate student and a client, Kelly (1969a) stated that he would:

> Try to get him to pin-point the issues, to observe, to become intimate with the problem, to form hypotheses, to make test runs, to relate outcomes to anticipations, to control his ventures so that he will know what let to what, to generalize cautiously, and to revise his dogma in light of experience. (p. 61)

For Kelly, then, treating his clients as scientists allowed them to experiment with viewing difficulties in a different light. In this way, Kelly suggested that the process of working through problems was similar to the process of scientific inquiry and that "only as the therapist approaches his client's problem as a scientist, and invites his client to do the same to the limit of his ability, can he avoid the tyranny of dogmatism and the professional exploitation of his clients" (Kelly, 1969a, p. 53). Furthermore, Kelly stated that in the client therapist relationship, the "psychologists is his [the client's] fellow experimenter, not an unctuous priest," (Kelly, 1969a, p. 53) suggesting that meaning making need not be a solely individual process and also making room for the prospect of relational meaning making as seen in the commonality and sociality corollaries. Thus, I believe an undue emphasis has been placed on the *stance* of the scientist (as an objective removed observer) rather than the originally intended scientific *process*. If, in fact, the emphasis for the person as scientist should have been placed on the scientific process, then many more possibilities for a both/and (meaning both individual and relational) constructivism become possible.

There is nothing about the process of scientific inquiry that prohibits strategic consultation with a co-experimenter or a well-informed colleague. Moreover, the process of qualitative inquiry actively encourages personal involvement in research (Arvay, 2002) and completely discounts the position that scientists need to be (or could possibly be) objective removed observers. It remains true that there are some who would prefer the process of scientific inquiry (or meaning making) to be a very private and personal process, yet there are others who crave the input of others and seek out the consult and advice of those close to them. Thus it seems plausible that meaning making could contain both a personal/individual and a relational quality. It could be that meanings are created both through personal meaning making processes and also by sifting through the meanings that are extracted from close personal relationships—rather than simply being either an individual or a relational process.

For me, the lines of separation between these two positions (individual or relational) have always seemed arbitrary because my meaning making tends to have a both/and rather than and either/or quality. The events of September 11 and the shifts in meaning making necessitated for so many, have further reduced the need for a true theoretical separation between Constructivism and Social Constructionism. Through conversations with others about 9/11, I feel that we begin to make meaning together. I borrow pieces of their personal constructions to help me form my own as I suspect they do with me. Perhaps I add the unique perspective of a new mom, a worried, fretful, overprotective, "will the world be safe for my child" new mom, while my friend adds the perspective of a daughter from a military family. I begin to understand the issue of safety and protection from her perspective and she begins to see the benefits of peaceful co-existence from mine. Regardless, it seems that meanings are *both* created together though our languaging about the events and their aftermath, *and* our personal creation of meanings.

Therapeutically, because of its emphases on constructed and co-constructed realities, constructivism is in an ideal spot to help with the shift in meanings necessitated by the events of 9/11. Constructivist psychotherapists pay attention to the existing core constructs that both help clients to make life meanings and also stop them from finding the life satisfaction they seek. When childhood ways of construing events have lost their utility but continue to be dominant in their adult meaning making endeavors, it is the constructivist psychotherapist who assists clients as they renegotiate early meanings to better fit their adult lives.

Additionally, because we have not been known for having a "firm grip on reality" or even that there is one true objective reality to grasp, helping others to reconstruct or simply construct life meanings in light of the events of 9/11 seems to be a natural step. Helping others to view the world as it "really is" seems much more foreign and inappropriate or cruel than it did before. When one's core belief systems are shattered along with millions of others, who is to say what is real? What is true? Life is no longer predictable and thus many have reported anxiety, sleeplessness, worry, depression etc. With the removal of predictability comes a choice point for many (although not always an active conscious choice). Many questions arise: Shall I change my belief systems to fit this new information?

Shall I find completely new ways of believing? Shall I hold steadfast-
ly to my old systems of belief and try to poke and prod this new
information until I can make it fit? And who in my life will support
my "choice" of meaning making at this time? If I find a new way of
believing, who else believes in this way? Who will help me as my
beliefs begin to falter when confronting new situations? What will
happen to those who shared my former belief systems? Will they still
be close to me? Will this cause a rift between us? In such a national
and even global crisis, each individual person dances through meaning making first with external partners (the media, friends, family
filtering information), then as a solo (taking it into ones own world
of meaning), subsequently bouncing between the two. Within this
shared tragedy, it is compelling to tell one's story and to hear the
many stories of others, and how they make their own meanings. A
both/and constructivism enables us to be well positioned to work
with both the personal and interpersonal aspects of these com-
pellingly necessary shifts in meaning making.

RECONSTRUCTING MEANINGS

The tragedies of September 11, 2001 had a universal impact.
For some the impact could be considered remote and only brought
to light on the anniversary of the attacks. For others the impact could
be felt more personally because of the rupture in their personal feelings of safety or their feelings of empathy for those directly affected
by the tragedies. For others still, the impact could be felt deeply on a
daily basis because of personal losses and stress reactions. Regardless
of the unique personal impact the events of September 11 had or are
having on individuals, it is clear that the tragedies of that day
required a shift in, or at least a reexamination of, the ways in which
our constructs guide our lives. Kelly (1955/1991a, 1955/1991b)
would have considered the emotions that were produced as an aftermath of 9/11 constructs of transition; indicating a move from our
previously held way of understanding ourselves or the world to a
new or revised way. Below, I will briefly detail how these constructs
of transitions can be understood in light of 9/11 and then move on
to levels of personal change suggested by Kelly (1969c), including a
relational perspective, which I believe is in keeping with the case for
both/and constructivism.

Returning once again to the person as scientist metaphor,
when a scientist (or a person) discovers that the assumptions on
which they have been basing most of their predictions and anticipa-

tions are invalid, they begin to experience anxiety—defined by Kelly (1955/1991a) as the failure of our constructs to be able to predict or anticipate. The events of 9/11 clearly produced feelings of anxiety for most (if not all) people living in the United States; the events were so unpredictable, that for many nothing in life seemed stable. Interestingly, after a brief period of self-reflection about what caused some groups of people to hate the U.S. to such an alarming extent, the focus of the country seemed to turn to an investigation of how we could have been blindsided by the attacks to the extent that we were. We needed to know why we did not predict the attacks and what would be needed in the future to make these kinds of events more predictable. Even our terrorism alert or code system is set up in order to help anticipate the likelihood of a future attack, perhaps in an effort to reduce anxiety by making terrorism more predictable. However, for some, because the attacks imposed a change in core constructs or ways of making meaning, simply knowing when or if future terrorist attacks may occur is not sufficient to significantly reduce anxiety. Instead, these people experience threat, defined as an awareness of an imminent and personal change in core ways of making in meaning. In Kelly's (1969c) own words:

> This is threat. To feel that one is on the threshold of deep changes in himself and his way of life is, I think, its essential feature. Threat is, from this point of view, an impending personal experience, not a set of ominous circumstances. (p. 284)

Thus, the threat experienced after 9/11 involves a very personal (and perhaps relational) shift in meaning making. How these shifts are manifested can be understood by examining the eight levels of personal change proposed by Kelly (1969b) and discussed below.

LEVELS OF PERSONAL (AND RELATIONAL) CHANGE

Kelly (1969b) proposed that all personal movement (meaning elaborating the range of options available to make different choices) is brought about through changing constructs. By constructs, Kelly was referring to the ways in which we make sense of the world. By anticipating events (or people, places, objects etc.) and seeing them not as "entirely strange and unique occurrences, but as recurrences," (Kelly, 1969b, p. 230) we are able to link an event to another event and also to contrast it with those events that are different. This ability to perceive both likeness and difference in events helps to build constructs, however constructs also give meaning to

318

events. For example the construct that "anger equals pain" could have been created from a childhood where a parent would act out physically when angry. In adult life, however, the construct then gives meaning to current events and helps the client to avoid all confrontations that could lead to anger. Thus the construct "anger equals pain" has lost it's utility and revisions become necessary, an anxiety producing situation (as discussed above). Some of these revisions can be considered minimal, only requiring a reordering of constructs to reduce the experience of anxiety (i.e., reconstruing the self through existing ways of making meaning), while others require more detailed fine-tuning of constructs or, in the more extreme examples, complete abandonment of prior ways of understanding the world and the subsequent creation of new constructs. How one approaches these changes is discussed below.

In all of the following levels of personal change, I propose there is a corresponding relational component that has been previously neglected. Constructivist scholars have tended to promote the traditionally masculine view of psychological health—a view that that is mostly focused on individuality and personal agency (Goldberger, 1996). However, there is an alternate view of psychological health that prioritizes relational affiliation and connection in the search for self-understanding (Doherty & Cook, 1993; Gilligan, 1982; Jordan, Kaplan, Miller, Striver, & Surrey, 1991; Miller, 1991). More specifically, the self-in-relation model proposed by Jordan, Kaplan, Miller, Striver, and Surrey (1991) and Doherty and Cook (1993) asserts that there are many who create and elaborate their personal meaning making systems through their close personal relationships. Although this view is typically associated with women, what seems to be of most relevance to constructivism is to recognize multiple ways of making meaning rather than to emphasize potential gender differences. Constructivism is concerned with the unique ways in which meanings are made (Neimeyer & Bridges, 2003), and thus accepting both an individualistic and relational way of making meaning seems theoretically consistent. Thus, because I do not believe a relational approach is at odds with constructivist epistemology, I will attempt to extend the relational perspective to the levels of personal change proposed by Kelly (1969b). Doing so will give further examples of both/and constructivism. Additionally, I will offer examples of the potential shifts in meaning making brought about by the tragedies of September 11.

Level 1: Contrast Reconstruction

At this level of change a person adjusts his or her meanings by moving from one polar end of a construct to the other end (i.e., from "people are basically good" to "people are basically evil"). This attempt to make no real change to one's core construct system, but instead simply relocate oneself within the existing system, was referred to by Kelly (1955/1991) as "slot-rattling." Slot-rattling indicates that there was not a change on a continuum (i.e., basically good, somewhat good, neutral, somewhat evil, basically evil), but instead a shift between extremes. Relationally, this shift can produce unstable interpersonal connections and it is not uncommon for a rapid reversal to occur. However, if a contrast reconstruction occurs within the framework of larger construct system changes, the shift can become an enduring one. Yet, without relational support for the contrast shift in meaning making (i.e., people are basically evil), a shift will usually be made again that returns the person to the former way of understanding the world (i.e., people are basically good), albeit with slightly less commitment.

Level 2: Use of a Different Construct

At this level, change is experienced as an attempt to understand events and relationships through different previously extant constructions. Often this is experienced as a "casting about" trying to make sense of a tragedy or crisis through the means currently available. Each failed attempt to fit the events into preexisting constructs can produce more anxiety. Conversely, anxiety is reduced when a way to make meaning of an event is located. The events of September 11 left many people "casting about" (both literally and figuratively) attempting to make a modicum of sense out of the tragedies. Constructs related to safety, spirituality, fairness, evilness, peace, and forgiveness (among others) were tried on to find a way to understand the events of that day. However, because the events metaphorically happened to all of us, we were not left to "cast about" alone. Instead we tried on our constructs with our friends, family, public figures, and spiritual leaders. Although we may not have used the same constructs as others to understand the tragedies, we were able to gain access to possible construct choices for making meaning through these relationships.

Level 3: Make the Preverbal More Explicit

Similarly to the second level, this third level involves using existing constructs to understand events and relationships. The main difference here is that many of the constructs that are elaborated are preverbal ones that operate pervasively within the system. By creating verbal constructs that attempt to give voice to preverbal ones, we begin to make meanings more explicit. The relational aspect of constructivism is ideally situated to help at the third level; it is through our relationships that we get to know our meanings more completely (Jorden et al., 1991). For example, a man may not fully understand the anxiety he was experiencing after 9/11. Ultimately, he finds a way to understand shifts in his perception of safety, and his belief that God works in mysterious ways. However, there remains a felt sense of anxiety and general trepidation, especially around his frequent business trips that require air travel. Through conversations with his wife, he acknowledges that flying feels less safe to him, yet to him this does not seem to adequately explain the anxiety he experiences on his trips away from home. After further exploration both with his wife and through personal reflection, he begins to understand the tacit preverbal meaning-making construct of "good vs. bad" father. Having been abandoned by his own father at an early age, he ritually kisses his young children goodbye with a softly muttered "I'll be back soon." Thus, not only was air travel less safe, it was also placing his firmly held, but perverbal construct that "good fathers do not leave" in jeopardy. Once awareness of this construct occurred, it became possible to locate a more appropriate construct in his meaning making system for those parents who died on September 11, and thus for his own feared loss (i.e., bad things happen to good people sometimes).

Level 4: Hierarchical Restructuring

By further elaboration of existing construct systems it becomes possible to reorder the constructs based on new priorities and discovered inconsistencies. This level of change falls into the "fine-tuning" category, yet it requires a close examination of the inconsistencies within meaning making constructs and looking at their impact on the overall system. Often having a close "other" to help in the examination, elaboration, and restructuring of meanings can facilitate what could be an arduous and potentially painful process. For some, core constructs revolved around good things happening to good people, safety in their own homes or at work, an omnipotent God (i.e., all knowing, all powerful, all good), or the power and impenetrability of the United States. For these people, perhaps constructs concerning God working in mysterious ways, or the presence of evil in the world, held a subordinate position. In light of 9/11, inconsistencies become evident in core constructs such as "good things happen to good people." Thus, shifts in the hierarchy of constructs become necessary; though admittedly not comfortable shifts.

Level 5: Testing for Predictive Validity

Once again we arrive at the person-as-scientist metaphor, wherein the process of hypothesis testing is performed to test one's meaning-making structures with actual outcomes. As we endeavor to make sense of 9/11, we take either our newly formed constructs or our adapted existing ones and check them out with our friends, family, and the world at large. For example, exploring the construct that "to be happy I must be sure that I am completely safe" could be tested after 9/11 when the certainty of complete safety is impossible. Through relationships with others and personal exploration, it becomes possible to understand the possibility of happiness in an unsafe world. As constructs are tested and retested, it becomes more possible to increase the correspondence of constructs with actual outcomes.

Level 6: Changes in the Range of Convenience

This level of change requires changing how constructs are applied—either to increase the range of convenience (i.e., apply them more generally) or to decrease the range of convenience to the point of making the construct almost obsolete. For example, increasing the range of convenience of the construct that "good things happen to good people" could result in incorporating unexpected or unexplained acts of violence, accidents, and natural disasters. Thus, the construct then becomes something like "in general good things happen to good people and bad things happen sometimes anyway." In the opposite case, restricting the range of convenience of the construct "a safe world equals a happy life" allows for a fulfilling and potentially happy life despite the enormous shifts in personal and global experiences of safety, and the realization that the world is no longer ultimately safe. The construct then becomes "safety equals happiness, but being less than safe does not prohibit happiness," a construct with conceivably little personal meaning.

Level 7: Alter Meanings of Existing Constructs

At this level, new meanings are constructed out of existing ones. Although the changes may be subtle, the fact that a construct was recreated (closely aligned with an existing one) allows for

322

changes in the order of constructs and the range of convenience they possess. Relationally, discovering how a trusted and respected other construes the events of 9/11 can help to increase the utility of constructs in understanding the events of 9/11 and the experience of everyday living. For example, the construct of "revenge versus forgiveness" could be closely related to "people are basically good or basically evil" and thus, a reconstruction of the second construct to "mature versus mistaken" (after considering the meaning making of a respected friend or family member) alters the need to be fully entrenched on the revenge pole of the first construct.

Level 8: Creating New and Abandoning Old Meanings

In this last level of change, an attempt is made to create entirely new meanings and, thus, it can be considered the most significant level of change. Often these meanings are created through detailed self-exploration, relational meaning making, and perhaps even therapy. For many, the events of 9/11 required this kind of change. Additionally, old ways of making meaning quickly lost their utility and needed to be abandoned in order to reduce the experience of threat and anxiety. The meanings that were created concerned the personal, relational, local, and global ways of understanding the world and will have ramifications for generations to come.

CONCLUSION

As can be seen in all of the levels of change, personal transformations in light of 9/11 can have both an individual and a relational component. It is important to note that I am not prescribing that there must be a both/and component to all ways of making meaning. Indeed, there are some people for whom a relational component would never be an option; for them all meanings are made individually and personally. Yet, for others the relational is the main arena for meaning making. Both of these processes of meaning making have a place in constructivism. If we accept that all personal realities are experientially valid, then all avenues to creating these realities are also experientially valid. My goal in this chapter was to show that both/and constructivism is not opposed to the underpinnings of constructivist epistemology. To the contrary, it can help make constructivism more inclusive with regards to the many different ways in which meanings are made.

REFERENCES

Arvay, M. (2002). Putting the heart back into constructivist research. In J. D. Raskin & S. K. Bridges (Eds.), *Studies in meaning: Exploring constructivist psychology* (pp. 201-223). New York: Pace University Press.

Burr, V. (1995). *An introduction to social constructionism.* New York: Routledge.

Doherty, P., & Piel Cook, E. (1993). No woman is an island: Women and relationships. In E. Piel Cook (Ed.), *Women, Relationships, and Power: Implications for Counseling* (pp. 15-47). Alexandria, VA: American Counseling Association.

Gergen, K. J. (1999). *An invitation to social construction.* Cambridge, MA: Harvard University Press.

Gilligan, C. (1982). *In a different voice: Psychological theory and women's development.* Cambridge, MA: Harvard University Press.

Goldberger, N. R. (1996). Women's constructions of truth, self, authority, and power. In H. Rosen & K. T. Kuehlwein (Eds.), *Constructing realities* (pp. 167-193). San Francisco: Jossey Bass.

Jordan, J., Kaplan, A., Miller, J. B., Stiver, I., & Surrey, J. (Eds.). (1991). *Women's growth in connection: Writings from the Stone Center.* New York: Guilford Press.

Kelly, G. A. (1991a). *The psychology of personal constructs: Vol. 1. A theory of personality.* London: Routledge. (Original work published 1955)

Kelly, G. A. (1991b). *The psychology of personal constructs: Vol. 2. Clinical diagnosis and psychotherapy.* London: Routledge. (Original work published 1955)

Kelly, G. A. (1969a). The autobiography of a theory. In B. Maher (Ed.), *Clinical psychology and personality: The selected papers of George Kelly* (pp. 46-65). New York: John Wiley.

Kelly, G. A. (1969b). Personal construct theory and the psychotherapeutic interview. In B. Maher (Ed.), *Clinical psychology and personality: The selected papers of George Kelly* (pp. 224-264). New York: John Wiley.

Kelly, G. A. (1969c). The threat of aggression. In B. Maher (Ed.), *Clinical psychology and personality: The selected papers of George Kelly* (pp. 281-288). New York: John Wiley.

McNamee, S. (1996). Psychotherapy as a social construction. In H. Rosen & K. T. Kuehlwein, (Eds.), *Constructing realities: Meaning-making perspectives for psychotherapists* (pp. 115-137). San Francisco: Jossey-Bass.

McNamee, S. (2002). The social construction of disorder: From pathology to potential. In J. D. Raskin & S. K. Bridges (Eds.), *Studies in meaning: Exploring constructivist psychology* (pp. 143-168). New York: Pace University Press.

McNamee, S. (2004 [this volume]). Relational bridges between constructionism and constructivism. In J. D. Raskin & S. K. Bridges (Eds.), Studies in Meaning 2: *Bridging the personal and social in constructivist psychology* (pp. #). New York: Pace University Press.

Miller, J. (1991). The development of women's sense of self. In J. Jordan, A. Kaplan, J. Miller, I. Stiver, & J. Surrey (Eds.), *Women's growth in connection: Writings from the Stone Center* (pp. 11-26). New York: Guilford Press.

Neimeyer, R. A., & Bridges, S. K. (2003). Postmodern approaches to psychotherapy. In A. S. Gurman & S. B. Messer (Eds.), *Essential psychotherapies: Theory and practice* (2nd ed., pp. 272-316). New York: Guilford Press.

Raskin, J. D. (2002). Defending constructivist ethics after September 11. *The Humanistic Psychologist, 30*, 281-291.

Rothstein, E. (2001, September 22). Attacks on U.S. challenge the perspectives of postmodern true believers. *The New York Times*, p. A17.

CHAPTER 15

The Permeability of Personal Construct Psychology[1]

Jonathan D. Raskin

"THE CONSTRUCTIVISTS ARE COMING!"

A 1988 *Family Therapy Networker* cover either warned or proclaimed (depending on your perspective), "The Constructivists are Coming!" This impending arrival has not gone unnoticed by personal construct psychologists, arguably the original psychological constructivists. But the relationship between personal construct psychology (PCP) and constructivism remains controversial. In her excellent 1995 biography of George Kelly, Fay Fransella (1995) cautioned against subsuming PCP under the rubric of constructivism. Though she indicated that in principle she had no problem with PCP being considered constructivist, she worried that some people "appear to be substituting a philosophy for a psychological theory" (p. 130), which is problematic for psychotherapy because when it comes to helping clients "you need more than the guidance of a philosophy" (p. 132). In the seven years since Fransella's (1995) book appeared, the influence of constructivism on PCP and psychology in general appears to only have increased. I have noticed this in my role as president of the North American Personal Construct Network (NAPCN). The last few NAPCN conferences have all explicitly made efforts to incorporate constructivism into the program and have increasingly welcomed prominent constructivist speakers from outside PCP, including Michael Mahoney, Sheila McNamee, Sandra Rigazio-DiGilio, and John Shotter. In addition, NAPCN is in the process of changing its name to the Constructivist Psychology

---

[1] A version of this paper was presented at the 15th International Congress on Personal Construct Psychology, Huddersfield, England, UK, July 2003.

Network—a more inclusive name that appeals not only to PCP'ers, but also to those who might identify themselves more generally as constructivists.

While I sense a great deal of excitement on the part of the NAPCN Steering Committee as NAPCN moves towards its name change, I remain acutely sensitive to concerns—expressed in a variety of ways by a variety of PCP'ers (Chiari, 2000; Fisher, 2003; Fransella, 1995, 2000)—about PCP being washed out in a flood of constructivism. After carefully listening to all the constituencies within NAPCN as the name change issue has proceeded, I have tentatively concluded that the heart of the PCP versus constructivism matter revolves not so much upon Fransella's (1995) contrast between constructivism as an all-too-broad philosophy bordering on a shallow eclecticism versus PCP as a sophisticated and clinically specifiable psychological theory. Admittedly, my conclusion has been influenced to some extent because, while I admire her work a great deal, I do not much care for Fransella's distinction between constructivism and PCP. After all, it is easy to criticize a straw-figure version of "constructivism-as-ill-defined philosophy" lacking clinical particulars if one ignores the many specific constructivist theories and therapy approaches garnering attention, none of whose adherents would likely identify with the creed Fransella ascribed to them, namely "that as long as you are a constructivist and abide by that philosophy, you can do what you like, certainly in the realm of psychotherapy" (p. 130). Surely intricate and nuanced theory combined with detailed and explicit clinical application can be discerned in a fair share of therapies commonly classified as constructivist, including but not limited to White and Epston's (1990) narrative therapy, Ecker and Hully's (1996) depth-oriented brief therapy, Eron and Lund's (1996, 2002) narrative solutions therapy, Hermans and Hermans-Jansen's (1995) self-narrative therapy, Jay Efran's structural constructivist therapy (Efran, Lukens, & Lukens, 1990), and the cognitive constructivist therapies of Guidano (1991) and Mahoney (1991, 2003). These therapies all spring from explicit psychological theories and their concomitant notions of how persons come to experience problems in living. They also all thoroughly explicate ways to proceed clinically, often times in greater detail than Kelly did in presenting PCP. Kelly, after all, encouraged clinicians to make use of any and all currently available counseling strategies, something many PCP therapists have often taken as an invitation to incorporate other clinical approaches and techniques (constructivist or not) into their work. More to the point, I do not find the theories that Fransella homogenized under the constructivist banner to be ill defined and superficially eclectic, nor do I find PCP to be so clinically airtight that admitting constructivist elements inevitably must weaken it by watering it down. Thus, her distinction fails to resonate with me.

Because I do not find the portrayal of constructivism as an "anything-goes" approach to theory and therapy convincing, I suspect that something else is going on when we PCP'ers wring our hands about the specter of constructivism intruding into our idyllic Kellyian universe. I think we experience threat and anxiety. We experience threat because as we move into a world where it becomes ever more difficult to remain isolated from the constructivist goings-on around us, we realize that immanent changes to our theorizing and thinking lurk up ahead. At the same time, we experience anxiety because we realize that much of the newfangled constructivist theorizing, even when it seems exciting to us, falls outside of PCP's original boundaries. As PCP'ers struggle to modulate their theoretical systems in response to the fragmenting impact of constructivism, they encounter anxiety. Thus, when Fransella (1995) cautioned, "if personal construct theory is allowed to be subsumed under the umbrella of constructivism as if it were nothing but constructivist, Kelly's philosophy may well survive, but his theory will sink without trace" (p. 131), I interpreted her remark not so much as an indictment of constructivism but as an expression of threat and anxiety within the PCP community as it strains to deal with the impact of constructivism. As the Networker said, "The Constructivists are Coming!" Anxiety and threat in the face of this are to be expected.

PERMEABILITY AND THE CONSTRUCTIVIST NEXT DOOR

Threat, Anxiety, and Hostility: "All in the Constructivist Family   "

As a native New Yorker raised in the suburbs of New York City during the 1970s, I always liked the television sitcom All in the Family. To this day, I do not believe television has produced a better portrayal of Kellyian hostility than Archie Bunker. Behind all his blustering and semi-illiterate prejudicial ranting lurked a man tormented by the ever-present experiences of threat and anxiety. The Queens neighborhood Archie lived in was, from his vantage point, being invaded. Blacks, Jews, Asians, Puerto Ricans, and gays were all settling into his once all-white, all-heterosexual (or so he thought) neighborhood. Everything Archie believed about gender, race, and sexuality was being challenged. The show's humor came from the fact that rather than trying to make sense of ongoing socio-political developments by openly engaging them and seeing where they might lead him, Archie resisted social change by hostilely cramming events into a procrustean and outmoded worldview. In many respects, Archie perfectly personified Kelly's (1955/1991a) hostile construer: "If people do not behave the way he predicts, he will make them! That will validate his construction of them!" (p. 512/377). Hence, Archie's liberal son-in-law did not have a point; rather, he was a meathead! Though most of us repudiated Archie's specific beliefs, I think we tuned in to watch him every week because we nevertheless identified with someone desperately trying to cope with threat and anxiety by hostilely clinging to constructions that were not working especially well anymore. After all, most (if not all) of us are hostile sometimes.

While certainly PCP'ers are a far cry from Archie Bunker, like Archie they too find themselves having to deal with the threat and anxiety that results from new people moving into their neighborhood. Constructivists have purchased the house next door (and several others on the block) and are showing up at neighborhood get-togethers with increasing frequency. PCP'ers had better figure out what to do and soon lest the neighborhood be overrun. If we turn hostile in response to our threat and anxiety by insisting that PCP is the only bet for successfully transporting meaning making from our fragile suburban neighborhood into the larger metropolis of psychology, then I am afraid we risk our standing in city and suburb alike. There may be a tremendous price to pay for proving our predictions right. We may win the bet (at least in our own eyes), but as a consequence become so marginalized by remaining theoretically pure and isolated that we lose our ability to earn ourselves needed attention—not to mention a living in the increasingly intellectually integrated twenty-first century psychology metropolis! And once we lose our means of earning a living, it won't be long before the bank forecloses on our house and we wind up homeless and irrelevant, wandering aimlessly around what will by then have evolved into a PCP-less constructivist neighborhood. As Kelly (1969a) observed about hostility, "it may be fun, but it's bad" (p. 272).

Threat, Anxiety, and Change

In PCP, there are several responses one can have to threat and anxiety besides hostility (Kelly, 1955/1991a, 1955/1991b). Anxiety begins when a construction is insufficiently permeable, making it unable to "admit into its range of convenience new elements not construed within its framework" (Kelly, 1955/1991a, p. 79/56). One solution is to loosen one's constructions, allowing them to apply to a wider array of elements. Thus, we could loosen our ideas about what counts as being consistent with PCP, allowing constructivist approaches to be more readily included. This does not result in a change in our construction of PCP itself, but instead simply allows PCP to be subsumed under the broader heading of "constructivism" (or vice versa!) by providing a greater ability to endure ambiguity in specifying precisely the relationship between PCP and constructivism. Of course, the drawback of loosening is that the ways we think about PCP and constructivism may indeed become too loose, failing to provide a meaningful or reliable way to consistently specify a relationship between them. I think this kind of loosening happens quite a bit when discussing how particular constructivist theories relate to constructivism more generally. It may even be what Fransella (1995) was referring to when she worried about constructivism being an all-encompassing term that forbids no position—a criticism also latched onto by more vociferous opponents of constructivism, albeit with a more alarmist tone (Held, 1995; Mackay, 2003).

The counterweight to loosening is tightening. Instead of moving towards a more ambiguous (or, at worst, incoherent and unspecifiable) interpretation of how PCP relates to constructivism, the tight construer battens down the hatches. For example, one might conclude that PCP is decidedly not a type of constructivism. Thus, constructivism does not require attention, or at least no more attention than other current theoretical templates such as behaviorism and psychoanalysis. Tightening can be quite anxiety reducing by allowing us to suspend the whole unpleasant and stressful discussion about PCP and constructivism. Instead, we can focus purely on PCP proper, with lengthy and intricate discussions about what Kelly meant when he said this or wrote that. We can flesh out the theory itself without worrying ourselves about what anyone outside of our tight nit community might be saying or doing. Perhaps this sheds some light on the complaints I sometimes hear about there being an insular quality to the PCP community. While I have not experienced it that way, the fact that many others have gives me pause. My concern is that this insular quality may be a side effect of tight construing in the face of external threats, a side effect with the unfortunate consequence that we are periodically derided as "Kelly worshippers"

(Desai, 1995). While I consider the "Kelly worshipper" characterization unfair, at the same time we may inadvertently perpetuate such a view when we tightly construe PCP by sticking almost exclusively to Kelly's writings and other "pure" PCP texts. When PCP scholars isolate themselves from broader discussions about constructivist happenings within psychology and related social science disciplines, they isolate themselves from important intellectual conversations and significantly reduce their ability to influence the direction these conversations take. This avoids the PCP-constructivism issue, but does not solve it. In Kelly's words, the tight construer "does not 'face his problems'; hence he does not find new solutions to them" (1955/1991a, p. 498/367).

Kelly suggested that rather than simply loosening or tightening one's constructs in the face of anxiety, one might modulate them and make them more permeable (Kelly, 1965/1969c). In making one's constructs more permeable, one simply achieves "the capacity to embrace new elements" (Kelly, 1955/1991a, p. 80/56). When PCP'ers embrace constructivism, they likely do so from within a superordinate PCP structure. Even so, the process of making one's constructs more permeable is often more difficult than it sounds because "not everyone has set out to erect constructs for himself that are permeable enough to encompass and modulate the extremes of loose and tight thinking. And not many teachers have ever thought to suggest that he should" (Kelly, 1965/1969c, p. 128). When it comes to constructivism and PCP, making one's constructions more permeable proves to be no less arduous a task for PCP'ers than for anyone else. It involves allowing new elements in, even though doing so might be threatening because it inevitably requires us to revise our constructions based on experience.

This means that our constructions of PCP will change; the theory will no longer remain the same one Kelly posited back in 1955. It might not even remain the same one written about it the brand new *International Handbook of PCP* (Fransella, 2003) or defined extensively for the lay public in the recent *Internet Encyclopaedia of PCP* (Scheer & Walker, 2003). Change is threatening, and often involves loss—something even young children soon realize. When my seven-year-old daughter recently came home from her last day of school for the year, she expressed pride in having met the challenges of first-grade and excitement about the inevitable complexities of proceeding to Grade 2. However, she also expressed sadness about leaving something with which she was comfortable and accustomed.

How did she describe this hodgepodge of feelings combining growth and loss? As "bittersweet." Like seven year olds, academics are not immune to the bittersweet emotions that accompany life's endless progression. Unless we retreat into "Archie Bunkeresque" hostility, PCP is bound to change and our most-cherished constructions must change with it. Kelly saw this coming when he subtly reminded us that good scientific theories must be modifiable if they are to survive and continue to be relevant:

> A theory should be considered as modifiable and, ultimately, expendable. Sometimes theorists get so pinned down to deductive reasoning that they think their whole structure will fall down if they turn around and start modifying their assumptions in the light of their subsequent observations. (Kelly, 1955/1991a, p. 30/22)

In other words, PCP must continue to evolve if it is to survive. While threat and anxiety over immanent changes to the makeup of both our theory and intellectual community may make it often appear counterintuitive, opening PCP to an influx of constructivist theorizing is one such way to ensure PCP's continued survival. For applying the principle of modifiability to a theory means that any theory, PCP included, is "an eventual candidate for the trash can. Such an outlook may save the scientist a lot of anxiety, provided he has flexible overriding convictions that give him a feeling of personal independence of his theory" (Kelly, 1955/1991a, p. 31/22). This is not meant to imply that PCP has outlived its usefulness and should be pushed aside. Quite the contrary, it is simply meant to say that PCP is itself a construct system, one that—in keeping with the Experience Corollary (Kelly, 1955/1991a)—must inevitably evolve as it is used to successively construe new occurrences. Constructivism is only the latest of many new occurrences PCP has encountered along the way. Of course, the difficulty in this process is that there is no guidebook to help us construe PCP in light of constructivism. Ironically, it is in this area—how to construe PCP with regards to constructivism— that Kelly's theory once again may prove its utility.

GETTING IN THE MOOD: ACCEPTING THE INVITATIONAL

An Invitation to the Invitational

Kelly encouraged us to employ language according to the *invitational mood* (Kelly, 1964/1969b). The invitational mood bridges the gap between what Kelly saw as objective and phenomenological uses of language. When speaking objectively, we often assume that the words we use directly map the world we seek to understand; that is, "the subject-predicate relationship inheres in the subject itself" (Kelly, 1964/1969b, p. 148). As an example, Kelly (1964/1969b) examined the statement "The floor is hard." Kelly (1964/1969b) observed that from an objectivist position "the sentence's validity stems from the floor and not from the speaker" (p. 148). By contrast, when speaking phenomenologically, we usually assume that we refer to the contents of our minds rather than the qualities of the world itself. When we say the floor is hard, according to a phenomenological perspective "it is presumed that such a statement portrays a state of mind of the speaker and does not necessarily represent anything more than that" (Kelly, 1964/1969b, p. 148). Kelly's invitational mood marked his attempt to move beyond the traditional contrast between objective and phenomenological uses of language, one which neither imprisons us within our supposed objective descriptions of the world nor reduces our verbal proclamations to little more than mental musings disconnected from every day life. Adopting an invitational mood towards the floor, we might say, "Suppose we regard the floor as if it were hard" (Kelly, 1964/1969b, p. 149). Rather than leading us to a finite conclusion, language becomes a way of positioning us in relationship to the future by encouraging certain expectancies—we function "as if" the floor were hard without presupposing that this must be our final answer. Importantly, the invitational mood does not require us to negate one construction of things before entertaining another:

> Suppose, instead, we employ the language of hypothesis. We say, in effect, "To be sure the floor may be regarded as hard, and we know something of what ensues when we cope with it in light of such an assumption. Not bad! But now, let us see what happens when we regard it as soft." (Kelly, 1964/1969b, p. 160)

Responsibility and the Invitational

In a book pondering the future of PCP, Spencer McWilliams provided a thoughtful and personal account of his own evolution as a personal construct psychologist, using the invitational mood as a framework for doing so (McWilliams, 1996). He titled his paper "Accepting the Invitational," but he could just as well have titled it "Accepting Responsibility" because one of the major themes he addressed was the importance of taking credit for one's constructions: "I believe that to acknowledge further our active role in construing we must use a language that requires us to take conscious responsibility for our personal participation in creating meaning" (McWilliams, 1996, p. 70). In considering the relationship between construing and language, McWilliams (1993, 1996) suggested the adoption of E-prime, a form of speaking in which all versions of the verb to be are eliminated as a way to emphasize the responsibility of the speaker in formulating what is being said. McWilliams' (1996) stated goal was "to find a more genial way to speak in a manner that requires me to recognize the hypothetical nature of my interpretations and helps me avoid attributing permanent qualities to events that continually change" (p. 70). While McWilliams (1996) acknowledged that simple adoption of E-prime alone does not solve the problem of mistaking our constructions for reality itself, it may help us along the way.

Stressing the centrality of active persons taking responsibility for their constructions is something that Kelly hinted at when he referred to the *personal involvement* of researchers in the research that they conduct (Kelly, 1964/1969c). McWilliams strikes me as the personal construct psychologist who has most effectively zeroed in on the centrality of taking responsibility for one's constructions rather than passing them off as objectively discovered entities (McWilliams, 1993, 1996). In my own, far less thorough way, the idea of taking responsibility for one's constructions has infused my work on the hazards of diagnosis and the medical model of psychotherapy. Elsewhere I have suggested that mental health professionals would do well to accept responsibility for the diagnostic systems they construct by stressing their own *human involvement* in the creation of these systems (Raskin & Lewandowski, 2000). The concept of human involvement is not limited to psychotherapy and diagnosis, however. It can be used as a way to encourage people to think about the respective parts they play in creating means for understanding all areas of life, which might otherwise simply be seen as objective representations of how things are.

In this line of thinking, we often minimize or disguise our own invested roles in the ways we construe events by ascribing foundational justifications to our constructions. Then we discredit alternative constructions by pointing out how these constructions are inconsistent with said foundations. Obviously, if "the floor is hard" becomes a foundational and unquestionable construction, then "the floor is soft" can never be entertained because it is inevitably incorrect. I tend to believe that this "absolute foundationalism" is the kind of thinking that trips up critics of constructivism when they say, "What is real is never dependent on our constructions, hence constructivism is incoherent and forbids no position" (Held, 1995; Mackay, 2003). These critics remain committed to an indicative, rather than invitational, view of language—and therefore they cannot entertain the idea of multiple, often competing, hypotheses without in the end identifying some as right and others as wrong. They find it impossible to consider the question, "What if we acted *as if* what is real were dependent on our constructions?" From the "human involvement" perspective, all of us are invariably committed to particular constructions of how things are. Thus, in keeping with McWilliams (1993, 1996), I invite readers to consider the relationship between PCP and constructivism via the notion of human involvement, which I use to encourage us to see ourselves, not our theories, as ultimately responsible (both individually and collectively) for the constructions we hold of ourselves and our theories.

HUMAN INVOLVEMENT , PCP, AND CONSTRUCTIVISM

PCP "*as if*" Constructivism

In light of the above discussion about human involvement and taking responsibility for our constructions, let us to return to the issue of PCP and constructivism. Adopting an invitational mood and then taking responsibility for the constructions that result can help us productively transform the debate about whether PCP does or does not fit within the confines of constructivism. That is, let us employ the invitational mood as a way to suspend, for the time being, judgments about whether particular attempts to combine PCP and constructivism are ultimately consistent with PCP in some kind of final way. Instead, let us adopt an "as if" perspective. What happens when we act as if PCP is consistent with Gergen's social constructionism (Gergen, 1985, 1991, 1994) or von Glaserfeld's radical constructivism (von Glaserfeld, 1984, 1995) or Maturana and Varela's structure determinism (Maturana & Varela, 1992)? What possibilities unfold when we act "as if" specific Kellyian concepts merge nicely with particular constructivist ideas? As an obvious example, what occurs when we act as if Kelly's Sociality Corollary and social constructionist notions of relational co-construction of meaning are consistent?[2] Note that we are not saying that sociality and the relational emphasis of social constructionism are, in a once and for all sort of way, consonant and interchangeable. Just as Kelly did with his "the floor is hard" example, after exhausting as many possibilities for productively construing sociality as consistent with social constructionism, we might turn around and start entertaining what might result when we begin acting "as if" these terms are incompatible.

Social Constructionism, PCP, and Selfhood

Of course, this process is already underway. Among the many chapters in this volume whose authors focus on integrating constructivism and constructionism, Paris and Epting's (2004 [this volume]) contribution amalgamates PCP and social constructionism. In their chapter, they tackle the difficulties involved in integrating what is commonly seen as PCP's agentic individiualism with social constructionism's presumed social determinism. This apparent discrepancy in fundamental theoretical principles tends to be one of the more vexing problems people have identified when grappling with social constructionism and PCP. However, Paris and Epting encourage us to overcome it by acting as if personal and social are little more than two sides of the same coin. They argue that social determinism should not be confused with the constitution of individual identities. They discuss the game of chess to demonstrate their distinction between something being constituted as opposed to determined:

> The activity of chess and the role of chess player, are constituted by the rules that make up the game of chess, and without which it would not be chess. We can only think and do chess by first knowing the rules. However, the way we play the game, the particular moves that we, as well as our opponents, decide to make, the very outcome of the game, are not determined in the sense that the rules of chess cannot be said to cause any particular move, strategy, or outcome of any particular game. (Paris & Epting, 2004 [this volume], p. 3)

In their interpretation of social constructionism, identities are socially constituted to the extent that they are governed by consensually accepted ideas about the types of "selves" people can choose among and the ways those selves are typically established within the social realm. However, people maintain agency within the socially constituted reality that results because they are free to pick

---

[2] This issue has been taken up somewhat by PCP'ers (Kalekin-Fishman & Walker, 1996), though the implicit message often seems to be that, in the end, PCP trumps social constructionism with its own superior, if often neglected, application to group realities.

and choose the selves they plan to pursue, albeit their agency is governed by the socially shared assumptions that engulf them.[3] Of course, people can opt to resist the "rules of the game" by declining to choose from among the presently available options for selfhood, but when they do they are simply encouraging a larger social renegotiation of these socially agreed upon rules. Further, their resistance only has meaning within the confines of these rules because it is the rules themselves that regulate the entire enterprise in the first place. In other words, the meaning and significance of laying claim to particular varieties of selfhood makes little sense without the backdrop of a shared social context, a context people collaborate in constructing and sustaining.

While it remains implicit, Paris and Epting—like all scholars advancing particular readings of one or more academic texts—are basically encouraging us to act "as if" their proposed "social constitution versus social determinism" construct is legitimate. This invites us to entertain the many possibilities for creative synthesis between PCP and social constructionism, which may prove fruitful for personal construct psychologists and social constructionists alike. In the spirit of the invitational mood, it seems pointless to argue about whether Paris and Epting's take on social constructionism and PCP correctly adheres to the tenets of either theory. Rather, let us assume for the time being that it does and ask ourselves, along with Paris and Epting, to take responsibility for trying on (and, when push comes to shove, advancing or repudiating) particular readings of these theories. If we do this, then we allow ourselves to expand our horizons and, perchance, open new vistas for theory, research, and practice.[4]

---

[3] Wandrei (2003) recently examined the "interpenetration" of individual and social constructions in relation to "agency-in-practice," which challenges the traditional understanding of agency as something that originates solely from within the person. Instead of rejecting human agency (as radical forms of social constructionism sometimes do), Wandrei (2003) posited the development of agency as something that unfolds *epigentically*—as an emergent part of the person's biological structure, but a structure whose processes are simultaneously shaped by being immersed in a socio-cultural context. In this conception, the social and individual mutually construct and constrain one another (Wandrei, 2003); agency springs both from the biologically emergent processing abilities of individuals *and* the socially constituted constructions that engulf all human endeavors.

FIVE HYPOTHESIS

In case it is not clear by now, I am advocating that PCP'ers embrace the invitational mood and see what unfolds should they invite those intriguing yet somewhat intimidating new neighbors, The Constructivists, over for an afternoon tea or summertime barbeque. Some individual PCP folks are already doing this, but the PCP community's overall investment in this endeavor seems sketchy and tentative at best. Therefore, I ask more directly: What might happen if PCP, as a movement, began to concertedly act "as if" constructivism had more to offer? Nobody yet knows the outcome and the risk of threat and anxiety is certainly great. However, in keeping with Beverly Walker's (1992) portrayal of the personal construct psychologist as a "risk-taking adventurer" as opposed to a "conservative dogmatist," below I present five hypotheses about PCP and constructivism, all of which I hope are taken in the spirit of a credulous approach and the predictions of which are put to the test of experience.

Hypothesis 1: PCP Will Sink Without a Trace unless it Becomes more
Permeable

This first hypothesis is unsettling, but one my experience leads me to reluctantly believe. NAPCN (soon to be the Constructivist Psychology Network) is struggling to expand its membership. Yes, about a half dozen thirty and forty something year olds consistently attend the conferences. However, they are substantially outnumbered by the retiree generation and while we do our best to keep our graduate students involved in PCP, it is a difficult task.

To a lot of first and second time conference attendees, the PCP community seems friendly and quaint, but it is not where their professional future lies. Why? I return to my earlier suggestion that personal construct psychologists have been too insular and narrowly focused on PCP. This is not a new observation; Neimeyer (1985) made it nearly two decades ago in his review of the development of personal construct psychology. More recently, Fisher (2003) observed it anew, noting that we PCP'ers—like the muppet characters on the classic Jim Henson television show Fraggle Rock—have often found ourselves an intellectually isolated lot. Agreed, one could argue that personal construct psychologists are visionary theorists

---

[4] Importantly, Paris and Epting's approach not only potentially leads to changes to PCP, but it also requires modifications to social constructionism. The theoretical evolution cuts both ways.

whose emphasis on human meaning has not caught on yet within mainstream psychology. But how does that explain the consistently high attendance at "Constructivism in Psychotherapy" and similar conferences, even though constructivism is no more mainstream than PCP? The 2002 NAPCN conference in Vancouver was good, but attendance paled in comparison to the conference that immediately followed it at the same venue. That conference: The Second International Conference on Personal Meaning. It is my observation that unless the PCP community makes PCP more permeable than it has to constructivism and related meaning-focused theories, PCP will eventually die from benign neglect. This observation may apply best to North America, but it is important for the Europeans and Australians to be aware of it, too.

Hypothesis 2: Constructivists Are Interested in PCP

As much as we need to open ourselves more fully to the constructivist movement, we also need to aggressively share PCP with our constructivist neighbors. This should not be difficult, as many of the constructivist approaches often considered threats to the continued existence of PCP explicitly acknowledge their intellectual indebtedness to Kelly and his theory. While we PCP'ers have often noted the wandering eye of our colleagues as they have begun to flirt with constructivism, we are likely less aware that the infatuation is mutual. In my readings of constructivist therapy texts, I am struck by how often Kelly is mentioned as an important influence. Kelly's theory is explicitly incorporated into Ecker and Hulley's (1996) depth-oriented brief therapy (Ecker & Hulley, 1996), Eron and Lund's narrative solutions therapy (Eron & Lund, 1996), Efran's structural therapy (Efran et al., 1990), and the cognitive constructivisms of Mahoney and Guidano (Guidano, 1991; Mahoney, 1991). Sheila McNamee (2004 [this volume]) even acknowledged the theoretical significance of Kelly for her brand of social constructionism—something that might surprise some PCP'ers who have generally experienced social constructionism as hostile towards PCP (Warren, 1998). In effect, constructivist authors of all types seem readily amenable to learning more about PCP and using it in their work. This does not mean there cannot be hearty disagreement at times. It simply means that rather than being washed out by constructivism, greater contact between PCP and constructivism can only help PCP get stronger and more influential by placing it in the midst of a lively and energetic dialogue and letting its advocates speak their minds.

Hypothesis 3: PCP and Constructivism Can Strengthen One Another

Many of the issues currently facing constructivism are ones Kelly and other PCP'ers anticipated long ago. I believe Kelly's writings can be used to good effect in negating many of the "anything goes" criticisms currently leveled at constructivists. Again, by accepting the invitational, constructivists and PCP'ers alike can focus on human involvement by emphasizing the commitment of their critics to particular philosophical constructions, which are then stated as objective facts. Sociality, embodiment, and assessment are all areas where PCP has much to offer constructivism. Similarly, I think that constructivism can embolden PCP'ers to more firmly assert much of what Kelly said long ago, even if he said it in somewhat cautious tones lest he alienate more traditional colleagues. That is, as someone who sees PCP as more closet constructivism and less critical realism, I believe constructivism is important in PCP's continued evolution.

Hypothesis 4: There Will Always Be Room for "Classical PCP"

Just because many PCP'ers support a robust dialogue with constructivists does not mean they have given up on PCP. Rather, I think they support the dialogue because they see it as a way to enhance PCP and share it with a wider audience. Along these lines, if PCP'ers modulate Kelly's theory in ways that make it more permeable, then PCP will flourish. This permeability will allow PCP'ers to creatively develop new approaches to both constructivism and PCP. Sharing PCP with a broader array of meaning-interested scholars and practitioners may produce more widespread interest in Kelly's original work. So, by taking a less reverential approach to PCP and allowing the constructivists in, we may ironically increase PCP's popularity and influence by familiarizing a greater variety of persons with it.

Hypothesis 5: These Hypotheses Require Revision and Replacement Over Time

None of the above hypotheses are once and for all. As they are put to the test, they will inevitably require revision and replacement. It is my hope that for the time being they may provide a useful guide for those, like myself, who struggle with the relationship between PCP and constructivism.

CONCLUSION : IT'S IN THE WAY THAT YOU USE IT

Clearly there are a good many PCP'ers out there who find themselves open to constructivism—until they sit down and read some. Even if they like aspects of it, they ultimately find it difficult to restrain their critical instincts (a side-effect of too many years of graduate school, perhaps?) and these instincts spring forth with a vengeance in the identification of a laundry list of reasons why constructivism does not gel with PCP. Even though I am an advocate for advancing linkages between PCP and constructivism, I must concede that I, too, have gone to graduate school and so am not immune from this critical tendency, myself. However, I have argued that the "as if" philosophy behind the invitational mood, combined with an emphasis on taking responsibility for our constructions of PCP, may prove helpful in moving our critical selves past the "Is PCP constructivist?" quagmire.

That is, the "PCP as consistent with constructivism" hypothesis can be put to the test by trying it out in the course of our everyday practice as personal construct psychologists. After all, behavior is an experiment! Of course, even among collegial PCP'ers, hypothesis testing is never easy or without controversy. Consider when the editors of the *International Journal of Personal Construct Psychology* renamed it the *Journal of Constructivist Psychology*. They were testing out the rather audacious "PCP as constructivism" hypothesis by acting as if PCP was a type of constructivism. Not surprisingly, some PCP'ers reacted negatively—namely, those who were still acting as if it was not. Regardless of whether one supported the name change decision, through our ensuing behavior we put our hypotheses about PCP and constructivism to the test, and when our hypotheses were confirmed, we invited others to act as if our position was correct. However, rather than running off to cite Kelly passages with biblical passion and getting lost in an argument over whose interpretation of PCP is most correct, we might instead claim responsibility for the constructions of PCP we are exploring and continue to test them out through experience.

George Kelly smugly seemed to enjoy people acting as if his theory was a type of behaviorism, existentialism, humanism, cognitivism, and so on (Kelly, 1970). In his own inimitable (and sometimes irritating!) way, he usually declined to endorse these classifications. Maybe he wanted us to take responsibility for our views of PCP instead of accepting whatever he might have thought. Perhaps this was just as well because, whether he meant it to or not, it allowed those attracted to his theory to each take responsibility for a particular approach to PCP and to proceed "as if" one or more theoretical classifications fit (or, "as if" none of them did!). In the present chapter I, too, have proceeded based on an "as if," one which encourages

342

PCP'ers to act as if PCP could be enriched through greater contact with constructivism. This reminds me of the song "It's in the Way that You Use It," by Eric Clapton, who seemed to implicitly grasp the relationship between constructing meaning and accepting responsibility for the ways we apply it. I acknowledge my human involvement in the "PCP as constructivism" venture and believe the PCP community would do well to take it up, too. We may not know yet where it will lead us, but throw in a dash of constructive alternativism and the possibilities are endless!

REFERENCES

Chiari, G. (2000). Personal construct theory and the constructivist family: A friendship to cultivate, a marriage not to celebrate. In J. W. Scheer (Ed.), The person in society: Challenges to a constructivist theory (pp. 66-78). Giessen, Germany: Psychosozial-Verlag.

Desai, H. (1995, May). Ways in which personal construct psychology has (and has not) turned into a religion. NAPCN News, 4-5.

Ecker, B., & Hulley, L. (1996). Depth-oriented brief therapy. San Francisco: Jossey-Bass.

Efran, J. S., Lukens, M. D., & Lukens, R. J. (1990). Language, structure, and change: Frameworks of meaning in psychotherapy. New York: Norton.

Eron, J. B., & Lund, T. W. (1996). Narrative solutions in brief therapy. New York: Guilford.

Eron, J. B., & Lund, T. W. (2002). Narrative solutions: Toward under standing the art of helpful conversation. In J. D. Raskin & S. K. Bridges (Eds.), Studies in meaning: Exploring constructivist psychology (pp. 63-97). New York: Pace University Press.

Fisher, J. M. (2003). Fraggle Rock: A study in isolationism. In G. Chiari & M. L. Nuzzo (Eds.), Psychological constructivism and the social world (pp. 98-104). Milan, Italy: FrancoAngeli.

Fransella, F. (1995). George Kelly. London: Sage.

Fransella, F. (2000). Personal construct psychology by the year 2045. In J. W. Scheer (Ed.), The person in society: Challenges to a constructivist theory (pp. 440-448). Giessen, Germany: Psychosozial-Verlag.

Fransella, F. (Ed.). (2003). International handbook of personal construct psychology. Chichester: John Wiley.

Gergen, K. J. (1985). The social constructionist movement in modern psychology. American Psychologist, 40, 266-275.

Gergen, K. J. (1991). The saturated self: Dilemmas of identity in contemporary life. New York: Basic Books.

Gergen, K. J. (1994). Realities and relationships. Cambridge, MA: Harvard University Press.

Guidano, V. F. (1991). The self in process. New York: Guilford.

Held, B. S. (1995). Back to reality: A critique of postmodern theory in psychotherapy. New York: Norton.

Hermans, H. J. M., & Hermans-Jansen, E. (1995). Self-narratives: The construction of meaning in psychotherapy. New York: Guilford.

Kalekin-Fishman, D., & Walker, B. M. (Eds.). (1996). The construction of group realities: Culture, society, and personal construct theory. Malabar, FL: Krieger.

Kelly, G. A. (1969a). Hostility. In B. Maher (Ed.), *Clinical psychology and personality: The selected papers of George Kelly* (pp. 267-280). New York: John Wiley.

Kelly, G. A. (1969b). The language of hypothesis: Man's psychological instrument. In B. Maher (Ed.), *Clinical psychology and personality: The selected papers of George Kelly* (pp. 147-162). New York: John Wiley. (Original work published 1964)

Kelly, G. A. (1969c). The strategy of psychological research. In B. Maher (Ed.), *Clinical psychology and personality: The selected papers of George Kelly* (pp. 114-132). New York: John Wiley. (Original work published 1965)

Kelly, G. A. (1970). A brief introduction to personal construct psychology. In D. Bannister (Ed.), *Perspectives in personal construct psychology* (pp. 1-30). San Diego: Academic Press.

Kelly, G. A. (1991a). *The psychology of personal constructs: Vol. 1. A theory of personality*. London: Routledge. (Original work published 1955)

Kelly, G. A. (1991b). *The psychology of personal constructs: Vol. 2 . Clinical diagnosis and psychotherapy*. London: Routledge. (Original work published 1955)

Mackay, N. (2003). Psychotherapy and the idea of meaning. *Theory and Psychology, 13,* 359-386.

Mahoney, M. J. (1991). *Human change processes.* New York: Basic Books.

Mahoney, M. J. (2003). *Constructive psychotherapy.* New York: Guilford.

Maturana, H. R., & Varela, F. J. (1992). *The tree of knowledge: The biological roots of human understanding* (R. Paolucci, Trans., rev. ed.). Boston: Shambhala.

McNamee, S. (2004 [this volume]). Relational bridges between constructionism and constructivism. In J. D. Raskin & S. K. Bridges (Eds.), *Studies in meaning 2: Bridging the personal and social in constructivist psychology* (pp. 37-50). New York: Pace University Press.

McWilliams, S. A. (1993). Construct no idols. *International Journal of Personal Construct Psychology, 6,* 269-280.

McWilliams, S. A. (1996). Accepting the invitational. In B. M. Walker, J. Costigan, L. L. Viney, & B. Warren (Eds.), *Personal construct theory: A psychology for the future* (pp. 57-78). Melborne: Australian Psychological Society.

Neimeyer, R. A. (1985). *The development of personal construct psychology.* Lincoln: University of Nebraska Press.

Paris, M. E., & Epting, F. R. (2004 [this volume]). Personal and social construction: Two sides of the same coin. In J. D. Raskin & S. K. Bridges (Eds.), Studies in meaning 2: Bridging the personal and social in constructivist psychology (pp. 3-36). New York: Pace University Press.

Raskin, J. D., & Lewandowski, A. M. (2000). The construction of disorder as human enterprise. In R. A. Neimeyer & J. D. Raskin (Eds.), Constructions of disorder: Meaning-making frameworks for psychotherapy (pp. 15-40). Washington, DC: American Psychological Association.

Scheer, J. W., & Walker, B. M. (Eds.) (2003). The Internet encyclopaedia of personal construct psychology [On-line]. [Retrieved from http://www.pcp-net.de/encyclopaedia on August 18, 2003]

von Glaserfeld, E. (1984). An introduction to radical constructivism. In P. Watzlawick (Ed.), The invented reality: How do we know what we believe we know? Contributions to constructivism (pp. 17-40). New York: Norton.

von Glaserfeld, E. (1995). Radical constructivism: A way of knowing and learning. London: The Falmer Press.

Walker, B. M. (1992). Values and Kelly's theory: Becoming a good scientist. International Journal of Personal Construct Psychology, 5, 259-269.

Wandrei, M. L. (2003). Agency-in-practice: An interpenetration of individual and social construction processes. Journal of Constructivist Psychology, 16, 287-322.

Warren, B. (1998). Philosophical dimensions of personal construct psychology. London: Routledge.

White, M., & Epston, D. (1990). Narrative means to therapeutic ends. New York: Norton.

About The Editors

Jonathan D. Raskin, Ph.D., is an associate professor of psychology at the State University of New York at New Paltz. His scholarship generally focuses on applying constructivism to psychotherapy, abnormality, and ethics. Dr. Raskin co-edited *Constructions of Disorder: Meaning-Making Frameworks for Psychotherapy* (with Robert A. Neimeyer; American Psychological association, 2000) and *Studies in Meaning: Exploring Constructivist Psychology* (with Sara K. Bridges; Pace University press, 2002). He serves on the editorial boards of the *Journal of Constructivist Psychology, The Humanistic Psychologist*, and the new Internet Journal, *Personal Construct Theory and Practice*. Dr. Raskin is licensed as a psychologist in New York, where he maintains a small private practice.

Sara K. Bridges, Ph.D., is an assistant professor of counseling psychology at the University of Memphis. Her scholarship examines both constructivism and sexuality. She is particularly interested in a constructivist approach to human sexuality, especially as it relates to counseling. Dr. Bridges co-edited *Studies in Meaning: Exploring Constructivist Psychology* (with Jonathan D. Raskin; Pace University Press, 2002). In addition to her scholarship, she is a coordinator for the Constructivist Psychology Network conference to be held in Memphis in June 2004.

APPENDIX: ABOUT THE CONSTRUCTIVIST PSYCHOLOGY
NETWORK (CPN) [FORMERLY NAPCN]

THE ORGANIZATION
Starting during 2004, the North American Personal
Construct Network (NAPCN) changes its name to the Constructivist
Psychology Network (CPN). It continues to be a network of persons
interested in personal construct psychology and related constructivist approaches to psychology, relationships, and human change
processes. It is largely comprised of psychologists, but there are also
members from related disciplines. Those interested in personal constructivism or related areas of constructivist, constructionist, narrative, or postmodern approaches to psychology are encouraged to
join.

MEMBERSHIP INFORMATION
CPN membership is open to anyone. An annual membership
includes a subscription to the *Journal of Constructivist Psychology* (4 issues
per year) and receipt of the CPN newsletter, the *Constructivist Chronicle*.
Dues can be paid in either US or Canadian dollars. To join, complete
form included in this volume, which lists 2004 dues.

CPN CONFERENCES
CPN sponsors its own conference in even numbered years.
These conferences allow for constructivist scholars to gather and
share ideas within an academic and collegial conference setting. In
odd numbered years, CPN co-sponsors an international congress
with the European Personal Construct Association (EPCA) and the
Austral-Asian Personal Construct Association (APCA). The international congress provides a forum for an even wider array of constructivist scholars wishing to communicate with one another.

NEXT CPN CONFERENCE
The University of Memphis, TN (June 17-20, 2004)

CPN NEWSLETTER
CPN publishes a newsletter, the *Constructivist Chronicle*, twice a
year. The newsletter contains conference information, updates on
new books and articles related to constructivist psychology, and fea-

ture articles on events and people within the constructivist community.

CONSTRUCTIVIST PSYCHOLOGY SECTION
CPN, in conjunction with Division 32 (Humanistic Psychology) of the American Psychological Association (APA), has established a new interest section in Division 32: the Constructivist Psychology Section (CPS). Joining Division 32 and CPS entitles CPN members to a 15% discount on CPN dues! Both CPN and Division 32 membership forms are included in this volume.

CURRENT CPN OFFICERS

President: Jonathan D. Raskin, State University of New York at New Paltz

Treasurer: Stephanie Lewis Harter, Texas Tech University

Newsletter Editor: Robert H. Mole, Calgary Catholic School District

Steering Committee Members:
Sara K. Bridges, The University of Memphis
Jay S. Efran, Temple University
April E. Metzler, Lehigh University
Kenneth W. Sewell, University of North Texas

MEMBERSHIP APPLICATION
CONSTRUCTIVIST PSYCHOLOGY NETWORK

Name: _____

Address: _____

_____

_____

_____

Highest Degree: _____

Date Awarded: _____

Institution: _____

Are you a student?   Yes _____   No _____

2004 Dues: CPN membership only
(Consider joining Division 32 and its Constructivist Psychology Section for
discounted CPN rates; see below)

United States: $66 US (professional rate) / $36 US (student rate)
Canada: $100 CDN (professional rate) / $55 CDN (student rate)
Outside North America: $76 US (professional rate) / $46 US (student rate)

2004 Dues: CPS and CPN membership
(Must be a member of Division 32 of the American Psychological Association
for these rates; see Division 32 membership form in this volume)

United States: $56 US (professional rate) / $30 US (student rate)
Canada: $85 CDN (professional rate) / $47 CDN (student rate)

Send payment to: Stephanie Lewis Harter, Ph.D.
                     Psychology Department
                     Box 42051
                     Texas Tech University
                     Lubbock, TX 79409-2051, USA.

351

Subject Index

assessment in, 79-81
client reluctance to change, 279-280
client-therapist relationship, 280-281
cognitive, 328
and cognitive therapies, 73-74
diagnosis in, 79-81
epistemology of, 70-71, 83
facilitating change, 281-283
and humanistic/experiential psychotherapy, 74
identifying client in, 76-78
maladjustment in, 278-279
objectives of, 78-79
perception vs. interpretation in, 71-73
and psychotherapy integration, 74-77
and September 11 attacks, 316-317
shared characteristics of, 278
therapeutic relationship, 280-281
Constructivists
as interested in PCP, 340
Constructs
altering existing meanings of, 322-323
changes in range of convenience, 322
changing, 318-319
contrast reconstruction, 320
creating new and abandoning old, 323
hierarchical restructuring, 321-322
making preverbal explicit, 320-321
testing for predictive validity, 322
use of a different construct, 320
usefulness, 16
Context shifts, 187
marriage as context shift, 187-188
Context-centered group therapy, 185-189
as acceptance-based treatment, 188

blackboard illusions in, 194
contract for social phobia workshop, 192-195, 217
Eastern philosophy in, 188, 196, 207
eyes-closed exercises, 197, 206
outcome data for treatment of social
phobia, 208-214, 215
participant reactions to for social
phobia, 212-214
roots of, 188
for social phobia, 190-208
Contextualism, 53
Contextualist worldview, 54-55
Container model of storylistening, 88-89, 108-109
"Continuing the connection," 231-232, 233, 235, 236
correlations for, 232
Conversation
constructivist, 69, 83
as metaphor for meaning, 69
Core constructs
and contrast reconstruction, 320
defined in PCP, 30, 57
development of, 119
and hierarchical restructuring, 321-322
and the social, 30
as superordinate role constructs, 60
Core ordering processes, 273, 274
Core role. See Role
Creative power of the self. See Self, creative
Creative self. See Self, creative
Credulous approach, 125
Cultural practices. See Practices
Culture, 20
in aftermath of September 11 attacks, 239
Cybernetics, 188

Constructivism, radical
Radical inquiry, 80
Range of convenience, 57, 322
Realism
limited, 51, 52, 300-301
Reality, 10, 11, 274, 300-301, 316
and belief, 299-301
as constructed, 16-18, 272
nature of, 5, 11
perceived vs. interpreted, 71-73
Recursion, 56, 57, 58, 59-61, 65
defined, 53
vs. repetition and iteration, 53-55,
61
Reductionism, 269
Reflexive Narrative Mode, 141, 144,
154
Reflexive Narrative Process
Sequences, 141, 146
Reflexivity, 79, 291-292
Relational, 19-20
Relational change, 318-319
Relational constructivism, 267
and Adlerian therapy, 269-277
Relational coordination, 48
Relational meaning, 41-44, 315, 316,
318
to unify constructivism and constructionism, 41-44
Relational politics, 19
Religion
in aftermath of September 11
attacks, 239
as quest. See Religion-as-quest
Religion-as-quest
as correlated with, 242-245
and existential search, 245-247
ideological tensions in research on,
253
overview of, 241-245
re-examining, 245-247
three components of mature reli-

gion, 242
Religiousness
as intrinsic or extrinsic, 242, 245
Repertory grid, 81, 121, 223
Research methodology
hermeneutic, 82
narrative, 82
qualitative, 82, 315
Research practices
human science. See Human science
research
personal involvement in, 335
and promoting justice, 240
Responsibility
and the invitational, 334-336
and PCP "as if" constructivism,
338-339, 342-343
Rogerian conditions for change, 280-
281
Role, 59, 60
defined in PCP, 30-31
personal construction of, 65
Role Construct Repertory Grid. See
Repertory grid
Role relationships, 80
Role theory, 116

Science
as rhetorical move, 79
and child sexual abuse, 15
and "just research," 240-241
and psychotherapy, 82
and religion-as-quest, 244
Scientist's stance, 315
Second-order change, 188
Selective attention, 274-275
Self, 10, 17-18, 20, 59, 65, 292, 297-
298, 299-301, 306, 307
construction of, 26-29
constructive alternativism and, 294-
295
core constructions and, 293-295

www.ingramcontent.com/pod-product-compliance
Lightning Source LLC
Chambersburg PA
CBHW022346280326
41935CB00007B/94